Metamodernism

Metamodernism

The Future of Theory

JASON ĀNANDA JOSEPHSON STORM

THE UNIVERSITY OF CHICAGO PRESS
CHICAGO AND LONDON

The University of Chicago Press, Chicago 60637
The University of Chicago Press, Ltd., London
© 2021 by The University of Chicago
Published 2021
Printed in the United States of America

30 29 28 27 26 25 24 23 22 21   1 2 3 4 5

ISBN-13: 978-0-226-60229-5 (cloth)
ISBN-13: 978-0-226-78665-0 (paper)
ISBN-13: 978-0-226-78679-7 (e-book)
DOI: https://doi.org/10.7208/chicago/9780226786797.001.0001

Library of Congress Cataloging-in-Publication Data

Names: Josephson-Storm, Jason Ānanda, author.
Title: Metamodernism : the future of theory / Jason Ānanda Josephson Storm.
Other titles: Future of theory
Description: Chicago ; London : The University of Chicago Press, 2021. | Includes
bibliographical references and index.
Identifiers: LCCN 2020054701 | ISBN 9780226602295 (cloth) |
ISBN 9780226786650 (paperback) | ISBN 9780226786797 (ebook)
Subjects: LCSH: Philosophy, Modern—21st century. | Post-postmodernism. |
Postmodernism. | Social sciences—Philosophy. | Ontology.
Classification: LCC B805 .J67 2021 | DDC 149/.97—dc23
LC record available at https://lccn.loc.gov/2020054701

♾ This paper meets the requirements of ANSI/NISO Z39.48-1992
(Permanence of Paper).

Contents

PART IV. KNOWLEDGE AND VALUE

Preface and Acknowledgments

This is my most personal and most abstract monograph. If Freud and Nietzsche are right, there are probably reasons these go together. This monograph emerges from a particular impasse in religious studies—an impasse to which I have myself contributed. Over the last few decades, many scholars in religious studies have come to reject the analytical utility of the category *religion*. My first book contributed to this movement by shifting the focus away from Euro-American scholars and revealing how Japanese officials, under extreme international pressure, came to terms with the Western concept of religion by "inventing religion" in Japan. The problem with this kind of genealogical research is that it inadvertently forecloses the possibility of generalizations, leaving viable mainly two kinds of scholarship: that which endlessly repeats and valorizes the act of deconstruction, and that which narrowly focuses on irrelevant and microscopic case studies. I have increasingly come to feel that both modes are dead ends. So how do we find our way out of this impasse and into a brighter future of theory? This is a question I am compelled to try to address; this monograph is my attempt.

What is metamodernism? It aspires to be a theoretical revolution. It charts a number of things: a process social ontology, a new multispecies semiotics, a revaluation of the place of values in the human sciences, and an alternative to the sterile opposition between realisms and anti-realisms. It seeks to establish a new model for producing humble knowledge that is capable of tracing the unfolding of de-essentialized master categories in their full complexity. It is about the future of the disciplines—not just my home disciplines, but the whole of the human sciences.

This represents a departure for me. Reflexivity is something I have been promoting for my entire scholarly career (and I am not stopping now). Turning the techniques of a discipline inward on itself regularly appears theoretically sophisticated and intellectually ambitious, and sometimes even gets praised as revolutionary. But limiting one's research to critical scholarship about scholarship tends to undercut the work of the disciplines and to reduce them to little more than ideological formations themselves—an act which is, essentially, destructive rather than creative.

It seems that deconstruction generally takes less effort and is better rewarded than construction. Despite all the controversy it inevitably evokes, it can be seductive to take the stance of an epistemological anarchist and to start exploding fundamental concepts and then reveling in the chaos as disciplines disintegrate. I have largely made my career out of such an attitude. I think this kind of work is valuable, but it is simply not enough.

After something has been destroyed, something new must be built, and for something new to be built, a movement is necessary. That movement, I hope, is metamodernism. Progress is made by collectives, not individuals. I am asking the reader to come with me and experience a paradigm shift—one that turns on my previous work not in order to repudiate it, but to work through my own critical presuppositions and out the other side so that a new of way of thinking can be born.

Like many of my scholarly cohort, I have come to feel as though I am living in the shadow of the previous generation's ideological conflicts. My parents are both analytic philosophers, and I originally majored in philosophy myself before I became alienated from it due to its exclusion of Asian philosophy. As a graduate student in Oxford, Paris, and Palo Alto, I had a strong interest in "theory" and made pilgrimages to lectures by such luminaries as Giorgio Agamben, Jacques Derrida, Bernard Faure, René Girard, Bruno Latour, Richard Rorty, Michel Serres, Cornel West, and Slavoj Žižek, among others. As I have been writing this book, I have been working through those influences, sometimes pitting various biological and intellectual progenitors against each other as I push to find a way out of the impasses that have come to constrain us. This has not been easy. I could have struggled with these philosophical forebearers forever and yet not felt myself fully ready—but I bit my tongue too long, so now I'm spitting blood.

This project originally came to me in Vienna in 2011, when I met an old friend for a drink at a café. My first book was poised to come out and my friend wanted to know how I was going to follow it, given that it was in some respects a critical genealogy of my whole subfield. The key insight he rightly suggested is that forthcoming projects might have something to do with what was going to come after postmodernism. Inspired by our conversation, I almost immediately began writing a few rough chapters of this book, and then I set about organizing and hosting a conference on "After Postmodernism." But soon thereafter I ended up shelving this very important project in order to write *The Myth of Disenchantment*. I originally thought that these two projects were connected—since in one I was trying to unravel "modernity" and in the other I was confronting and working through postmodernism—but they quickly diverged. This book remained in my thoughts, however, throughout that process.

In the course of writing, I took a break of four months to welcome my magnificent daughter into the world and to focus on her instead of scholarship, and this extended hiatus ended up producing a significant change in the work's tone. My earlier drafts were motivated by the destructive energy employed in the process of deconstructing deconstruction, according to my old mode; but the revisions I produced following my daughter's birth are rooted in compassion. It might not look like it, but this book is a love letter to my daughter, grounded in hope for our capacity to build a better world for the next generation.

This work was written and initially peer reviewed before COVID-19 became pandemic. Its final rounds of editing happened during self-isolation (with a toddler) while the virus caused rampant suffering in the world beyond our walls. My parents were sick and, although confirmational testing was unavailable, there were many anxious days when I worried for their health, but thankfully they recovered. They were lucky. Every day, I read obituaries of those less fortunate. Many days I nearly wept, worrying about the fate of our world.

It is much too early to say what impact this soft apocalypse will have on all of our futures. There will be a tendency to bookend history, to place this pandemic as a watershed. A world is ending, or perhaps has been ending for a long time. But an ending is also an opportunity for a new beginning. My hope is that the metamodern theory propounded in this project will help open the doors to a brighter future: the future of theory after postmodernism.

.

I would like to thank a number of people from around the globe whose conversations have been of immense benefit to me over the last decade or so. Thanks are due first of all to my parents and brother—John, Susan, and Seth Josephson—who are all scholars in their own right; to my dear friend, the mathematician Jeremy Bellay; and to three key friends at Williams College: Denise Buell, Jeffrey Israel, and Christian Thorne. In many respects the seeds of this creative project emerged from my productive conversations with these individuals.

I also want to mention the places where I have discussed some aspects of the work and received valuable feedback, including the American Academy of Religion conference, Duke University, Harvard University, Kyōto University, Northwestern University, Ohio University, Princeton University, Syracuse University, Tōyō University, Universität Heidelberg, Université de Genève, Université de Lausanne, Universiteit Antwerpen, University of California–Berkeley, University of North Carolina–Chapel Hill, and Vanderbilt University. But I owe a special debt of gratitude to the three institutions that have been my primary hosts during the writing process—Universität Leipzig, Ruhr-Universität, and Williams College.

This project benefitted from discussions with Richard Boyd, Balakrishnan Chandrasekaran, Ryan Coyne, Rita Felski, Sarah Hammerschlag, Andreas Hölke, Terence Keel, Volkhard Krech, Kathryn Lofton, Ron Mallon, Bojana Mladenovic, John Modern, Matthew O'Connell (who suggested the term "metamodernism" to me), Tania Ramalho, Bernie Rhie, Craige Roberts, Mark Schmanko, Myrna Perez Sheldon, Suman Seth, Knut Stünkel, Mark C. Taylor (whose big shoes I have been trying to fill here at Williams), Manuel Vásquez, and Tisa Wenger. Thank you all for the insights you brought to this material. I also learned much from students in classes I taught on Nietzsche, Social Construction, Word Virus, Theory after Postmodernism, and several iterations of the Religion Department's senior seminar. For the tedious work of written feedback on drafts of various chapters, thanks are also due to Zaid Adhami, Linda Ceriello, Seynabou Diop, Giovanni DiRusso, Georges Dreyfus, Andrew Durdin, Ezra Feldman, K. Healan Gaston, Warren Goldstein, Eleanor Goodman, Ruth Groff, M. Gail Hamner, Adrian Hermann, Jacqueline Hidalgo, Andre Hui, Andrew Jewett, Syd Jones, Susanne Ryuyin Kerekes, Lucas Klein, Christoph Kleine, Hans Martin Krämer, James Manigault-Bryant, Keith McPartland, Soban Mehmood, Avery Morrow, Eli Nelson, Ahmed Ragab, Josh Reynolds, Hubert Seiwert, Olga Shevchenko, Christina Simko, Claire Sufrin, Michael Thate, Phillip Webster, and Saadia Yacoob. I will always be in your debt.

I also want to thank Kyle Wagner, Alan Thomas, and the editorial board of the University of Chicago Press for believing in this project and helping shepherd it to completion. I'd also like to thank Evan Young and Mary Corrado for copyediting and Emily Han for indexing.

This book results in part from research conducted at the Kolleg-Forschungsgruppe "Multiple Secularities—Beyond the West, Beyond Modernities" at Leipzig University. The Kolleg-Forschungsgruppe is funded by the German Research Foundation. Research in Europe was also made possible by the World Travel Fellowship, Käte Hamburger Kolleg, Dynamiken der Religionsgeschichte, and the generous support of Williams College.

This book is dedicated to my two hearts—my wife, Dalena, and our wonderful daughter, Athena. Both are a constant source of inspiration and hope.

Jason Ānanda Josephson Storm
Williamstown, Massachusetts, 2020

Note on Texts and Citations

The main text of this book is just the tip of the iceberg; the endnotes are heavily interwoven with diverse secondary literature in varied philosophical traditions and academic disciplines in multiple languages. The manuscript as originally written was much too long for conventional publishing standards, so the process of preparing it for publication has resulted in a number of orphaned chapters on topics such as power, causation, Adorno, Derrida, Foucault, Hegel, Quine, and the history of postmodernism. I will likely publish some of these separately. Further content related to the book and links to these fugitive pieces as they appear will be available at a dedicated page on my professional website: https://absolute-disruption .com.

Although translations are few and far between compared to my previous books, those from Japanese, Chinese, French, Spanish, Italian, and German are my own unless otherwise noted. Japanese, Korean, and Chinese names in the text are presented in the traditional order — surname (in small caps) followed by given name.

Opening

[The] metamodern [is an] extension of and challenge to modernism and post-modernism.

MOYO OKEDIJI, *Transatlantic Dialogue: Contemporary Art in and out of Africa*

Categories decay. The human sciences* used to presuppose the possibility of intellectual progress, but for decades now a host of scholars have called into question the universality of the disciplinary objects and their utility as analytical categories. Conceptual analysis — once the bedrock of the philosophical enterprise — has failed. In many sectors of the academy, it now seems naive to presume the coherence of categories such as "art," "literature," or "religion," much less the possibility of *progress* or *knowledge*. The crowning insight of many disciplines in the human sciences — often reserved for senior majors and graduate students — is that their core conceptual categories are intellectually or ethically compromised. In most colleges and universities, students move unawares from the department of non-religion to the department of non-literature to the department of anthropology (in which they had better not attempt to evaluate culture).

For a while, the excitement of these negative positions — and, conversely, anxieties about them — were wrapped up in the term *postmodernism*. In this they came to meet with other forms of skepticism: epistemological, linguistic, and ethical. Even disciplines that had dodged the category critiques often found themselves caught in so-called postmodern problematics. Skeptical dogmas of all sorts proliferated. Doubt was praised over understanding. Truth was said to be a sham. Knowledge was nothing more than power. Philosophical problems were recast as problems of language, but then language itself became a problem. Communication was rendered suspect. Translation was believed impossible. Scholars became skeptical about the capacity of the word to reflect the world. As epistemological issues multiplied, they banished values from the human

---

* "Human Sciences" are humanities plus social sciences. But as I envision them, the human sciences should study not only humans (as a species of animal), but also our multispecies ecology and environment.

sciences, arguing that ethics were incompatible with objective scholarly inquiry or moral relativism. But ethical negativity also prospered in academic moralizing, if now primarily expressed in terms of disparagement and condemnation. For a time, many scholars imagined themselves to be masters of suspicion. Even today everything seems problematic and almost every thinker morally questionable. Such cynicism can be paralyzing.

This is intellectual life under the sign of the negative.

Postmodern skepticism was supposed to be liberating, but it failed us. Faced with the skeptical arsenal of "deconstruction," scholarship across the humanistic disciplines was dominated for a time by a kind of post-structuralist poetry and political posturing rooted in the play of homonyms.[1] Worse, by way of backlash, it has lately been overwhelmed by waves of radical particularity that are generally hostile toward all generalization. Both of these moves are errors that are leading us into intellectual dead ends. It should be no surprise that as analytical objects disintegrate, centrifugal forces push us further apart. Even theory—which once aimed to be a grand interdisciplinary synthesis—has begun to fracture along demographic lines. Intersectionality has too often been replaced by competing class and race reductionisms.[2] Indeed, over the last few decades, scholars have increasingly rejected the possibility of communication and meaningful generalizations, while scholarship succumbs to fragmenting hyperspecialization.

Scholarly retreats to the sociological survey, the micro-history, or the archive are not solutions but rather temporary gestures. As bad as word-play was, the renunciation of abstraction (which seems to be the scholarly move of the moment) ultimately abandons communication so completely that our efforts fall into dissolution. Deconstruction may have largely functioned as the self-inflicted martyrdom of a weak intelligentsia; and yet it would be an equally grave mistake to try to reverse course and retreat directly into the insincere comforts of a false universalism. It is not enough to be positivists, as though we did not know better.

Postmodernism left behind a set of philosophical challenges and models that linger in academic life. This matters because even if you do not consider yourself a theorist, even if you have no stated interest in postmodernism or the project of philosophy, if you are a scholar in the humanities or social sciences today you have almost certainly imbibed, without realizing it, a set of unquestioned convictions that originated in postmodernism.

There is a temptation in the face of the abyss of skepticism to recoil from its edge and to attempt to reconstruct the disciplinary master categories, reassert the supremacy of facts, or exchange skeptical doubts for partisan presuppositions—but this is, in effect, to answer negation with restoration disguised as redefinition. This would be a fatal mistake, a blind alley. It would result in merely the deferral of the central problematic. The decay of master narratives has led to a near-universal distrust of universals, while deepening particularity seems to promise nothing but further disintegration. We scholars need a better model that rejects both modernist essentialism and postmodernist skepticism; a way that is beyond both hyperspecialization and obscurantism; a way that is neither purely inward-gazing nor outward-assimilating, that can sustain the necessary tension in which self and other function in interdependent relationships.

We need to chart a new course.

Many people are dissatisfied with the current moment and are searching for a way out. The last fifty years have allegedly seen the human sciences undergo a series of course corrections. Philosophers began writing about *the linguistic turn* of the 1950s and 1960s. This opened the floodgate to at least three more "turns," as *cultural*, *interpretive*, and *historical turns* appeared in the late 1970s and early 1980s.[3] Then, in the late 1980s, there was a *cognitive turn*.[4] By the early 1990s scholars were compiling sources for *the postmodern turn*.[5] By the mid-1990s there was another *historic turn* (or perhaps it was merely the earlier historic turn reasserting itself).[6] Rather than growing weary, scholars kept going, and the late 1990s and early 2000s saw discussions of both a *turn to religion* and a *corporeal turn*.[7] The last couple of decades have seen a blinding series of turns, including (in rough chronology) the *speculative turn*, the *visual turn*, the *participatory turn*, the *affective turn*, the *material turn*, the *transnational turn*, the *pragmatic turn*, the *sensory turn*, the *historical turn* (now for the third time, perhaps having forgotten its history), the *mobility turn*, the *temporal turn*, the *spatial turn*, the *reparative turn*, the *animal* or *nonhuman turn*, a (perhaps antagonistic) *human turn*, and the *ontological turn*.[8] Scholars have also recently proposed a *pedagogical turn*, a *practice turn*, a *quotidian turn*, and an *empirical turn*, although it is not clear whether any of these will catch on.[9] At almost the same time I began writing this introduction, the Japanese scholars ISOMAE Jun'ichi and KAWAMURA Satofumi were calling for a Levinasian *alterity turn* (他者論的転回), while the American literary theorist Mark Seltzer was promoting what he refers to as a *turn turn*.[10]

Many of these represent the same movement by different names. They are typically promoted by scholars in one field in complete ignorance of what is going on in other disciplines. This is perhaps why so many allegedly different "turns" repeat the same set of topics—bodies, matter, visuality, emotions, affect, recurring invocations of history itself, and so on. This is also why scholars supporting allegedly identical turns come to conflicting conclusions (e.g., the ontological turn in anthropology is nearly the mirror opposite of the ontological turn in political theory). Although there are some bright exceptions, these repeated calls for turns tend to produce not so much intellectual innovations as the translation of older scholarly vocabulary into new jargon. Scholars in other disciplines keep rediscovering art history and material culture. We replace every reference to "structure" with "assemblage" or "network." The supposed revolutionary nature of these turns is largely confined to rhetorical gestures whose conventionality is masked by appeals to the language of radicalism and polemical condemnations of their proximate peers.[11]

There seem to have been enough "turns" at this point to imply the compulsive repetition of a trauma or perhaps a dizzy running in circles. But perhaps we are always turning away because we know neither where we have been nor what we are aiming for.

Many of these turns and related anti-postmodern philosophies (such as New Materialism, Speculative Realism, and Affect theory) suffer a common set of flaws. Undeniably each has some valuable insights, but by underestimating postmodernism's philosophical problematics they have often failed to capitalize on its gains or inadvertently walked the same blind alleys and roundabouts it evoked. New Materialists, for instance, have borrowed much of their intellectual edifice and specific analytic categories (actant, agency, assemblage, network, anthropocentrism) from the linguistic turn and often the very poststructuralists to which they now see themselves opposed. Speculative Realists have merely transposed into ontology the skepticisms of the antirealists, and in doing so largely agree with their supposed rivals. Affect theorists, in attempting to align psychological theories of affect against the poststructuralists, are actually agreeing with many poststructuralists who also imagined that emotions were outside of discourse, and arguing against many psychologists who have come to see emotions as culturally constructed rather than extradiscursive.[12] All that is to say, many contemporary scholars are defining their projects against postmodernism, but without realizing how much of their basic intellectual frameworks they have inherited from it.

 Postmodern skepticisms cannot be evaded; they must be worked through. And there is an array of beneficial results waiting at the other end for anyone patient enough to take the effort. To gesture at some of these potential gains:

Postmodern doubt can be made to doubt itself, and when cleansed of its negative dogmatism and lingering longing for lost certainties it can show us the way toward humble, emancipatory knowledge. Antifoundationalism can become a new foundation. Postmodern cynicism and moral outrage can be transmuted into positive ends—Revolutionary Happiness and multispecies flourishing. Irony and despair can become fierce joy and hope. Beyond anti-essentialism is not a new essentialism, but a world of becoming. Rather than defending the master categories from criticism, we can grant and build on those criticisms—because if all these sundry critiques are granted, they actually tell us something fundamental about the social world and the nature of the categories themselves. Put differently, regardless of the status of postmodernism, this monograph provides a new theory of the social world (applying not just to humans but also other animal species) and a new ethical model for the human sciences. Taken together, these insights and others point the way to a bright future for epistemic and ethical enterprises across the disciplines. The stakes for *all* scholars in the humanities and social sciences couldn't be higher. Nietzsche philosophized with a hammer; here I mean to philosophize with lightning.[13]

To herald the coming movement I hope to inspire with a name, I am using the term "metamodernism."[14] Only a handful of significant theorists have used this term previously, so associations with it are mostly unformed, but I am primarily following in the footsteps of the Nigerian art historian Moyo Okediji, who described metamodernism as an artistic attempt to both extend and challenge modernism and postmodernism together.[15] (For other uses of "metamodernism" see note).[16] Taking Okediji as my initial inspiration, I am applying this form of metamodernism in a positive philosophical mode for the first time. In that respect, previous scholars of "metamodernism" or "metamodernity" are welcome to take this book as an attempt to construct a particular metamodern philosophy and not an attempt to define the entirety of metamodernism per se.

I will return to the term "metamodernism" repeatedly throughout the book, and will build upon this initial perfunctory gesture at characterization, but for the moment just remember that the "meta-" prefix here is primarily meant to suggest a higher- or second-order position beyond (post)modernism. Put differently, the main emphasis in metamodernism should be on this "meta" and not the "modernism." But as we build to a greater understanding of everything that metamodernism entails, I will draw inspiration from many "postmodern" and "modern" philosophers, recovering parts of their theories in order to construct this new one. (Hence, what follows may occasionally look shockingly modernist and at other times startlingly postmodernist.)

So how might we move beyond postmodernism? There is another way that has not yet been tried. I would like to put forward an approach that is neither deconstruction nor restoration—as a substitute, I think we need to find *the negation of the negation.* This is because the various postmodern philosophies seem ideally suited to dialectical analysis. We might therefore think that G.W.F. Hegel, the putative "master of the dialectic," could shed some light not only on where postmodernism has been, but also on what it might productively transform. After all, aren't all the various "anti-," "post-," and "de-" prefixes merely different ways of defining a position as the antithesis or negation of its predecessor?

This project does not rely on Hegel's authority. It is not meant to suggest a return to Hegelianism. Hegel's dialectic is merely a source of inspiration. But his account of the movement of thought, especially the negation of the negation, is valuable insofar as it suggests the crucial moment on which the dialectic advances.

In brief, I see the negation of the negation as different and distinct from an older positivity; it is a further radicalization of the negation.[17] No mere rejection of the preceding system, it has actual content. In a geometrical sense, we can imagine tracing the boundaries of a complex figure. This is the first negation, which separates the figure from the ground around it. In the negation of the negation, both the specific contradictions *and* the preceding order are integrated into the form of the second-order negation, which means that a two-dimensional metaphor for visualizing such a figure becomes insufficient. The preceding system is not only cancelled out but is also assimilated into the new system. It has to account for the older totality even as it traces the foundation across which antinomies appear. It therefore preserves in its movement the contradictions of various inherent negativities. To deepen the geometrical metaphor, it is like rotating the figure into a new dimension of space (adding features along a new axis) or turning the figure inside out to produce a new object that provides a place for the old antagonisms to appear unresolved. Hegel's dialectic could thus be thought of as a three-dimensional spiral, passing over its starting point while perpetually ascending.[18] It is a return, but a return in a higher key. Thus, to proceed would seem to require building on the older skeptical gesture to articulate a new concept (hence, *meta*modernism).

To skirt a cliché, we need a Copernican revolution. We need to revolve the human sciences on their axis. This is not a turn in the fixed plane of disciplinary horizons (as so many other turns have been) but rather a three-dimensional reorientation. Rather than running in circles, we need to spiral upward. The center must move if we are not going to fall into further fragmentation.

In sum, I aim to move beyond deconstruction by radicalizing it or turning it inside out. While it may sound paradoxical, negating negativity is actually the beginning of a positive gesture that authorizes the new accumulation of knowledge. It seems absurd that while the natural sciences seem to be making consistent progress, the human sciences seem to be continually circling the drain. In a gesture that may look like pulling the plug, I believe there is hope for the future.

This is a book for people who are sick of "Theory." People who are tired of gratuitous namedropping; anti-authoritarian arguments from authority; shallow insights masked in obscurantism; self-loathing humans claiming to represent the agency of microbes; Americanization masquerading as diversification; and most crucially, theory that is merely jargon overlaid on predetermined political judgments. This a book for people who wish that more scholars in the humanities and social sciences chose theories based on empirical adequacy instead of prior ideological commitments. For those people, this book provides a set of empirically testable theories in the philosophy of the human sciences. If taken seriously, it will provide new methodological openings that should lead to fresh scholarly inquiries into the nature of our human and nonhuman environment. It does not presume that you must care about the meaning of postmodernism other than as a springboard for serious theorizing. This work is no mere posturing—it has pragmatic implications for how we should do our scholarship. It is also a meta-work about theory formation itself, and as such it tells us something significant about theories (and about generalizations in general) in the human sciences. It tells us which sorts of theories are likely to hold, which sorts of theories need more substantiation, and which theories must be terminated.

This is also a book for people who are content with the current fragmented theoretical landscape—people who shrug their shoulders at the question of where theory (or philosophy) goes from here; people who are *not* kept up at night by the putative impasse between modernism and postmodernism; people who perhaps even feel liberated from the need to think about questions of epistemology since a broader shift toward phenomenology opens up space for them to focus on questions of identity and politics in ethically motivated subdisciplines. This work draws on and allies itself with current works in feminist theory, critical Black studies, postcolonial theory, science studies, queer theory, and environmental studies. Indeed, it can help further many of the ambitions behind these movements. This is because understanding sources of skepticism about climate change, the causes of anti-Black racism, secular hegemony and their entanglement requires a broader understanding of the social world, which this monograph aims to contribute. This work thus proffers a re-theorizing of the social sphere, including a fresh theory of the formation of social categories (applicable to race, religion, gender, art, and so on). If we want to change society, we need to understand it better.

This book provides a positive vision of a possible ethical and political goal rooted in compassion and multispecies flourishing, a vision of how we might struggle together toward utopia in dystopian times. For those readers who are not yet disenchanted with the various strains of pessimism that have recently come to dominance, this book makes a case for why they should be, because the alternative to progress is being caught in the same impasses that have ensnared us for so long. We must seek the way out and forward, because once we do we will be able to build a better world together.

In addition, this book provides a big picture in which various theoretical subdisciplines can situate themselves. Given that postmodernism and allied theories are waning, metamodernism aims to provide a new grand synthesis. It charts the way that normative and epistemological commitments should be intertwined and suggests openings for further dialogue.

Scholars in religious studies and related disciplines will want to know that this is the first full-length work to line up the various critiques of disciplinary master categories ("religion," but also "science," "art," etcetera) and trace out their affinities and shared conceptual roots. Doing this is not only historicizing; it also suggests an innovative approach to scholarship across the disciplines that would have been out of reach for anyone embedded in a singular disciplinary horizon. Thus, metamodernism represents a major intervention with implications across the humanities and social sciences. It is intended to be a concise prolegomenon to a new research program that will be generative to work in a diversity of fields.

This book is for all readers, but perhaps the most important reader is a scholar or graduate student in the human sciences who has a research project they are passionate about. To make this work accessible to such a reader, I have intentionally avoided jargon, obfuscation, and bullshit. This is nevertheless a very academic book, and its unadorned prose is quite dense, such that a careless skimmer may find themselves caught in inadvertent traps. For a reader to get the most benefit, this book must be read carefully, with the hermeneutics of charity, and with resistance to disciplinary territorialism.

0.1 Into the Abyss: Postmodernism Unraveling

At the start, I want to make some effort to specify my target—or at the very least my terminological choice about the thing we are in the process of eclipsing. To take a typical example of what I have in mind, the entry on "Postmodernism" in *Encyclopedia of Activism and Social Justice* (2007) reads as follows:

> [Postmodernists argue that] language does not reflect reality outside of it and no theory—scientific or not—can objectively represent the social and

natural world which solely consists of texts, inter-texts, interpretations and discourses. . . . Postmodernism can be philosophically associated with an unsystematic skepticism against faith in rationality, objectivity, and scientific knowledge. The rise of epistemological anti-realism and ethical relativism seem to be the main characteristic features of Postmodernism in philosophy.[19]

[handwritten marginalia: = end of some-thing]

This sample definition presents a concise and fairly representative summary of many scholars' default assumptions about postmodernism. The entry's author also accurately observes, "It has been repeatedly suggested that what is new in this epoch is . . . that it is the end of something: the end of ideology, the end of history, the end of philosophy, [or] the end of reality."[20]

This is a good depiction of what the academy under the sign of the negative looked like, regardless of what term was used to describe it. But many characterizations of postmodernism include a similar list of features. Although not always with the same succinctness, postmodernism in philosophy is typically associated with: 1) antirealism; 2) an emphasis on endings, which has often included disciplinary autocritique; 3) an extreme version of the linguistic turn that characterizes the world in terms of texts; 4) a broad climate of skepticism; and 5) ethical relativism (sometimes called "ethical nihilism")—all of this is regularly bundled together under the term "postmodernism."[21]

Here is the thing: all five of these are genuine theoretical issues irrespective of anything called postmodernism. Much of this monograph will be working out these problematics in turn and it will demonstrate how addressing them correctly actually permits a reconceptualization of epistemology, ethics, and social ontology. But there are two further points I want to elaborate before we do: first, these conundrums do not correspond to the thinking of any specific thinkers; and second, these issues are older than most accounts of postmodernism give credit.

For starters, the properties of a generic postmodernism might suggest its rough interchangeability with a small group of similar terms. Since the 1980s, four terms have been increasingly used in the Anglophone academy to chart a semi-overlapping and inconsistent terrain: *deconstruction, poststructuralism*, *"French Theory,"* and *postmodernism*. Initially, these might suggest a set of expanding circles—*deconstruction* naming the work of Jacques Derrida and his followers; *poststructuralism* growing to include other responses to structuralism such as those by Roland Barthes, Jean Baudrillard, Michel Foucault, Luce Irigaray, Julia Kristeva, and Jacques Lacan; "French theory" seemingly expanding this circle still further to suggest a greater range of French thinkers from Pierre Bourdieu to Giles

Deleuze to François Laruelle; and finally, *postmodernism* bringing art, literature, and philosophy together and broadening out from the Francophone context to include German and American thinkers like Martin Heidegger, Walter Benjamin, and Richard Rorty.

This approximation has distinct flaws. These are exonyms, as almost none of the primary theorists named above actively embraced these terms to describe their movements. These thinkers would not have agreed with being sorted into one camp or the other (there were no self-described "*post-structuralistes*" in France). The terms are also used inconsistently; what one philosopher will criticize as deconstruction, another will characterize as postmodernism or poststructuralism. The terms' conflation is apparent in frequent messy hybrids like "deconstructive postmodernism" or "postmodern poststructuralism."[22] Given how blurry the boundaries are among terms, one might get the sense that we are not talking about a multiplicity of movements but one variegated movement referred to variously.

All four movements are often assumed to be European in origin and described together as a European "invasion" of American philosophy, but independent specialists have repeatedly made the opposite observation about each of these terms—namely, that what gets called deconstruction, poststructuralism, and French theory bears very little relation to any recognizably European projects and is instead closer to an American subversion or parody.[23] Hence, there seems to be a consensus among historians of these movements that this whole cluster of theories—whether referred to as *poststructuralism, postmodernism*, or *deconstruction*—is an American invention.[24] More precisely, there is a strong case to be made that these movements have resulted from a North American engagement with a number of predominantly French (and sometimes German) theorists from different disciplines, whose works, after having been reformulated in the Anglophone academy, were then re-imported in modified form back into Western Europe. I basically agree with this historiographical intervention as far as it goes. But we could take it further.

Before we move on, I want to reconstruct in the barest of brushstrokes how we got here. Anglo-American philosophy's attempt to reformulate itself as a "scientific discipline," along with increasing overspecialization, primed scholars in other human sciences to look elsewhere for grand theorizing.[25] Thus, the role previously accorded to philosophy came to be occupied instead by imported European forms of "theory." Literature departments were already prepared to import philosophy because of the preexisting popularity of literary expressions of existentialism. These departments soon became key sites for the formation of the so-called poststructuralist or postmodern canon (note the irony of canonizing an

anti-canon), which was produced by drawing together European thinkers from different disciplinary backgrounds that were often opposed to
each other. This canon became increasingly linked to emancipatory political struggles both within existing departments and in complement to
the birth of women's studies and many ethnic studies programs (which
had sprung up in part to address the needs of an increasingly diversified
student body).[26] The critical response to these critiques by establishment
figures only served to solidify a sense of a counter-movement. Looked at
from this vantage, "French theory," "postmodernism," and "poststructuralism" were not so much separate movements as a spectrum of Anglo-
American appropriations of continental theory, which were marshalled
together to address preexisting domestic intellectual concerns and then
re-exported to Europe (and the rest of the globe) as a fresh bricolage of
skeptical dogmas.

I use *postmodernism* to talk about this whole spectrum of theories, but
to their proponents and critics they were often referred to as *postmodernism, deconstruction, poststructuralism*, or *French theory* (the differences
between these will mostly be irrelevant in what follows). Under these
names, a set of skeptical doctrines, yoked to emancipatory politics, effectively served as a model—a method—even a program for intellectual life.
The issues they evoked were not new. They represented preexisting elements in a new constellation. What was historically new was their sway. It
was difficult for a younger scholar to enter the humanities and many of the
social sciences from the 1980s until the mid-2000s without assenting to
the prescribed premises discussed below. In many of the disciplines these
got entangled with category decay and autocritique. The consequences of
this entanglement continue to impact scholarship today.

Much of what we regard as the novelty of these movements has been
with us for a long time, much longer than is conventionally supposed by
even those historians aware of these movements' American backgrounds.
This deeper history can be excavated. It is important not because of some
arbitrary fetishism of origins, but rather because the key philosophical
positions associated with philosophical postmodernism can be found
happily coexisting alongside other commitments normally taken to be
antithetical to the movement. The discovery of this will be part of what
frees us from postmodernism's long shadow.

·

We can start with the term "postmodernism" itself. Tantalizing references
to the "postmodern" or "postmodernists" began appearing in English-,
German-, and Spanish-speaking contexts at the dawn of the twentieth cen-

tury.[27] For instance, in *Die Krisis der europäischen Kultur* (1917), the German philosopher Rudolf Pannwitz had already begun arguing that a calamity in European intellectual and cultural life had produced an ethical vacuum leading to a new type of person that he called "the postmodern man" (*postmoderne mensch*).[28] The appearance of this text and even the term *postmodern* more than a century ago allows us to see that characterizations of the postmodern condition are far from new. Nor was Pannwitz unique. The first English book with "postmodernism" in its title came out in 1926.[29] On a basic philological level, what these examples show is that the term *postmodern* became lexically available shortly after 1901, when variants on the term *pre-modern* appeared and came into common usage in a number of European linguistic repertoires. No sooner had "modernity" become the quintessential periodization than it became possible to imagine its future eclipse.

Now it is the postmodern that is waning, even as we continue to be haunted by it. This is because the most influential studies of "postmodernism" in culture—by Jean-François Lyotard, David Harvey, Fredric Jameson, and Charles Jencks—explored artistic, philosophical, and cultural trends of the 1970s and 1980s that have mainly fallen out of vogue in the years since.[30] For example, paradigmatically postmodern authors (like Alain Robbe-Grillet) seem passé today; the weight given to television in theories of postmodern cultural analysis is equally dated; and the same could be said about almost everything associated with the so-called postmodern zeitgeist, from postmodern architecture to painting. Even Jameson's identification of postmodernity with "Late Capitalism," while prescient (especially insofar as we still live in a media-saturated consumer society), still depicted a pre-internet, pre-2008 financial collapse, pre-precariat, pre-credit default swaps, pre-pandemic, pre-surveillance capitalism version of the global economy.[31]

Even at its heights, postmodernism seemed to refer not to a global pattern, but to narrow and selective groupings of Euro-American cultural production. Philosophers in the rest of the world often wondered about whether they could be "postmodern before being modern."[32] "Postmodernity" was unevenly distributed at best. This was true even in North America: while theorists like bell hooks and Cornel West drew on postmodern philosophy, they also criticized how badly the theorizing of postmodern art and culture described Black American artistic and cultural production.[33]

In addition to postmodernism being outdated and parochial, many descriptions of what defined it are also inaccurate. Lyotard famously argued that the defining feature of postmodernity was that the "grand narrative has lost its credibility." But in his moment, as today, metanarratives were far from vanishing. Even when philosophers rejected master narratives, non-philosophers still expounded plenty of master narratives. Narratives of progress, secularization, democratization, enlightenment, and the like were retold by politicians, filmmakers, tech entrepreneurs, psychologists, and even many scholars. Much of the postmodern canon was even rooted in its own pessimistic grand narratives about the fallenness of Being, colonialism, the death of God, or disenchantment. In this last respect, modernism is more similar to postmodernism than is typically described, because many avowed modernists were also pessimists about progress, and references to secularization and rationalization were often framed as laments. All that is to say, *contra* Lyotard, that the death of metanarratives was celebrated prematurely. It was not the defining feature of the post-modernity of his era, and even today I see no end to metanarratives.[34]

.

There is another philosophical opposition we need to shed. One common way to define "postmodernism" is as a rejection of "positivism."[35] When this "positivism" is identified with a specific philosophical movement it is usually the "logical positivism" of the Vienna Circle.[36] The surprise therefore is that the logical positivists shared a number of positions that have since become associated with postmodernism, and others that turn out to be common to an Anglo-American school of literary theory known as New Criticism. We can see this if we return to the common features associated with postmodernism (the history of disciplinary autocritique will be explored separately in chapter 2).

First, *antirealism*. As I discuss in chapter 1, Derrida and company were not the antirealists they are often accused of being.[37] But Rudolf Carnap, the most famous of the Vienna positivists, *was* an antirealist. As he put it in *Der Logische Aufbau der Welt* (1928): "It is shown that the thesis of realism, asserting the reality of the external word . . . are pseudostatements, sentences without factual content."[38] The surprise for many contemporary neo-realists who see themselves as defenders of science is that Carnap and company argued that realism was unnecessary for the natural sciences.

Second, *the linguistic turn*. Few charges are as widespread as the claim that postmodernism represented a relativistic "linguistic turn."[39] But the phrase "the linguistic turn" was initially coined by Gustav Bergmann in 1953 to describe a movement in logical positivism.[40] Key features of the linguistic turn, though, go back even earlier—to New Criticism.[41] For instance, the "death of the author" was explicitly theorized in the 1940s (decades before Roland Barthes) by members of New Criticism.[42] Furthermore, C.K. Ogden and I.A. Richards introduced Ferdinand de Saussure to many Anglophone readers in *The Meaning of Meaning* (1923), a work which also addressed claims often associated with (post)structuralists, such as the arbitrariness of the sign, the power of discourse, and the idea that language determined or socially constructed concepts. It even presented a version of the prison-house of language metaphor (often misattributed to Nietzsche).[43]

Third, *generalized skepticism.* The pioneering disability studies theorist Tobin Siebers has argued that postmodern and poststructuralist skepticism are better thought of as "Cold War criticism," first articulated by theorists connected to New Criticism in the 1940s who cultivated "the project of opposing thought to itself" and formulated a "skepticism about endings, intentions, interpretations . . . and claims to truth and falsehood."[44] Siebers held that this largely functioned to project a sense of political or intellectual urgency on what was in practice inward-looking and depoliticized criticism. We can see, for instance, the attack on "totalizing systems of thought" as a vestige of critiques of "totalitarianism," a term which was deployed primarily by American anti-Communists to lump together Stalinism and Nazism. Although I emphasize alternate sources of skepticism in chapter 6, I think Siebers is right that a general climate of skepticism, irony, and doubt began long before the supposed heyday of postmodernism.

Fourth, and finally, *ethical relativism or ethical nihilism.* As I show in chapter 7, the common claim that postmodernism is a rejection of ethics is false. Most postmodernists have been moralists. But influential positivists—like A.J. Ayer—did actually reject ethics as mere emotional statements. Moreover, long before postmodernism was accused of ethical nihilism, positivism was accused of the same thing. For instance, Karl Popper contended that "positivism" was an "expression of ethical nihilism; that is to say, of an extreme moral skepticism."[45] Nor was he alone in making similar accusations about a Logical Positivist rejection of ethics.[46]

In precis, four of the main charges against postmodernism—its putative antirealism, "the linguistic turn," generalized skepticism, and ethical nihilism—can be equally laid at the feet of Logical Positivism and New Criticism. But the striking thing is that, in positivism at least, these positions were largely disconnected from pessimism and cynicism, and the positivists were, if anything, optimistic and intensely pro-science. Given this, postmodernists seem like the positivists' disillusioned cousins. Moreover, these various philosophical problematics—alongside the term "postmodernism"—were already available in the Anglo-American academy by the 1950s (if not earlier). But it took time for them to be hybridized into what amounted to a coherent intellectual model. While there are reasons one might want to distinguish between deconstruction, poststructural-ism, and the like, historicizing their origins has suggested that they are in many respects better thought of as different aspects of the same move-ment. Thus, they must be overcome together.

•

In summary, postmodernism—as an intellectual style—has been hard to grasp in part because it cannot be found principally in the writings of French theorists whom most scholars seem to mash together or get wrong anyway. The poststructuralist criticism of an American film theorist who has only read the most cited fragments of Deleuze and Baudrillard has more to do with his or her particular disciplinary formation than with the writings of either French philosopher. This means that we will neither overcome nor perfect postmodernism by developing a more exhaustive reading of any "primary" theorist.

Postmodernism and its sub-movements live secondhand in a range of different disciplinary compilations. As Thomas Kuhn argued, textbooks often reveal a "community's paradigms" because introductory works sug-gest the simplistic exaggerations and secondhand critiques that often function as established truths throughout academic disciplines and are reinforced as part of the disciplining process itself.[47] Postmodernism was taught to burgeoning scholars either to inspire particular philosophical commitments or to function as a research model, or even sometimes as the reverse—a whetstone against which to sharpen counter-arguments. It was a pastiche that emerged from an amalgamation of disparate frag-ments pieced together in textbooks and edited volumes and reconstructed by secondary figures.

Most canonical postmodernist theorists were not actually antirealists, ethical nihilists, or universal skeptics. That said, antirealism, ethical nihil-ism, and skepticism are actual philosophical problems. Indeed, they sug-gest certain fundamental questions about reality, values, and knowledge that any serious scholar in the humanities or social sciences will have to address. I am not an anti-postmodernist; rather, I think that most of what has been understood as postmodernist theory is susceptible to diminish-ing returns, and that those returns have already diminished beyond the point of usefulness. Postmodernism's moment has passed. It's time to work through it and past it.

Metamodernism is what we get when we take the strategies associated with postmodernism and productively reduplicate and turn them in on themselves. This will entail disturbing the symbolic system of poststruc-turalism, producing a genealogy of genealogies, deconstructing deconstruction, and providing a therapy for therapeutic philosophy. Like a snake devouring its own tail, the very (in)coherence of postmodernism as false unity can be productively disrupted, shattered and disaggregated. This alone will not be sufficient to either prove its validity or move us past it; after all, it is a move anticipated by the main theorists associated with the movement itself. The surprise, however, is that granting most of these skeptical challenges will provide us with a new vantage on the theoretical enterprise as a whole.

·

To head off a misunderstanding, I am not using the term "metamodernism" to describe a period or collective zeitgeist. While the metamodernism I am describing here is not incompatible with such projects, I am skeptical of both sweeping periodizations and the whole notion of broad epistemes for the following reasons.

Grand periodizing concepts such as modernity, postmodernity, and metamodernity are generally incoherent. As I argued in *The Myth of Disenchantment*, the term "modernity" is itself vague.[48] There can be value in vagueness, but "modernity" rests on an extraordinarily elastic temporality that is elaborated in disparate and value-laden ways in different regions and periods. Modernity is as much a *spatial* as a temporal category, and to call a culture modern was typically to ally it with newness and to consign its other to some form of colonization. Modernization also picks out different uneven processes (e.g., urbanization, rationalization, globalization), while modernism captures various dispersed artistic, scientific, or philosophical movements. To speak of "modernity," "modernization," or some broad "modernist" episteme is to select from within these and to bundle them together. Enunciations of modernity are not just vague; they are doing a lot of covert work, and "modernity's" main feature is its capacity to reify a rupture or breach, which it marks as the expression of a single horizon of temporality. Moreover, as I showed in *The Myth of Disenchantment* most versions of this rupture never really occurred (e.g., we were never disenchanted). Modernity is used paradoxically to indicate equally a diversity of historical and geographic ruptures, a set of contradictory processes, and a cross-cultural episteme and to describe a continuous now-time used for different "nows" from the fourteenth century to the present. All of these are erroneous.

Characterizations of the current epoch as *postmodern* are also misguided because the concept of "postmodernity" contains a kind of core misrecognition. Postmodernity has never really worked as a periodization. Discussions of *modernism* and *postmodernism* often refer to the same canon of early thinkers; for example, Nietzsche, Freud, Marx, Kafka, Samuel Beckett, and James Joyce were often defined as "paradigmatic modernists" before being claimed as paradigmatic early "postmodernists."[49] Indeed, the appearance of the term "postmodernism" is roughly contemporaneous with characteristically "modernist" art movements like Cubism and Dadaism. While *postmodernism* is often described as a counterreaction to *modernism*, the meaning of both terms often overlapped inasmuch as they both suggested transcending "modernity." Later, postmodernity came to be presented as a second rupture after the initial "modern" rupture. In this respect, both periodizations rest on the idea of a fundamental break from the past, which, while inflected differently, often presumes the very notion of modernity I have previously worked to dispel.

Neither "modernity" nor "postmodernity" is doing us much good as a conceptual lens; if anything, they seem to be masking serious theoretical disagreements under a superficially shared terminology. I don't want metamodernism to fall into the same trap. Claiming that metamodern culture oscillates between modernist and postmodernist modes would be adding further obscurity on top of two already overly general periodizations.

Chronological periods can be useful as shorthand. But, as I will argue, periodizers typically go about their work backwards by emphasizing similarities instead of the causes of those similarities (see especially chapters 4 and 6). Many of what are supposed to be a period's defining features are not uniformly available. Furthermore, *contra* Kuhn, multiple competing research paradigms are often operative simultaneously in the same discipline (e.g., string theory versus loop quantum gravity). The concept of worldview is itself incoherent. My point here is that it would take a lot of evidence to persuade me that there were ever any generic, epochal paradigms or worldviews. Postmodernism, even at the height of its dominance, was never the sole operative research paradigm in the human sciences. Nor was there a single episteme "modernists" shared.

Metamodernism has been used by other scholars to characterize artistic, cultural, and religious movements. This work is valuable on its own. But metamodernism should not be thought of as a pervasive zeitgeist (at least, that is not what I aim to describe here). If periodizations are ways of describing technological, political, cultural, or philosophical constellations, then I think we could adapt what William Gibson said about the future, and note: if metamodernity is here, it's not evenly distributed. I would thus like to encourage finer-grained periodizations (both spatial and temporal) and alternate ways of conceptualizing history and uneven or nonlinear historical trajectories (returns, hauntings, prefigurations).

•

All told, postmodernism is not the only movement that will be eclipsed. In what follows, I work through and past much of what was thought of as "modernism" as well. I do not want to dismiss all differences between modernism and postmodernism, but there has been a shared conceptual terrain that gets ignored when the two are presented in polarization.

I cannot emphasize this enough: what I am trying to overcome is not some arbitrarily defined "postmodernism" or long-refuted positivism or modernism; rather, my actual target is a set of near hegemonic models for doing scholarship in the human sciences. Most fundamentally, meta-modernism is an attempt to give rise to the next phase of the dialectic, or to advance the movement of thought in Hegelian terms. Rather than just a response to postmodernism or an oscillation between modernist and postmodernist modes, metamodernism is an overcoming of both. But insofar as postmodernism is itself primarily a negation of the preceding mode of modernism, metamodernism *must* negate postmodernism in turn *without* merely returning to the previous system.

Thus, in Hegelian terms, metamodernism represents the sublation or *Aufheben* of all that preceded it. This book lifts up both modernism and postmodernism and shows that the places in which they overlap, as well as their shared conceptual strategies, are at the root of a number of philosophical neuroses. Metamodernism aims to lead us forward—not in the manner of a centrist politics that seeks to build itself in the space two opposing camps share, but in a *cancellation* of the two previous camps that works by demolishing shared philosophical assumptions in both terrains. Some oppositions will be rendered irrelevant; others will be undermined. A very select few will be hybridized into new forms. These will form the basis of new theorization.

But (and this is also a key point) metamodernism does not stand on my characterization of past movements. It is not an argument rooted in the authority of particular philosophical progenitors; nor is it an attempt to describe an already inchoate moment. It is rather an exercise of first-order theorizing. If successful, the results should be self-sufficient, my brief account of postmodernism here functioning only as a catalyst.

0.2 Overview of the Work

This book is about the future of not just one discipline, but all the human sciences. My suspicion is that the way forward for religious studies is also the way forward for other fields. Indeed, this work's founding impulse necessitates a meta-level view beyond that of any one discipline. To explain: a range of theorists have justly criticized academic disciplines for their increasing in-group partisanship, construction of disciplinary silos, exclusion of other disciplinary perspectives, and inward fragmentation.[50] Communication breakdowns across fields are common. Scholars are increasingly working on basically the same topics, but in total ignorance of each other. What one might call "territorial pissing" is widespread as academic departments are often pitted against each other for increasingly scarce funding.

This academic trend has been combined with a broader shift toward "epistemological insiderism," which Rogers Brubaker has defined as "the belief that identity qualifies or disqualifies one from writing with legitimacy and authority about a particular topic."[51] I do not want to repudiate insider scholarship in general (just as I think there is a place for specialization), but it would seem that identitarian preoccupations combined with hyperspecialization necessarily leads to navel-gazing. Across the humanities and social sciences, in counterreaction to previous generations' artificial fetishizing of putatively impartial distance, contemporary scholars are increasingly coming to position themselves inside the community they study and to delegitimize the scholarship of outsiders by attacking their identity positions.[52] The epistemic justification for this is often standpoint theory, which is sometimes *misread* as maintaining that knowledge is completely reducible to social standpoint. Paradoxically, this has led to scholars gesturing at other people's social standpoints[53] — for instance, straight white scholars validating their arguments by signaling their argumentative affinity with the standpoints of queer people of color. (Yet if knowledge were completely reducible to standpoint, then not only would this whole signaling business be pointless, but also there would be no reason ever to try to persuade anyone outside of one's own standpoint community.)

In summary, we are increasingly writing for ourselves and in ignorance of our intellectual neighbors. Despite the common rhetoric of interdisciplinarity, many attempts at crossing disciplinary boundaries fall victim to internal firing squads. Indeed, many scholars unfortunately mistake territorial pissing for rigor and blinkered hyperspecialization for depth, but a work that is narrow will miss an immense swath of common ground. The good news is that this is not inevitable. There is a way out by means of anti-disciplinarity and new forms of theoretical abstraction.

This is a stance I need to explicate, especially because in many sectors of the academy philosophy has a reputation for being nothing more than the perspective of "dead white men" who claimed to have access to the universal while simultaneously excluding/discrediting those whose experiences/ subject positions were being marginalized.[54] Similarly, it has often been observed that totalizing systems of thought aspire to explain everything and therefore frequently generate built-in mechanisms for automatically dismissing criticisms of their all-encompassing visions (e.g., if you reject the ubiquity of class struggle it must be because you have "false consciousness"). As a result, any claim to have produced a complete system or to have apprehended universals is now held suspect, and rightly so.

Yet, as Kwasi Wiredu has pointed out, while decolonizing philosophy necessitates the "unmasking" of "spurious universals," not all generalizations are necessarily false.[55] But the broader the generalization one aims to make, the higher the standard of evidence must be. The universal cannot be approached directly; it must be apprehended in the particular. This means that we must always be careful that our specific vantage on a totality has not led us to mistake a local formation for the whole. But if any moment ever called out for broad solutions and higher-order abstractions, it is this one, in which individualist solutions to collective problems are regularly ending in failure. We will never solve anthropogenic climate change, structural racism, or patriarchal hegemony if we are incapable of thinking in terms of totalities.

In this book I put forth a system for an era of anti-system, but with two significant qualifications: (1) It is a system premised on its own incompleteness. In a way, it is a *non-system system* based on an examination of the places in which certain systems have typically broken down, and rooted in a radicalization of skepticism that embraces its own finitude and eventually obsolescence. It presumes that epistemological progress comes not from the rational cogitations of an isolated ego, but via a collective struggle in which we mutually work to verify and falsify each other.[56] And (2) it is an *anti-universalist universalism* because it posits not homogeneity or stability, but the ubiquity of diversity, heterogeneity, and change. By emphasizing the pervasiveness of change, I am speaking to this very philosophy's own demise. Yet by embracing impermanence, we can still make progress together. Perhaps a god's eye view comes not from a singular vision but from many eyes.

Accordingly, what follows draws widely on disciplines outside both my primary intellectual home (Religious Studies) and my secondary fields (Asian Studies and Science & Technology Studies). This monograph will show some of this breadth, but this work is necessarily idiosyncratic and incomplete. I will leave it to readers from other disciplines to see which aspects appeal to them, and I hope that other inspired scholars out there will find ways to apply the techniques outlined here to their own research.

There is only so much that I can do in one book, but with the help of other committed interlocutors, the potential payoffs of this project can be great.

.

This book sets out from the five problematics associated with post-modernism: 1) antirealism, 2) disciplinary autocritiques, 3) the linguistic turn, 4) a broad climate of skepticism, and 5) ethical nihilism; and by working through each of them seriously and dialectically produces something new. They will become in turn: 1) metarealism, 2) process social ontology and social kinds, 3) hylosemiotics, 4) Zeteticism, and 5) a revaluation of values converging on Revolutionary Happiness. Again, these five areas have pragmatic consequences irrespective of anything called post-modernism. Theorists have spent a long time circling a small set of fundamental problematics. This is because, whether they are aware of it or not, all scholars in the human sciences need epistemology, ethics (or at least an intellectual goal), a notion of meaning, and a set of research methods for studying social kinds. This is my attempt to produce such. It is an open system in the era of anti-system.

The argument of the book proceeds as follows:

The initial chapter, "How the Real World Became a Fable," begins by reconstructing the shared theoretical commitments of a range of realist and antirealist philosophers. The surprise is that while a split between realists and antirealists organizes a host of polemical conflicts, members of these putatively rival camps actually share more than they realize. By dialectically working through the putative opposition, the chapter shows where realism and antirealism turn into each other.

I argue that "real" is primarily a contrastive or negative term, which gains most of its meaning from an opposing concept (e.g., a veggie burger is not real meat but it is real food). I suggest that we might want to call the position that grants the contrastive or modal nature of the real "metarealism," as it is beyond both realism and antirealism. The further challenge is that there is a long history of identifying the "real" as mind-independent and in contrast to the social or the mental. Many debates about realism have been haunted by an apocalyptic notion of the real as that which would remain if humans vanished. This clearly poses a problem for scholars in the human sciences who want to deploy the vocabulary of realism: one is left asking, if social phenomena are real, what are they real in respect to?

I answer this by analyzing mind-dependence, which has been surprisingly undertheorized. It comes in distinct types, which provide the key to unlocking different accounts of social construction. When combined with metarealism, they open the way to a social ontology that allows us to further specify gradients of the real, forms of social construction, and different modes of existence.

With this in hand, part II, "Process Social Ontology," offers a new account of the nature of the social world and theorizes afresh how social categories function and come into being.

In chapter 2, "Concepts in Disintegration," I stage the "postmodern" critique within the disciplines by working through the various challenges to the utility of the concept of "religion" in religious studies and to "art" in philosophy of art and then providing a kind of deconstructive dojo for taking down any discipline's main categories. These categories, on which we scholars in the human sciences have focused our disciplines, are all equally vulnerable to a finite set of skeptical challenges.

Scholars in disciplines who have been working to fend off criticisms of their central categories (I'm looking at you, political science) will want to know that if the core skeptical issues being raised are not addressed, it is only a matter of time before their discipline's most cherished concepts will be demolished. Scholars who think they have successfully rejected theory and re-entrenched their disciplinary methodologies (History) should know that they have only kept the skeptics from the gates as long as they have been able to put on blinders, and that even normal scholarship in their field is defenseless against robust and fundamental criticism on core conceptual grounds. Furthermore, while family-resemblance categories, polythetic concepts, and open concepts are a step in the right direction, they open up more problems than they solve.

One might imagine that these critiques of disciplinary master categories would undermine our capacity for knowledge and throw the disciplines into a morass of endless deconstruction. This is in many cases what has actually happened, but I show that it needn't.

The following two chapters, "Process Social Ontology" and "Social Kinds," demonstrate how the critiques of all the various disciplinary master categories are similar, and show that by *granting* these critiques we can describe—in inversion—the common features of what we could call social kinds. We (de)construct social kinds—with all their vagaries and contingencies—in common and predictable ways. Thus, if we abandon any notion of the uniqueness of any central category (including necessarily "religion") and indeed if we hollow it out such that it has no "essential" content then this will enable us to undertake a grand re-understanding of all the categories. Recast, the method of conceptual analysis advocated by two millennia of philosophers has run aground. But the way that conceptual

analysis has foundered tells us something significant about the mechanisms through which concepts and social worlds are produced and maintained. The other side of the dissolution of the disciplinary master categories is a new methodology for the human sciences.

Metamodernism demonstrates how various properties that make up
the social world are constructed. By working through anti-essentialism
in feminist theory, chapter 3 demonstrates how process metaphysics
points beyond merely skeptical anti-essentialism. It also explains why
we need to shift from a substance ontology to a process ontology of the
social world and how that solves a number of philosophical problems.
Chapter 4—which is in many respects the heart of the book—then examines an important theoretical framework in the philosophy of biology:
namely, homeostatic property-cluster kinds. Rather than reducing the social to individuals or abstract social forces, I argue that it is better thought
of in terms of social kinds. Once it has been fully elaborated, this theory
of social kinds entails new methodologies for the human sciences and
implies a host of potentially new research programs. It solves the problem of comparison and generalization across geography/culture/history.
In brief, metamodernism suggests a profound reorientation towards the
social world that will be of benefit to scholars in the human sciences and
lay people alike.

Chapter 5, "Hylosemiotics" (the only chapter in part III, but the book's
longest), begins from a standard account of postmodernism as the linguistic turn. Approaching the problem of the gap between world and representation dialectically permits us to resolve the skepticisms associated
with the linguistic turn by deepening rather than retreating from its implications. But it does so by shifting the model for philosophy of language
from human language onto the sign-making behaviors of a range of sentient beings. Hence, metamodernism shows how meaning can be received
from the environment and lays out a new panspecies material semiotics
called "hylosemiotics."

Many issues in the philosophy of language are turned on their head
when animals are included in the world of sign producers and consumers,
and when attention is given to the materialization of discourse. Metamodernism provides a new vantage on the way the world itself functions
as sign-bearing. It argues that meaning consumption and production
are not the same thing. This has significant consequences for the meanings of meaning. It also shows how, while communication is necessarily
fraught and prone to faults, translation is nonetheless possible. This hylosemiotics also addresses a core problem with much of New Materialism—
namely, the limitations of typical accounts of agency. Metamodernism

also provides a new system of sign-aspects that will be able to guide future scholars not just in the humanities and social sciences, but across the biological disciplines in their attempt to reconstruct how sentient beings communicate and come to understand the world around them.

Taken together, parts I, II, and III provide an innovative theory of the social world, both human and nonhuman, and suggest new methodological tools for studying it. The work could have stopped there, but there is another key knot associated with scholarship under the sign of the negative that needs to be untangled.

Part IV, "Emancipatory Knowledges," broadens out to address the entanglement between ethics and epistemology. Postmodernism often appears as an unsolvable Gordian knot because theorists regularly conflate epistemology and ethics. This part of the book starts from a provisional, analytical bifurcation of knowledge and norms—primarily to prevent common fallacious smuggling operations in which epistemological claims are rejected for ethical or political reasons, while positive normative projects are undercut by epistemological skepticisms.

Postmodernism is regularly associated with universalized forms of cynicism and doubt. But as chapter 6, "Zetetic Knowledge," argues, there is an alternative to corrosive forms of skepticism. We get there by being skeptical of skepticism. Skepticism inevitably harbors residual epistemological commitments; its very doubt is propelled by attachments to lost certainties and its own doxa and dogmas. When skepticism commits to purifying itself, learning to doubt its own propelling beliefs, then it ceases to be skepticism.

Deepening, rather than retreating, from skepticism leads us toward an adjustment of our standard of knowledge. The other side of skepticism is an orientation toward knowledge called "Zeteticism," to which I add a theory about how inference should function in the human sciences.

Philosophers typically bifurcate inference into induction and deduction, but they also tend to criticize both modes as deeply flawed. As an alternative, one section of the chapter recovers a version of abduction, or inference to the best explanation. It shows how abduction solves problems with induction and deduction. It also suggests that we should reconceive of inference on a spectrum from abduction to prediction. This has its own reward beyond simply curing us of our attachment to skeptical dogmas. Metamodern Zeteticism helps us to understand, concretely, how we should structure our thought, how we should evaluate evidence from our senses, how we should formulate generalizations and theories, and what status they should have once they have been produced. This epistemology will work in practice to produce humble, pragmatic, situated knowledges.

Finally, chapter 7, "The Revaluation of Values," presents a goal for the humanities and social sciences. It starts from the accusation that postmodernism is basically ethical nihilism or moral relativism. I argue that the reverse is actually true. A form of ethics has in fact prospered, but it has taken an almost resolutely negative form. Metamodernism turns postmodern ethics inside out and discovers a kind of critical virtue ethics directed toward what I call "Revolutionary Happiness" (capitalization intended and explained). This project conceives of Happiness not as pacifying contentment or euphoric haze, but rather as a more radical project that makes demands on the social order for the benefit of not just humans but also other sentient beings. Metamodernism thus rewrites the putative oppositions between fact and value to articulate a normative, embodied ethics or politics.

In sum, metamodernism can be conceived as a kind of philosophical therapeutics that leads through the disintegration of concepts and deconstructive vigilance to a kind of reconstructive capability directed at multispecies flourishing. Reading the book in order is therefore tantamount to a kind of therapy, but it may take more than one reading to appreciate this fully. If the project is successful, the very terms "postmodernism" and "modernism" will have been unmasked, their hostilities rendered moot, and even their most ardent followers will be presented with the necessity of reckoning with their fundamental self-misrecognitions. In this way, the work as a whole aspires to be a cure for modernism and postmodernism alike. It aims to transform the reader and heal them of a set of philosophical anxieties and phantom oppositions.

·

This book belongs to no existing camp. If anything, it is a "hopeful monster." I am a queer, mixed-race Jewish-Buddhist. But while this project has roots in my particular intellectual and all-too-human standpoint as well as in queer, feminist, and critical race theory, in addition to being inspired by Buddhist philosophy, it is not and should not be reduced to any of those.[57] It is also not merely postcolonial theory, though it is partially a product of a decolonizing impulse, it resists simplistic moralizing. It embraces instead Boaventura de Sousa Santos's call for an "emancipatory, non-relativistic, cosmopolitan ecology of knowledges."[58] This is neither analytic nor continental philosophy. That is to say, while the problematics I am trying to overcome were formulated within the American academy, this work aims to subtly provincialize Euro-American thought by way of a breadth of engagement with non-European (especially Asian) philosophical materials. I have read everything I could get my hands on, from philosophy of science to ethology, biology, psychology, sociology, anthropology, analytic and continental philosophy, and more. This is not eclecticism so much as an active counter-hegemonic reading program culminating in antidisci-plinarity. To reformulate Audre Lorde's famous phrase: the master's tools never really belonged to him to begin with.

PART I: METAREALISM

1: How the Real World Became a Fable, or the Realities of Social Construction

The 'real world'—an idea that is of no further use, not even as a compulsion—a useless idea, an idea that has become redundant, hence *a disproved idea—let's do away with it!*

NIETZSCHE, *Twilight of the Idols, or How to Philosophize with a Hammer*

To remove altogether the "realistic" temptation to use the word "world" in the former vacuous sense, we should need to eschew once and for all a whole galaxy of philosophical notions.

RICHARD RORTY, "The World Well Lost"

How did we get the idea that some people had stopped believing that the world was real? In many academic circles, "postmodern antirealist" is such a routine condemnation that the two terms are regularly assumed to be synonymous. Postmodernism, deconstruction, and poststructuralism are all commonly characterized as types of antirealism.[1] Realists often see themselves as saving modern philosophy from postmodernism. But the putative split between realism and postmodern antirealism is chiefly a phantom opposition. It organizes polemical confrontations while simultaneously obscuring the actual similarities and differences between various thinkers. Even philosophers who explicitly line up for or against "realism" as such are typically talking past each other or disagreeing about issues that are basically irrelevant for those of us working in the human sciences.

These organizing debates around realism could therefore almost be dismissed except for two things: the only way for metamodernism not to be inadvertently lumped together with antirealism or realism is explicitly to unravel at least some of the conflict; and more importantly, I want to suggest a better notion of what it means to refer to something as "real." Reassessing the semantics of the "real" will put us in a position to undercut another key opposition in the human sciences—namely, that between reality and social construction. Real things are often supposed to be mind-independent while socially constructed things are supposed to be mind-dependent. But, surprisingly, the crucial notion of mind-dependence has largely avoided serious scrutiny. In this chapter I remedy that.

Scholars in the human sciences who see themselves as realists or anti-realists will want to know why they'd do better to avoid such affiliations. Thus, the project will advance in what I want to suggest is the metamodern mode, which is dialectical, by transcending a perceived opposition, after which it will show the benefits of this kind of philosophical movement. Scholars who presume incompatibilities between real and socially constructed or real and mind-dependent will want to know that this presumption is incoherent. Scholars who have already argued that something can be both real *and* socially constructed will benefit from this chapter's articulation of a more sophisticated notion of the real.

1.1 Realism as Scientism

In his most famous work, Thomas Kuhn argued that when a dominant paradigm begins to collapse, scientists begin consulting philosophy, a subject toward which they are normally disdainful.[2] It seems that only when they are faced with accumulating anomalies and a deepening sense of crisis do scientists begin to take seriously the work of their more humanistic colleagues. But Kuhn's observation could just as easily be reversed, since when humanistic disciplines are in a state of paradigm collapse, they often invoke the natural sciences. Necessarily, there are good ways to use scientific findings in humanistic research.[3] But many gestures toward natural science in philosophy involve superficially misusing scientific terminology or quantitative methods.[4] Political theory can be spiced up with jargon wrested from pop neuroscience or complexity theory. Continental philosophy can be enlivened with phrases usurped from quantum physics or ecology. Literary analysis can be formalized by hastily adopting "big data" and pretending its subjects can be modeled like fluid dynamics, and so on.[5] These are largely rhetorical moves that are compelling at a superficial glance, but further analysis demonstrates that these apparent parallels are lacking in deeper shared substance. Science seems to be useful to humanists mostly when it reinforces positions the humanities already take as givens.

As bad as superficial gestures to science may be, however, the most fulsome expression of this response to paradigm collapse is espousing allegiance toward "realism" as such, especially when undertheorized. When a discipline's foundations are disintegrating, claiming to be a "realist" is often an attempt to both keep skeptics at bay and signal a shallow scientism. Indeed, the gradual breakdown of various guiding research paradigms in the humanities and social sciences has led to several decades of proliferating natural science–inspired "realisms" (e.g., critical realism, speculative realism, and so on).[6]

Some of these realisms are motivated by a backlash against the slow disintegration of the disciplinary objects—"religion," "art," and so on—discussed in chapter 2. To anticipate, with many disciplines becoming increasingly skeptical of the utility of their organizing categories, it should not be a surprise that the main thing some of these newer realists are interested in asserting is the reality of the disciplinary objects themselves. For instance, from its title, a "realist ontology of religion" might suggest a theological defense of the reality of some particular religious ontological claim, such as the existence of God. But when we turn toward self-avowed realists in religious studies, "realism" instead seems to announce one's belief in "a social reality that exists 'out there'" and a "realist interpretation of the term [religion]," which the author defines in terms of a repackaged nineteenth-century definition of "religion" as "an account that holds that there are forms of life predicated on a belief in the existence of superhuman beings."[7] I will address these notions of a world "out there" and "social reality" later, but I want the reader to register that what being a realist about "religion" seems to signify is not that any particular religious ontological claims are real, but that particular scholarly definitions should be protected from postmodern criticism.

We could approach this in a different way and ask what, beyond their disciplinary subject matter, are realists in the human sciences realists about? Although this is not meant to be exhaustive, many realisms are stand-ins for two contradictory things: a commitment to a "reality" that functions principally as a proxy for a non-specialist's notion of the current worldview of physics, and an emphasis on "the real" as something mind-independent. These two forms of realism are then often conflated with a defense of the social scientist's object of inquiry and presented in contrast to supposedly corrosive social constructionism or postmodern antirealism.

In the first case, many contemporary philosophers have seen the stakes of the debate over realism as being about the status of our current best scientific theories.[8] These commitments are clearly on display in the new realisms. Critical realism, for instance, often takes as its inaugural moment Roy Bhaskar's *A Realist Theory of Science* and his extension of those insights to social sciences in *The Possibility of Naturalism*. Similarly, allies of speculative realism have argued that "the only credible metaphysic is one that is sensitive to the philosophical implications of the natural sciences" and that "it is science itself that enjoins us to discover the source of its own absoluteness."[9] Yet, on a closer reading of their work, most so-called antirealists also grant that the conclusions of contemporary scientific research are approximately accurate.[10] Moreover, both realists and antirealists accept the relative reality of commonsense objects. So, what do they actually disagree about?

It would seem that realist and antirealist philosophers differ primarily in the nature of the strawman attacks they launch at each other. As Simon Blackburn summarizes:

> On the one hand it seems absurd . . . to question the reality of the objects of common-sense, or core scientific theory. On the other hand realism is often seen as demanding the mythical God's eye view, whereby we step out of our own skins, and comment on the extent to which our best scientific theory corresponds with an independent reality. . . . In the one view realism seems almost indisputably true, and in another equally obviously false or undiscussable. So there is every opening for debates in which each side talks past each other.[11]

Hence, although it is controversial, many philosophers have argued that the whole debate over realism is "dead" or basically a non-issue.[12] This is not the whole story, however, and I will discuss debates about "independent reality" further below. But it does seem that the realist vs. antirealist argument is largely a false opposition, and many (but clearly not all) scholars in the humanities and social sciences who declare themselves to be realists without specifying or really understanding current scientific models are basically just signaling their scientism.[13]

(Moreover, as I have argued elsewhere, literary realism has historically been in a feedback relationship to scientism—as literary accounts of what is real both reflect contemporary notions of science and produce new understandings of science.)[14]

1.2 Varieties of Mind-Dependence

The second challenge to any metaphysical "realism" in the human sciences is that there is a long history of identifying the "real" as mind-independent. A few illustrative quotations follow. To William Alston, "realism" means that "the things we encounter are 'mind-independent.'"[15] For Michael Devitt, a "realist" thinks that "An object has objective existence, in some sense, if it exists and has as its nature whatever we believe, think, or can discover: it is independent of the cognitive activities of the mind."[16] Bimal Krishna Matilal: "the realist believes that the world consists of some mind-independent objects, even discourse-independent objects."[17] Hilary Putnam defines the first commitment of metaphysical realism as agreeing with the statement that "The world consists of some fixed totality of mind-independent objects."[18]

If *realism* is primarily defined contrastively in terms of mind-independence, to me the obvious question is: what is the opposite case? Namely, what is mind-*dependence*? Astonishingly, mind-dependence is for the most part undertheorized. What is worse for these debates, it could mean very different things. It could be an *ontological, causal, classificatory*, or *universal* assertion.[19] I'll discuss the last in the next section, but in the following paragraphs I will think through the differences between these (and in chapter 4 I add an additional *representational* subtype of mind-dependence).

First, for an entity to be *ontologically mind-dependent* would be to say either that the entity exists in whole or in part as a mental phenomenon (e.g., qualia, subjective sensations, or thought itself) or that it continues to exist primarily because of ongoing mental attitudes or beliefs either individual or collective (e.g., a child's imaginary friend, which exists only as long as she believes in her; the sovereign who is only the sovereign insofar as people believe she is the sovereign; or money, which has value only as long as people are willing to treat it as such). Mental phenomena and collective belief types of ontological mind-dependence could be differentiated, as they have divergent research implications; but in general claims of ontological mind-dependence are used to suggest that the phenomena in question are in some sense mental and not purely material.

Second, for an entity to be *causally mind-dependent* would mean that it was either brought into being by a mind or that it has certain important features because of a mind. For instance, a motorcycle is causally mind-dependent because it was brought into being by the human minds that designed and built it. Similarly, we might say that a dachshund is causally mind-dependent as it has most of its breed-specific traits because dog-breeders have chosen to cultivate those traits. Note that causal mind-dependence does not require that the results be intentional. The depletion of the ozone layer would also be causally mind-dependent because it was the unintended byproduct of human decision-making. These causally mind-dependent phenomena are also physical phenomena. So, to say that a dachshund is mind-dependent is of little use when it is urinating on your shoes.

Third, for a grouping to be *classificatorily mind-dependent* would mean that it is the result of the classification activities of some kind of mind. For example, the classification of diverse minerals and organic materials into the category "gemstone" suggests that gemstone is a mind-dependent category determined by perceived aesthetic or economic value. *Classifica-*

tory mind-dependence need not be observer-relative. To explain: much of the debate around mind-dependence is confused with a similarly unhelpful opposition between subjectivity and objectivity. I hesitate to use either term, but it is worth noting that while music critic Robert Christgau's list of the best The Coup albums is subjective, that he has classified albums this way is objective. Or perhaps more helpfully, the Japanese language has a classificatory category (indicated by 匹) that lumps together into one category small animals, insects, fish, and demons. This is a mind-dependent category, but its existence is objective for the researcher attempting to describe Japanese linguistic categories.

Demarcating distinct aggregates is a subtype of classificatory mind-dependence. By way of example, the identification of a cloud as a cloud would seem to be partially dependent on someone picking it out as such. Otherwise, it would be just an indefinitely bounded set of fine water droplets. Similarly, whether a particular peak is part of the *same* mountain or a different mountain would seem to be a matter of mind-dependent individuation. This individuation could be particular to a person, but it also could be conventional to a community (e.g., as manifested in maps or agreed to by the scientific community). In either case, the aggregating depends on both selection and (to some extent) the material object being so categorized. That is to say, individuating aggregate phenomena, like other types of classification, is to some extent mind-dependent. (Chapter 2 will develop the claim that judgments of identity or similarity and difference are task-dependent.) Additionally, these first three levels of mind-dependence often overlap (e.g., a classification of the ways that different civilizations have produced money), but they needn't always co-occur.

To prefigure this and later chapters' larger issue of concern, the term "mind-dependent" could be swapped with "socially constructed" and still capture most of the relevant literature, which also tends to depict an opposition (that I will challenge) between "socially constructed" and "real." Although my typology of social construction/mind-dependence is more expansive, Sally Haslanger, for example, distinguishes between two different broad types of social construction—causal construction (if social factors caused something) and constitutive construction (if social factors played a key role in its definition).[20] Indeed, when scholars are arguing about the social construction of "X" they seem to mean that "X" is ontologically, causally, or classificatorily mind-dependent, but with the added feature that accounts of social construction often emphasize a group's (rather than an individual's) role in the production of "X." Moreover, as discussed below, social construction theorizing tends to lean into the contingency of "X" such that "X" might not have existed without social forces.

1.3 When Realism Becomes Antirealism and the Reverse

To return to the earlier argument, sometimes mind-dependence is taken into what might be an idealist or neo-Kantian register and is portrayed as a question about whether the world itself is *universally mind-dependent*. But this largely turns out to be a red herring based on a misreading of contemporary forms of idealism.[21]

To explain: ever since George Berkeley published the *Treatise Concerning the Principles of Human Knowledge* (1710), philosophers have been thumping on furniture in frustration and fantasizing about striking idealists and antirealists with rocks. For instance, a famous passage from James Boswell's *Life of Samuel Johnson* reads:

> We stood talking for some time together of Bishop Berkeley's ingenious sophistry to prove the non-existence of matter, and that everything in the universe is merely ideal. I observed, that though we are satisfied his doctrine is not true, it is impossible to refute it. I shall never forget the alacrity with which Johnson answered, striking his foot with mighty force against a large stone, till he rebounded from it, — "I refute it *thus*."[22]

Likewise, Bruno Latour has described the frequent attempts of philosophers to counter social construction by "thump[ing] on a table" to demonstrate the table's reality and intimidate their opponents.[23] Indeed this pattern of argumentation is sufficiently widespread that in some circles it is known as the "furniture argument," for the propensity of so-called realist philosophers to start banging on objects when confronted by their more skeptical colleagues.[24]

We might see a cousin of this critique in Marx and Engels' *The German Ideology*, which satirizes a "valiant fellow" who "had the idea that men were drowned in water only because they were possessed with the idea of gravity" and who dedicated his life to stopping people from drowning by convincing them not to believe in gravity.[25] In this Marx and Engels seem to be parodying a particular version of voluntarist idealism—by which I mean a version of idealism that recognizes a particular feature of the world as not only mind-dependent, but subject to individual choice. We can imagine a more contemporary similar "valiant fellow" asserting not only that "capitalism" is socially constructed, but that it might vanish if only we would stop talking about it.

Critics of postmodernism from the vantage of critical realism, speculative realism, or new materialism often seem to imagine that postmodern antirealism amounts to just such a voluntarism.[26] For instance, Manuel

Vásquez provides an unattributed misreading suggesting that Derrida denied the existence of the external world.[27] One can also find a similar contention by Andrew Collier, who in *Critical Realism* recounts an anecdote about a speaker presenting research on Sartre: "A deconstructionist asked her, in a pained and patronizing tone, whether she was claiming that there really had existed such a person as Jean-Paul Sartre, independently of what we might say of him. When she said yes, she was, she at once lost the attention of the deconstructionist contingent."[28] I think this particular "deconstructionist" was probably mind-dependent insofar as I'm skeptical that they existed outside of Collier's imagination (although I admit it is a recognizable exaggeration). But for the moment I want to ask: are these fair characterizations of idealism? Or postmodernism for that matter?

By way of counter-example, despite Samuel Johnson's attempts at refutation by kicking rocks, George Berkeley stated very specifically in *The Principles of Human Knowledge*:

> I do not argue against the existence of any one thing that we can apprehend, either by sense or reflection. That the things I see with mine eyes and touch with my hands do exist, really exist, I make not the least question.[29]

After all, any serious scholar of Berkeley would have reminded Johnson that Berkeley specifically argues that physical objects are not dependent on the mental state of a specific person.[30] Indeed, the main thrust of Berkeley's project was to show that God did not create a material world that itself then has to produce the world of sensory experience via some secondary and mysterious process; instead, God directly produces the world of experiences. If God wanted you to stub your toe, your foot would be hurting. Berkeley denied the existence of "matter" not because it is all in our heads, but because it is unnecessary to postulate a second-order real world behind that of appearances. To say that something is matter is just to say that it has an appearance. So there is no need to refer to matter as a supposed cause of experience. For Berkeley, it is not that reality does not exist, but rather that we have direct access to it. Keep this in mind, as direct access to reality is often presented as defining both realist *and* anti-realist positions.

The foremost transcendental "idealist" philosophers—Kant and Schopenhauer—did not deny the existence of a mind-independent world either; rather, in the broadest of brushstrokes, they shared the intuition that we come to know the world by way of our mental categories, but that noumena or things-in-themselves are not conditioned by those categories. As Schopenhauer put it: "nothing is so persistently and constantly misunderstood as idealism, since it is interpreted as meaning that the empirical reality of the external world is denied."[31] So here the supposedly anti-realist position is that there is an external reality, but that we lack access to it to some extent.

Although Friedrich Nietzsche started as a kind of skeptical neo-Kantian (under the influence of Schopenhauer), his later "anti-realism" was actually a denial of what is typically seen as Kantian idealism. While Nietzsche criticized truth, philosophy, and reason, his antirealist credibility is often established by reference to the section of *Götzen-Dämmerung* titled "How 'the Real world' at Last Became a Fable," which serves as the inspiration for this chapter's title. But Nietzsche's essay is regularly misread because it is taken out of context. Nietzsche's views are clearer in an early part of *Götzen-Dämmerung* where he argues that it is a mistake to "divide the world into 'real' and 'apparent' parts, whether in the manner of Christianity or in the manner of Kant."[32] Although describing himself as an opponent of idealism, his final position is closer to Berkeley's inasmuch as Nietzsche's point is that there is not a second "real world" or "thing-in-itself" behind the apparent world of sense experiences. Those keeping score should note that both pro- and anti-noumena philosophies are regularly accused of antirealism. Ironically, a philosopher can be called an antirealist for arguing either that we have complete access to reality or that we lack complete access to reality. Moreover, Nietzsche is arguing for something quite close to the positivist position discussed below.

So how do the postmodernists fit in? The first point I want to make is that canonical postmodernists were not exaggerated voluntarists of the sort criticized by many contemporary realists. They argued for a gamut of different positions. Many of them were basically skeptical Neo-Kantians. But the postmodernist thinkers who came closest to antirealism typically did so through the methodological suspension of linguistic reference (discussed in more detail in chapter 5).[33] Recast, what normally gets counted as postmodernist or poststructuralist antirealism is their internalist semantics, which was sometimes expressed in a skepticism about the capacity of linguistic categories to represent accurately a mind-independent world. But this was not the antirealism it is often made out to be.

More specifically, while Jacques Lacan and Jacques Derrida did embrace this kind of linguistic skepticism, the critics are wrong to say that they denied the existence of a world outside of discourse. As Derrida put it, "the other is 'the real thing'" that interrupts discourse. [34] This is even more clear in Lacan, who made the Real a core component of his influential tripartite registers (alongside the imaginary and the symbolic). Lacan described "the Real" as "that which resists symbolization absolutely," by which he meant that it subverted both the symbolic and the imaginary.[35] In sum, neither thinker actually expunged reality. Both of their projects rather suggested what could be called "traumatic realism"—that there is an (ineffable) extra-discursive Real that is glimpsed briefly in moments when discourse breaks down and therefore indicates the presence of something troubling discourse itself. So when New Materialists claim to be demonstrating to postmodernists "the stubbornness of the materiality of things" or shouting at them to take seriously the existence of a "real" world "out there," they are not saying anything new.[36]

•

Moreover, other supposed postmodernist antirealists like Richard Rorty were not antirealists so much as deniers of the distinction between realism and antirealism, which they often did in a manner similar to Nietzsche: by rejecting the existence of a gap between appearance and reality.[37] If anything, this would seem to suggest a position closer to naive realism than to its antithesis. But this is also a positivist position.

To explain: as mentioned in my "Opening," Rudolf Carnap argued that "asserting the reality of the external word" was a pseudo-statement without meaningful content. This probably sounds like textbook antirealism. But Carnap contended that there was no way to verify scientifically the reality of the world *outside* sense experiences, because there was no way to access the world *except* by means of sense experience. Kant's noumena, even if real, are irrelevant because, by definition, we could never encounter them. So like Nietzsche, Carnap and many of his fellow Logical Positivists rejected the need to conceptualize a real world behind that of appearance. But in contrast to some other similar positions, Carnap's indifference to accounts of mind-independent reality was driven by his scientism, not in spite of it. In contrast to philosophers today who see realism as the only way to defend scientific naturalism, Carnap argued that science did not need to postulate a mind-independent world. In broad strokes, Carnap was arguing for a pro-science antirealism. Indeed, some scholars have even argued that one of the main outcomes of Logical Positivism was undermining the need for mind-independent realism in the natural sciences.[38]

Despite their self-presentation, many of the new realisms have just found a way to shift the epistemological claims of skeptics into ontological claims. This is clearest in Quentin Meillassoux's Speculative Realism. Meillassoux made his reputation with his appeals to mathematics and science and his attack on "correlationism," a category which basically collapsed together Kant, Hume, and postmodern skepticisms. But in order to break the circle of correlationism, Meillassoux defined his realism in terms of a commitment to a quasi-Nietzschean "hyper-chaos." He argued that there is reality, but it is a reality that can shift unpredictably, not just contingently, such that the fundamental structure of the cosmos could rework itself at any instant.[39] Meillassoux's "realism" therefore posits the existence of a less stable, less predictable, and less comprehensible reality than that suggested by the "antirealist" he opposes.

Nor is Meillassoux alone in this (as will be discussed in chapters 3 and 5); a number of New Materialists have made what amounts to the same move insofar as they have formulated a notion of reality that is hugely attenuated—a reality of flux in which we cannot posit most of the things we might want to posit about reality (e.g., William Connolly), or a reality constantly being recreated in a process of entanglement such that every attempt to measure it transforms it (e.g., Karen Barad). In both these cases, the things we have said about Lacan and company we would need to say about these neo-realisms: namely, that their philosophy inadvertently suggests skepticism about the way ordinary linguistic categories represent a mind-independent world. Only the new ontologists presented this instability as a feature of the world, not a limitation of language. In sum, many of the new realisms just make a "realist" ontology out of what in other quarters counts as antirealism.

I do not want to weigh in on arguments about our capacity to access a mind-independent reality. My main point is that the oppositions that are supposed to define a grand split between realism and antirealism do not line up. Philosophers can be accused of being antirealists for insisting on a mind-independent world beyond that of appearances (like Kantians), but they can also be accused of being antirealists for the opposite claim— denying a mind-independent world beyond appearances (like late Nietzsche and early Carnap). Moreover, one could adopt either broad metaphysical realisms or antirealism and be either pro- or anti-science. Finally, as noted above, realism and antirealism have sometimes even turned into each other. All this suggests that much of the antagonism between realists and antirealists is incoherent or at least misguided.

1.4 Apocalyptic Realism and the Human Sciences, or Real as Socially Constructed

I want to begin this section by making a simple observation: metaphysical forms of realism are largely irrelevant to the human sciences because they block out the objects of inquiry from the beginning. Defining realism in opposition to mind-dependence amounts to what we might call *apocalyptic realism*, because to do so presumes a notion of the real as that which would remain if humans vanished.

If to be real is to be completely independent of humans, then anything we might choose to study in the human sciences would not be real from the start. So this notion of realism is already unsuitable. It would be misguided to assert that motorcycles, attitudes, dachshunds, or Japanese counting words are not real. This suggest that at minimum, realism in the human sciences cannot be apocalyptic in its basic formation. For that reason, at the very least, we need an account that denies the opposition between real and mind-dependent/socially constructed.

To say that a *social* entity is *socially* constructed might seem to be merely asserting the truism that a social phenomenon is social.[40] If that were all that was going on, we would have no need of a theory of social construction. But I think the repeated references to social construction across the humanistic disciplines are actually capturing something important.

Certainly, the phrase "social construction" appears most often in the literature to argue that a particular entity is not real. For instance, the British anthropologist Ashley Montagu has argued that "the term 'race' is a socially constructed artifact," adding that "there is no such thing in reality as 'race.'"[41] Calling something a social construct shifts the entity under discussion from the realm of nature into the realm of culture or mind-dependence. This is often taken as equivalent to the charge of unreality. As discussed in more detail in chapter 2, a standard strategy for demolishing a disciplinary master category is to assert that the category in question is "socially constructed" and by implication that it is unreal. But when thinkers like Montagu argue that "race" is socially constructed, they are suggesting that it is a product of culture not biology. The unstated premise that culture is in some sense illusory is a clue.

Many disciplines are split between constructivists and realists who largely talk past each other. At worst, social construction is even mistaken by its critics for a kind of idealist voluntarism in which individuals are thought to have the capacity to bring socially constructed things into being by merely believing or speaking them into existence. But these controversies aside, both pro- and anti-constructivists typically agree about the stakes of the conflict for a particular entity in question. As Ian Hacking and Sally Haslanger have both noted, social construction functions as a kind of "unmasking" or "debunking," and as such it works to render entities contingent.[42]

That said, on the ground, social scientists have spent a long time grasping at a way of capturing social life and the very concepts we use to interpret it, and have aimed to do so without being caught in the opposition between real and socially constructed. Some, like Peter Berger and Thomas Luckmann, have worked self-consciously toward this end.[43] But most scholars do so implicitly, through empirically driven case studies, without articulating or even necessarily being fully aware of their premises.

This grasping and striving have been taking place across the academy. But it can be seen especially clearly in the same disciplines—critical race and gender theory—that gave political urgency to the notion of social construction in the first place.[44] Succinctly put, even if "race" is socially constructed, it nonetheless has a big impact on people's lives. So, to say that "race" is unreal or illusory would seem to be missing the point. This has engendered, in some cases, a backlash against the notion of social construction within the very subdisciplines that gave it early life. But some critical race theorists have thus concluded that categories like race might be both real and socially constructed. I think this is an intuition many scholars in the human sciences would grant about their own particular subject matter, even if they have never theorized it explicitly.

Thus, in what follows (not just here but in subsequent chapters), I would like to provide scholars with a vocabulary applicable across numerous disciplines that all too rarely engage with one another—a vocabulary that can bring organization, precision, and clarity to our collective efforts. Moreover, while I am skeptical of "realism" and "antirealism" as broad philosophical banners, I do not wish to abolish references to the "real" as such from our disciplinary vocabularies. It can be useful, for instance, to say that the Satanic ritual abuse panic of the 1980s was both socially constructed and, in some sense, not real, while LaVeyan Satanism is both socially constructed and, in some sense, real (although it was not the source of abuse, as some claimed). If I am belaboring this point, it is because I believe that exploring the tension between socially constructed and real will provide us with a way to reconceptualize our scholarly categories.

1.5 Metarealism: Modes of the Real

Here is where this is all going: the main reason that both partisans of "realism" and blanket statements about the reality of social construction miss the mark is that "real" is primarily a contrastive or negative term that gains most of its ordinary meaning from an opposing concept. By way of explanation, to say of something that it is "real" does not say anything about the entity in question except to the extent that it excludes some particular way of being not-real. For instance, "real" is often distinguished from "illusory," "fictitious," or "fraudulent." But there are as many different ways to be not-real as there are kinds of things.[45]

A few examples will make this clear: The phrase "not the real Madonna" could mean a range of things—it could be a hallucination of Madonna, a fictional Madonna, an optical illusion that resembles Madonna; or it could be a statue of Madonna, someone who looks like a mutual friend named Madonna, a Madonna-impersonator, a singer whose voice resembles that of the pop star, a religious icon misidentified as depicting Madonna, or a forgery of Edvard Munch's famous painting "Madonna," and so on. Each of these hypothetical Madonnas is "not a real Madonna" in certain respects, but not in others, and crucially many of these not-real Madonnas are "real" physical objects or even people. The same is true of the positive version of the statement, since to refer to someone or something as "the real Madonna" could be an attempt to rule out a large variety of things, including visual hallucinations, misidentifications, category errors, fictions, or forgeries. In a nutshell, a bust of Madonna is a real statue, but not a real person.

Another example: to say a dream is "not real" doesn't mean that the dream never happened or was never experienced. The dream in question was actually dreamed. To say that a dream is not real means that the events experienced in the dream were not what happened in waking life. We can say that Satanic ritual abuse wasn't real if we mean that no children were actually being abused. We can say that "LeVeyan Satanism" is real if by that we mean it is an organization with actual members and thus is real in contrast to made-up or fictitious organizations. Race is unreal insofar as it is not a consequential biological category, but race is real insofar as it is not imaginary or irrelevant in relation to people's life experiences.

To be clear, this is not meant to be a species of relativism in the old-fashioned sense. Sometimes scholars argue that a given phenomenon is real because the people who believe in it really experience it. But this amounts to the claim that people who are really experiencing something are really experiencing something, which is a tautology. Instead of superficial tautologies of this sort, I want to encourage scholars to specify contrasting classes when using the term *real*. This would have the direct benefit of putting us in a position to be clearer about when we actually agree or disagree.

As argued above, many philosophical accounts of the real use mind-dependence as a contrasting case, but such an apocalyptical realism will not work in the human sciences (to continue the metaphor, we need to be postapocalyptic). Rather than defending or attacking realism as such, what we should be asking is: *if a specific social phenomenon is real, what is it real in respect to?* There is not going to be a one-size-fits-all answer. As I have been arguing here, there are many different modes of being real or unreal depending on what feature of the world we are considering. Indeed, many philosophical conflicts result from scholars holding different presumed but unstated contrastive categories.

·

To return to the categories outlined above, references to social construction usually amount to the claim that X is either ontological, causal, classificatory, or universally socially dependent, with the added implication that X is somehow not *real*. We now know that we should be skeptical of this latter implication, especially when a contrast-class to real is left unspecified. Moreover, many accounts of social construction turn out to be trivially true. To say that "nations" are socially constructed just means that social factors play a role in the formation of nations, which no one would really dispute. (That said, it is only trivially true if we stop at the issue of social construction itself and don't continue forward to the question of *how* it has been constructed, which can yield useful and productive insights, as we will see.)

But the most intense debates about social construction have been about classifications and whether specific scientific categories map onto the world. Thus, when referencing nonhuman entities, these debates are often really about natural kinds. For instance, debates around the social construction of "quarks" were not about ontological social construction, but about whether or not quarks are a natural kind.[46] I'll discuss natural kinds in chapter 3, but that scientific theories are socially constructed is another truism. All theories are classificatorily mind-dependent because they depend at least partially on human minds to think them up in the first place. Theories necessitate theorizers. This means that if there are any true theories, they must be socially constructed. Debating the "social construction" of quarks is a red herring. To foreshadow a claim I develop over the course of several later chapters, social construction is part of how we achieve knowledge of the world in the first place.

1.6 Conclusion: Modes of Reality; Modes of Existence

In this chapter I have been suggesting that contemporary realists and antirealists are often closer to agreement than disagreement, and that sometimes different philosophers can be assigned to the same camp for holding completely opposite views. This effectively nullifies the claim that these are two mutually opposed sides. Arguments for or against realism often signal broader ideological stances rather than definite positions about mind-independence. Furthermore, it turns out that most arguments over realism vis-à-vis mind-dependent and -independent phenomena are actually unhelpful for the human sciences. Our scholarship constantly grapples with mind-dependent but nonetheless "real" entities (again depending on contrast class). If realism is paradigmatically modern and antirealism is paradigmatically postmodern, then we can transcend both in the name of the metamodern. In this respect, the workaday human scientist who rejects the polar extremes of the social construction debates and instead strives, amidst the fast-moving current of ever-changing social process, to generate knowledge about the world will find a philosophical compass in metamodernism.

As I will address in greater detail in chapters 4 and 5, conversations about mind-dependence and social construction have historically depicted only humans as minds or constructors. But if we open up to the world of animals and other sentient beings, it will provide a fresh vantage on the whole debate. We worry a lot about whether certain categories are mind-dependent or human-relative. But these concerns could be relativized by comparison to other creatures. For instance, bats could have a category based on sonar ping similarity that groups all objects that ping similarly together. This would almost necessarily be a bat-relative category. But why would that make us doubt it for being "socially constructed"? Or cause us to think of it as necessarily any less "real?"

To coin a term, philosophy that grants different modes of the real is "metarealism"—a word that both signals the philosophy's relationship to the broader project of metamodernism and deploys the sense of "meta" as something that is beyond or higher-order relative to other concepts of the real. In this respect, we might say that metarealism refers to any philosophy that grants that the *real* comes in modes. Metarealists recognize that uses of the term "real" necessitate reference to a contrast class. From the vantage of metarealism, deploying "real" without contrast class (e.g., references to "real men" without explicitly articulating the alternative) is generally either confused or merely ideological. Metarealism is thus beyond both realism and antirealism. It rejects the shared terrain of modern and postmodern philosophy alike.

·

There is another fundamental issue these discussions of the reality of social construction have behind them—namely, the question of how it is that social entities can exist at all. To say of a physical object like a rock that it "exists" might at first pass seem to mean merely that it is composed of matter. But what does it mean to say that the Catholic Church *exists*? What does it mean to say that "Satanists" or economic recessions *exist*? These might look like the same question about *real in contrast to what* that I asked above, but I want to suggest that it actually implies something different.

Our first clue is that while *real* and *exist* are often taken to be equivalent, there are good reasons we might want to differentiate them. Some not-real

Madonnas are materially existing objects, while other not-real Madonnas lack physical instantiation. So the way that the statue is not a real person is not identical to its existence or nonexistence as a material object. Perhaps more importantly, there are classes of entities that are *real*—in various noteworthy senses—yet do not exist.

Different philosophers have argued variously that fictional characters, numbers, absences, destroyed objects, or dead people are both real and nonexistent.[47] Emphasizing the contrastive nature of real as I have above can clarify these debates. For instance, Lord Byron's *Memoirs* were *real* (insofar as they were actually written rather than merely imagined), but they no longer exist in physical form because they were burned by his literary executor. Another example: Sherlock Holmes is a *real* fictional character insofar as he can be distinguished from made-up fictional characters, but he too lacks physical existence as a human.[48] To clarify, I've just made up the character Papaya Dalolo, but she is not a real fictional character inasmuch as no one has written any fiction about her (at least not yet). Thus, it would seem that some entities can be real without existing.

There are also good reasons to further distinguish between *being* and *existing*. To explain, English is fairly unusual in that "to be" is both a predicating and an existential verb. We use "to be" both to describe the properties of things (the crow is black) and to suggest that something exists (the crow *is*, or there is a crow). But predication and existence do not have to be conjoined, and a number of languages (e.g., German, French, Japanese) have different verbs for the two modes. This is evidence for the position that we can make true predicative "being" statements about nonexistent objects.[49] "The silver mountain is made out of silver" might seem to be definitionally true, even though no such mountain exists. Similar arguments have been put forward about the properties of mathematical objects. Controversies about philosophy of mathematics aside, I think this suggests that having properties (*predicative being*) should be distinguished from some bare notion of existence as such.

All this is building toward the observation that, in addition to talking about different modes of the real, it also makes sense to talk about different *modes of existence*. I do not mean anything especially enigmatic by this expression. Events, for instance, exist differently from the way objects exist. Events are often said to be composed of "time-slices," while objects are typically thought of as existing in terms of their materialization.[50] The existence or nonexistence of absences (such as shadows, silences, cracks, and holes) has often been seen as paradoxical (does the crack in the Liberty Bell *exist*?), but we might solve this by saying that absences exist in a parasitic or negative mode.[51] Fictional characters *exist* in terms of having been represented (with fictional objects having representational properties just as physical objects have substantial properties).[52] Indeed, this actually seems to solve problems of how reference to fictional characters is possible. Fictional characters exist in their representation, but their properties are canon-dependent (which of course is why there are so many debates around what counts as canon).[53] We might think of biological entities as *existing* in terms of their being presently alive.

This list is not meant to be exhaustive by any means, but it suggests a line of approach that will become important. If socially constructed things are real, do they also exist? If so, how? Subsequent chapters will explore these issues, and in so doing will answer the question of exactly *how* social construction works.

PART II: PROCESS SOCIAL ONTOLOGY

2: Concepts in Disintegration & Strategies for Demolition

Anthropology is dead. . . . In and through its signal idea, the culture concept, death-bed anthropology appears determined to carry on for some time to come, if only in and through other disciplines and other disciplinary formations. Consequently, we write in the wake of anthropology, haunted by it.

SCOTT MICHAELSON & DAVID JOHNSON,
Anthropology's Wake: Attending to the End of Culture

The specter of "the end of the social," as such [has been] necessarily accompanied by the end of the social sciences.

PETER WAGNER, *A History and Theory of the Social Sciences*

Analytical concepts have been disintegrating throughout the human sciences. Religious Studies used to be able to presume its object of analysis. Our methodological pluralism and global coverage were underwritten by postulating the existence of "religion" as a universal aspect of human experience found in all cultures. It was often taken for granted that there were different "religions" that ostensibly shared a common essence, function, or perhaps even origin. Not only did this position organize religion departments; it was also supported by other disciplines—such as philosophy and political science—that tended to grant the universality of religion even as they distinguished their disciplinary objects from it. For a considerable period, the special task allotted to Religious Studies was to advance the understanding of the nature of religion. But those days are long gone.

For almost sixty years, a host of theorists have challenged the universality of religion and its utility as an analytical category.[1] It may surprise readers coming from other disciplines, but most scholars trained in Religious Studies today now consider it naive to presume "religion" as a concept. Indeed, while American religion departments are still structured the way they were back when we postulated "world religions" with a common essence, a generation of scholars has been formed in the context of claims that "there is no data for religion" and that "religion is solely the creation of the scholar's study" with "no independent existence apart from the academy."[2] The issue is still contested, but in many quarters the rejection of "religion" as an analytical object approaches the consensus view.

This poses a special challenge for our discipline. Religious Studies has no distinctive methodology. It has no special approach. It teaches no specific technical skill. It has no core principles. It has no single object language. It has no clearly delimited geography, people, or time period. The only thing we supposedly share is our commitment to a category— *religion*—we no longer believe in.

Like many disciplines, Religious Studies is in crisis. Confronting the dissolution of our object, scholars have attempted to buttress "religion" with references to increasingly faulty underpinnings such as phenomenological experience, evolutionary psychology, and culturally postulated supernatural agents. These efforts, while well-intentioned, seem to me to be like the philosophy professor from Trier University who constructed an elaborate planetarium with a waterwheel and an intricate system of pulleys and screws in an attempt to defend the classical centrality of the earth, tracing the orbit of the sun as a planet with Venus and Mercury as its satellites. In attempting to save the basic framework for the study of religion by supplementing it from within, I fear the discipline is in danger of enacting a similar procedure—charting one Ptolemaic epicycle after another in defense of an illusory center.[3]

In the face of various skepticisms about our central category, it might seem that we have but two choices: either we can endlessly repeat the act of deconstruction or we can continue to add "epicycles" by redefining our master categories in ways that move further and further from their common usage. Neither of these gets us very far.

But I have a message for my fellow scholars of religion—our dilemma is less fresh than it first appears. When we aren't bemoaning some generalized "postmodernism," we tend to portray the challenge to the category in Religious Studies as either a novel sign of critical acumen or an unprecedented phase of decay (depending on perspective). But we aren't alone. The disciplinary objects began their disintegration years ago, as I will demonstrate momentarily. Not only have many of the human sciences dissolved their central categories; most have also long since abandoned notions of working toward a shared object of inquiry. This apocalypse—if that's what it is—is old news. We are already postapocalyptic.

This is important because the critical turn in Religious Studies has inadvertently paralleled similar turns in other disciplines. Crucially, many of the proposed solutions for the challenge to "religion" that are being debated now have already been tried and have failed in other disciplines, in ways we can learn from. To be blunt, tracing these debates shows that many things currently being presented as cutting-edge theory in Religious

Studies are ultimately dead ends. This chapter, then, represents an urgent intervention with serious stakes for the discipline, and the details that follow are essential to making this case.

To provide some preliminary evidence for the historical disintegration of the categories: already in 1956, Morris Weitz had published a skeptical Wittgensteinian critique of the category *art*. In 1958, Dorothy Emmet had begun the decomposition of *society* as an object of analysis, Raymond Williams had popularized a proto-genealogical analysis of *culture*, and Norwood Russell Hanson had launched a parallel Wittgensteinian investigation of the conceptual foundations of *science*; while 1961 saw Walter Ullmann begin historicizing the notion of the *political* and H.L.A. Hart problematizing the definition of *the law*. While Wilfred Cantwell Smith instigated the process of dissolving *religion* in 1962, Thomas Kuhn was building on Hanson and others to launch a massive critical revolution in the notion of *science*. Rounding out the decade was Hayden White with the challenge to *history* and its narrative tropes in 1966. This was only the beginning.[4]

These skeptical challenges took different forms and the disciplines were mainly unaware of their neighbors' similarly urgent impasses. Some fields were profoundly destabilized by these critiques, while many others marginalized them. Over the ensuing half century, however, new thinkers have often deepened these criticisms and added other disciplinary concepts to their ranks. Many of the academy's key terms have faced dissolution. If I were writing exclusively as an intellectual historian, I could easily spend the whole monograph summarizing these positions, producing a catalog of landmark critical books and articles. But I want to warn you that any disciplinary object not yet criticized is ripe for future attack, so instead of exhaustively charting merely the existing critiques, I intend instead to spell out the steps many of these critiques have taken and to provide a checklist of sorts that outlines how they produced epistemological disorder. This is no mere sophistry. What I mean to show, rather, is that if we attend properly to these deconstructive strategies, we can get the demolition of the master categories to show us how they were constructed in the first place. The very strategies that have been used to annihilate our disciplines point the way out of both "modern" and "postmodern" philosophical projects and toward new metamodern undertakings.

•

To clarify the larger concerns of this chapter, there has been a fundamental breakdown in the classical view of "concepts" as such. For much of the more than two-thousand-year history of European philosophy, the core model for philosophical inquiry has been conceptual analysis. The philosopher asks "what is justice?" and then goes in search of justice's defining features. According to Aristotle, "a definition is an expression indicating the essence of a thing"; so the goal of philosophy was thought to be the pursuit of better definitions, which was supposed to proceed via the discovery of essences.[5] The organizing presumption was that the meaning of a concept is basically a definition that captures its essence and articulates the necessary and sufficient properties for membership in the category to which the concept refers. But despite a long history of philosophical attempts to refine definitions, this very model of the concept began to collapse in the early twentieth century under pressure from Ludwig Wittgenstein and others.

Today many analytic philosophers have come to think of conceptual analysis as a failed methodology that even the turn to "ordinary language" was unable to rescue. Jerry Fodor and William Lycan have argued that "the number of concepts whose analyses have so far been determined continues to hover stubbornly around none" and "no effort of analytic philosophy to provide necessary and sufficient conditions for a philosophically interesting concept has ever succeeded," respectively.[6] Perhaps hyperbolically, Paul Elbourne remarked: "Despite 2,400 years or so of trying, it is unclear that anyone has ever come up with an adequate definition of any words whatsoever."[7] Although the issue remains controversial, similar claims about the failure of conceptual analysis have been made by many other philosophers.[8]

Readers of continental philosophy are likely already familiar with an alternate set of critiques about the simultaneous limitations and necessity of concepts. For instance, Gilles Deleuze both emphasized the inherent problem of concepts vis-à-vis life or experience and defined philosophy as the "creation of concepts."[9] By way of another example, Jacques Derrida fashioned the neologism *différance* into several distinct critiques of concepts—including problems of deferred presence, infinite meaning deferral, and the relationship between iteration and conceptual change.[10] Likewise, György Lukács and other Marxist theorists have reinterpreted "reification" (*Verdinglichung*) as a political or normative critique of the objectification of concepts as such.[11] Concepts are often believed to produce reifying damage and to function as conduits for status quo power. Analytic philosophers and critical theorists frequently think of themselves as fundamentally at odds with one another, but on this one point, at least, they turn out to be surprisingly close: concepts, which we are fated to use, are inherently problematic.

While I want to begin by basically granting this point, it is not where I am going with my line of criticism. Instead I want to turn the critique of concepts inside out to see where it takes us. The first part of the chapter takes as a case study Wilfred Cantwell Smith's classical interrogation of the category "religion." The section after that provides an earlier and more paradigmatic version: namely Morris Weitz's criticism of art as a point of departure and a possible blueprint for autocritique. The section that follows demonstrates how the meanings of the key master categories were exploded beyond recognition, leaving disciplines in various states of skeptical crisis or flat-out denial. It does so by exploring a set of techniques that could be remobilized to produce epistemological anarchy in almost any field. Wittgenstein seems to be both the instigator of and an oft-proposed solution to many forms of autocritique. Thus, the penultimate section discusses some of the main attempts to limit conceptual dissolution with reference to Wittgenstein. Mainly these took the form of gestures toward family-resemblance and polythetic concepts, and I will show why these strategies failed. The chapter concludes with a reappraisal of what we have learned about concepts by tracing these modes of criticism.

To be clear about my ambitions, I am not here to either mock deconstructive criticisms or throw up my hands at the limits of concepts; rather, I intend to show how the by-now-routinized critique of the disciplinary master categories tells us something fundamental about social kinds. We need to amplify the strategies of demolition before we can move past them. But reconstructing the architecture of critique in a metamodern mode will then allow us to pinpoint the shared structures of the concepts we have been interrogating.

2.1 The End of Religion

Neither religion in general nor any one of the religions, I will contend, is in itself an intelligible entity, a valid object of inquiry or of concern either for the scholar or for the man of faith.

WILFRED CANTWELL SMITH, *The Meaning and End of Religion*

From the very beginning of Religious Studies' formation as an autonomous discipline, scholars have expressed discomfort with *religion* as an analytical category.[12] But the disintegration of the scholarly concept really commenced in earnest with Wilfred Cantwell Smith's *The Meaning and End of Religion* (1962). Smith's early genealogy of the modern concept of religion is in many respects paradigmatic both because of its position within the history of the discipline and because it echoes the critique of other master categories in different fields. In what follows, I want to chart the habits of thought Smith engendered and which, like the symptoms of a trauma, Religious Studies scholars (myself included) have been compelled obsessively to reenact.

Smith begins by tracing the etymology of the word "religion." The striking similarity of terms for religion in contemporary European languages points to their shared origins in the Latin *religio*.[13] But as Smith argues, *religio* only entered the mainstream of European vocabularies as part of the Protestant Reformation, at which point the term was basically synonymous with piety. There were not different kinds of *religio* or "religions" in this period, but more or less genuine expressions of piety, the singular *religio*.[14] Smith argues that the modern concept of religion as a general category appeared only over the course of the seventeenth and eighteenth centuries. It is worth underscoring that for Smith neither the Hebrew Bible nor the Greek New Testament contains a term analogous to the contemporary "religion."[15] So he suggests that the use of "religion" by scholars examining a pre-modern West, even if it appears in their sources, runs the risk of the cardinal sin of the historian—anachronism.

Even more strikingly, Smith notes that the ancient Egyptians, Iranians, Aztecs, Chinese, Japanese, Indians, Indonesians, Greeks, or Hebrews did not possess indigenous words for religion in their respective languages.[16] He suggests that it took the efforts of Euro-American scholars or missionaries, either alone or in concert with the locals, to produce new terminology to describe the "religion" of the non-European, in effect conjuring into being through a linguistic act a division between the culture's religious and political worlds. Likewise Smith observes the historically late, and largely Western, construction of the main terms for specific religions—"Boudhism" (1801), "Hindooism" (1829), "Taouism" (1839), "Zoroastrianism" (1854), "Confucianism" (1862)—none of which precisely corresponds to native categories.[17] Hence Smith argues that "religion" is inextricably tangled with the history of European expansion. The distinctions captured by the term are not native elsewhere. Thus, he concludes, *religion* is a foreign imposition.

Finally, Smith argues, individuals and their social relations disappear behind the concept "religion" as part of a process of "reification."[18] Religion is produced by means of a double abstraction: first, heterogeneous beliefs, practices, and institutions are subsumed under the concept of a particular religion, which is then imagined to be the repository of a coherence alien to it; second, a set of religions is incorporated into the category "religion" as such to describe what is purported to be universal to humankind. Each phase of this movement results in the loss of resolution, the blurring of distinctions, and the compression of the diversity of elements. Thus, it encourages scholars to blur normative and empirical registers; by listing, for example, the "beliefs of Catholics," they are in effect obscuring the difference between what Catholics ought to believe and what they do believe. Moreover, this process seems to be asymmetrical since the supposed features of "religion" as such (e.g., emphasis on faith, the transcendent, the divine, exclusivity) are largely an abbreviated Protestantism that does not really apply very well to other "religions." In sum, religion is an abstraction of an abstraction, and each phase in this process results in an un-recouped remainder.

So far Smith's challenge looks like a typical anti-essentialist critique of the sort that can be found in other disciplines. But the particularities of his project are apparent in Smith's formulation of his core claim as quoted in the heading of this section.[19] What could be glossed over as merely philosophical nominalism, however, betrays itself with the appearance of this "man of faith." Scratch the surface and Smith turns out be an odd sort of anti-essentialist, as he argues in a footnote that "apart from the proper names of persons, the only nouns that can stand up to final scrutiny are 'God' . . . and 'man'. . . . All else is either a conceptual abstraction and/or adjectival."[20] In effect, despite his use of the Marxian vocabulary of reification, Smith's nominalism rests on religious grounds.[21]

Smith demonstrates that to describe a given position as originating in religion is to say that it is merely perspectival, that it is merely one way of looking at the world. To call Christianity *a* religion is to deny its status as a universal description of the world; it is to render it thereby implicitly relative, if not false. This is a profound insight and worth dwelling on for a moment. Put in a different way, the abstraction "religion" should not be available to religious people, because the word automatically classifies whatever theology one holds—or whatever practices one embraces—as merely particular beliefs, and in that sense as optional. It represents the claim that one does not know the world so much as have a narrow perspective on it. The category "religion" is de-specifying in a manner that any inevitably particularized believer should find unsettling—and when, as is often the case, they *don't* find it odd, this is evidence that secularism has infiltrated the conceptual frameworks of even the pious. The category religion therefore subverts religion.

To recast this critique, as Smith himself does in a later essay, "'Religion' in its modern sense is at heart a secular concept."[22] To express this claim in a Hegelian mode, we might note that to introduce religion as a category, one needs to introduce its opposite, the secular. To set up an opposition between religion and secular, however, requires that one take up a position outside both categories. One has to be able to take up both as a totality. But this very act is a problem for religion because it means that there is an area into which religion does not extend. An Evangelical Christian might argue that one's relationship to God is at stake in all activity, in all spheres of life, hence that there is no genuinely secular realm; in this sense, the emplacement of the category religion undermines its referent. At the very least, Smith wants to remind us that in our contemporary epoch, to call something a religion is to set it apart from the "real world" of science and material reality. Imposing religion on a non-European group is relativizing (e.g., when the Parsi became practitioners of the Zoroastrian religion, the *Amesha Spenta* were reduced from a class of supposedly real entities to the components of religious belief); but then, so is imposing the category on European groups. As we'll see momentarily, the situation is different in other disciplines: for instance, to call something "art," while it often removes it from everyday life, tends to make it more available as art, rather than less.

In summary, Smith argued that religion was a construction originating late in European thought. There are no native terms for religion in other places or periods. Religion emerges as a concept by subsuming human social relations under a series of increasingly general categories that are subsequently reified. Religion describes a perceived relationship, no matter how disguised, to Euro-American Protestantism. Finally, religion itself is a secularizing concept. These are all claims that the field of religious studies has elaborated and debated over nearly the last sixty years.

So what might we do in the face of the concept's disintegration? Smith's crack at a solution was that we should stop writing about *religion* and *religions*, and instead should use the terms *religious*, *faith*, or *cumulative tradition*. As a consolation prize for the dissolution of the discipline's main terminology, these alternatives are Ptolemizations that do little to address the core issues. The term *faith*, with its heavily Protestant connotations, has just as many problems as *religion*. *Cumulative tradition*, like adding epicycles to an already faulty set of ellipses, is merely a wobbly near-synonym for the discredited "*religions*." Indeed, it is hard to see how the term *tradition* is any less relativizing than *religion*; if anything, it goes further than *religion* in demoting Judaism or Buddhism to mere customary practices. Hence, while his criticisms were well-founded, Smith's proposed alternatives failed to take hold in the field.

•

Although there is not space here for a full recap, the disciplinary autocritique of "religion" did not stop with Smith. The most representative version of the subsequent critique was perhaps Jonathan Z. Smith's, which rested on interrogating scholars' role in producing religion as a category. This latter Smith was joined by Talal Asad, David Chidester, Daniel

Dubuisson, Timothy Fitzgerald, Peter Harrison, Aaron Hughes, Richard King, TOMOKO Masuzawa, and Russell McCutcheon, who all deepened or altered the critique in various ways. A number of scholars have called into question the very field of religious studies by arguing that the treatment of "religion" as a putatively *sui generis* category masks the globalization of particular concerns endemic to Christendom and their subsequent presentation as universal aspects of human experience. In response, a further group of scholars—including ISOMAE Jun'ichi, Hans Martin Krämer, Adrian Hermann, Anna Sun, Tisa Wenger, and myself to name a few— recouped in various ways the voices of non-European actors that were the object of that discourse and showed their agency in the formation of "religion" or religions in their own context (see the note for a more extensive list of key authors).[23] In brief, the criticisms of *religion* that Cantwell Smith connected to his position as a "man of faith" were reworked, further secularized, and refocused on *religion*'s messy history and limited analytical value.

Even as these challenges to the category *religion* became increasingly prominent, many scholars felt the need to sidestep the critique. One can imagine why this might be the case. The critique itself threatened a number of important scholarly projects. It seemed to call into question the legitimacy of religious studies as a scholarly discipline and imperil the validity of the research of individual scholars. It also seemed to subvert many of the things that brought scholars to the study of religion in the first place, whether they were aiming to protect their personal faith from secularism, seeking a justification for the liberal principle of "freedom of religion," or even trying to build a theory of divine revelation. This was also true for those motivated by a desire to undermine the putative irrationality of religious fanatics, to showcase the incompatibility between religion and science, or to underscore religious violence against minoritized populations. All of these competing scholarly agendas might seem to require a category *religion* to underpin their arguments.

•

Part of what makes this difficult is that after the publication of *The Meaning and End of Religion*, there has been a sea change in the lexical meaning of "religion" in Euro-American contexts. This attention to definitions, even rejected ones, is important because scholars sometimes suggest that a specific culture does not have *our* definition of religion without trying to reconstruct what *our* definition is supposed to be. Although dictionaries have their limitations, they illustrate what I have referred to elsewhere as the shift from a *theocentric* to a *hierocentric* definition of religion.[24] In effect, older (although still "modern") European-language dictionaries generally defined "religion" in theocentric terms as the worship of God or gods, while the more recent versions of these very same works generally use hierocentric terms such as "the supernatural" or "the sacred" to stand in for the deity. That is to say, the *theocentric* definition of religion implied the reality of God and was rooted in a Christian theological presupposition that religion was centered around God's revelation to different peoples; while in the *hierocentric* definition references to God were replaced by a vague notion of sacrality or the transcendent that didn't do much better. It could almost go without saying, but the *hierocentric* definition is still a largely Christian concept—just a quasi-secularized one.

The theocentric concept of religion was also a genetic one in the classical sense, in that it was believed that there was a first religion or divine revelation from which all others descended or departed. That is to say, there was supposed to be a common ancestor to all religions. Furthermore, irrespective of whether scholars saw God as the initiator of a revelation from which most of mankind had fallen, or the end product of the evolution of Natural Religion that could not help but reason to a Supreme Being, a unitary divinity was believed to be at the beginning and end of this process. The terms "religion," "religions," and "the religious" were all understood as directed toward this originary God. In the early uses of the category "religion," Christianity was understood as the only true member of the category, while Judaism and Islam were portrayed as imitations of religion or not-quite-religions. This reference set expanded to include a list of religions such as Buddhism and Hinduism, but with the assumption that each of these religions was a way of worshipping God.[25]

Today, all but the most theologically minded scholars have abandoned that view. Nonetheless, it is worth emphasizing that the closest thing scholars have to a commonly accepted list of religions is largely based on a theocentric concept of religion that we have since disowned without revising the list of religions itself. Our textbooks and courses thus preserve an archaic taxonomy rooted in an idea that its members shared an essence we have largely repudiated. Hence, no attempt to restore the category of religion according to a new set of organizing principles will recover the classical taxonomy that produces the common contemporary list of religions.

That the term "religion" has changed so much in the last thirty years suggests that there is no common meaning of the term shared by speakers of English, much less other languages. To clarify this point, Gottlob Frege famously provided an account of meaning in terms of a combination of 1) sense (*Sinn*), that is to say, its description or cognitive significance; and 2) reference (*Bedeutung*), namely, the thing indicated or referred to by the concept.[26] Religion has had a significantly different sense at different periods even within the history of the English language, and very few languages have shared that sense at any given time. Moreover, religion has referred to a shifting set of extensions—no pre-modern individual and few non-European languages have shared the same list of religions. Does everybody consider Scientology a religion? Evidently not, as some courts in France, Spain, and Germany have ruled that it is actually a profit-making venture only masquerading as a religion.[27] According to this account of meaning, *religion* is a problem because across different languages and epochs it lacks both a shared sense and a shared reference.

The importance of these shifts goes beyond mere scholarly pedantry. "Religion" has consistently changed in recent times because its definition is a valuable territory for anyone to possess. The pace of change has only intensified. At least since 9/11, much of the globe has been inundated with competing proposals that the boundaries of religion should be adjusted. In the United States, for instance, language from the anti-cult movement, meant to delegitimize claims to the special rights due to *religions*, has been increasingly applied to fundamentalist Christianity by the secular Left, to Islam by the "Judeo-Christian" and secular Right, and to both by ascendant New Atheists. In parallel, religious exemptions have been increasingly weaponized by conservatives to continue to litigate culture war issues that had otherwise been settled by popular will (e.g., contraceptive mandates, same-sex marriage, and so on). Taken together this has meant both raised stakes for redefining religion in a way that suits a particular group's interests and correspondingly significant shifts in the meaning of the category.

Looked at a little bit differently, because "religion" has a central organizing function in many contemporary categorizations and common object language vocabularies, it won't work to pretend "religion" is simply a metalanguage term or redescriptive scholarly category and redefine it according to some baroque scholarly criteria. The gap between a scholarly understanding of religion and its function in various cultural lexicons is too great. Nor is it sufficient to merely track its appearance in a set of object language texts, precisely because when English speakers were using the word "religion" even two centuries ago it did not mean either what scholars or what English speakers today understand it to mean—besides which, classical scholars were often imposing the term upon groups of practices that had no analogous categorical terms that applied to them.

Religion might therefore seem to be nearly untranslatable. Brent Nongbri, for instance, has argued that no pre-modern terms can be defensibly translated as "religion" because to do so necessarily excludes important meanings of the older terminology and sneaks in modern assumptions.[28] But even seventeenth-century English speakers presumed a different sense of the word than a typical native English speaker does today, and necessarily suggested a different reference set. So that would mean that if the lines "It is religion that doth make vows kept, but thou has sworn against religion" were not written in English, even according to a broadly Fregian account of meaning we could not translate "religion" as religion.[29] Even works from thirty years ago or in different contemporary English-speaking communities might suggest the same problem. On these grounds, "religion" in English could not be translated into English if it weren't already in English. This might seem to be a paradox.

I want to note a further issue with the category of religion that is not just a problem of translation. As I have demonstrated elsewhere, the introduction of the category of "religion" into a culture that lacks such a concept produces demonstrable and sweeping changes—intellectual, legal, and cultural.[30] In brief, the category has globalized such that discourse about "religion" is now accessible in every corner of the world, co-created by centuries of self-identifying secularists or religionists, as well as colonial administrators, diplomats, missionaries, subalterns, scholars, newspaper editors, and anyone else who joined the conversation in any given language. This has led toward massive institutional changes and legal shifts, and even produced a new discourse on religion. Few can resist holding an opinion on religion; the idea of needing such an opinion, which was largely nonexistent around 1700, has now become nearly universal. Concurrently, the category has also become heterogeneous to the point that any illusion of universal agreement on the boundaries of religion can no longer be maintained.

To this, I would add that much of the genealogy of the category of "religion" is still unwritten. We have seen that religion is a transnational category, intertwined with imperialism, colonialism, and global systems of power. But like many other master categories, scholars have been very invested in placing religion on one side or another of what amounts to an East–West binary (now in the name of anti-Orientalism). Yet, as I have been arguing for some time, most putatively Western concepts were not exclusively Western. Bluntly put, Europeans have had a long history of claiming credit for things that they did not invent. Postcolonial neo-Orientalism rejects too much when it states that the concept of religion is *exclusively* European in its formulation (even if religion is heavily weighted toward a Christian prototype). For this reason, there are ongoing reappraisals of the extent of the "Europeanness" of religion (and ancillary concepts like *secularity* and *science*) and the recovery of the voices of non-European actors who helped form all of these concepts.[31]

•

"Religion" has been under attack as a concept since before "postmod-ernism" is supposed to have appeared. Even so, the architecture of the critique is familiar. Religion is shown to have no essence; it is shown to be a modern, predominantly European concept; and it is shown to be in contradiction to the very thing it claims to study. It then might seem un-clear how to move forward if the definition of religion is broken as well as the most commonly identified group of religions—a taxonomy compiled and organized according to a concept of religion we have long since re-jected.

Before concluding this section, I want to note that some articulations of "religion" already anticipate a reading of postmodernism in which all positions or forms of knowledge are reduced to belief. As we have already observed, labeling something religion while locating it beyond the reach of reason and therefore marking it as unassailable also reduces it to a rela-tivist position. Quentin Meillassoux describes a central feature of our cur-rent moment by coining the term *"enreligement"* (enreligioning), adding that the "modern man is he who, even as he stripped Christianity of the ideological (metaphysical) pretension that its belief system was superior to all others, has delivered himself body and soul to the idea that all be-lief systems are equally legitimate."[32] He is arguing that what used to be considered conflicting knowledges or intellectual positions are now pre-sented as equally valid beliefs. Accordingly, many of the things Smith says about religion can be said about the other objects in the academy. Instead of ubiquitous secularization, everything has been "enreligioned"—turned into religion, but in the belittling sense in which everything is merely one faith among others. Indeed, have not expressions like "faith in science" and "faith in reason" become widely repeated clichés? Meanwhile, the "beliefs" of professional climate scientists are placed in the public dis-course on equal footing with those of amateur global warming skeptics. This is not a new observation, but "religion" has become our preferred idiom for communicating not a dogmatism, but a relativism. It is my intu-ition therefore that Religious Studies is the key to finding our way forward.

That said, my prescription for Religious Studies is a purgative. We can-not continue to hold onto the innateness or uniqueness of "religion." All attempts to reaffirm the contours of our discipline by producing alter-nate theories of "religion" or replacing "religion" with near synonyms are doomed to failure. Instead, I think the discipline needs to be reorganized around the suspension of religion as a fundamental object. From the out-set I want to distinguish this suspension from the simple act of rejecting the object as such. To completely delete the term *religion*—the ostensible goal of a bare secularism—is self-defeating because to do so would undermine the concept of the secular itself. We need rather simultaneously to recognize the contingency of religion and to track the causal processes that anchor its properties. This will permit us to see how not just "religion," but all the disciplinary master categories have been produced. Restated, I aim to disintegrate the object—to forgo the definition of "religion," to give such definitions up as unnecessary.

But first I want to show how the critique of "religion" was but one of a similar set of challenges to different disciplinary objects in the same period. We need to look at these because we haven't even seen yet all the possible critiques of "religion." Equally importantly, it will turn out that the way to study "religion" is to locate it among all the other shattered scholarly categories. Standing on the rubble of all the combined categories should put us in a position to avoid the pitfalls of both false essentialism and skeptical historicization. In abstract terms, after the categories have been fractured, we can see what they have been hiding and discover a new basis for a reconstructed humanities and social sciences.

2.2 The End of Art

The objects approach zero as their theory approaches infinity, so that virtually all there is at the end is theory, art having finally become vaporized in a dazzle of pure thought about itself, and remaining, as it were, solely as the object of its own theoretical consciousness. . . . Art had come to an end.

ARTHUR DANTO, "The End of Art," in
The Philosophical Disenfranchisement of Art

Art was one of the first scholarly master categories to begin unraveling.[33] At the dawn of the twentieth century, various artists started producing anti-art intended to defy notions of authorship and to attack the category of art itself.[34] For instance, in the mid-1910s, Dadaists began buying previously manufactured objects—like coatracks, snow shovels, and urinals—and declaring them "readymade" art.[35] As the Dadaists became increasingly famous, it is no surprise that philosophers found themselves forced to respond to these provocations. In this respect the critique of art initiated a tradition of autocritique, setting the terms for many later acts of demolition.

The most influential early work in this line was Morris Weitz's "The Role of Theory in Aesthetics" (1956); it is worth discussing on its own terms because it provides a critique that scholars in other fields will likely find eerily familiar. Weitz begins by noting that aesthetics has traditionally been preoccupied with producing different answers to the question "what is art?" He argues that this whole line of approach is misguided because it falsely presumes that works of art share a common essence or a common nature. If one looks at the diversity of works considered to be art—e.g., paintings to ballet to sculptures to piano concertos to signed urinals—it is easy to see that there are no necessary and sufficient conditions for membership in the category. No matter how you define *art*, the definition will end up either too narrow and exclude works commonly recognized as art, or too broad and include things not generally recognized as art. There is no particular set of features or properties that can serve to characterize and distinguish "art" from everything else. There are no clear boundaries to the category. Art cannot be defined. Thus, Weitz concludes, a theory of art is logically impossible.[36]

Instead of asking "what is art?" Weitz suggests that philosophers should be asking: "what kind of a concept is art?" His answer is that art is an "open concept," by which he primarily means that it is a *family-resemblance* concept in Ludwig Wittgenstein's sense of the expression. In *Philosophical Investigations* (1953), Wittgenstein had famously argued that many general concepts have a *family-resemblance* quality. Using the example of "games," he observed that membership in the category is not determined by necessary and sufficient conditions or an exhaustive set of properties common to all games.[37] Card games, ball games, and video games do not share a common essence. Rather, games have various asymmetrical strands of similarities, just as my daughter might seem to share certain features with her relatives, such as having green eyes like her mother, black hair like me, a temperament unlike either parent but resembling her paternal grandmother's, and so on. All in all, with the benefit of historical hindsight, it is possible to see one whole version of the skeptical critique telegraphed in Wittgenstein's late writings, and indeed Wittgenstein was a frequent reference in criticisms of the disciplinary objects before his position was usurped by Saussure.

Weitz argues that *art* is a family-resemblance concept in this respect. It is based in unevenly shared similarities rather than in a definition. By "open concept," Weitz also means to indicate a distinctive feature of art—namely, that it is continuously evolving. Not only are new works of art constantly being produced, but artists are continually finding new ways to defy the very boundaries of art itself and to transgress the concept's limits. In this respect, one cannot exhaustively enumerate either works of art or the conditions under which the concept of art is appropriate. As Weitz puts it, "the very expansive, adventurous character of art, its ever-

present changes and novel creations, makes it logically impossible to ensure any set of defining properties."[38] Trust future artists to disrupt any
possible definition of art.

To these standing critiques of the category Weitz adds the observation
that art is also an "evaluative" concept. To call something a work of art is
often as much an act of praise as it is a description. Defining *art* is therefore also often doing normative work in promoting the particular artistic
movements or styles that appeals to the theorist. For instance, to say "this
abstract painting is art" or "this signed coatrack is not art" is not so much
a neutral description as a statement of aesthetic values or subjective judgment. Accordingly, this means that attempts to define art often serve covertly to justify the critic's admiration for a particular work. By saying "art
is successful harmonization," what the theorist really means is that they
find a particular painting aesthetically appealing. For Weitz, the history of
aesthetics has been just an unfolding sequence of subjective evaluative
preferences disguised as a philosophical quest for meaning.[39]

Weitz's critique works on an immanent semantic level. He argues that
there is no necessary and sufficient conditions for membership in the category *art*, *art* has no real essence, its meaning is always evolving, and objects hitherto classified as *art* have no inherent common features. Thus, he
concludes that all attempts to define *art* are hopeless. The whole discipline
of aesthetics—insofar as it understands itself to be more than a normative
or subjective exploration of personal taste—is fundamentally misguided.

•

Naturally, there were many attempts to suture the wound in the category
opened by Weitz and his peers. Following "The Role of Theory in Aesthetics," a flurry of new ways to anchor the definition of art were proposed and
generally refuted.[40] Scholars of religion might want to know that in the
1960s there was a renewed attempt to ground art in "aesthetic experience"
(just as some religion scholars today are returning to notions of "religious
experience" as essential). But this project failed, as it was observed that
there were no psychological features common to all so-called aesthetic
experiences and that it would be equally impossible to anticipate all the
preconditions for such experiences in the future.[41] Phenomenology could
not be made to ground a category of art. Other attempts to define art (e.g.,
institutionally) were ultimately no more successful. If anything, the skeptical crisis deepened. It did so in part because in addition to the semantic
critique above, theorists began presenting historicist and then cultural
relativist challenges to the notion of *art*.

The historicists' case against art was rooted in the observation that the

model for notions of art as an autonomous or *sui generis* category presumed the unity of the collection of classical "fine arts"—painting, sculpture, music, poetry, dance, and architecture—but it was easy to see that
this collection of arts was the product of an arbitrary culturally and historically contingent grouping.[42] According to this line of reasoning, discussions of the meaning of "art" in general were inextricably bound up in
an eighteenth-century European shift that repositioned disparate crafts
under a common taxonomy as arts, and also produced a new orientation
based not on their diverse materials and mode of production but on con-
noisseurship and notions of the experience of the observer. It was only
then that debates around the meaning of art as such became possible.
Hence, "art" appeared as a modern European invention.

Having historicized the conceptual category, it did not take long for a
range of Euro-American scholars to argue that other cultures "don't have
our concept of art."[43] Although imprecisely phrased, this conclusion followed logically from the Wittgensteinian and historicist critiques described above. When concepts were equated with definitions, it was possible to adjudicate whether definitions in different languages agreed. But
having rejected definitions based on necessary and sufficient conditions,
it became nearly impossible to figure out whether two family-resemblance
categories were identical. Moreover, if *art* was not an autonomous category of human experience but an arbitrary cluster of "arts" that emerged
only in a specific period of European history, then it was almost necessarily the case that other cultures would lack identical conceptual edifices.

Finally, there was what one might think of as a Weberian or avant-garde
critique of art. That critique observed that identifying something as "art"
functions to separate it out or intensify the conceptual work that the processes of autonomization and differentiation undertake socially, so that
there are now a set of special practices—legal, governmental—that no
longer pertain to it.[44] Recast, to conceptualize something as "art" is to
remove it from the everyday—to separate it from every other kind of social practice, to render it independent and in that sense transcendent. Art
is supposed to have primarily an aesthetic rather than a functional role.
Ordinary objects are considered tools, not art. Art becomes property of
the museum and the gallery, something displayed instead of used. In response to this trend, the avant garde attempted the reunification of *art*
and *everyday life*, which meant that both terms had to dissolve.[45]

The critique of art bears an uncanny resemblance to that of *religion*.
Again, we see a pattern in which the concept is exposed as modern, culturally relative, normative, and in fundamental contradiction with its area
of study. In the next section I explore the parameters of the autocritique
as a genre and explain the strategies behind the destruction of the dis-

ciplinary object. After that section, I address the most obvious counter-strategy, which finds scholars appealing to Wittgenstein's notion of family-resemblance to save categories in decay. But this common quick fix is doomed to failure.

2.3 Strategies for Demolition

Philosophy is a struggle against the bewitchment of our intellect by means of our language.

LUDWIG WITTGENSTEIN, *Philosophische Untersuchungen*

Autocritique has a method. More, it has conventions and teachable poses. Such paradigm-demolishing has paradigms of its own. Like any genre, it follows more or less customary structures, patterns, and schemes. In truth, it is eminently iterable. If autocritique means turning a discipline on itself, in this section I take the next step by turning autocritique itself inward or providing an autocritique of autocritique. Again, art and religion were not the only categories to meet with their putative ends. Indeed, starting in the 1950s, various disciplines went through rounds of autocritique. They were articulated in different academic idioms, even though various critics were often unaware of each other. As a result, dissolving scholarly objects often defaulted haplessly into one another, e.g., religion scholars were rejecting "religion" in favor of "culture" at just the moment when anthropologists were swapping "culture" for "literature," itself increasingly out of favor with English professors, and so on.

These various critiques deployed an overlapping set of intellectual moves, and it is possible to abstract from them a set of strategies for destroying disciplinary objects (for the sources from which the following is generalized, see the mother of all endnotes).[46] To be clear, the epistemological and rhetorical strategies underpinning autocritique, though routinized, are no less valid for that. Do not mistake my tone: I am deadly serious. Despite the intentional provocation of what follows, I do not think these strategies are mere sophistry. Rather, they rest on real philosophical issues, which tell us something fundamental about the way we have been misunderstanding categories and their relationship to the world. In what follows, I will demonstrate how this works—offering what is basically an anarchist cookbook or deconstructive dojo for subversive academics.

2.3.1 IMMANENT CRITIQUE

(1-1) STEP ONE—collect competing definitions. Nearly every scholarly master-object has been defined in multiple and contradictory ways. In some cases, you can list hundreds of rival attempts to pin down the meaning of the object in question. A survey undertaken in 1952 suggested that "culture" had as many as 164 different definitions.[47] Often, subdisciplines operate under implicitly different or unexamined notions of the disciplinary objects that give shape to their particular subject matter. You can begin the autocritique by calling out these inconsistencies. Do literary scholars study a special class of writing called "literature"? (Forgive the scare quotes; they are indigenous to the mode.) Or do they study the figurative and rhetorical dimensions of all writing, or all language? Do literary scholars write about film? But if so, then in what sense is film "literature"? Many disciplines are divided into distinct camps that represent both conflicting notions of their master-object and rival approaches to the discipline. Disciplines are defined by their shared objects of inquiry; but if no one can agree what that shared object is then perhaps it isn't shared after all.

(I-2) STEP TWO — expose internal contradictions. Having collected definitions, identify the *inherent contradictions* of the scholarly object. Demonstrate that the object cannot be captured with a classical definition based on necessary and sufficient conditions. You can show that attempting to fix the definition either forces unintended inclusions or excludes commonly accepted members of the category. Every attempt to define "society" seems to leave out some human groupings that in frustratingly inchoate ways one knows to be "societies." The object will also have vague boundaries and implicit gray areas. Policing the conceptual object will appear fraught. It will be possible to demonstrate that the object's common definition (intension) and its reference (extension) are irreconcilably out of sync. No definition of religion generates the list of commonly accepted religions. "A set of beliefs about God" might sound like a succinct definition of religion until you realize that it forces you to exclude Buddhism, Confucianism, and many other "religions." The same phenomena will sometimes count as members of the category and sometimes not. Sometimes the coatrack is art and sometimes it is a place to hang your jacket. The taxonomy will be unstable or at least multiple. Many objects will also be shown to contain inherent paradoxes, or at least dialectical tensions. For all these reasons, it will be possible to argue that there is no single essence common to all generally accepted members of the category. The notion that the disciplinary object is an irreducible *sui generis* phenomenon or a "natural kind" will collapse.

(I-3) STEP THREE — disaggregate the concept. Once you have rejected definitions based on necessary and sufficient conditions, your next move is to say the same things about your disciplinary object that Wittgenstein said about "games." In other words, you can contend that the conceptual object should be seen as the product of family-resemblance or heteroge-

neous and semi-overlapping networks of similarity.[48] Once you have rejected, as excluding too little, the definition of "long prose fiction" for
"novel," you can go on to argue that "novels" share *some* but *never all* of
the following features: length, fiction, prose form, multiplots, the forgo-
ing of supernatural plot devices, an abundance of realistically described
detail, multiple voices, and so on. You can leave undertheorized the exact
number of features required to be a member of the category.

Variations on this theme often result in a discipline formulating a new
notion of concepts in general, including: an "open concept," a concept
with an "open texture," an "essentially contested concept," a "family-
resemblance concept," a "prototypically centered taxonomy," or a "polythetic category."[49] Once an object reaches this state of disaggregation it
will be possible to show that self-consciously opening the concept in any
of the above modes produces more rather than fewer contradictions. Open
concepts expand voraciously, the open texture of language makes it impossible to bound or adjudicate, essentially contested concepts turn out
not to have essences, polythetic categories decompose into competing
groupings, family-resemblance presumes the very thing it is trying to explain (discussed below), and so on.

(1-4) STEP FOUR—collapse the implicit binary. Even without all the preceding steps, it is possible to show that formation of the scholarly object
required excluding another term (or terms), and this act of exclusion will
turn out to be partial or incomplete. Instead of a Wittgensteinian notion
of concepts defined by similarity, an alternate route is to grant a quasi-
Saussurean notion of the concept as differential—but this will introduce
its own set of contradictions. The notion of "culture" is predicated on a
distinction between "culture" and "nature," even as numerous examples
contravene this very division (the colony of bacteria growing on a petri dish
are a "culture"), calling into question the term's meaning and boundaries.
Usually you can show that the binary tension inherent in the category is
loaded and gets its effect from other implicit antagonisms. The notion of
"society" rests on an opposition between the "social" and the "individual,"
in which the "individual" stands for autonomy, free will, and the blank slate
of nature, over and against the "social," understood as organization, rules,
and the civilizing process. It is a value-laden opposition whose core un-
ravels under closer examination. Crucially, insofar as one defines concepts
differentially, these very distinctions will come to seem unmaintainable.

(1-5) STEP FIVE—introduce nominalist skepticism (optional). An alternate route to the immanent critique of the category is by way of a nominalist challenge to abstraction. You can always argue that a scholarly master category subsumes a heterogeneity of individual phenomena under
an immaterial concept. Be relentlessly specific. There is no such thing as

"the economy," which cannot be studied as such. There are only millions of "irreducibly"—and note that word; the nominalist will use it often—millions of irreducibly distinct instances of production and exchange: country-dwellers in Vermont selling firewood by the roadside; Midwesterners trading gifts at Christmas; freelance accountants balancing books in their home offices; robot factories making mirrorless cameras in China; and on and endlessly on.

Often the analytical object can be unsettled by showing that the abstraction is itself reified or granted an artificial coherence. Nobody lives in "society"; there are no institutions or laws that obtain for societies in the aggregate. We never encounter a "society" in total or as such. We inhabit distinct social formations, on the understanding that this term is itself a placeholder for the specification that the concept demands—an itemized analysis of *this* as opposed to any other social formation. It is possible to argue that the scholarly category is the result of a misplaced concreteness that mistakes an abstraction for a concrete reality.[50] Quantitative data often masks qualitative differences. What it means to identify as "Hispanic" is not the same in Florida as in Texas. When you say that the "state" is hostile to the dispossessed, what do you mean by "the state"? Is the state a simple or perhaps not-so-simple thing, a concrete, bounded set of institutions—centralized institutions, in the first instance, housed in the government districts of the nation's capital? Or is it a distributed process and power, and so not a thing at all, present in every locality, coextensive with the national geography, interwoven with the life of all its citizens, themselves its permanent and mutually surveilling deputies?

If all else fails, you can always charge other scholars with confounding the model for the thing being modeled, or confusing the map for the territory. Society is only the product of the sociologists' research. Isolated "words" are a fiction of linguistic analysis. Economists, convinced that the market is the "great aggregator of all information," are committed to arguing that no model can match the market in this regard. The model of the market will always know less than the market and should not be mistaken for it. This leads to the charge in a host of disciplines that their own disciplinary objects are merely scholarly projections and not things in the world.[51]

2.3.2 RELATIVIZING CRITIQUE

An alternate route to the disintegration of the scholarly object is to relativize it by provincializing it either historically or culturally. Often, though not always, these moves will go hand in hand.

(R-1) STEP ONE—historicize. You can begin by analyzing the object's etymology. Show that the general term used in the discipline has had fundamentally different meanings in different historical moments, and that its recurrence in different periods masks fractures, ruptures, and important conceptual differences. The term "science" entered English and French in the twelfth century as a synonym for "knowledge," but it referred in particular to logically demonstrable truths based on reasoning from first principles. "Science" implied logic in contrast to empirical experimentation. Experimental knowledge was regarded as probabilistic, dependent on imperfect senses, and accordingly uncertain. So, a "scientific experiment" would have been a contradiction. But in the nineteenth century, the meaning and status of philosophy and science switched. The natural sciences, rather than philosophy, were seen as the paragon of certain knowledge.[52]

It should also be emphasized that the historicist critique does not have to take the form of intellectual or discourse history. You can formulate it as an account of some combination of material, legal, political, cultural, institutional, and social changes. The birth of a modern notion of "madness" as mental illness produced new places of confinement, caused legal statutes to be written, gave rise to a whole new class of mental health professionals, altered the subjectivity of those who came to understand themselves as mentally ill, and transformed family relationships in demonstrable ways.[53]

Tracing shifts in meaning, often alongside explorations of the manner in which the term has functioned differently in various communities, serves to destabilize the object. It is generally possible to demonstrate that the current scholarly usage of the object is at least in part the product of a semantic history that is in some sense unavailable to it (diachrony impinging on contemporary synchrony).[54] The current meaning of "religion" emerged partially from an opposition between "religion" and "superstition" that we have mainly forgotten.

(R-2) STEP TWO—identify the victims (genealogical critique). Having traced the shifting meaning of the object in some particular language or set of languages, you can show the impact of power on these changes (in other words, identify the victims). *Art* constitutes itself by excluding the artisan. Often it will be revealed that certain groups have promoted the concept for their own benefit, to the detriment of others—that the object has served political ends. The identification of different perpetrators and victims will result in Marxist, feminist, postcolonial, or antiracist critiques or some combination. The notion of *culture* served primarily to position anthropology in relation to other disciplines, and to legitimize the European colonial project. Anthropologists reinforced the inequalities that existed between European elites and the rest of the world by objectifying indigenous peoples under the ahistorical category of the "primitive" and by essentializing "culture" and "cultural difference" as part of the process of legitimizing European expansion and civilizing missions. Discussions of *culture* often just mask racism and legacies of colonial domination. Excavating these issues is intensely valuable, and given the widespread horrors of colonialism, racism, sexism, homophobia, and capitalist exploitation it is almost inevitable that nearly every conceptual object will be found to have some suspect relationship to them.

Historicist or genealogical critique sometimes takes the form of a "genetic fallacy"—namely, the assumption that a belief is true or false because of its source. But it needn't. Indeed, a semantic history of this sort is often a causal narrative. It is possible to demonstrate that current thinking on the subject is a legacy of older debates or conceptual understandings. Moreover, genealogy of this sort is fundamentally destabilizing insofar as it is able to provide a causal account that obviates reference to truth. For instance, it is possible to give a causal explanation of why someone believes in gravity (they were taught about gravity in high school, their teachers were taught a particular version of gravity for specific reasons, and so on) without necessarily needing to reference the truth of any particular theory of gravity.

(R-3) STEP THREE—Relativize the cultural context (optional). Even if you omit steps one and two above, you can still contend that in some non-European culture or cultures, "they don't have our concept of the object." In sloppier versions of this argumentative formula, what is meant by "our concept" is implied but not explored. In more sophisticated formulations, however, after establishing the object's semantic field, it is possible to show that no term exists or existed in the non-European language equivalent to the European term or covering anything close to the same range of meanings. The Japanese had no indigenous term for "religion."[55] Chinese has no native term for "word," nor do Chinese languages exhibit the divisibility of speech into the easily segmented phonetic and semantic compounds common to European languages. Therefore, "there are no words in Chinese."[56] Melanesians have no indigenous concept of "society," nor do they distinguish the individual from the collective in the same way that European cultures do.[57]

When combined with some version of the immanent critique above, you can argue that the standard non-European translation term is a neologism or that it has a different prototypical center or a different definition, exists in a different theoretical constellation, or relies on different conceptual exclusions. *Alpanā* is not the native word for "art" in Hindi, but originally described a specific craft produced by groups of women, who, after having been symbolically purified, arose before dawn, chanted mantras, and constructed images of the gods.[58]

This kind of critique can be justified in terms of notions of fundamental untranslatability or the incommensurability of different conceptual systems. To really understand why a Trobriander refers to a plot of land as *buyagu* (garden-site), one has to understand not only contrasting terminology like *odila* (bush) and *yosewo* (uncut bush outside the garden-site), but also the whole of the Trobriand Islands' social, cultural, legal, and agricultural system.[59] "Space" fundamentally changed its meaning in physics from Euclid to Einstein. For Euclid space was homogenous, flat, and unchanged by the placement of matter. But for Einstein none of that was true: space could be curved, heterogenous, and shaped by the presence of matter. Moreover, not only did "space" mean something different in relativistic physics, but "time," "force," "matter," and "energy" all changed their meaning and conceptual relationships to each other as well.[60]

2.3.3 ETHICAL CRITIQUE

(E-1) A DASH OF ETHICS. In addition to any of the criticisms above, you can also argue that the object is "evaluative" or normative in its usage or construction. To determine the boundaries of the "political" is itself a political decision, benefiting some partisan groups over others. To confer on a particular thing membership in the category is often interpreted as an expression of value or subjective preference. To deny that a John Cage composition is "music" or to deny that a Mondrian square is "art" are both expressions of taste. Values turn out to be inexplicably linked to the object, and attempts to purge them often turn out to be self-defeating. In some cases the object encodes covert forms of racism, sexism, and/or imperialism (see also the genealogical critique above). "Culture" does most of its work by removing something from nature (removing or displacing fixed notions of race or gender, for instance), but then "culture" itself becomes read as a source of essential difference, reinscribing all the things it was meant to displace. We denaturalized race and gender as biological categories only to turn them into cultural prisons. In some modes of criticism, the evaluative nature of the object is merely taken to suggest that scholarly value neutrality or analytical objectivity is impossible. History is impossible to write without a plot: any given historical study must be written as a romance, a comedy, a tragedy, or a satire, and the choice between these is ultimately ideological.[61] In either case, you can excavate the subterranean values of the object to undercut its critical capacity.

•

Marshalling some combination of the above criticisms could allow you to deploy a still-topical catchphrase and argue that the object has been "socially constructed." But here I would suggest caution. The critiques above have led many scholars to argue that their category of analysis does not exist or perhaps need not have existed. They demonstrate that the object in question is mind-dependent or historically conditioned or socially produced. But then they unmask it as such and triumphantly declare that "there is no such thing as race" or that "quarks are not real" or that "homosexuality is meaningless," or (especially when directed toward a putatively natural category such as mental illness, biological species, or even H_2O) they declare that the object in question is not a "natural kind." My account of metarealism (chapter 1) would caution against this last move. While analyses of social construction are valuable and negativistic gestures are great for attracting controversy, you might want to resist this final assertion that if the object is socially constructed then it is empty, nonexistent, or unreal, as this final flourish tends to undercut the rest.

•

I want to emphasize that the immanent, relativizing, and ethical critiques can be conducted independently. The methods do not need to be actualized in sequence. Critics mix and match. Indeed, different disciplines have already embraced many of these moves to varying degrees. In this respect, some disciplines (e.g., cultural anthropology) have internalized the autocritique more forcefully while others (e.g., economics) have rendered the critical position taboo and largely excluded it from the discipline. One might speculate that some disciplines have resisted these criticisms not on intellectual grounds, but because they are supported by extra-academic institutions that reinforce their scholarly objects.[62] For instance, government agencies have a financial investment in pragmatic solutions, and therefore, groups funding research on voter preference do not want to hear there is no such thing as "politics." Nevertheless, even in fields that have not yet made the critiques manifest, they linger like ticking time bombs, ready to be set off by epistemological anarchists.

These recipes represent argumentative approaches that can be deployed on virtually any conceptual category in the human sciences—not just master categories, but ancillary terms as well. Religious Studies began by dissolving "religion" and then quickly moved on to disintegrating concepts of particular religions ("Hinduism"). The follow-up move is often to digest other lower order conceptual vocabularies ("the sacred"). For the record, these tropes work in part because they exploit genuine epistemological fissures, and being routinized does not make them any less effective.

•

I may now have given the impression that all scholarly objects are identical. Plainly, this is not the case—today the category "art" might tend to aestheticize, "religion" to relativize, "culture" to de-naturalize, "science" to universalize, and so on. These master categories clearly do different work.[63] My main contention is that many of these categories fell apart in the same period and that similar strategies can be used to disrupt them in the future. But the differences may also be emphasized.

That said, in much of the academy, two main master categories have come to absorb the deconstructive impetus toward disciplinary decay. Scholars shedding notions of religion, literature, art, etcetera have often turned toward "culture" or "politics" as replacement terms. Even scholars less conscious of the disciplinary critiques above have often suggested that everything is "political" or everything is "cultural." But the concepts of "culture" and "politics" are themselves vulnerable to the same sort of challenges discussed above. Indeed, there has been a robust critique of "culture" in anthropological circles alongside culture's rebirth in the rest of the academy. Moreover, while the critique of "politics" in political theory has been somewhat marginalized, most of the critical strategies above apply to "politics" equally well, and the concept is just as susceptible to destabilization. Accordingly, the clearest corollary of the above is that scholars have nowhere to retreat.

•

Before moving on, I want to suggest the implications of these strategies for one more category—namely, *science* itself. If the "end of science" is not normally told according to the tropes discussed above, it is because science is our contemporary synecdoche for knowledge as such. In the age of rising climate change denialism and post-truth politics, it would seem to be if anything even more foolhardy to question the coherence of science. But we cannot protect "science" unless we engage with these skeptical concerns. This is because science is vulnerable to many of the same critiques deployed against the other categories.

Science, in other words, can be provincialized according to a now predictable set of deconstructive strategies.[64] Although Thomas Kuhn was not a skeptic and did not mean to relativize science, *The Structure of Scientific Revolutions* (1962) epitomizes some of the intellectual moves I have been discussing.[65] It appeared in the same time period as the other works above, and despite being overlooked by most commentators, Kuhn used Wittgenstein's notion of family-resemblance as a starting point for the project.[66] Kuhn's argument basically consists of R-1 and R-3 critiques insofar as it is both historicist and rooted in the problem of the limits of translation. Beyond Kuhn, as several philosophers have observed, there is no single scientific method that all the sciences share.[67] Knowledge is produced differently in different scientific disciplines. It is also not possible to demarcate clearly the boundaries of science. The meaning of science appears today in part through its putative opposition to superstition and pseudo-sciences.[68] But this is an opposition that cannot be fully maintained. Every attempt to define science to include astronomy but exclude astrology turns out to either leave out a well-recognized science or include a denigrated pseudo-science.[69] We could add a dash of the ethical critique. To call something a science is clearly a term of prestige, and in many circles conveys a normative force (e.g., "science says breastfeeding is good"), and so on.

I have only touched on some of the critiques; but my argument might already suggest the question "does this critique of science mean knowledge is impossible?" Thankfully, the answer is no. As I argued in chapter 1, many of the debates about "realism" versus "antirealism" are really about confidence in the contemporary scientific cosmology. Yet if science is not a unity, then all these conversations about science's cosmology are mistaken. Instead of a grand problem with "the scientific worldview" we should really be thinking of the longevity of different localized theories. Whether or not quarks are an artificial projection of a specific set of cultural assumptions or an accurate description of some component of the universe is a question for physicists in a field that already has methods for adjudicating such issues. Restated, the social construction of quarks is not a grand issue for science as a whole, because *there is no science as a whole to be attacked or defended*.

Even if science has often stood in for knowledge, giving up on the unity of science doesn't mean giving up on knowledge; it means we must come to a better understanding of diverse knowledges. In chapter 6, I argue for Zetetic knowledge. Indeed, one straightforward conclusion of that chapter is that there are better and worse justified truth claims. Some of the better justified claims are likely associated with the sciences, but many are not.

To explain, the assertion that "Louis XVI was executed in 1793" is a

well justified statement. We could say we know that it happened insofar as we have many eyewitness testimonies, and it is unlikely (though
not impossible) that any future evidence will change historians' minds
about that fact. But it is not a scientific claim (as we use the word "science" in English). Some "scientific" claims have lots of robust evidence
for them (e.g., anthropogenic climate change), whereas others do not (e.g.,
string theory). Some claims in the humanities have more or less evidence
for them as well, regardless of their pretension to scientific status. All of
which is to say that we do not actually need an inflated and universalized category of science to support knowledge. As I argue in chapter 6, we
need instead a theory of knowledge. A successful epistemology needs to
be found, not abandoned.

·

This critique can also be rendered infinitely meta. One could note that if
all the things discussed in this chapter are often referred to as "concepts,"
then the concept of concept could be subject to the same kind of critique.
Philosophers have used "concept" as a technical term to mean different
things (something that takes a truth value, what translations share, a set
of rules for synthesizing experience, a conception of the world as a whole),
while outside philosophy the term "concept" primarily refers to mental
representations. Meanwhile, empirical work in psychology and cognitive
science has produced four different grand, and likely contradictory, theories of mental representation.[70] Taken together, not all concepts are alike,
nor do they belong to the same "kind," and the term *concept* itself can obscure this important difference.

·

I want to take a step back and say why the proliferation of autocritiques
should itself be surprising. In their early formalization in the nineteenth
century, scholarly disciplines aimed to define closed planes or systems.
The formation of a discipline often rested on the notion that one could at
least provisionally apprehend a totality, such that the discipline is in principle capable of basically complete or self-sufficient descriptions of the
phenomena it examines.[71] For example, for physics to come into being as
an academic specialization, it had to be able to assume experimentally
that physical effects have only physical causes. Physics was founded in
part on the study of matter and the supposition that the mathematics of
material interactions was at least analytically separable from biology, psy-

chology, and so on, even if physicists often suggested that their results had wider implications.[72] But in general, fundamental progress in a given field has been identified with the production of a greater understanding of the discipline's particular object.[73]

In contrast to their natural scientific siblings, the human sciences often emphasized less complete planes of explanation than putatively autonomous categories of human life or experience; still, the construction of particular analytical objects was similar. To give a concrete example: Anglophone English departments were historically grounded in the assumption that *literature* represented at least a superficially distinctive arena of research and teaching.[74] The natural sciences have often been conceived in a reductive hierarchy such that explanation at one level is partially based upon another level. Although there have also been a number of explicitly hybrid disciplines (e.g., biophysics) as well as various significant territorial disputes, to the extent that they have maintained their autonomy in the academy each academic discipline has tended to assert priority over a particular investigative horizon and the techniques that go along with its exploration. To be a scholar in a given discipline has historically meant engaging with the discipline's shared object.

For the last half century, however, many quarters of the academy have increasingly become preoccupied with autocritique. Instead of just exploring common objects, we have been chipping away at them. In this respect, the academic disciplines have turned inward, thereby undercutting their very notion for being. This critique is not always paralyzing, but it is surprisingly common; and it suggests epistemological instabilities at the very heart of the human sciences. Before I conclude this chapter, I want to turn to one proposed solution—namely, appealing to family-resemblance concepts—and show how this alternative fails.

2.4 Family-Resemblance, Polythetic Concepts, and Other Category Errors

Almost from the beginning, philosophers identified more and more problems with Morris Weitz's positive project to ground art in an open or family-resemblance concept. This is important because Weitz's project has been paralleled in other disciplines that also turned to family-resemblance concepts or related schemas when their core conceptual categories ran into trouble. For instance, in religious studies, a modified Wittgensteinian schema known as "polythetic classification" has enjoyed unusual longevity in attempts to define religion. Although I recognize that there is something valuable about understanding categories in terms of loose clusters (see chapter 4), here I want to suggest problems with conventional Wittgensteinian strategies when they are used as routes toward the reconstruction of disciplinary objects.

Some of the impetus for these recuperative strategies has come from Eleanor Rosch's pioneering research in cognitive linguistics. Inspired by Wittgenstein, Rosch demonstrated that many conceptual categories exhibit *typicality* effects.[75] Many categories are asymmetrical and tend to center on a prototypical member that comes to stand for the category as a whole; for instance, many English speakers consider a ROBIN a better example of the category BIRD than a PENGUIN, even though by definition both are equally birds.[76] There is much that is significant in Rosch's insights.

Despite prototype theory's value for understanding linguistic taxonomies, when theorists have attempted to transform it—or other versions of Wittgenstein's family-resemblance theory—into scholarly or scientific praxis they quickly run into problems. One of the main issues with prototype theory has been compositionality, meaning the problem of the combination of different concepts/categories. As Jerry Fodor has observed: "a goldfish is a poorish example of a fish, and a poorish example of a pet, but it's a prototypical example of a pet fish. So similarity to the prototypic pet and the prototypic fish doesn't predict similarity to the prototypical pet fish. It follows that if meanings were prototypes, then you could know what 'pet' means and know what 'fish' means and still not know what 'pet fish' means."[77] But there are more difficulties with family-resemblance models than the compositionality issue of prototypes.

The first problem is that the extension of open or family-resemblance concepts to include new members requires us to judge similarity. If there were no set of necessary and sufficient conditions to qualify something as a work of art, it might seem that one could decide to classify a new work as art if it were similar to a previously identified work of art. It has been tempting for scholars to take a prototypical or paradigmatic example (e.g., da Vinci's *La Gioconda*) and then go looking for objects that resemble it. The obvious problem with this is that if category membership is determined by resemblance to a certain prototype, then problems of definition are merely deferred to the original, as prototype theory cannot explain how the prototype itself came to be a member of the category.[78]

More importantly, as WATANABE Satoshi and others have pointed out, everything resembles everything else in some respect.[79] A skull is like the moon in that they are both material objects, vaguely spherical, appear to be the same shade of gray in certain light, and appear in a particular Octavio Paz poem.[80] It would be a mistake, however, to conclude anything significant about this resemblance. In any arbitrarily determined set, member objects are going to have some properties in common, but this does not mean that they are part of a natural grouping or kind.[81] (I will return to and expand on this point in chapter 4.)

Furthermore, even if all members of a given set share a common quality or property (*tertium comparationis*), that would not imply that this similarity was itself significant or defining. For instance, games are activities, but being an activity captures more than "games." Even if all games are activities, not all activities are games. Hence games cannot be defined as activities, even if that is a feature they all share. On a sufficiently high level of abstraction one will always be able to find some common denominator to a predetermined list, but that is not sufficient to justify it as the defining feature of a given concept.[82]

Comparative judgments of similarity also vary based on the circumstances and purposes of the comparison. Take sorting luggage at the airport: from a pilot's perspective bags are more similar the closer they are in weight; from a fashionista's perspective the most similar bags might be those that share a color or brand; a baggage handler tasked with stacking bags might emphasize similarity by shape; from a given passenger's perspective the most similar bags are the bags they themselves own, and so on.[83] Similarity is not an absolute property of a set of objects, nor is it an innate clustering of qualities.[84] Perceptions of similarity say more about one's perspective, purpose, and perhaps prior linguistic categories than they do about anything else. This has direct implications for how we construct scholarly objects.

Faced with two identical urinals made by the same company, one would be hard-pressed to argue that one is art and the other is not on the basis of similarity as such.[85] The Dadaist's famous urinal "Fountain" is hardly more similar to da Vinci's *La Gioconda* than it is to its non-art toilet-sibling. That one can see a resemblance between different artworks does not mean that any two artworks are more similar to each other than they are to other non-art. Moreover, starting from a prototypical example and listing all the things that are similar to it would eventually capture everything. While the liberating aspects of universalized resemblance will be discussed in chapter 4, if everything is similar to everything else then one cannot reconstruct a category merely by comparing like objects.

The *family* in family-resemblance is also doing covert work.[86] In its non-philosophical usage, "family-resemblance" typically refers to individuals who share common genetic heritage. Literal family similarities are thus the result of a shared genetics or a deeper structure. To refer to "games" or "art" in terms of family-resemblance suggests that they share an underlying non-manifest connection. But to describe family-resemblance without establishing deep connections is to presume the relationship first, and

only then to interpret different qualities as evidence for shared membership in the category. For instance, the urinal in the restroom seemingly
shares a family-resemblance with toilets and other bathroom fixtures, and
one could list the qualities these objects have in common; but the same
urinal placed in a gallery and taken to be art would seemingly tend to
share a family-resemblance with sculpture, bringing other features of the
piece to the fore.[87] In either presumption of family or category, different
qualities will seem to predominate. In summary, describing something
as a *family*-resemblance *presupposes* rather than explicates a similarity.[88]

Taken together, these criticisms suggest serious flaws with using family-
resemblance as a way to construct a scholarly category. Polythetic classification is no better. The notion of polythetic definition or classification
comes from the American philosopher Morton Beckner, who, inspired by
Wittgenstein, described what he called "polytypic concepts."[89] Instead of
a *monothetic* class with a single set of properties or criteria for membership, Beckner suggested that an aggregation of individuals might share
a heterogeneous cluster of properties, such that some members of the
group have, say, properties f_1 and f_2, while others might have properties f_2
and f_3, and so on. In a polytypic group, no single property is possessed by
all members, and generally no single member has all the properties that
define group membership. Put in terms of similarity, members of a polytypic class are not all equally similar to each other.

Subsequent theorists expanded on this model and changed the name to
"polythetic classification."[90] Scholars have been tempted to use polythetic
definitions to ground the category *religion*. For example, a 1967 article
listed nine "religion-making characteristics" and then argued that "when
enough of these characteristics are present to a sufficient degree, we have
a religion."[91] But in the philosophy of science (with a few exceptions), polythetic classification has largely fallen from popularity because of a set of
easily recognizable problems.

First, polythetic classes are often decomposable into monothetic subclasses. For instance, one could differentiate a subclass of religions that
share characteristics 1 and 2 from one whose members share characteristics 3 and 4 but lack 1, and so on. But the possibility of doing so suggests
that one does not need to posit a polythetic grand class. Hence, the very
notion of something as a polythetic class instead might seem to suggest
that what looked like one category is really a group of different, but self-
consistent monothetic kinds.

Second, if we break down those monothetic subclasses, we often see
that they themselves are asymmetrically applied. That is to say, polythetic
features are themselves often polythetic. For instance, the listed third
religion-making characteristic is "Ritual acts focused on sacred objects."

But "ritual" itself turns out be a polythetic class: after all, what do a marriage ceremony, hand-shaking, a Homa fire offering, the slaughter of pigs in New Guinea, a toast while taking a drink of beer, and the recitation of the Kaddish have in common, aside from all being called "rituals"? To cover all the properties required for a thing to be called a ritual might call for the production of a further nested polythetic class. The same thing could be said of "the sacred." Hence, the polythetic definition of religion devolves into further categories requiring even messier polythetic definitions.

Third, there is nothing intrinsic to the notion of polythesis to suggest how many different properties one would need to share to be a member of a given category. How many of the nine "religion-making characteristics" are necessary for something to count as a religion?

Fourth, most of what we want to do with categories has to do with making generalizations or projecting properties. For example, saying something is a "bird" is supposed to bring with it projectable properties (e.g., that it has feathers, lays eggs, and so on). But there seems to be no rationale for the ability to generalize across polythetic classes. Just because something has properties f_1 and f_2 does not mean that all members of the class have that property. Indeed, the very disconnect or disjunction implied by the necessity of resorting to a polythetic class would seem to undercut notions of a projectable set of properties. Members of a polythetic category by definition do not share any particular necessary properties except category membership. So one might be tempted to say that "religions are ethical," but if religion is a polythetic class composed of members with clusters of differing properties, there is no reason to suggest that any statement about "religion" is generalizable to all religions. Although I provide a solution in chapter 4, on their own polythetic taxonomies undermine, rather than support, generalizations. In this respect, polythetic classes seem to shed the very thing that was supposed to have made them useful in the first place.

Finally, and most importantly, formulating a polythetic definition requires a preestablished group. Scholars seem to need to assume that the aggregated individuals are members of the same class before figuring out what properties they heterogeneously share. Again, like family-resemblance concepts, polythesis presupposes the very thing it is trying to explain.

In summary, while family-resemblance might work as a characterization of linguistic categorization, it will not work to reconstruct the objects of disciplinary inquiry. The notion of similarity is too vague to ground a concept; trying to start with a prototype just pushes back the problem; and even the notion of family-resemblance or a particular "open concept" presumes rather than explicates the category in question. Polythetic definitions turn out to be even worse: they postulate rather than explicate themselves; they are inevitably decomposable into further polythetic categories; they fail to answer how many polythetic features are necessary to make up a class; and they provide no justification for generalizations. Indeed, one could restage the same arguments against Hart's notion of an open texture in legal theory and Gallie's notion of essentially contested concepts in political theory, which are both variations on the same Wittgensteinian insight.

All that said, there is something right about the insight that many categories are composed of loose clusters of attributes; the problem is that neither prototypes nor family-resemblance can explain how the relevant categories are anchored (for an alternative, see chapter 4).

2.5 Conclusion: Legitimation Crisis

Broadly speaking, the human sciences are experiencing what Jürgen Habermas calls a "legitimation crisis," a catastrophe of self-justification that arises when "a social system allows fewer possibilities for problem solving than are necessary [for its] continued existence."[92] I think this applies to our subject because almost no matter how you look at it, the human sciences have lost much of their problem-solving capacity, and so have forfeited much of their legitimacy. But here I am most interested in one particular aspect of that legitimation crisis—specifically, the notion many scholars have that their discipline's intellectual projects have run aground. Given how intimately disciplines have been tied to their objects, one might well ask: what might cause a discipline to call into question, challenge, or even abandon its primary object? How did art historians give up on art, anthropologists abandon culture, and so on?

The way the academic disciplines organized themselves around their core disciplinary objects left them vulnerable. There were deep-seated problems with the earlier notions of concepts, both theoretical and pretheoretical. When skepticism became a promising intellectual or professional path, these liabilities were there to exploit. Put differently, the foundations of the human sciences were faultily constructed. The problem was rooted in the very heart of the disciplines and their focal disciplinary objects.

To be clear, there is a common philosophical substratum to the arguments above: they did not just happen as part of some ill-defined cultural zeitgeist, but rested on the discovery of a set of philosophical issues.

The evidence of this chapter could itself be historicized as follows:

Starting in the early 1930s, Ludwig Wittgenstein began explicitly working to refute a classical theory of concepts.[93] Although it had been challenged before, a classical view of concepts had a long history associated with both Platonic and Aristotelian philosophical lineages.[94] In brief, concepts were supposed to be grounded in definitional structures explicating their essences and describing the necessary and sufficient conditions for their use. The aim of philosophy and then the special sciences was to discover or sharpen the definitions of real concepts, which were supposed to reflect accurately the divisions of nature or culture.

But the early twentieth century propelled all this into chaos. Wittgenstein argued that many general concepts lacked an exhaustive set of properties common to all examples of the category. Concepts do not share common essences and cannot be captured by means of necessary and sufficient conditions. The posthumous publication of his *Philosophical Investigations* in 1953 further disseminated this line of critique. Similarly, critiques of the limits of conceptualization appeared independently in analytic and continental philosophy. Unbeknownst to each other, scholars also began attacking the particular concepts around which various disciplines had been established. They did this as part of these broader philosophical critiques, but mainly they seem to have come to the issue independently by focusing closely on the disciplinary objects.

While often sharpened or perhaps amplified by poststructuralist, postmodernist, and postcolonialist theory, these moves generally preceded such movements. In point of fact, sifting through the secondary literature one can find many of these assaults on the scholarly objects in the 1950s and early 1960s. The citation chain is also interesting, because in many disciplines a whole new round of criticisms emerged in the 1980s that generally omitted reference to the critiques of a generation earlier. These new challenges were often formulated by reference to Derrida or Foucault or Edward Said, and frequently pointed to Saussure where previous thinkers had positioned Wittgenstein. These critiques became part of the way postmodernism was construed within the disciplines. This is not to say that these later arguments were identical, but they deployed similar moves for similar purposes. The disciplinary critiques are variations on a small number of themes—which suggests that the critiques emerged when they did in part because of a fundamental reappraisal of the meaning of concepts in general.

•

To restate what I want us to carry forward, I have presented the typical strategies for categorical critique. They have been mixed and matched in their applications across the disciplines, but the strategies are generally similar. Many disciplines have found their central concepts destabilized. Disciplines that have thus far managed to ward off such critiques are ripe for disintegration. By all the signs, critique seems more likely to spread than to disappear. And so it should. Often we need to know that we are not imprisoned in the categories that have been used to define us. Destructive criticism is therefore necessary—not just for the discipline but for individual scholars—to clear the ground and shatter our old preconceptions, before we can achieve the simultaneous deconstructive vigilance and reconstructive ability our work requires. In this respect, I have been aiming to teach budding scholars a set of strategies for staging further criticisms.

But crucially, the *commonalities* of these critiques also tell us something fundamental about the nature of our social categories. If every category is different, the main thing they seem to share is that they can all be challenged in an analogous manner. The concepts in the human sciences fractured in similar ways because they are in some significant sense similar concepts. If this is the case, a new understanding of concepts and even knowledge can be built—not on a defense of the categories, but from the structure of the critiques themselves. Chapter 3 builds off these "postmodern" critiques, turning them inside out, to begin to produce a new metamodern notion of social kinds.

3: Process Social Ontology

*The world is but a perennial movement. All things in it are in constant motion.
. . . I cannot keep my subject still. . . . I do not portray being: I portray passing.*

MICHEL DE MONTAIGNE, "Repentance"

In perhaps his most influential short story, "Tlön, Uqbar, Orbis Tertius," Jorge Luis Borges imagined an ancient language that lacked nouns and instead used "impersonal verbs, modified by mono-syllabic suffixes (or prefixes) functioning as adverbs. For example, there is no noun that corresponds to our word 'moon,' but there is a verb which in English would be 'to moonate' or 'to enmoon.'"[1] Borges would not need to look so far today, since a similar trend occurs in various theory circles which have now spent several decades purging themselves of particular nouns, substituting (for instance) *minoritized* for *minorities, enslaved* for *slaves, male-identified* for *male, racialized* for *race, criminalized* for *criminal, unhoused* for *homeless*; in linguistics, *standardized* English for *standard* English, and in religious studies *canonized* over *canon*, and so on.[2] These word choices are typically explained as an attempt to emphasize actions or choices over fixed or inherent characteristics.

I mention this terminological shift not to mock it, but to uncover the philosophical commitments behind such changing language. Indeed, in many respects I think it is a positive move, but one in need of further theorization (which this chapter will provide). In brief, much of its origins can be seen in an "anti-essentialism" that became increasingly prominent in the American academy after the 1980s. There were many converging earlier sources of the critique of essences: existentialism, feminism, Marxism, critical race and postcolonial theory all often portrayed anti-essentialism about human categories as emancipative.[3] Additionally, the epistemological grounds for anti-essentialism came from the failures of the grand project of definitions in philosophy discussed in chapter 2. But a significant further source for criticisms of essentialism was the construction of postmodernism, which amplified these other critiques and knit them together with various forms of linguistic skepticism.[4] We can see this epitomized in Roland Barthes's statement that the "disease of thinking in essences . . . is at the bottom of every bourgeois mythology of man."[5] All that is to say that these intertwined critiques have produced unwitting and default anti-essentialisms in many disciplines in the human sciences.

While anti-essentialisms have been extremely valuable in challenging entrenched notions of all sorts, they have also run into predictable difficulties and dead ends. Anti-essentialism in feminist theory provides an important exemplar. In brief, the critique of essentialism was initially a powerful force against presuppositions about gender and thus facilitated a revolution in critical scholarly inquiry. But according to Naomi Schor, by the 1990s accusing scholars of "essentialism" had become "the prime idiom of intellectual terrorism and the privileged instrument of political orthodoxy . . . the word essentialism has been endowed within the context of feminism with the power to reduce to silence, to excommunicate, to consign to oblivion."[6]

Yet anti-essentialist feminism in the same period encountered a political impasse because of the observation that if there was nothing that defined women, then how could one emancipate them? As Diana Fuss has observed, various theorists began asserting that women (or lesbians) were defined by the fact that, in contrast to men (or heterosexuals), their essence was to have no essences.[7] On these accounts, femininity is defined in terms of its indefinability; lesbianism is the only sexual orientation that is not a sexual orientation; or the one thing all women share is that they have nothing in common. The contradictions of these essentialized anti-essentialisms were only too easy to criticize. Meanwhile, according to Sherene Razack, de-essentializing gender in feminist theory had also resulted in re-essentializing race as the primary source of difference, setting feminism and critical race theory on a collision course.[8] Moreover, as anti-essentialism became increasingly generalized, it ultimately became a skepticism not just about entrenched notions of gender, but also about all possible generalizations. Altogether, anti-essentialism became a dogmatic orthodoxy in feminist theory in the same period in which it became snarled in various contradictions that came to call the whole scholarly project into question. Rejecting talk of "essences," Jane Roland Martin observed, meant that "we followed a course whose logical conclusion all but precludes the use of language."[9]

Feminist theory is not alone on this trajectory—many fields seem to have reached a similar impasse. While there are certainly defenders of "scientific essentialism" in analytical philosophy, anti-essentialism has become so entrenched in many disciplines that its most vocal opponents are often "anti-anti-essentialists," who grant many of anti-essentialism's main claims while calling for purely pragmatic essentialisms either epistemologically (nominal essences) or politically (strategic essentialism).

But each of these has been attacked on anti-essentialist grounds.[10] To be fair, many of these issues persist as merely verbal disputes because scholars have been operating with unrecognized differences in their notions of "essences" (although of course this has been an issue since the beginning).[11]

In this chapter I argue that a process social ontology makes better sense of the evidence that justified the emergence of anti-essentialism in the first place and it can do so without falling into the sinkhole of an ever-expanding "anti-essentialism" that means nothing can be said. Regardless of the status of process thinking as an ontology more generally, social entities are best understood in terms of processes. But if anything (and this is where anti-essentialists are right), ordinary language and "folk psychology" about the social world regularly commit the fallacy of substantializing social kinds, and then (equally importantly) asking of them the wrong sorts of questions based on these assumptions.[12] I touch on the implications of process thought for anti-essentialism later in this chapter, but regardless of the status of anti-essentialism, a process sociology ontology is crucially important for the project of this monograph because it allows us to see the disciplinary master categories in a new light and thereby suggests a novel mode of systematic theorizing for the human sciences.

For those unfamiliar with "process metaphysics" or "process ontology," it is primarily identified with Alfred North Whitehead's philosophy of becoming.[13] But he was not alone in his thinking; a number of philosophers—a handful in the European tradition and many more globally (such as classical Chinese, Indian, and Nahua philosophers)—have argued for the ontological primacy of process over substance, of becoming over being.[14] Process theorists generally reject the notion that everlasting substances are the most basic constituents of existence and argue instead that what appear to be enduring entities are really temporary stabilities in unfolding processes. They also often reject the grounding assumption of much of analytical philosophy: that what is real is what is pure, independent, or unadulterated. Process thinkers tend instead to describe existence in terms of dynamics, change, transformation, impermanence, creation, destruction, entanglement, emergence, interdependence, and interrelation.[15]

As noted above, part of the rationale for the epistemological value of a process social ontology is that it permits us to make sense of various species of anti-essentialism, including the disintegration of our analytical categories. I will argue that once the disciplinary categories are seen as process kinds, we are on our way to understanding (and even granting) the critique of the disciplinary objects. It will turn out that many of the things that purportedly rendered impossible a social scientific account of cultural categories are instead the opening suppositions that make such a study possible. Having demolished concepts in the last chapter, in this chapter I begin rebuilding a new, "de-essentialized" notion of social categories from the rubble of the disciplinary objects. Chapter 4 will develop this project in more detail as we populate the social world with specific "social kinds." But both chapters share a specific way forward—one that understands critique not as precluding the study of the disciplines, but rather as a useful pointer toward the ontology of the social world.

To clarify my intentions here, *ontology* has recently become a buzzword in a range of disciplines, but unbeknownst to many involved, it is regularly used in directly contradictory ways. Some theorists use the term ontology to describe how their ethnographic subjects construct their worlds. To do ontology in this mode requires bracketing out the world as such to focus on the worldviews, ways of living, or world-making practices of the people being studied. A scholar in this mode is not asking whether, say, kachina spirits exist, but studying the way kachinas factor into the "ontology" of Hopi culture and ritual practice.[16] Following Michael Lynch, we could refer to the first of these projects as "ontography" or writing about world-making practices.[17] In contrast, other theorists are using ontology more in the term's original meaning, to refer to theorizing about what exists and how things exist. To do ontology in this latter mode is to make claims about the world itself rather than about the worldview of a specific group. Both modes are potentially useful, but using the word *ontology* for what amount to incompatible endeavors means that many scholars are in fact talking past each other—worldview vs. world. I am broadly skeptical of the coherence of the idea of "worldviews."[18] So here I mean to be doing ontology in the classical sense, but rather than investigating existence as such, I am primarily interested in the basic existents of the social world. (A further metaontology is described in chapter 5.)

3.1 A World in Motion

Our first hint about the processual nature of social kinds is a broad observation that has often been used as the main evidence for anti-essentialism and has sometimes even been deployed to challenge the possibility of social science as such—namely, that social phenomena are heterogenous and subject to constant variation and transformation.[19] As Charles Taylor argued, the success of "the natural sciences is bound up with the fact that all states of the system, past and future, can be described in the same range of concepts," but the human sciences address "open system[s]" and "we cannot shield a certain domain of human events" from any other. Hence, the human world consists of constantly chaotic and interlocking systems. Moreover, "conceptual innovation . . . in turn alters human reality," leading to "radically unpredictable events."[20] In brief, Taylor argues that it is hard to produce inductive generalizations about society because it is constantly in flux.

Coming from a very different disciplinary vantage, the French cognitive scientist Pascal Boyer has argued that cultural representations "undergo mutation, recombination and selection," and that consequently "the process of [cultural] transmission seems guaranteed to create an extraordinary profusion of baroque variations."[21] Indeed, anthropologists have increasingly recognized that cultural transmission is underdetermined, meaning that "tradition"—and culture as a whole—is actually constantly changing.[22]

For a long time, psychologists and linguists have been making similar observations.[23] Despite popular notions of established linguistic meaning, fieldwork in a range of communities has shown significant regional and temporal variation. As historical linguistics has demonstrated, semantic change is frequent and can be quite rapid (e.g., the shift in the meaning of the word "gay" from primarily meaning happy to meaning homosexual in the span of a couple of decades). It is often assumed that speakers in the same linguistic community share common cultural concepts, but except in those rare areas in which we have been explicitly taught and our beliefs have been semi-standardized (such as being coached in specific definitions according to a common educational standard), the acquisition of most concepts comes from inferences based on fragmented material. Most of us have a piecemeal smattering of ideas about the world based on implicit references, stray examples, anecdotes, and stories; therefore, we disagree about more than we realize. For example, according to one study, even native-English-speaking undergraduates disagree over the meanings or categorization of basic terms such as "clothing" and "furniture."[24] All that is to say, a certain amount of variation and change is the norm rather than the exception.

Likewise, the British economist Tony Lawson has argued against economic models privileging stabilities and regularities on the grounds that "social reality" is "highly transient [and constantly] being reproduced and/or transformed through practice."[25] Roughly similar claims have been made by sociologists and philosophers, as well as many other theorists, about their specific domains.[26] For instance, sociologists Michael Omi and Howard Winant observed that "while race is still popularly understood as essence," it is rather "an unstable and 'decentered' complex of social meanings constantly being transformed by political struggle."[27] It would seem that not only are social categories constantly changing, but by some accounts the rate of social change in general is even increasing.[28]

These various findings are often taken to imply that the systematic study of culture and society is impossible, but this interpretation of their implications is incorrect—we can actually come to understand a social world in motion. In the first instance, we can trace how things have changed in the past without their current dynamics necessarily undermining our analysis. For example, a lot of good work has been done that examines the historical and cross-cultural unfolding of "race" as a category, which is no less useful given the heterogeneity of the category and its tendency to change. In the second instance, all that is necessary to have knowledge of the social world is for the rate of knowledge gain to be larger than the rate of change.[29] Difference and variation make prediction hard (and prediction has never been a strength in the human sciences), but they do not preclude analysis of the past or the present. Moreover, understanding the processual nature of the social world would make our investigation of it more accurate.

Indeed, the primary implication of the observations recounted above is that it entails an inversion of the classic social or anthropological account of social change. While older theorists tried to come up with different schemes to explain change and variety, change is ongoing for a host of reasons and heterogeneity is much more typical than homogeneity. So a whole generation of theorists got it exactly backward—the thing that needs to be explained is not social change or cultural differences, but relative *stability* or *similarity*.[30] (Basically, I am proposing an anti-universalist universalism, as I argue the default is variety and difference.) Put differently, scholars have spent vast amounts of effort trying to apprehend the roots of social/cultural change and difference as if these were exceptional or at the very least in need of explanation. But what we really need to understand is stability and homogeneity, which from much of the evidence rehearsed above (as well as from the vantage of a process social ontology) are the actual anomalies in need of explanation. I will return to this in chapter 4.

But first I want to focus on another implication of the Heraclitean quality of the social world and explore how an account of its processual nature can help clear up some of the category critiques outlined in chapter 2. What does it mean to think of social kinds in terms of processes? In some respects, it will take this chapter and the next to explain. But to get there requires that we first make a brief detour through the notion of "natural kinds" in contemporary philosophy. A discussion of natural kinds is important because many people have a tendency to mistake social categories for natural kinds and then, when they do not function like natural kinds after all, to demolish them altogether, rather than pausing to consider how social kinds might function differently.

3.2 Natural Kinds

For readers unfamiliar with the expression "natural kinds," the basic idea is that while various conceptual categories divvy up the world in conflicting ways, there exist some collections of individuals with common, consistently identifiable properties that we can refer to as "kinds."[31] Analytic philosophers often refer to these groupings as "natural kinds" or "real kinds" and often describe them by way of a metaphor recouped from Plato (or equally ZHUANGZI) as representing the "joints of nature." At the level of ordinary language and perception, the world would seem to be populated by natural groupings like wolves, oak trees, quartz crystals, and rosebushes. These categories are projectable insofar as, say, the features or properties of one wolf are more or less generalizable to other wolves. Further, it would seem that while some linguistic categories are arbitrary (e.g., "my favorite pets"), others designate these genuine groupings or natural kinds.

Natural kinds are often described as key to problems in both semantics and philosophy of science and have accordingly been the subject of significant contemporary debates. Philosophers John Dupré, Ian Hacking, and Muhammad Ali Khalidi all list some subset of the following features as commonly associated with an "essentialist" model of natural kinds.[32]

1. *Essence.* Natural kinds share a bundle of properties in view of their "essence" and therefore their properties are projectable. In this context, saying that natural kinds have *essences* typically means that they are supposed to have "essential" properties that determine membership in the kind, such that a generalization about one individual member of a natural kind in view of their kind-ness is said to hold for all members of the kind.

2. *Definability.* Natural kinds are supposed to be both definable and clearly delineable. There are no gray areas about membership in a natural kind. Natural kinds are delimited by clear boundaries that can in principle be discovered and demarcated. It is also often supposed that a natural kind can be defined by discovering its essence.

3. *Necessity and sufficiency.* "Each of the properties associated with a natural kind is possessed by every individual that belongs to that kind, and any individual possessing all of them belongs to the kind in question."[33] Natural kinds are supposed to be definable based on discovering these necessary and sufficient conditions.

4. *Mind-independence*. Natural kinds exist in nature independent of human minds and the basis for their classification is inherent in the structure of the world itself.

5. *Intrinsicality*. Members of a natural kinds are supposed to possess the properties they do intrinsically, independent of their connection to anything else.

6. *Microstructure*. Natural kinds are often supposed to share a common "microstructure" (e.g., the common atomic structure shared by all members of a particular chemical element).

7. *Modal Necessity*. Natural kinds are supposed to have the properties they have in every possible world in which they exist.

8. *Law of Nature*. There are supposed to be invariant laws of nature that apply to particular kinds; thus natural kinds can be thought of as crucial to theorizing of natural laws.

9. *No-Crosscutting*. Natural kinds do not crosscut each other. Something cannot be part of multiple natural kinds unless the kinds are part of a consistent, nested hierarchy (e.g., species, genus).

10. *Discoverability by Science*. Natural kinds are discoverable by science. It is also often said that natural kinds figure in the formation of natural laws.

An essentialist or "classical theory" of natural kinds tends to assume all or most of these features. The classical theory has something going for it— for instance, chemical elements seem to fit all of these features, and the argument could be made that some other classifications in physics and chemistry do as well.

That said, the main thing I want the reader to take away from this list is that *none* of the features associated with classical natural kinds works for the kinds we typically focus on in the human sciences. Indeed, if you take the list of ten features associated with natural kinds and compare it to the critiques of the disciplinary master categories in chapter 2, you will see that they effectively cancel each other out.

By way of illustration: *religion* and the other disciplinary master categories lack "essential properties." Religion cannot be defined in terms of necessary and sufficient conditions. There would seem to be few if any properties possessed by all members. Religion lacks mind-independence, intrinsicality, and microstructure. It lacks "modal necessity" insofar as we can imagine possible worlds either without "religion" or having "religions" with properties very different from ours. It is not clear if there are any lawlike generalizations that apply distinctively to members of the kind religion. "Religion" is not a *sui generis* category; hence, most examples of religion exhibit cross-cutting. The question of discoverability by science is rendered messy by debates about the nature of the social sciences. At the very least, "science" itself is a master category of the sort I am interested in investigating. So "discoverable by science" produces recursion. In sum, the disciplinary master categories are not classical natural kinds.

Substances have often been seen as the ideal subject for theories of classical natural kinds. But theorists working on the various life sciences have independently observed that many of the defining features of classical ideas of natural kinds do not apply to various important biological kinds, such as "species" and "disease."[34] While biologists often see their subject in terms of natural groupings, the kinds they work with do not seem to be as invariant, clearly definable, independent, or lacking in gray areas as the natural kinds philosophers have spent their time theorizing. Despite the status of animal species in particular as paradigmatic natural kinds in some philosophical arena, they do not actually fit the classical theory very well. "Wolves," for example, do not fit many of the defining criteria of natural kinds above (see note).[35]

This has important implications. Anti-essentialists in the humanities and social sciences often see themselves as opposed to biological essentialism, or they stage social categories in opposition to biological natural kinds. Indeed, much of humanistic anti-essentialism has worked by suggesting that the variability and heterogeneity of a particular category means it is not biological. The surprise is that there is a well-established critique of essentialism in biology as well. Most biologists do not think that species (and other biological kinds) have essences, by which they mean that they "have been unable to find an essential trait that occurs in all and only the members of a particular taxon."[36] Biological kinds generally have exceptions.[37] Biological kinds and social categories exhibit similar heterogeneity and variation (although social kinds tend to be more varied and are necessarily capable of more rapid changes). Recognizing biological anti-essentialism does not mean that everything reduces to biology or that some of the anti-essentialist critiques of biologizing social categories were unwarranted; rather, it means that repudiating "essences" or critiquing "essentialism" is not the best way to communicate those insights. Put differently, many of our social kinds are not biological categories and should not be mistaken for such (e.g., race), but rejecting essentialism isn't the right way to distinguish between biological and social kinds, because many biologists also reject essentialism about biological categories and some have even argued that there are no natural kinds in biology.

One could respond to this in two ways: either by chipping away at the notion of natural kinds so that it better fits biological kinds more generally, or by suggesting that biological entities do not fit the category of natural kinds. To my mind this issue is largely a matter of semantics, but it is no surprise that there has been a long history of process thinking in the biological sciences, if not elsewhere.

Strikingly, biologists focusing on such diverse subjects as metabolism, evolution, life cycles, and ecological interdependence have all converged on process-based thinking by working out the details of their own domains.[38] It is astonishing that the human sciences have thus far (with a few important exceptions) failed to do the same.

3.3 *Process* Social Kinds: A First Pass

While few people would deny the processual nature of culture or society, the dominant modes of discussing human affairs are typically oriented in a mode more appropriate to substance thinking than to process thinking. We often talk about "capitalism" or "neo-liberalism" as if they were bounded entities with clear borders and agency of their own, instead of dynamical processes. Our main terms for the disciplinary master categories are still caught up in substance-like language such as *art* and *religion*, and we ask of them such substance-type questions as: "is a given exemplar *a* work of art or *a* religion?" But when approaching social kinds in this manner, our basic questions often amount to category errors. There is a reason Marxist theory, anti-essentialism, and process metaphysics all converge on critiques of the fallacy of "reification" (*Verdinglichung*, literally "making something into a thing") and "misplaced concreteness."

Beginning with the disciplinary master categories I was deconstructing in chapter 2, we can produce a list of generalizations about their qualities (or lack thereof) that stands in stark contrast to an essentialist account of natural kinds. Doing so should give us a preliminary set of features that the disciplinary objects (or as we'll now refer to them, "process social kinds") share. They are:

1. *High-Entropic*. As noted above, the term "essence" is the subject of significant controversy. But the critique of essentialism has often amounted to the observation that various social kinds have significant variation (regional and temporal) in their meaning and/or properties. To borrow a notion from thermodynamic systems theory, one could say that the disciplinary master categories are "high-entropic" because they are multi-variant, diverse in their instantiation, consistently changing, and often lacking in equilibrium. Furthermore, it would seem there are few if any properties possessed by all members of a social kind category.

2. *Undefinable*. Definition, especially by necessary and sufficient conditions, is basically a failed project. It might work for a small number of natural kind categories (e.g., defining gold in terms of its atomic number), but it won't work for any social kind. In part this is because humans generally do not base mental representations on definitions. Taken together, 1 and 2 above lead toward critiques I-1, I-2, I-3 and R-3, discussed in chapter 2.

3. *Niḥsvabhāva or Interdependent*. This is a technical term from classical Indian philosophy that can help us clarify something important. The Sanskrit word *svabhāva* can be translated as "own-being" or "intrinsic nature," and it generally refers to something that is "unconditioned, not dependent on other entities."[39] To be *niḥsvabhāva* is to be lacking in *svabhāva*. I introduce the term here because one of the central features of social kinds is that they are not independent, but interdependent. In other words, their properties emerge from their relationship to other entities. As Bimal Krishna Matilal has observed, an object lacking in *svabhāva* "has no absolute values of its own but has a value only with respect to a position in a system."[40] In that respect, the existence and properties of social kinds are causally dependent on their local environment. Moreover, as we have seen in the category critiques, many social kinds come into being by way of an exclusion of a contrasting kind (hence critique I-4).

4. *Cross-cutting*. Social kinds cut across each other. This is in distinct contrast to natural kinds. It is sometimes supposed that a given entity can only be a member of one (non-nested) natural kind; e.g., something is either gold or silver but not both. Yet social kinds often display just this tendency. The same action can be both religious and political. The same tennis ball may be categorized as a piece of sports equipment, a dog toy, an art installation, or a planet in a child's mobile, depending on the context.[41]

5. *Abstractions/Reifications*. Social kinds—like most linguistic categories except personal names—tend to be abstractions or generalizations. There is usually something lost in the process of generalizing. Moreover, there is a strong tendency for people to take social kinds and reify them—that is to say, treat them as though they are entities with their own agency or as though they are natural kinds.[42] (This leads toward critique I-5.) Part of the work of scholars in the human sciences is to find a balance between over-generalization and over-particularization. This may mean finding a sweet spot in a given work, or it might mean successive works tacking back and forth between the two modes.

6. *Historically/Culturally Contingent*. As discussed in chapter 2, much of the conversation around social construction is about historical contingency. In effect, if history had been different, the entity in question would have been different in some important way. It is hard to do counterfactual history well, but social kinds tend to have properties that have changed over time and in that respect different historical outcomes might have produced social kinds with different properties. (Moreover, these changes can often be reconstructed to expose the function of contingent systems of power.) Further, many social kinds exhibit a high degree of difference between cultures or languages, which often either lack the kind in question or construe it differently (hence critiques R-1, R-2, R-3).

7. *Normative*. Social kinds tend to have normative registers. They suggest values. The normativity inherent in the human sciences has bothered a lot of scholars. But I will argue that it needn't. The final two chapters of this book will be devoted to making the case for bringing our hidden values to the surface in such a way that they help to further intellectual progress (hence critique E-1).

8. *Mind-dependence*. As I argued in chapter 1, there are different kinds of mind-dependence, including ontological, causal, and classificatory versions. To say that something is mind-dependent could suggest that something exists primarily because of ongoing attitudes and beliefs (e.g., a given dollar bill is money only as long as a group of people believe it is money), or it could be a causal account of how it came into being (e.g., Banksy's mural "The Son of a Migrant from Syria" is mind-dependent because it was envisioned and then created by a human mind, but it is a physical object), or it could just be a description of an *ad hoc* classification (e.g., my daughter's collection of her favorite rocks). In all these senses, it would seem that disciplinary categories are mind-dependent.

This is a very provisional list. In chapter 4 I will articulate and give nuance to these points in greater detail, but even in broad outline they suggest that we need to conceptualize social kinds with features diametrically opposed to those associated with classical notions of natural kinds.

The most important implication of the above, however, is that thinking of the disciplinary master categories as process kinds allows us to see them in a new way. This is because, at the most basic level, processes have a different grammar than substances—they are verbs rather than nouns. Thus, the scholars who substituted verbs for nouns I mentioned in the opening of this chapter are on the right track. To think of social kinds as processes is to emphasize their function as patterned activity and constant change, rather than as "building blocks," containers, or shared concepts. As John Searle has observed, for "social objects . . . the grammar of the noun phrases conceals from us the fact that, in such cases, process is prior to product. Social objects are always, in some sense we will need to explain, constituted by social acts; and, in a sense, the object is just the continuous possibility of the activity."[43]As he elaborates: "social *objects*, such as governments, money, and universities, are in fact just placeholders for patterns of *activities*."[44] I think Searle is basically right (and indeed this assertion complements Judith Butler's exploration on the role of various discursive processes in the "sedimentation" of sexed and gendered bodies), although unfortunately the rest of Searle's work largely fails to capitalize on this insight.[45]

I will complicate this in chapter 4, but at the very least what makes an object "money" is not what it is made of (metal, paper, computer bits), but the process of its manufacture and the potential activity of its use. Moreover, the same material artifact can be used as a weapon, a work of art, or an object of worship. So the real question should not be "is this object art?" but "*when* and *how* is this object art?"[46]

•

Reconceptualizing the social world is not primarily a matter of terminology or metaphor. I am not trying to rid us of our nouns. Rather, I am pointing out that focusing on substances over processes in the human sciences leads toward different modes of investigation. Think of the difference between an analysis of gold (an archetypal substance) and an analysis of a thunderstorm (an archetypal process). Gold has discrete boundaries. It can be identified by investigating its chemical properties (e.g., a trioxonitrate acid test). Gold's essence and properties result from the fact that it has seventy-nine protons in the nucleus of its atoms. Hence, its atomic number (79) can be used to define gold insofar as all gold atoms are supposed to have the same number of protons. In an analysis of substances, change is often the problem to be explained. So if different samples of gold behaved differently or changed over time, that would necessitate an explanation.

Thunderstorms, by contrast, lack discrete boundaries. The edge of a given storm is typically vague. Whether one is studying a single storm or multi-cell clusters can be relatively ambiguous. Thunderstorms have typical properties, not necessary properties. They are usually accompanied by winds, heavy rain, sometimes sleet or hail, but they can have no precipitation at all. Thunderstorms are not autonomous substances; rather, they are assembled from components (e.g., air, water, pollen grains, etcetera) and their manifestation is contextual and hence relational (e.g., typically requiring the presence of a combination of moisture, an unstable air mass, and thermals to produce a lifting force). Rather than being static entities, thunderstorms go through stages (from cumulus to mature to dissipating). They produce and are a product of atmospheric conditions (or more precisely, what we call a thunderstorm is a sequence of changes in the atmosphere), and so on. All that is to say, if the logic of substances is based on distinct boundaries and relative stability, the logic of a process is one of components, context, stages, cycles, phases, and conditions.

Processes lack sharp boundaries. They have fuzzy edges. Many processes are unowned (e.g., a heatwave) and thus have no inherent substance of their own.[47] A process has no permanence. It cannot help but change over time, unless it is to be a spent force. The coherence of a process is causal; they are identified by what they do, not where they are. Processes recruit other processes and are recruited in turn. They are conditioned and relational, rather than autonomous and essential. It makes no sense to look only for the pure process, as if it existed on its own or in an uncontaminated form. Change is the rule for processes, and stability or persistence is the exception.

Thinking in terms of processes allows us to break down the distinction between social entities and events. What is called an "entity" or "state" at any given time is revealed to be a slow process, while events are just fast processes.[48] To treat social kinds as processes is also to emphasize their function as loopings of matter and meaning. This will be explored in greater detail later in this book; for now it will suffice to say that we approach the mental through the material and the material through the mental. That social kinds are process kinds means that while they are the sites of language, they are not merely language, because they include non-conceptual elements—elements that by themselves resist reduction into language.

A process social ontology has implications for how we understand subjectivity. An older stratum of theory in the social sciences tended to presume that people had stable identities and encountered stable social structures. But the basic structure of human subjectivity (or perhaps the phenomenological ground of experience) is itself processual. As Rowland Stout argues, processes are more salient in consciousness than in events, since "I know what I am doing in a more direct way than the way I know what I did, and this applies similarly to what I am feeling, thinking, seeing, etc. The subjective perspective . . . is a perspective on their ongoing mental life—their life as a process."[49] For this reason, both phenomenology and an explanation of human mental life need to reckon with the importance of experience itself as a dynamical process. Moreover, a processual view allows us to envisage what we might term (after Édouard Glissant) an "ontology of relationality," or a sense and function of subjectivity that is more concerned with the unfolding relations (personal, structural, global, political, what-have-you) that constellate as/in subjectivity than with some reified "identity" that emerges from these relations.⁵⁰ Instead of old-fashioned accounts of identity positions, this allows us to emphasize the relational co-emergence of individuals and their environment.

Strikingly, conceptualizing social kinds as unfolding processes allows us to grant (and even make sense of) much of the critique of the disciplinary objects discussed in chapter 2. Six of the eight main features of the disciplinary master categories revealed by turning the critique inside out include being high-entropic, undefinable, *niḥsvabhāva* or interdependent, cross-cutting, tending toward reification, and being typically historically/culturally-contingent. All of these make sense as critiques of processes that have been misunderstood as substances.

To return to the anti-essentialism with which we began this chapter, several philosophers (DeLanda, Deleuze, Dupré) have observed that process gives us a natural critique of "essence."⁵¹ Processual kinds are change, definitionally. Furthermore, genealogy, for instance, gets most of its mileage out of demonstrating that a "unity," previously perceived as universal and transhistorical, turns out to be historically conditioned. But generalizing this basic argument would be admitting that *all unities* are the product of just such contingencies. Paraphrased, all social entities turn out to be formations in the Foucauldian sense. But arguing that a social entity is unreal because it lacks an "essence" or because it changes over time is equally a mistake. When all we were doing was destabilizing essences, we often left ourselves unable to say anything at all for fear of accidentally essentializing. But when we realize that we were really reacting to the perceived opposition of the processual nature of the social to the supposedly fixed and rigid identity of natural kinds, we can relax in the insight that to exist as a social entity is to be conditioned, to be the product of causally unfolding processes. Thus, we can make certain generalizations while also recognizing that we are talking about processes in flux, and that whatever we say now can and will likely be subject to change in the future. Nevertheless, our observations can be incredibly useful—they can help us to gain a more accurate picture of the stage of unfolding we are in now, as well as those that have come before.

•

So how do we know we are talking about the "same" processes? In a Heraclitean sense, we never have the "same" process at all. This can be illustrated with a parable known in classical Indian philosophy as "Menander's Chariot" (which is a similar but better formulation of the famous parable of Theseus' ship). The *Milinda Pañha* ("Questions of King Menander") portrays a dialogue between King Menander and the monk Nāgasena. When I teach this to undergraduate students, I refer to Menander's "racecar" to update the parable. The thought experiment goes like this: Menander is a racecar driver. After each lap his car completes, the pit crew replaces a piece of the racecar with a new part. Say after one lap, one percent of the car has been exchanged with new material, and so on. Eventually the pit crew has replaced every single part and the car is made out of one hundred percent new parts. The question is — *at what point does it stop being the same car?* Students usually reply either that it is always the same car or that it stops being the same car after the first change. But at this point I introduce the further wrinkle that the pit crew has been secretly hiding parts in a warehouse and in boxes, and they have accumulated all the original matter of Menander's racecar. Which of these is the real car — the original matter or the currently functioning car? What would happen if the pit crew took these components and assembled them into a second vehicle?

The relevance of this parable to biological and social kinds can be made explicit. Like Menander's racecar/chariot, the cells in the human body turn over roughly every fifteen years (some much faster, some slower).[52] Similarly, the ontology of corporations (and other social groups) encounters an issue because replacing members can lead toward the same seemingly paradoxical conclusion that the corporation is always different corporations.[53] Since attaining canonical form in Plutarch as Theseus' ship, a version of this thought experiment has had a long life in European philosophical thought, where it is often used to argue for some version of mereological nihilism.

But the *Milinda Pañha* has a different conclusion. First, it suggests that the chariot is only provisionally or conventionally the same chariot. Any entity composed of parts or aggregates lacks a single or essential nature. So in this respect, a process is in some sense always changing, and therefore lacks autonomous or permanent identity (again, think of Heraclitus never stepping in the same river). This seems to be a largely skeptical response. But the *Milinda Pañha* goes one step further, and suggests that the conventional identity of the chariot is similar to a lit torch being used to light another torch. Is it the same flame? No. But Nāgasena argues that the flames share a causal continuity.[54] Restated, whatever the degree to which Menander's chariot is the same chariot, it is the same because it shares a process or causal continuity. You are not the matter of your body, but to the extent that you are provisionally you, you are an unfolding process with a particular causal history.

Another key point is that unlike objects, processes can fork (one chariot can become two). To recast this in more contemporary terms, we can use the example of the Tigris River. In some respects, the Tigris is a different river every day, insofar as it contains different matter. The Tigris literally forks, and it is pragmatically relative to a given project whether any given tributary counts as a part of the same river. But rivers with no causal or process continuity to the Tigris are definitely not the same river. So the Tigris and the Mississippi are not the same river in any meaningful sense.

The main upshot of this is that when analyzing processes, as opposed to identities, we describe relations and causal continuities. Social kinds do not exist outside of time. Social kinds mean or function differently at distinctive moments and places and in relationship to other entangled processes. That said, social kinds are not fully unbounded, but result from the partial accumulation of past interactions. Instead of necessary history or arbitrary flux, we have path dependence. Outcomes are partially conditioned by environment and previous outcomes. In this we have recovered the discipline of history, without presumptions about the handing down of essence.

3.4 Conclusion: Beyond Anti-Essentialism

The disciplinary categories are vulnerable to the same sorts of critiques because they function similarly. Moreover, as I have been arguing, many of the deconstructive criticisms of the disciplinary master categories amount to identifying errors stemming from reification, atemporality, and misplaced concreteness—in other words, faults rooted in misidentifying the processual nature of social kinds. Indeed, one could argue that the human sciences have consistently mistaken social kinds for natural kinds. Thus, we have either vainly emulated the *modus operandi* of the natural sciences or, when certain knowledge was not forthcoming, completely rejected the possibility of explanatory knowledge. But as I have been arguing, neither path is necessary if we understand our subjects not as static universals but as historically conditioned unfolding processes. Although we have to be careful about importing "just-so" stories or misguided forms of reductionism, the human sciences are more like biology than they are like physics, and we need to approach our subject matter accordingly.

All this means that we need to stop trying to analyze social kinds as if they were classical natural kinds. A significant thread in the debate around natural kinds, as evidenced by Khalidi and others, is to expand the notion of natural kind until it is broad enough to include things like social kinds. While I am sympathetic to these efforts, what this approach overlooks is that social kinds have a different basic structure than natural kinds. The preliminary list of process social kinds' features above already suggests that social kinds are better formulated by inverting (rather than extending) the features typically associated with classical notions of natural kinds. My further reservation is the suspicion that "natural kind" is itself probably not a "natural kind term," or at the very least that the abstract structure of "kinds" in physics, mathematics, geology, and sociology differs enough across these disciplines that the respective "kinds" cannot be covered by the same grounding theoretical abstractions.[55] For this reason, I think trying to come up with a notion of natural kinds that fits all special sciences will almost necessarily fail (or it will become so vague and general in its effort to capture everything that it will ultimately be unhelpful).[56] It would be a mistake to assume that the term "natural kind" is itself a "natural kind" that would allow us to reconstruct the categories in all the natural sciences, much less include categories in the human sciences. To put a finer point on it, *the world we study in the human sciences is not jointed*. It is not divisible into clearly demarcated kinds. But even so, we can still study the social world.

Sometimes philosophers argue that social kinds are radically different from natural kinds, but they draw from this the conclusion that the human sciences are not real sciences.[57] While I would agree that the human sciences are not nomological disciplines, I will argue in chapter 4 that one of the things holding back rigorous theorizing in the human sciences is the very lack of a theory of social kinds itself. So I will start from the suspicion that social kinds are different from classical natural kinds, but that the human sciences also produce genuine knowledge.

The problem is that many of the academic disciplines have taken idealized versions of physics (or in this case perhaps chemistry) to be the prototypical example of science. There are few things outside minerals and chemical elements that fit the notion of classical natural kinds articulated above. Despite my early argument I do not mean to presume a simple opposition between substance and process. Archetypal natural kinds like atomic elements actually have their properties based on their history (say, in atomic fusions produced in the nuclear furnaces of stars); but that said, from the vantage of the lifespan of the entire human species, their properties seem to be stable. So atomic elements may appear eternal, even if they are the product of particular (albeit long time-scale) processes. Social kinds—like biological kinds—do not exhibit even that stability. Moreover, social institutions, ethical values, nation states, and social movements are continually producing new ethical, political, artistic, and intellectual for-

mations and so on. As I demonstrate in greater detail in chapter 4, social kinds are typically materially instantiated, but that does not guaran-
tee their atemporality. Human artifacts, for instance, generally change
and decay even if some do so very slowly. For these reasons, not just the
meaning, but even the referents of our scholarship are constantly shifting.
Therefore, the human sciences cannot fix or eternalize their concepts. But
that should not limit our capacity to carry out research.

Research itself is a process. To explain, in chapter 6 I will argue that the
very way we come to knowledge about the world is through processes like
abduction. In this respect "the method of identifying an object is itself a
process. Therefore, things cannot even be recognized as things without
some process."[58] We wouldn't know about substances or their properties
without process. Thus, there are many reasons we might want to think of
processes as an ontological fundamental. At the very least, reorienting
ourselves to the processual nature of social kinds, necessarily including
knowledge and science, should give us a better vantage on many things,
including scholarly praxis itself.

To circle back to the chapter opening one last time, a process social ontology also has a distinct advantage beyond mere anti-essentialism. Many
anti-essentialisms lack an account of essence. They often assume that any
generalization (or hint of universalism) is itself tantamount to engaging in
taboo essentialist thought. As Fuss has observed, many scholars essentialized essentialism and treated it as though every gesture toward similarity
or shared properties was equally pernicious.[59] This was a mistake. Once
we started saying that "the essence of X was that it lacked an essence," we
should have realized our critique had become muddled. But an emphasis
on processes lets us move past that skeptical impasse. While I think we
tend to focus too much on revising preferred terms while letting background assumptions persist unchallenged, this insight has been in front
of us all along with the linguistic trend toward verbs. It is probably the
case that the only thing all the "slaves" in different cultures had in common was the process of having been "enslaved," so rather than treating
all generalizations as false, we can say quite a bit about the enslavement
process.

There has already been a small turn toward Whitehead in some theory
circles. While I'm not as enamored with Whitehead specifically, I am sympathetic to all types of processual thinking. That said, many of the New
Materialists and Deleuzians who have evoked process metaphysics do
so in order to emphasize flux and arbitrary change. They use processes
to smuggle skepticism into their ontology (which parallels the problems
with speculative realism discussed in chapter 1). But many of those theorists who want to use Whitehead to get to chaos have not done their home-

work on processes. Processes can be highly varied and probabilistic, but if studied they are not generally unpredictable (e.g., chemical reactions). Moreover, most of the turn to Whitehead is about doubling down on his quasi-theistic monism (hence William Connolly's weird catechism).[60] More importantly, many theorists in the humanities who have thus far turned to processes seem to be using process primarily as a metaphor. They gesture at the processual nature of things without articulating actual specific processes or giving an account of how they might work. Their processual thinking often functions as mere posturing. The process social ontology I have been articulating here is no mere rhetorical stance, and in chapter 4 I chart specific processes and show how studying them could change our research methods.

I also want to note that all of this also pushes against a common interpretation of Roy Bhaskar's "critical realism" in the social sciences. In *A Realist Theory of Science*, Bhaskar argues for a distinction between an "intransitive, natural world" and a "transitive" domain of human theorizing that aspires to correspond to that world.[61] In *The Possibility of Naturalism*, he further suggested that "the 'social world,' though different than the 'natural world,' can also be thought of as an 'intransitive' realm, to which the 'transitive' theories produced by social research attempt to correspond."[62] Although critical realists have understood Bhaskar in different ways (not all of them incompatible with my account), it should be clear that the evidence marshalled above argues against thinking of the social world as an intransitive structure that exists behind the shifting appearances of social phenomena. Rather, a process social ontology suggests that the social world, just like theorizing about that world, is in a state of constant change, yet those transformations can be analyzed.

To restate what I want us to carry forward to the next chapter: to think of social kinds as fixed objects with essences is a massive error. But brute anti-essentialism is too imprecise a response. Adopting a process ontology instead allows us to understand the objects studied by the human sciences as dynamic components of the social world. This does not rule out the possibility of knowledge with respect to the objects of study; rather, it enables new means for both classification and study of social kinds without presupposing them as static categories, permitting us to build a new theory of social kinds on the rubble of "postmodern" critiques.

4: Social Kinds

This is the language of identity, of social kinds or categories, of considerations that are bound up with those kinds or categories.

KWAME ANTHONY APPIAH, *The Ethics of Identity*

What is the social world made of? The obvious answer—individual people—was for a long time dominant in the social sciences. Under the banner of methodological individualism, a number of social scientists argued that there was no such thing as society distinct from individual humans and their intentional actions, often reconstructed in terms of rational choice theory. This mode of theorizing had distinct advantages in terms of simplicity and clarity. But in many sectors of the academy, methodological individualism has fallen out of vogue. At the very least, thoroughgoing versions of methodological individualism have generally collapsed because of their inability to explain group norms, institutions, corporations, and other collectives, including the economy as a whole.[1] That is not to say that explanations at the individual level are necessarily incorrect, but rather that they are often incomplete and that there are many reasons to engage in the study of groups, emergent phenomena, and higher abstractions. It would seem that society is more than an aggregate of the individuals that make it up.

So what are the alternatives? For a long time, the main rivals to methodological individualism were various kinds of methodological holism, which generally tended to construe the social in terms of towering and diffuse wholes such as cultures, social forces, social structures, or social facts. While there has been some valuable work on social groups, large-scale methodological holisms often lead to the errors of reification and misplaced concreteness discussed in chapters 2 and 3. Moreover, most accounts of social structures and social forces have been maddeningly vague, often suggesting a kind of dualism in which a social world that is at once elusive and all-encompassing functions as a parallel realm overlaying the material world. More importantly, there has been significant difficulty in figuring out how to understand the relationship between individual agents and the production of social wholes, structures, or forces.[2] While moderate holisms have something going for them, they typically omit the crucial question of how the social world functions and comes into existence.

So what makes up the social world? I will argue here that the social is not reducible to individuals or amorphous social forces, but consists in a range of different social kinds, best understood as temporary zones of stability in unfolding processes, which are instantiated in their materialization.[3] The social world is built not just out of social animals, but also out of their materialized signs (e.g., the no-smoking sign or an ant's semio-chemical trail are social kinds with particular social functions). Let's approach this from a different angle.

Humans have the capacity to produce new kinds of entities, such as hammers, money, traffic jams, professors, punk rock, Buddhist monks, and, of course, the disciplinary master categories—religion, art, science, politics, and so on. At least provisionally, these things would seem to be "social kinds," according to the minimal definition provided by the Icelandic philosopher Ásta, since they are collections "of phenomena defined by a property or feature that is a *social* property or feature."[4] That said, we will eventually need a more elaborated account of what it means to be a *social* kind (which I supply below). But Ásta usefully highlights the observation that our ordinary world is populated by entities seemingly brought into being socially and about which we make frequent inferences. The term "social kinds" is a fairly high-level abstraction, encapsulating everything from artifacts, social roles, and institutions to norms, events, and the like; but it is my contention that thinking in terms of the *kindhood* of social kinds will allow us to see the social world in a new light.

To head off a potential misunderstanding, "process social kinds" are not *social* in contrast to cultural, political, artifactual, economic, or symbolic kinds. My notion of process social kinds is intended to be a higher-order category that would include all those kinds as well. Based in part on the process ontology I argued for in chapter 3, the distinction between social kinds, social roles, and social events is not important to this theory. Moreover, unlike many previous theorists of the social, I will also expand my account of process social kinds to include some sorts of nonhuman agents. This is going to be even more important in the semiotics I articulate in chapter 5. But any naturalized theory of social kinds is going to have to reckon with the social kinds produced by social animals—such as matriarchs of elephant herds, queen bees, worker ants, beaver dams, wasps' nests, and so on. Social kinds are not the sole provenance of humans; so we are going to have to transcend presumed binary oppositions between the natural and the social or between nature and culture. But while our purposes require an expansive meaning of the "social," it would be a mistake to expand the category infinitely, as do followers of Latour's ANT.[5] Rather, in what follows, my notion of social kinds builds on the account of mind-dependence I articulated in chapter 1 (with the understanding that minds are not exclusive to humans, but also that not all entities have minds). To put it concisely, I mean "social" primarily as a proxy for socially constructed or mind-dependent.

Both commonplace language and academic scholarship are full of generalizations about social groups, artifacts, institutions, events, and the like. To be sure, not all generalities about social kinds are equally apt. But unless we are going to rule out most research in the human sciences and nearly all commonsense ideas about the social world (that is, dismiss all meaningful discussions of McDonald's, Republicans, or the Catholic Church), we would seem to be implicitly presuming something like social kinds that anchor those statements. Philosophers often look to notions of emergence to explain some of the gaps between individual agents and their function in groups. But conventional philosophical accounts of emergence will not work for all social kinds because many social kinds are not part/whole relations.[6]

Crucially, inferences about these social kinds often go beyond inferences about human individuals. This is because hammers and traffic jams, while they are brought into being by humans, do not have the same properties humans do, and generalizations about hammers and traffic jams are not reducible to generalizations about individual people. Bluntly put, a typical hammer has properties (e.g., a head with a solid, impact-resistant mass useful for delivering a forceful blow) which are not the properties of an average human being. Even social groups composed entirely of humans exhibit this divergence in properties. For instance, the Williamstown Congregational Church (WCC) and the Williamstown Board of Selectmen (WBS) could have completely identical membership, but the same set of people would be capable of doing different things when they constitute the two different groups. The WBS has powers the WCC lacks (e.g., the WBS can approve warrant articles, but the WCC cannot). Moreover, there are true statements about groups that do not reduce to true statements about members (e.g., "the WCC was established in 1765" is a true statement, but "Anne, Bridget, Ed, & Rachel were established in 1765" is false, even assuming that those four individuals constitute an exhaustive list of members of the church). So while groups are ontologically dependent on the people that compose them, to reduce groups to the properties of the individual members is to miss something important.

Another issue is that social kinds are typically multi-realizable. For instance, money can be made out of totally different materials—from gold coins to paper bank notes to digital bits—all while still being money. So it is clear that the properties of money go beyond the properties of any particular type of material. By way of another example, ink's social effects are dependent on its visibility, but that visibility can be achieved by a range of colorants with completely different origins and chemical compositions. While some New Materialist thinkers have attempted to suggest that the meaning of an assemblage is equivalent to the matter that composes it, the ubiquity of multi-realizable social kinds pushes against this kind of reductionism.

Still, while there is a long history of treating social and material properties completely separately, social kinds exhibit both in ways that are more entangled than has generally been supposed. Physical properties are part of what give social kinds their social powers, and physical objects are brought into being by social forces. Making a hammer out of wood and steel is the imposition of a function on raw material as well as the creation of a member of a social kind. But most of the properties of something thus constructed are physical. Moreover, looping effects often make the biological and the social difficult to disaggregate (e.g., dog breeds are social kinds which have particular biological characteristics because of the way they have been bred). In brief, many social kinds interweave what could be called social, physical, and even biological properties.

To understand these better, we need to figure out: what is it that brings social kinds or objects into existence? And what is it that gives them their specific powers/identities? I answer these questions in this chapter by modifying a notion of homeostatic property-cluster kinds that emerged from theorizing about biological species and by drawing on resources from the process social ontology discussed in chapter 3.

4.1 Homeostatic Property-Cluster Kinds

To get us started thinking toward an account of social kindhood, I want to repurpose some key insights from the philosophy of biology. The American philosopher Richard Boyd is famous for a series of articles whose aim is to reconstruct a notion of natural kinds centered on biological species (instead of chemical elements) as the paradigmatic example. To summarize, in Boyd's account, "natural kinds" have three main features:

1. Natural kinds are homeostatic property-clusters
2. determined by the causal mechanism that brings about their shared properties.

3. The accommodation thesis—the naturalness of a kind is determined in relationship to a disciplinary matrix.

Boyd's account of natural kinds hinges on treating natural kinds as *"homeostatic property-cluster kinds"* whose identities are determined by the mechanisms that bring a cluster of typically co-occurring properties together.[7] Natural kinds are defined in terms of loose clusters of typically shared properties. Unlike the fixed or static properties associated with classical natural kinds, his account presumes that a kind's properties change over time. He argues that it is shared changes in the property-cluster or the underlying homeostatic mechanism that preserve the cluster's identity.[8] One implication of this account is that similarity (or common properties) is not a sufficient criterion for membership in a homeostatic property-cluster kind. This makes his account distinct from theories like that of family-resemblance. A shared *causal mechanism* is required as well. A scientist cannot merely use the criterion of similarity to determine membership in a given kind; there have to be common homeostatic mechanisms. This is a vital insight, to which I will return repeatedly.

In addition to his definition of natural kinds, Boyd also argues for what he calls the "accommodation thesis"—namely, that being a natural kind is a matter of degree and it is specifically relative to a particular "disciplinary matrix."[9] But as he puts it elsewhere, "successful induction and explanation always require that we accommodate our categories to the causal structure of the world."[10] Natural kinds have to conform at least partially to actual "causal structures," but "the methods by which we learn about them are importantly historically situated, socially and politically constructed, and non-foundational."[11] I return to this accommodation thesis and reconfigure it in chapter 5.[12]

To provide an example of what Boyd had in mind, no particular essential properties are necessary and sufficient for membership in the species "jaguar" (*panthera onca*). But he argues that *panthera onca* is a "natural kind" in biology because members of the species tend to share a fairly stable cluster of properties and they do so because of specific causal mechanisms (especially genetic inheritance and environmental pressures), which have tended to select for their typical shared traits. Consequently, if we know that a given individual is a jaguar, we can predict that it will likely have a subset of species-typical properties, such as distinctive black spots, strong jaws, large canine teeth, and so on, as each of these traits has been selected for evolutionarily (although due to mutation and the like there will be exceptions). Once we begin to understand the mechanisms that select for various traits, examining even one jaguar will increasingly permit inductive generalizations about other members of the species and how likely they are to share traits, even if the specific properties of "jaguars" continue to evolve over time.

In sum, biological species are determined not by virtue of their shared properties but by the causal structures that hold those shared properties in "imperfect homeostasis," namely interbreeding, shared ancestry, and environmental pressures. Therefore, in Boyd's account, biology as a discipline would tend to converge on something like a species concept because "species" is doing some work in biological theorizing and there is at least some kind of causal structure/homeostatic mechanism that "species" picks out, even if imperfectly.

As noted in chapter 3, I am fairly suspicious of the classical notion of "natural kinds" and I think there are diminishing returns in trying to fashion a newer notion of natural kinds that would open up to include social kinds, even as I agree with much of what Boyd has to say. There is also something inherently confusing about Boyd's assertion that the "naturalness" of a natural kind is relative to a particular discipline. Yet Boyd's account of kinds as homeostatic property-clusters is an especially useful starting place for theorizing about *social* kinds because he is right that any good account of kinds as such will have to weave together the relationship between properties, the mechanisms that cluster those properties, and the role of both in the generalizations we make about them.

The rest of this chapter is either a sharpening of Boyd or a more or less novel account of social kinds built upon the skeleton of Boyd's theory, depending on how you want to distribute the credit. But it probably resembles a Soviet Era joke about official truths. *Question: Is it true that cars are being given away in Moscow? Answer: Yes, that is true, except for a few small errors—It isn't Moscow, but Leningrad. It isn't cars but bicycles. They are not being given away, they are being stolen. But otherwise, it is a true statement.* In this case, I think the notion of "homeostatic property-clusters" is, broadly speaking, a good way to think about the kinds used in social scientific discovery. But instead of "properties" I think we would more helpfully speak of "powers," with properties as a subset of those. In the place of "homeostasis," I would put "homeostasis and heterostasis." In the place of "homeostatic mechanisms," I would put "anchoring processes" (which I will try to specify and subdivide). I also will limit the discussion to *social* kinds by emphasizing the mind-dependence discussed previously. Some of these are only minor adjustments; others have major implications. The rest of the chapter will present and then work out in detail an account of social kinds based on these insights.

4.2 A Process Cluster Account of Social Kinds

Here is a succinct description of what I have in mind:

> *Social kinds* are 1) socially constructed, 2) dynamic clusters of powers, 3) which are demarcated by the causal processes that anchor the relevant clusters.

(This is not a definition, but a theoretical description intended to guide research.) Also, bear in mind the other features of social kinds discussed in chapter 3: A) social kinds are the products of unfolding processes and thus tend to be high-entropic or varied both temporally and spatially (hence tend to be historically contingent); B) they are *niḥsvabhāva* insofar as their properties emerge via their relationships to other social kinds; C) social kinds crosscut each other so that the same entity can be the intersection of different kinds; and D) what makes them "social" kinds is that they are mind-dependent in a way I will explore further in the following section.

We also need to begin with a provisional distinction between concepts and kinds. Concepts, understood in this chapter as *mental representations*, can be differentiated from kinds, understood here as *the entities to which concepts refer*. Concepts enter into the formation of social kinds, but the anchoring processes that produce kinds need not have concepts in them, nor are the properties of kinds reducible to the concepts people have of them. For a concept to play a causal role in an individual's actions they must first have the concept, but a social kind is not merely whatever a given individual conceives it to be.

To explain: according to many philosophers like Hilary Putnam and Saul Kripke, natural kinds exceed their reference. They have properties that those referring to them often don't know about. For instance, I can competently refer to "gold" without knowing all or even most of gold's properties (solubility, thermal conductivity, tensile strength, etcetera). Indeed, natural sciences are supposed to advance in part by discovering previously unidentified properties of natural kinds.

As I argue in more detail below, social kinds also exceed their reference, and research in the human sciences often proceeds by discovering hitherto unknown properties of social kinds. For instance, I can talk about "investment bankers" without knowing exactly all of what being an investment banker entails. Moreover, the *social kind* "investment banker" might have causally relevant properties that none of us know about. To be sure, an individual's *concept* of "investment banker" is normative and part of the social field, and thus the concept helps make the kind what it is, but not generally without a gap. Concretely, this means that there are things even investment bankers don't know about their own profession (as Karen Ho ably demonstrated in *Liquidated: An Ethnography of Wall Street*).[13] In the human sciences, disciplines frequently refer to what amounts to the same social kind by different names. Moreover, within disciplines, shared terminology can mask significant conceptual divisions. All that is to say, concepts factor into social kinds but are not identical to them. Social kinds are ordinarily enmeshed in evolving social practices. These practices are often in significant tension with common concepts of the kind. Indeed, frequently the gap between the manifest concept and the operative social kind is what sustains the kind's existence.

4.2.1 SOCIALLY CONSTRUCTED

In chapter 1, I gave an account of social construction as a broad theoretical intervention. There I suggested that accounts of "social construction" can generally be parsed into ontological, causal, or classificatory accounts of mind-dependence. To briefly recap, for a phenomenon to be socially constructed means that either: (*ontologically*) its existence is dependent on sustained beliefs or social practices; (*causally*) it has been brought into being or been given particular properties by beliefs or social practices; or (*classificatorily*) it exists as a category because it has been classified as such—or some combination of the three. But while in that chapter I explored the meaning of social construction, in this and the next two sections I want to talk about how social construction works in practice. Put differently, the question is—how do social kinds exist? To provide a concrete example: what makes a particular piece of paper a dollar bill?

In an influential account, John Searle describes social construction in terms of "institutional facts" being imposed on "brute facts"—to translate his vocabulary we might say he thinks social kinds are imposed onto physical kinds. Searle focuses on a particular kind of imposition—namely, when people task an object with "meaning" or "standing for or representing something else."[14] He argues that this proceeds by means of a formula that amounts to "X counts as Y in context C" (e.g., this paper counts as money in the United States).[15] Searle notes this imposition can have unintentional side effects. The designation of particular pieces of paper as currency with a certain value permits buying and selling—an intentional effect. But once a trade cycle is brought into being, there will be emergent patterns like recessions (even if they are not named as such)—an unintentional effect.[16] But "social reality," Searle summarizes, is created by "the collective intentional imposition of function on entities that cannot perform these functions without that imposition."[17]

Although there is not space here to go into my full disagreement with him, I think Searle is correct that representational meaning is one significant type of property that a social kind can possess. (I provide an alternate and fuller account of meaning in chapter 5.) But Searle's explanation about how collective intentionality takes effect is remarkably conventional (pun intended). In particular, he argues that humans bring new social kinds into existence by means of "declarations" or speech-acts which basically become established social conventions.[18] As a classic example, the declaration of a minister that a couple "is now married" gives the couple the rights of married citizens in the country that recognizes the marriage.[19]

The problem is that many ways to assign social functions do not take the form of declarations. Race is not produced merely by speech-acts. Blackness does not take hold by someone pointing at someone else and explicitly declaring that they "count as Black in America." Moreover, many of the social statuses Searle thinks are established by means of "collective intentionality" turn out to be contested by at least some sectors of the same society. Sovereign citizens, for instance, do not recognize United States currency; certain fundamentalists reject national laws around same-sex marriage; and so on. One could argue that this just means that the status of the dollar bill and marriage have not yet reached the point of "collective intentionality" for American society as a whole, but it is surprisingly hard to find anything that everyone in a given society agrees about. Searle also misses the contestations involved in the production of so-called collective intentionality. In this respect, he lacks a theory of "power."[20] That the US government has a greater say in what counts as marriage than the Westboro Baptist Church is better explained in terms of power rather than in terms of collective intentionality.

I detail a semiotics in chapter 5, but an insight that unifies both that semiotics and my analysis of social kinds is that *meaning is not restricted to language*. Just as an ant can produce a warning sign for other ants by leaving a chemical trail, humans produce a vast social world by way of not just spoken and written words, but also coffee machines, traffic lights, and paintings.

Social kinds don't just represent. They are better thought of in terms of the imposition of a broad range of properties or capacities. Declarations, speech-acts, and social conventions are insufficient to explain fully the conferral of properties. I do not make a hammer a hammer by declaring the raw materials a hammer. I must forge the hammer into being. So to return to the question that began this subsection, how are social kinds produced if not primarily by convention or declaration? There are multiple ways to produce new kinds, and in the following section I lay bare the mechanisms through which social construction brings new kinds into being by different anchoring/clustering processes that produce social kinds.

Here is what I want you to hold onto from this section. By *social* kind, I mean socially constructed kind. Not all things are socially constructed in any meaningful sense. Stars are not socially constructed (although necessarily our *theories* about stars and *words* for stars are — see chapter 5). By social construction, I mean mind-dependence in either *ontological, causal,* or *classificatory* modes. To these, we should now add a further key type of mind-dependence: *representational.* Sometimes to be socially constructed means to be produced as a sign, to be given the power to represent. Again, to anticipate chapter 5's semiotics, there are both voluntary and involuntary signs; the first is causally-socially constructed while the second is typically classificatorily-socially constructed (for a given token to be interpreted as a sign it has to be linked up to other tokens of what is taken to be the same sign).

4.2.2 DYNAMIC CLUSTERS OF POWERS

Boyd's notion of homeostatic property-cluster kinds needs two broad adjustments to make it work as an account of social kinds. First, we should think in terms of powers rather than merely properties; and second, we should recognize both homeostatic and heterostatic clustering.

In the first case, one consequence of a process view of social kinds is that it necessitates a shift from kinds being demarcated by what they *are* to kinds being demarcated by what they have the potential *to do* or *have done to them*. There is much disagreement in analytic philosophy about what it means to possess a "property." But in ordinary language to possess a property is generally understood to mean that something possesses a particular set of characteristics rather than a capability or a pattern of likely activity in given circumstances. For instance, my wooden desk possesses the property of "being brown." But it gets trickier when we observe that my desk also possesses the property of "being about 150 miles from James Baldwin's grave." It seems hard to imagine that this latter property says anything important about my desk, and harder still to imagine this as a meaningful property my desk suddenly gained in virtue of it having been moved from its point of manufacture to my office.

To get around this problem, some philosophers have argued for a theory of actual properties as those which have causal powers.[21] In this account, what it means to have the property "being brown" is to have the power to reflect light in a certain spectrum under specific conditions. There are no specific causal powers associated with being a particular distance from

Baldwin's grave, at least as far as I know, so that would not be a "causal property" in their account.

Although I have a more expansive notion of social causes than most philosophers (discussed in my next monograph), I think the identification of properties with causal powers is broadly correct. Just do not assume that by "cause" I mean deterministic or mechanistic causation. To avoid confusion, I also want to be clearer about terminology. Some philosophers treat the terms *power, disposition, capacity,* and *property* as synonyms, while others distinguish the terms according to their own particular technical usage.[22] In this book, I generally use "powers" as the higher-order category that includes such subtypes as *dispositions, capacities,* and *properties,* which I will discuss in a moment. As my usage of the term "power" might strike the reader as idiosyncratic, I should note that I'm planning a whole follow-up monograph to explain in greater detail the relationship between my account of powers and power.

For researchers in the human sciences, it can be especially useful to distinguish between actualized and unactualized powers. So I will often find it useful to use the term *properties* to indicate actualized powers and the terms *capacities* or *dispositions* to indicate potential powers.[23] To explain: the table salt in front of me possesses the *property* (actualized power) of being a white crystalline solid with a low electrical conductivity, but the same object if heated to 801° C has the *capacity* (potential power) to become a liquid known as "molten salt" with a high electrical conductivity. My table salt has this capacity even if it never actually gets that hot.

Capacities are especially relevant to social kinds. The framed unspent Thai baht banknote in the local Thai "Sushi" Restaurant has the capacity to be used as money, even if it never has been and never will be used as such. Capacities in turn can be subdivided into those that appear frequently (we'll call those *tendencies*), those it is advantageous to possess (*abilities* or *privileges*), and those that it is disadvantages to possess (*liabilities*).[24] But it is worth observing that the same capacity could be an ability in one context and a liability in another.

It is also important to note that the powers of social kinds are necessarily interactive. As Phyllis Illari and Federica Russo have summarized the literature, "powers are a feature of a system, not a particular object."[25] For instance, a heart lacks its signature powers in isolation (e.g., to pump blood it needs the entire circulatory system). Hence, the powers of a heart originate in interconnection with those of other systems in the body. This is equally true for social kinds, which as I have been arguing are *niḥsvabhāva*. Social kinds do not exist in isolation. By way of another concrete example, in order to actualize or manifest the baht's capacity as currency someone has to actually spend it, which requires the actualizing of the powers of a range of different people (e.g., buyer and seller). The baht's powers are not solely its own, but are necessarily relational.

To prevent a misreading, powers do not have to be positive. Powers can include obligations and opportunities, liabilities and abilities. By way of illustration, contemporary Latinx Americans share the capacity—or more precisely liability—of being more likely to be hassled by US American immigration authorities. In another example, taking a job as a bank teller bestows new capacities—an obligation to attend work regularly and the right to draw a wage from the bank. Social kinds function in ways that confer a mix of effects on their holders. Many social kinds are even transient. For instance, being a customer in a café is participating in a particular social kind, although being a customer is only a weakly anchored (see below) social kind insofar as it only confers a few powers in the form of rights/ obligations.

The powers conferred on a given social kind often vary significantly temporally and geographically. Social kinds are varied but not infinitely varied. It is better to think of social kinds in terms of a space of bounded variation about which one can make useful generalizations, rather than in terms of a centering ideal from which individuals depart.[26] Restated, a social kind should be seen not in terms of its similarity, with individual variations being seen as departures from the norm; rather, the idea of a typical member is itself an abstraction from the variation built into the kind itself. Further, unlike the Weberian notion of "ideal type" whose relationship to the category it exemplifies is generally not part of the theorizing, this theory of social kinds necessitates a description of the constraints on the variation built into the social kind. Accordingly, the next section explains how anchoring processes limit variation.

It could almost go without saying that there are no such things as social laws (at least not as many theorists have imagined them).[27] Generalizations about social kinds will have exceptions. In this we see another parallel to biology, insofar as biological "laws" are best thought of as descriptions of patterns with more or fewer exceptions. Put differently, social kinds are *cluster kinds*, which means that not all members of the kind have the exact same powers. An albino jaguar with no teeth is still a jaguar. But, as Anjun Chakravartty observes, we can still make *ceteris paribus* qualified generalizations about cluster kinds as long as we recognize that "the number of exceptions will vary according to the extent to which members of kinds figuring in the relevant generalizations share the same causally efficacious properties."[28] Our ability to generalize about the color of jaguars will be dependent on the proportion of jaguars with spots. In sum, descriptions of social kinds are typically limited to delineating what would normally be their cluster of powers in the absence of other intervening causal factors.

Second, in the philosophy of biology there has also been some push-back against Boyd's notion of homeostasis as the defining feature of a property-cluster. It has been argued that an emphasis on similarity or "homeostatic" mechanisms misses an important aspect of biological species—namely, that species exhibit not just similarities but stable differences. For example, mandarin ducks (*aix galericulata*) display prominent sexual dimorphism; during the mating season males and females exhibit very different coloration and plumage, to the point that observers often mistake them for members of different species. The biological world is full of stable differences of this sort, from genetically identical plants that take on totally different morphologies when they grow in different climates to the stable "caste system" of termites. At the minimum, then, Boyd's account of natural kinds should be expanded to include not just homeostatic mechanisms, but also "heterostatic" mechanisms that maintain regularized variation.[29]

Social kinds too can maintain both relatively stable similarities and differences. For instance, to be a member of the social kind "South African citizen" in apartheid South Africa included not just certain stable shared legal capacities (e.g., drinking age), but also regularized legal differences between White and Black South Africans. I am interested in the enforcement mechanisms that produce semi-stable forms of both similarity *and* difference. It might be helpful therefore to think of the "cluster" in some social kinds as sometimes synonymous with "conflictual space."

Social kinds tend to have modestly stable (if ultimately dynamic) clusters of powers or common patterns of similarity and difference. But identifying shared clusters alone is insufficient to determine membership in the "same" social kind. Sometimes totally different kinds have identical powers (e.g., being a police officer and being a soldier apparently both confer the legal right to kill under certain circumstances, but this similarity doesn't mean that police officers and soldiers are members of the same kind). For multiple entities to be members of the same kind, or for us to be able to ground robust generalizations (see chapter 6), requires that the kind be anchored by the same causal processes.

By way of reminder, social kinds are necessarily process kinds, which means that statements about them are *only* going to be true within a specific temporal and geographic horizon. In the language of analytical philosophy, social kinds require locational predicates.[30] We can make true statements about social kinds, and we can certainly attribute clusters of powers to them, but these need to be historically and contextual specified.

This is less of a liability than you might think. We often make statements whose truth is dependent on explicit (or implicit) designations of time and place. For instance, to say "the population of Boston is 4,875,390" presumes a particular definition of the metropolitan area and a particular time-sample (July 1, 2018). Likewise, there are no true statements about the powers of a social kind without similar kinds of specifications. Recast, any account of a social kind's cluster of powers is going to necessitate some kind of specification about time and place.

4.2.3 CAUSAL PROCESSES THAT ANCHOR CLUSTERS

Another key insight I get from Boyd is that cluster kinds are determined by the causal "mechanisms that bring about their co-occurrence." In that respect, looking for the causes that produce the co-occurrence of powers (actualized and potential) takes what was most useful about Wittgensteinian family-resemblance theory (its capacity to explain heterogenous classes with loose clusters of attributes) and solves two of its key problems: namely, infinitely expanding similarity and uncertainty about when generalizations are apt. Put differently, in order for a kind not to yield correct generalizations only by accident, there must be a causal reason that explains why it shares powers with others of its kind.[31] A couple of examples will help illustrate. The kind "green-colored minerals" is only a weakly generalizable kind because there is not one causal reason that different minerals are green; and knowing that a given crow is black, but not the causal reason why crows are black in general, limits efforts to generalize from one crow to the population as a whole. This means that describing the powers of specific social kinds is only part of the picture; we must also discover the underlying causes that produce clusters of powers.

As I have argued repeatedly, change and variation are the norm for social kinds. It is persistence, similarity, and stable differences that need to be explained. So the question that should attend research into social kinds is, when is it appropriate to assume that anything discovered about one particular member of a social kind is projectible onto the social kind generally? This turns out to be tantamount to asking what it is that gives social kinds their shared cluster of powers. It is worth emphasizing that both questions are important, even if the generalization at hand still requires temporal and spatial specification. This is less relevant in that smaller number of cases in which one can survey the complete set. But this is especially important if you want to generalize beyond a specific finite sample. If you wanted to expand beyond the subset of nineteenth-century French women about whom you have specific evidence, you would need an account of why French women in that period shared whatever trait you are investigating. Or you might ask, does my reading of Élisa Mercœur's poem apply to other French authors in the period, or was the poem idiosyncratic? If it does apply, why? If not, why not? For research projects, many of us ask ourselves basic questions: How do I start generalizing? Can I generalize further? Are my findings relevant beyond my specific case study? The first step to answering these questions is discovering the causal processes that have produced the power-cluster or specific properties we care about (see below).

The following therefore provides an account of multiple distinctive, causal, anchoring, or stabilization *processes* that give social kinds their shared properties and powers.[32] The reduplication of process language here is fully intended. I want to emphasize that social kinds are processes that require other processes as catalysts. In what follows I discuss three broad, if often interwoven, types of processes: *dynamic-nominalist, mimetic,* and *ergonic.* But I do not mean this list to be exhaustive. There is room for future research on the subject. It is also important to note that any given process might be weak or strong depending on the degree to which it works to produce shared powers.

Before getting into the typology, I want to clarify what I mean by *anchoring.* In a recent work, the philosopher of social science Brian Epstein makes a distinction between "grounding" and "anchoring."[33] His notion of each is fairly complicated, but in brief, *grounding* refers to the conditions that make something a particular kind of social object (e.g., what makes a particular screwdriver a screwdriver, or a particular piece of paper a dollar bill). *Anchoring,* by contrast, refers to whatever sets up the grounding conditions or frame principles for membership in the social kind and bestows on it the properties the social kind possesses. In Epstein's metaphor, anchoring is the "glue" that sticks the properties together. I'm less interested in Epstein's account of grounding, but here I am merging his account of anchoring with what Boyd and his followers in philosophy of biology have described as "homeostatic mechanisms" and then elaborating from these inspirations a typology that should be especially relevant for many kinds of research in the human sciences.

First, *dynamic-nominalist processes.* Ian Hacking describes "interactive kinds" as coming into being via what he calls a "process [of] dynamic nominalism, because it so strongly connects what comes into existence with the historical dynamics of naming and the subsequent use of name [*sic*]."[34] To translate Hacking's insight into the idiom of this chapter, some social kinds share powers because of the way they have been named or classified. Hence, this is a way to be more specific about what I have referred to as classificatory social construction. A lot of the conversation about social construction has assumed that most social kinds come into being via "discourse" or classification. I think this is good as far as it goes, and indeed many social kinds (e.g., citizen) come to share specific properties primarily because of dynamic-nominalist processes.

But I want to emphasize that it is generally not the act of classifying as such that produces similarities. There has been a critique of taxonomies and classifying in general in certain sectors of critical theory. But it tends to overlook the observation that not all classifying is equally pernicious. We classify things all the time. Choosing what to eat for breakfast requires an act of classification. What I want to emphasize here are the mechanisms that enforce or make particular classifications consequential. For the social kind to take hold, there have to be role adoption or enforcement processes to stabilize the cluster of powers.

Hacking thinks that interactive kinds are produced by feedback loops or role adoption in which people can "become aware of how they are classified and modify their behavior accordingly."[35] This is an important insight, and it seems to address some of the properties of a particular subset of human social kinds. As Kwame Anthony Appiah observed about social identities: "Once labels are applied to people, ideas about people who fit the label come to have social and psychological effects. In particular these ideas shape the way people conceive of themselves and their projects."[36] There are a number of social kinds that come to share properties in this way, but the notion that it comes from pure feedback between the classification and the recognition of such suggests a weak anchoring process because it relies on subjects adopting the classification and getting caught in the relevant feedback loop. Role adoption does not explain much if people are capable of rejecting the label or, as is more often the case, redefining what it means. In brief, self-identification requires policing to be stable.

Nevertheless, role adoption does not describe the limit of classificatory processes. Many of the kinds we are most interested in have come to share the powers they do because of specific classificatory enforcement processes (cultural, social, institutional, legal, and so on). Examples are bountiful: legal processes that confer particular capacities on certain groups (e.g., the ability to vote) which have built-in mechanisms to ensure compliance; the boundary policing that goes on in academic disciplines; social norms of shaming or reciprocity that encourage or prevent certain kinds of behaviors; tax codes that provide religious exemptions to organizations that take on certain properties; and so on. As will be explored in greater detail below, I think that many of the disciplinary master categories only share the properties they do because of dynamic-nominalist classificatory processes of this sort.

This attention to anchoring processes also allows us to flesh out how role adoption functions in greater detail than Hacking theorized. A more formal kind of role adoption happens when people agree to take on jobs or become citizens in a nation. In cases like these, the role adoption can have a stronger clustering effect because there are implementation mechanisms (positive financial incentives or disincentives such as being fired or deported) that reinforce the properties associated with the role. Moreover, often social kinds are produced by overwriting existing differences with new meaningful distinctions. For all these reasons, an analysis of dynamic-nominalist categories typically proceeds not by searching for a broad definition of the category in question, but by trying to figure out whose interests are served by the construction of the category and how those interests have resulted in attempts to constrain the category's meaning.

Before we move on to other types of anchoring processes, I want to emphasize that classificatory processes often rest as much on *exclusions* as on *inclusions*. Again, part of the way that "religion" has come to function as a social kind has been through the act of distinguishing it from "superstition" and "science." To this one might add the notion of "conceptual web" theory drawn from cognitive semantics.[37] This theory captures the observation that many concepts are demarcated relationally vis-à-vis neighboring concepts. The meaning of "mutton" does not lie solely in its difference from "sheep," but also (*contra* Saussure) in other relations of perceived similarity—say, with "pork." For this reason, when we are looking at dynamic-nominalist anchoring processes, we need to address both articulations of similarity and difference and, necessarily, attempts to police the boundaries of neighboring concepts, loosely defined.

In *The Invention of Religion in Japan*, I suggested that dynamic-nominalist processes were the only way to produce social kinds.[38] But it turns out that there are other relevant anchoring processes.

Second, *mimetic processes*. By mimetic process I mean the anchoring processes that come from repeated copying under environmental constraint. The inspiration comes from what Ruth Millikan refers to as "historical kinds," by which she means those natural kinds that have shared properties because of historical copying processes often combined with a consistent environment that tends to stabilize or limit variation.[39] Copying alone (whether of genes or "memes") tends gradually to produce increasing variations unless there are mechanisms to reinforce fidelity to the original.[40] We might think of biological heredity, which, combined with mutation, produces a limited range of variation with the characteristics of a given species evolving over time, but constrained by a physical environment that tends to render nonviable certain forms of radical mutation.

Mimetic processes are different from dynamic-nominalist processes because they do not require classification. Pre-cultivation plant species shared features not because of any classification system (except perhaps their own), but because of the processes of genetic inheritance. Similarly, many human bodily habits are acquired imitatively and unconsciously. Wittgenstein's disciples, for instance, were famous for imitating his particular way of putting his hand on his forehead.[41] Many infants learn to clap even before they have acquired their first words. Yawns are contagious. Dance moves are copied. To be sure, most human mimetic processes are also dynamic-nominalist insofar as the kind in question is explicitly named, but it is often the mimesis rather than the classification that determines the crucial properties.

A further implication is that mimetic kinds often share more properties than ahistorical kinds because properties that are only contingently associated may be copied together.[42] For instance, there is no reason that an all-bamboo diet and having bold black and white coloring should have been selected together except that pandas are descended from a common ancestor. In this respect, the features of historical kinds lack "modal necessity" because alternate histories could have resulted in the survival of different species or caused a given species to inherit different properties. For instance, a fortuitous combination of a genetic mutation and climate change happened to pandas about 2.4 million years ago; had it not, pandas likely would have either gone extinct or continued to be omnivores like their closest genetic relatives.[43]

Millikan explicitly argues that many kinds of interest to the human sciences, "such as ethnic, social, economic, and vocational groups," are best understood as sharing traits because of mimetic processes. This is due to the fact that "Members of these groups are likely to act similarly in certain ways and to have attitudes in common as a result of similar training handed down from person to person (reproduction or copying), as a result of custom (more copying), as a result either of natural human dispositions or social pressures to conform to role models (copying again)."[44] But a number of philosophers have seen the human predisposition to imitation or mimesis as fundamental to both individual learning and birth of culture more generally.[45] (One might also think of Pierre Bourdieu's notion of *habitus* or René Girard's insight that it is not just behavior, but desires or goals that are often copied.)[46] In sum, many social kinds share properties because of reduplication processes combined with social pressures toward conformity. Fads and fashion trends are paradigmatic examples.

Again, in the case of social kinds, mimetic processes may overlap with dynamic-nominalist ones. But attention to the former allows us to explain the co-occurrence of properties at an even finer-grained level of detail. For instance, all American McDonald's franchises may share a certain cluster of properties as part of being jointly classified as fast-food restaurants, but they share even more features in common (e.g., golden arches) because they have all been copied from a shared prototype. There is nothing in the name "fast-food restaurant" or codes around restaurants that specifies a particular décor or the co-occurrence of heat lamps and cartoonish mascots. But these can be explained in part by way of reduplication processes protected by copyright and trademark laws and variation intended to copy the associations while not violating those same laws.

There is a subtype of mimetic processes we might want to call "path-dependency" to suggest the relevant literature in economics, sociology, and political science. There are different ways to define path-dependency, one of which describes "self-reinforcing sequences" rooted in the reproduction of preexisting institutional patterns, often augmented by something that amounts to increasing returns.[47] The most famous example of path-dependency in economic theory is that of the QWERTY keyboard. To make a long story short, perhaps the best explanation for the arrangement of the keys on anglophone keyboards is because of self-reinforcing sequences that made it more advantageous to duplicate an earlier standard rather than adopt a new one.[48]

Finally, *ergonic convergence*. Sometimes kinds share properties through a process of selection or design intended to fulfill a certain function.[49] Of the three types of anchoring processes discussed in this section, ergonic convergence has the greatest potential for being misleading (in part as it is too easy to define functions retroactively). But when used judiciously, it has value.

The inspiration for this notion comes from philosophy of biology. Convergent evolution—namely, the independent evolution of analogous biological structures—is a hallmark of evolutionary theory.[50] Perhaps the most famous example is the complex eye. The eyes of cephalopods and vertebrates do not have a common origin, but rather have converged on a function.[51] So even though squid eyes and goat eyes have different origins and material constituents (and are both equally creepy), they share common powers because they were selected for similar functions. Similar examples include bird, bat, and insect wings; carcinization or the repeated tendency of crustaceans to evolve into crab-like forms; and seed dispersal in plants, all of which have different origins but are nonetheless usefully understood as common "kinds" with overlapping clusters of power.[52]

Convergence can also explain shared powers in social kinds. Think of an electric hot water heater.[53] All such heaters contain a thermostat that switches off the current as the water begins to boil. But there are many different ways of assembling physical components to make a thermostat, from using bimetallic strips to mercury bulbs to expanding gases to thermocouples. Each of these utilizes a different physical mechanism to produce the same result, because they were designed to fulfill a common function. Restated, the fact that hot water heater thermostats share the tendency to shut off the current as the water reaches a preset temperature is because they were selected for that function.

Another example is the spear, which seems to have been developed independently not just by different human societies but by chimpanzees as well.[54] While types of spears may have been produced by mimetic processes, the parallel convergence on making pointy sticks is an example not of classificatory or mimetic processes, but rather of ergonic convergence. There is a simple physics equation ($P = F/A$; pressure is determined by force over area) that crudely delineates the core of what makes a good spear, and trial and error will lead toward a convergence on a similar object, given similar material limitations.

One could add that sometimes ergonic convergences emerge because of the ideological, economic, and institutional functions they fulfill. We could talk about them in that respect as teleological kinds. For example, as (especially Marxist) art historians have noted, different art movements converged on similar forms because they were directed toward fulfilling this intersection of needs or "cultural niches."[55] In other words, there may be economic, ideological, or institutional pressures that encourage convergent properties. There is a reason most college application essays follow the same basic formula (and one could say the same thing about much of the fiction produced by MFA programs).

Social kinds with independent origins can converge because they have been constructed to satisfy similar needs or goals (practical, ideological, economic, etcetera). One might think of armies that tend to share the properties they do because they are teleologically structured organizations directed toward the goal of fighting wars.[56] In this respect, ergonic processes exhibit what could be described as Weberian rationalization toward specific ends. But we have to be very careful about providing accounts of convergent functions in these respects.

Accordingly, before we move off the subject, four qualifications are necessary.

First, in biology, convergent evolution is believed to produce analogues, not homologues. In other words, the wings of a butterfly and a bird are similar by analogy, not identity. But social kinds can merge in a way that unrelated biological species cannot. Still, even when ergonic convergence has been demonstrated, it does not mean that one is necessarily talking about an identical kind. For instance, bird wings, bat wings, and insect wings have some aerodynamic similarities, but they are also significantly different: bird and bat wings have bones, insect wings do not; bird wings use feathers, bat wings use flaps of skin, insect wings use modified scales, and so on. This means that ergonic convergence is a limited source of potential generalizations because we don't necessarily know which features are broadly applicable. This is especially true of convergence on economic or ideological niches. That different monarchical societies might converge on similar structures for the legitimation of sovereignty does not mean that these structures are generalizable. They suggest analogy rather than identity.

Second, most social kinds do not fulfill a common function. There is not one single need that motivates all religion or all art. More than a century of scholars searching for one have failed. So we have to be careful to avoid the older pitfalls of heavy-handed functionalist theorizing. There is a long history of functionalism in anthropology, psychology, and sociology. In the hands of some thinkers, sociological functionalism amounted to the claim that an institution or social kind exists because of its benefit to society. Similar arguments have been restaged by evolutionary psychologists who use natural selection to justify the claim that particular social organizations or cultural forms are innate because they contribute to the survival of the species (or did at some imaginary dawn of human origins). Against this mode of theorizing, I share with the neuroscientist Steven Rose the sense that much of evolutionary psychology amounts to little more than a collection of "unprovable just-so stories," formulated after the fact and lacking in any serious evidentiary basis.[57] As contemporary philosopher of biology Alan Garfinkel has observed, "many of these 'human nature' explanations are like explaining the existence of restaurants by saying that people have to eat. We can grant that it is human nature that people have to eat, but, we want to ask, why should that necessitate restaurants?"[58] Although eating serves a common biological function, restaurants are underdetermined by this function.

Third, we need to avoid accounts of ergonic convergence that lack explanatory mechanisms for cluster stabilization. Strikingly, the arguments of evolutionary psychologists are often mirrored by "critical" social theorists who assert that an institution or social kind exists precisely because of its detriment to society (e.g., "Crime exists because society needs a scapegoat").[59] Indeed, critical theory has its own just-so stories in which the function of certain social structures is supposed to be fostering oppression or benefiting neo-liberalism. Accordingly, limited forms of critical theory and evolutionary psychology can devise similar explanatory narratives. For example, if one finds a correlation between population size and increased male violence, the evolutionary psychologist might try to explain it by saying that increased violence is an evolutionary mechanism for keeping population in check, or a critical theorist might explain the same violence by saying that it is because the ruling class encourages worker violence as a means of suppression. These models share a naive sociological error: namely, explaining actions by their consequences instead of their causes.[60] In brief, the problem with these sorts of explanations is that they do not provide a causal mechanism that could affect individual or collective decision-making.[61] Male violence would only be *caused* by the need to limit population size if it turned out men were motivated (albeit unconsciously) to kill out of concerns about overpopulation (which seems generally far-fetched). [62]

Finally, functional convergence typically only explains a subset of the powers of a given kind. For instance, the primary function of a heart is to pump blood. We know that this is its primary function, because this is what the heart has been selected for evolutionarily. But the heart has both functional and nonfunctional powers (e.g., making a beating sound is nonfunctional). Thus, we should expect ergonically converged hearts to tend to share the functional powers and not the nonfunctional ones. As one might expect, while vertebrate hearts all share a common ancestor, earthworms have specific muscular areas that function like hearts insofar as they contract to pump blood, but to my knowledge these "hearts" don't make a beating sound. In sum, we have to be very careful at determining which powers are being functionally selected for.

All told, when identifying ergonic convergence, it is important to identify not just the need, but also the niche or environment that constrains response to the need, as well as the causal mechanism or process that can explain individual or collective decision-making. That said, ergonic convergence is particularly important for an analysis of artifacts. Many (but not all) artifacts are understood primarily based on their common function (e.g., what makes a calculator is that it calculates, what makes a hammer is that it can be used to hammer). Moreover, non-artifactual social kinds often had original functional purposes which they have lost, and one can do significant work by clarifying, unmasking, or, in a different mode, restoring the functional registers of specific kinds.[63]

•

To recap, I see three broad types of anchoring processes: *dynamic-nominalist processes, mimetic processes*, and *ergonic convergence*. This list might be extended. For instance, a fourth possible anchoring process might be *etiological processes* (causal history), to the degree that there are kinds which gain their membership from point of origin or recognizable descent. (Think of champagne: a wine only officially, though not vernacularly, counts as a champagne if it is grown in the Champagne region.) But etiology tends to be quite weak as far as anchoring properties are concerned. Despite many scholars' preoccupation with them, origins generally do not tell us very much on their own. The beginnings of a social kind are not usually enough to explain why particular properties have been passed down or stabilized. So I'm hesitant to treat etiology as a significant source of anchoring.

A given kind can also be anchored by different processes over time. Likewise, anchoring processes sometimes conflict.[64] But they function as anchoring processes because they work to produce the social kind and to glue the powers of the social kind in some form of at least provisionally stable homeo- or heterostasis. In a nutshell, anchoring processes describe how social construction happens.

The interactivity or looping quality of social kinds need not preclude knowledge of them. Social kinds can be transformed by being analyzed, but, as noted in chapter 3, if we can gain knowledge of them at a faster rate than they are transformed, then studying them is still useful. That said, there is a lot work that needs to be done on how scholarly inquiry functions to stabilize or undermine its objects of study. Academic disciplines in the human sciences can produce feedback that results in greater coherence in the area that they then study, and in that respect we have to account for the ways that scholarship itself functions as an anchoring process.

For this reason, I have been calling for a "reflexive human sciences" for some time.[65] It is important to study how academic disciplines shape the very fields they focus on. For instance, we need to study how sociology as a discipline changes society (e.g., sociological surveys affect their subjects' manufacturing of new kinds of social identities); how anthropological theory changes the people they study (e.g., creating new tribes and authenticating some forms of indigenous culture over others); how literary theory needs to work to interpret the vast volume of novels and poems that have been written with literary theory in mind. In Religious Studies I have been working on how the academic study of religion—in a range of disciplinary formations—tends to transform the "religions" that it studies.[66] There is a place for a higher order reflexive philosophy of the human sciences that reckons with the observation that the human sciences are in a sense porous and tend to transmute the areas that they purport to study. All that is to say, increasing awareness of how our scholarship alters its objects, far from precluding research, allows us to be better scholars.

It is also worth noting that we can now say something more specific about how and when social construction fails. Social kinds frequently melt away or significantly change their powers over time because of weak

anchoring mechanisms or changes in the anchoring mechanisms themselves. For instance, Joshua Abraham Norton, despite declaring himself
"Emperor Norton of the United States," failed in his attempt to possesses
the powers associated with sovereignty because he lacked constitutive anchoring processes to confer those powers on himself. Many social kinds
change their creators. You can invent a gun and die by its bullets or do-
mesticate grains and end up changing the structure of your descendants'
mouths.

There is one last hunch I want to mention before moving on. Many
kinds, including most of the disciplinary master categories, might be
best thought of as "historical individuals." To explain, the philosopher of
biology Michael Ghiselin made the unusual argument that species are
"individuals." From this he concludes that: "1) [species] names are proper,
2) there cannot be instances of them," and "their constituent organisms
are parts, not members."[67] Individual organisms are not members of a
general kind, but parts of a larger whole. Species get their identity from
their historical instantiation and they are born and die, as do the individual organisms that make them up. Once all the existing tigers are gone,
there will no longer exist any remaining species "tiger." While I am not
persuaded that this works as a theory of species, I have the suspicion that
some social kinds are historical individuals in this way. Would "religion"
exist if all references to the term "religion," as well as all the existing religions, were eliminated? Could "religion" be revived with zero knowledge
of the original concept? This is doubtless true of the specific "religions"
(e.g., Confucianism qua Confucianism could not be rediscovered without
reference to a particular historical trajectory). That said, I suspect that
the point cannot be generalized. Not all social kinds are historical individuals. This is definitely not true of functional kinds. Spears can be discovered without ever knowing of the existence of previous spears. So perhaps whether a kind is a historical individual likely depends on specifics
of the kind as well as the anchoring processes that produced it. All that is
to say, I frame this insight as tentative because more work is needed on
the subject.

•

To recap the broader argument: *social kinds* are the kinds of entities our
terms, concepts, and theories refer to (e.g., a national economy is not
identical to any given individual's concept of that economy). But we must
also consider the added complexity that because social kinds are typically
the product of interactive feedback loops, some social kinds are indeed
transformed, differentiated, or even brought into being either intention-

ally or unintentionally by concepts of them (e.g., preexisting systems for exchanging goods and services in Madagascar were changed in measurable ways by the introduction and imposition of a notion of the Malagasy "economy"). Furthermore, what makes an entity a member of a kind is both 1) clusters of powers, or what the entity can do, and 2) the causal processes that caused the entity to have that cluster of powers in the first place. Likewise, most entities are members of multiple cross-cutting social kinds. While many of these kinds emerge from dynamic-nominalist processes that specifically designate the kind in question (in other words, they are glued together discursively alongside structures of power that reinforce the classification), other kinds do not primarily gain their properties due to classification or naming. Some social kinds emerge secondarily from causal processes without being stated or even intentionally formulated as kinds. For instance, recessions came into being (and their particular cluster of powers mainly persist) as a side effect of having capitalist markets, not from being named as "recessions."

4.3 Deconstructing and Reconstructing Social Kinds

People frequently refer to social kinds. Our daily conversations are sprinkled with discussions of bat mitzvahs, migrant workers, Starbucks, and so on. We seem to do so competently enough that, at least on the surface, we have shared topics of discussion even if we do not share concepts or definitions (and indeed, most people when pressed cannot provide definitions for most of their vocabulary).

We can get by without really sharing concepts in part because the world is doing some of the work for us. This is as true of "social" as it is of "natural" worlds. Although reference is not the whole of meaning, as noted earlier, I do not need to know the properties of copper or migrant worker to refer to either, because both kinds exceed their reference. This is probably uncontroversial in regard to copper, but the term "migrant worker" is also an attempt to capture a kind—that is to say, a power-cluster—that encapsulates more than just the term. Many social kinds exhibit the added complications of being interactive kinds, which means that our collective (as opposed to individual) conceptions of "migrant worker" gradually affect the properties of the kind in question. But as I have been arguing, social kinds do not come into being solely through the act of being named. I can come up with a new term, but that in itself will not work to anchor a stable social category, at least not without a lot more effort from other people. So we don't have to worry about the subjectivity of my concept of "migrant worker" as long as I am discovering the kind's properties by way of something empirical rather than merely intuiting what the term means.

This has a significant implication: people—scholars and non-academics alike—have varying degrees of knowledge about specific social kinds and their properties. Moreover, people in general typically tend to have mistaken assumptions about process kinds (and necessarily also about anchoring processes). There exists a body of psychological research suggesting that most people tend to treat some, but not all, social kinds as tantamount to natural kinds.[68] People tend to treat categories like "religion" or "race" as universals that express fundamental essences and involve rigid category membership, whereas they tend to treat other kinds, especially artifacts (e.g., "chairs"), as though membership in the category were subjective, vague, and a matter of context. Likewise, many of the essentialized social kinds are highly entropic categories with diverse instantiations and quite different properties depending on time period, culture, and so on. Yet people often mistake the features of local social environment for features of the collective (e.g., all of our friends vote for a specific presidential candidate, and thus we assume mistakenly that everyone is voting for her).

Taken together this suggests that there are two different general kinds of work—deconstructing and reconstructing—that need to be done in regard to specific social kinds. Indeed, an ideal project might begin by deconstructing common views of its object and then work on reconstructing the formal properties of the object in question. The following pages explore these two modes and the implications of my account of process social kinds for scholarship and ordinary life.

•

The methodology that will be most familiar to scholars in the human sciences is the deconstructing or de-reifying mode. Sally Haslanger has rightly observed that "social construction" is primarily used in "debunking projects," which attempt to denaturalize specific entities or suggest that something that seems only thinly social has a thick script associated with it.[69] As noted repeatedly, one of the most common critiques of the disciplinary categories is that the category in question has been reified or treated with misplaced concreteness. As Marx and Engels put it, each new class gives "its ideas the form of universality, and represent them as the only rational, universally valid ones."[70] Sometimes we need to point out that this is not the case for a specific category. Indeed, one of the biggest obstacles to cross-cultural research is overgeneralizing based on one's own cultural categories (I will return to this below). All that is to say that even in its typical form this kind of deconstructive work is valuable.

But to make it better we need to tweak it in five core respects.

First, debunking strategies are often presented as unique to a specific kind and typically as a way of suggesting that the kind in question is in some sense "unreal." Scholars often want to say "there is no such thing as X" or that "X is socially constructed" and therefore nonexistent. The argument in question is typically established by way of exploring ruptures or discontinuities, exposing structures of power, or demonstrating temporal or regional variation. But as I argued in chapter 1, "real" is a contrastive term that necessitates a contrast class. Mind-dependence does not mean that a kind in question does not exist, nor does it mean that it is unreal (except in a specific contrast). Moreover, social kinds tend to be highly variable. Change is the norm not the exception. We also now know that anchoring processes (a.k.a. systems of power) are necessary for determining the properties of all social kind terms. If we recognize that all social kinds can be debunked and that their heterogeneity renders them no less "real," then it undercuts the deconstructive force of much skeptically tinged scholarship. We have to stop acting so surprised when we find out that a social kind is socially constructed. To be socially constructed is to be relational and processual, not nonexistent. So the affective tone of much critical scholarship needs to be reconsidered. Moreover, against many typical scholarly genealogies, a social kind's history is only relevant to the current case if its effects on the kind's power-cluster or anchoring processes can be demonstrated. Kinds do not automatically inherit essences from their origins (e.g., even if the American Modern Art movement was initially funded by the CIA, it would not mean that modern art is necessarily imperialist). We need to avoid the genetic fallacy.

Second, another implication of the model of social kinds I have been proposing is that there is no "essential" purity to social kinds, and that any claim that there is has merely masked the kind's origins. Hybridity is more than the typical—it is closer to the rule. This means that the opposition between a given category and its putative opposite can be collapsed. The social world is disjointed, so the category boundaries are necessarily permeable. This licenses creolization or the production of explicit hybrids. We have been producing cross-fertilized categories without realizing it, but have been unnecessarily compelled to justify them. For instance, rejecting the presumed dualism between "religion" and "politics" opens the door to political theology. This works because any given thinker or movement is rarely exclusively religious or exclusively political. We don't have to choose, for instance, if a work is philosophy or religion or politics, and any of those choices would be an imposition. De-reifying social kinds should open the way to even more crossings, to our ultimate benefit.

Third, genealogy typically confines itself to the tracing of language or discursive power. This is why genealogy tends to reproduce canon. But

because we now know that social kinds are not reducible to the terms
for them, we can be more sophisticated. We can begin our research into
a given social kind by exploding it in order to try to see what it has been
hiding. We can go beyond the canon to let voices speak that have otherwise been silenced or ignored. Further, as Theodor Adorno argued, there
is a chance, particularly if we proceed dialectically—that is to say self-
consciously and self-critically—to use concepts to get beyond concepts,
or in another idiom, to use language to outwit language. The end result
of this process for Adorno will be that concepts will lose their seeming
transparency and will no longer be confused with the things they represent. [71] This is an insight we need to extend to social kinds. Ordinary ways
of speaking about the social world and its categories are typically in error.
Hence, we can commence our investigations by incorporating the negation, or we can internalize the critique. This means that we cannot assume
the transparency of the central terms of our analysis, but we should not
mistake the terms for the things-in-themselves. (We do not have to suspend all terms at once, but only one set at a time.)

Approached differently, if words are like a net used to trap fish, this
means not forgetting the net (because if we do so the fish will slip away)
or worse, mistaking it for the fish, but instead looking under the net. Let
me borrow an example from mathematics. In mathematics it is not uncommon to introduce a category by asserting a collection of equivalence
classes. This produces a new system. For example, if you assert the equivalence of 12 and 0 you get a clock. 17 now corresponds to 5, etcetera. If you
reverse it and unbind equivalences of the clock, you suddenly get the inte-
gers back. 17 is now autonomous, no longer equal to 5 and closer instead
to 16. Designating something as a member of a particular social kind produces equivalence classes. So reversing the process should result in an ex-
plosion of variety. Rather than merely terminating in complexity or a rejection of abstraction, it should allow us to specify the world of differences
that the previously presumed unity had attempted to subsume, or had at
the very least partially masked.

Fourth, this account of social kinds should also suggest rebinding or
category shifting. A focused analysis of "Star Trek fandom as a religion"
could be a worthwhile project. But it would have to do more than just note
properties shared by Trekkers and say Southern Baptists; rather, it would
have to be able to identify the *same set of underlying anchoring processes*
that serve to produce those shared power-clusters. It would have to tell us
why they are similar rather than simply presuming they share membership in the category "religion" based on their shared properties. We probably do not have a word for the social kind that includes both the shared
powers between Trekkers and Southern Baptists and the causal processes

that anchor those shared powers, but from a certain scale of analysis, a kind like that could exist and explaining the causal mechanisms that produce it would do valuable work.

Finally, and most importantly, I need to emphasize that deconstructive methods also require a full knowledge of how the social kind in question has been put together. Sometimes learning how a social kind has been socially constructed makes it look harder to change rather than easier. This can be daunting, but justice projects are not furthered by self-deception. To undermine anti-blackness in America requires a full knowledge of the various anchoring processes (enforcement mechanisms, role filling, economic needs) that are working to produce "race" as a social kind in our contemporary world.

To recap: from now on, every social kind term should be read as if in quotes (including of course, my use of "social" in social kind). Scholars should not just adopt their metalanguage terms from their culture's object language and expect the terms to function without remainder. There are times when it is necessary to deploy the de-reifying jujitsu discussed in chapter 2. Sometimes we need to demolish the social kinds we believe are imprisoning us. Even to understand social kinds, we often need to begin with their detonation—pushing them to their limits, bringing unstable antinomies to the surface, and then forcing our conception of the social kind to explode in a flash of new possibilities that reveals what it had previously hidden. We are left with what remains.

•

But demolition is not the only kind of work we might want to do. There is necessarily a need to reconstruct social kinds. Reconstructing social kinds could be empirical, as there is plenty of work to be done discovering the power-clusters of specific social kinds. The theory of social kinds provided in this chapter directs our attention to social kinds in new ways. We need more work that recasts research about kinds into property-clusters, figuring out what process are anchoring those clusters, and so on.

But reconstructing social kinds could also be normative (e.g., arguing that we *should* use the term "philosophy" to cover the oral traditions of Ghanaian Akan sages).[72] Progress in both scientific and humanistic disciplines has been by way of "conceptual engineering" or changing the usage of terms.[73] Although in practice these arguments often say they are clarifying what a given term "really" means, I think (for reasons I will articulate in greater detail in chapter 7) that normative arguments are clearer when explicated as such. Linguistic advocacy is only going to work insofar as we are capable of putting into place specific anchoring mechanisms that produce the new properties we want in question (e.g., institutional resources) that produce the new properties we want in question.

But the next couple of pages elaborate another implication of the theory I have been articulating here: namely, that it suggests a new approach to comparison.

•

I believe this theory of social kinds solves the problem of comparison that has bedeviled Religious Studies and many other human sciences. Following Aristotle, many philosophers have argued that observed similarities alone do not provide an explanation—in essence, to observe "that something is so" does not tell us "why it is so"—and lacking this "why," we are limited in the kind of generalizations or knowledge we can produce about a subject.[74] A project that amounts to the statement that all "red" things are "red" has not contributed much knowledge. Similarity without an underlying cause is not much more than an analogy.

In rejecting comparison, scholars often argued that the problem was that "the issue of difference has been all but forgotten."[75] This critique of comparison—when assimilated to Edward Said's otherwise valuable condemnation of Orientalism—has at times been amplified into the claim that Asia (or, more often, the Middle East) is so radically different that one cannot describe it in terms or concepts drawn from European languages. But despite purporting to be anti-orientalism, this line of argumentation is basically just a neo-orientalist portrayal of an inherently incomprehensible and "mysterious Orient" that Said would have condemned. So, to the partisans of difference, I could add the observation that difference is no more meaningful than similarity. Everything is also different from everything else in some respect. For instance, I am a different person than I was this morning insofar as I trimmed my hair and, having heard BewhY's "가라사대," I have now changed my attitude toward his music. So there is no particular reason to fetishize either similarity or difference.

Comparisons can be illuminating when they render the familiar strange or the unfamiliar comprehensible, but most comparative scholarship tells us little about the intermediate category of comparison itself. For instance, similarities between Shintō and Haudenosaunee rituals do not mean that they are both examples of the same type of religion (putatively "animism"), nor would comparing their beliefs or practices explain the meaning of "animism." Comparison can provide information about either of the subjects to be compared, but not the category often supposed to be the axis of comparison. Moreover, as I observed in chapter 2, similarity itself is trivial and task dependent. So the utility of such comparison on its own would be limited.

But now we know that tracing similarity of power-clusters that share the same anchoring process can tell you when generalizations are apt. The better we understand the causal processes that glue the properties together, the better we will be able to predict where these properties will hold and where there will be exceptions. Thus, while apparent similarity or difference might be a good starting place for research, to rise to the level of explanation requires that we specify first that the causal, anchoring processes that have produced the kinds are shared; from that basis we can go on to analyze their similarity. This is what I have been trying to do for social kinds.

Having observed that social kinds are best understood as interwoven complex processes with ambiguous edges and significant variance both temporally and spatially, we might think of them in mathematical terms as high-entropy objects or objects with a high degree of complexity. Social kinds could also be described as possessing high Hausdorff dimensionality, like fractals.[76] Indeed, most objects in complex systems are high-dimensional because they are impacted by multiple systems. Accordingly, one could just argue, as F.A. Hayek did, that an overly simple attempt to describe a complex phenomenon is almost necessarily false.[77] How does one study immensely complex things?

If contemporary work in complexity theory is correct, then the answer is by identifying locally coherent structures within that system, making approximately true statements on different scales, or identifying the relevant impacting system. To explain this last point: even if the object of study is being impacted by multiple systems, for any specific purpose they might effectively be only part of one system. For instance, a word such as "tire" could be part of a number of different meaning systems (it could refer to feeling fatigue, a loss of interest, a specific part of a car, and so on). But in ordinary conversation we constrain its meaning through context to a small number of possible meanings or relevant systems. We can do the same in our theories. A consistent problem is the assumption that all of our theories need to describe universal patterns; but that means the exception always disproves them. Instead we need to be thinking in terms of productive generalizations. As Karl Mannheim observed, our vantage on the social is local and necessarily partial, but recognizing that finitude and attempting to go beyond it can at least partly allow us to ameliorate our limitations.[78]

Despite some debates in the secondary literature, pragmatism is required at two levels: that of the property-cluster and that of the anchoring mechanism. Many of Boyd's followers have been tempted to argue that identifying the homeostatic mechanism alone should allow one to pinpoint the boundaries of a given kind.[79] But the problem is that different levels of abstraction produce different notions of what counts as a *single* causal mechanism.[80] For example, at one degree of resolution, the center in the brain known as the hippocampus is composed of multiple distinct causal mechanisms such as excitatory and inhibitory neurons, glial cells, and support cells. But looked at from a more abstract vantage, the hippocampus itself is a single causal mechanism involved in the encoding of memory. Yet, as I have repeatedly remarked, the social world is disjointed. Not only do social kinds cross-cut each other, but our vantages on complex social kinds also often cross-cut each other (e.g., the same organization could be analyzed economically, architecturally, symbolically, and so on—with each type of analysis only capturing the vantage of a single complex entity). This means that for those of us working in the human sciences, whether a particular set of entities count as members of "the same" social kind or represent merely related kinds is often going to be a matter of pragmatic stipulation for the purposes of a particular generalization, rather than a simple fact of the matter.

Since there is no essential way to classify a given phenomenon (e.g., as religious or political), different classification schemes will make sense for different projects. But not every classification will turn out to be useful. Not all proposed social kinds describe actual clusters of powers. Our vernacular, and even scholarly, vocabulary about the social world is littered with terms which lack definitive references or which transmit mistaken assumptions. Even terminology with practical utility often misses what gives a particular social kind its properties and therefore fails to explicate when generalizations about it are likely to hold. To repeat an earlier observation, a kind is ultimately worthless if it produces inductive generalizations only by accident. Even our best terminology rarely depicts in full detail the properties or anchoring processes of a particular kind, but to the extent that our terms pick out actual property-clusters/anchoring processes we can work together to refine our theoretical formulations or accommodate our linguistic practices to better describe the kind in question. So even to be identifiable as worthy of accommodation, a kind has to at least incompletely track both shared power-clusters and shared anchoring processes.

This suggests two different kinds of pragmatic strategies toward social kinds, which we might call *aggregating* and *disaggregating*. To aggregate is to look at what examples share across a larger scale, although to do so necessarily ignores some differences; to disaggregate is to increase the resolution and look at a finer-grained scale that has less explanatory utility. Both are useful. To avoid miscommunication, both require that time and place specifications be explicit. The value of both strategies will rest on their ability to describe actual causal processes and power-clusters.

Questions of scale will necessitate pragmatic decisions about whether to consider a particular case to be one or more social kinds, but this does not mean that anything goes or that social kinds are defined by theorists primarily on an *ad hoc* basis. Rather, the necessity of aggregating or disaggregating a social kind (as well as its power-clusters and anchoring processes) will tend to be relative to a specific explanatory project, so making a mistake about scale will negatively impact research findings.

To harken back to what I said earlier in this chapter, social kinds are not identical to the terms for them. Sometimes the same social kind can be referred to by different words. We can see this, for example, in the succession of expressions for "place to urinate or defecate," which in American English went from *water closet* to *latrine* to *toilet* to *bathroom*, as new expressions were coined to replace older ones that had become offensive but then became offensive themselves.[81] Most social scientists are not trying to avoid talking about pissing, but our vocabulary exhibits similar redundancies, especially as different disciplines describe what amounts to the same social kind with divergent specialized terms. Whether given expressions are references to the same or similar social kinds is typically going to be task dependent based on the aggregating or disaggregating discussed above (e.g., the change from *latrine* to *bathroom* also roughly coincided with architectural differences that may or may not be relevant to a particular theory, and thus may or may not count as different social kinds).

Even more pernicious than references to the same kind by different expressions is when one term is used to refer to multiple social kinds (e.g., "Viking" as a cultural grouping or a raiding practice). A similar problem is when identical terminology masks divergent notions of the precise property-clusters and anchoring processes of a particular social kind. A disagreement about whether political science is a "science" may rest on unwitting disjunction between two different accounts of what makes something a science.

Verbal disputes about social kinds are ubiquitous because people often do not realize that they have very different notions of shared vocabulary. In chapter 5, I discuss meaning itself in more detail, but I observe that even native speakers of the same language often use terms in overlapping but not identical ways. Moreover, people are often wrong about how social kinds actually function. For these reasons the common practice in much of the human sciences of reducing a subject to what a particular set of interlocutors say about it (e.g., "religion" is whatever people say is religion) is likely to lead to problems.

Alternatively, the theory of social kinds I have been providing here suggests three *prima facie* responses to disputes of this sort. First, we can specify and then ascertain empirically which power-clusters and anchoring processes are determinate for a particular social kind in the relevant context. For instance, a disagreement about whether Islamic occult science is science might actually turn on the properties of being a "science" in context and what caused those properties to co-occur.[82] In a related mode, we can explore the gap between the manifest concept (i.e., the overlap in what people say the term means) and the operative properties of the social kind (i.e., how the kind or kinds referred to by the term actually function in practice).

Second, as David Chalmers has suggested, the disputants might suspend use of the disputed term and each try to make their argument without using it.[83] In so doing, they might discover that their disagreement is not about the properties of a particular social kind, but rests on something else. For instance, disputants might exclude the word "science" and discover that the core of the argument is an empirical question about Islamicate technological discoveries compared to Europe.

Finally, we might try an updated version of what Chalmers has called the "subscript gambit"—namely, to introduce multiple new terms distinguished with subscript (replace X with X_1 and X_2) to differentiate social kinds covered by the same term. For instance, one might say the social kind I am trying to capture—call it Science$_1$ (specified by a place and time period, a power-cluster, and anchoring mechanisms)—is not what is being discussed by the disputants above; that might be better called Science$_2$, which refers to a different set of properties and anchoring mechanisms. This method can resolve disputes by clarifying when disputants are actually talking about different things—but with the caveat that not all subscript or disaggregated terms are going to be equally valid and disaggregating may merely shift the issue onto more kinds that need to be explicated. Many descriptions of social kinds do not accurately reflect the kind in question (we can be wrong about the properties we ascribe to the referent of a term).

•

If the concept of social kinds I put forward in this chapter is taken seriously, it suggests a whole new domain of research in the human sciences. In addition to shifting our orientation toward de-reifying projects, a new paradigmatic kind of reconstructive project would be to take a particular sample, describe its cluster of powers, discover which anchoring processes determine the cluster it possesses, and then figure out whether those anchoring processes exist elsewhere.

One implication of this account of social kinds is that it gets us around one of the problems of research in the human sciences. Older modes of scholarship often proceeded with a universalized definition or regulative concept, which they then used as a lens to interpret their data. The model was either conceptual analysis or stipulated definition. But we know now, that it won't work to just specify a new definition without debunking the term first, because the average reader is going to bring their own particular sense of the kind's reference and properties to bear on the term. Besides, many people will continue to use the word without awareness of the new definition, increasing the possibility of two sides talking past each other without even realizing where they disagree. Indeed, one could evoke the Derridean suspicion that scholars stipulate a new definition of a commonly used term precisely because they want to encourage slippage. But even more importantly, as the account of reference above implies, most stipulated definitions won't work for social kinds because the definition in question is only as good as its capacity to capture the actual cluster of powers associated with the kind referenced. For this reason, unless they begin empirically with an investigation of power-clusters, most stipulated definitions are doomed to failure. Many projects have run aground because, lacking an introspective sense of the fragility of their own concepts, they tended to overstate their universality or they went looking for the wrong things in the first place.

As noted above, a common response to these failures has been for scholars to conduct their work primarily by restating the language of their sources. If a person says they are a "sovereign citizen," what ground does the scholar have to challenge their statement? This might seem to make intuitive sense. Repeating the words of one's sources might seem to avoid the issue of messy definitions. The problem is that there are many reasons why scholars might want to disagree with their sources. Verbal disputes are ubiquitous and our concepts often diverge without our realizing it. Granting the definitions of interlocutors also tend to lead toward majoritarian assumptions that I think many researchers would reject. If you merely relied on the words of your sources, many people would tell you that dolphins are fish and tomatoes are vegetables. Similarly, people are often mistaken in their accounts of gender, race, religion, and a whole host of other social kinds.[84] There are often significant disconnects between manifest concepts (common shared, or overlapping, meanings of terms) and the operative social kinds in practice. While not ignoring what people say about their social worlds, it is therefore the scholar's duty to do more than just reiterate what has been said; we must investigate the foundations that underlie the existence of the social kinds being discussed if we want our scholarship to have a meaningful impact.

Put another way, the view outlined in this chapter suggests that social kinds are not just identical to people's concepts of them—although, again, concepts often play a causal role in kinds' formation. For example, many white US Americans don't know all or many of the properties associated with being Jewish in our current historical moment; hence there is room to enumerate those. This is rendered extra difficult in regard to social kinds because the social world and the kinds that make it up are constantly changing (even many American Jews, myself included, don't know what all the properties associated with being Jews were at different periods or places). Social kinds also typically have properties that emerge in relationship to other social kinds, so a sense of the complex relational ecology is necessary to trace all the relevant properties of a given kind. Also, social kinds tend to vary more by context (time/place) than most people assume. All this means that scholars frequently need to differentiate a term's common usage from the actual social kind (and necessarily power-cluster and anchoring processes) to which the term refers.

The closest cousin to analysis of this sort would be a Foucauldian genealogy. But as noted, genealogy gains most of its force by showing discontinuity, rupture, variation, and change. Yet, as I have argued, variation and change are the norm in the social world. Social kinds are process kinds. So we must presume discontinuity and difference. The oddity is any similarity or stability at all. For metamodern process kind analysis to take place, the thing that needs to be explained is not discontinuity, rupture, or change, but why any properties should stabilize at all. Thus, it is the mirror image of a Foucauldian genealogy.

4.4 Conclusion: Changing the Social World

I have been arguing that the social world is not reducible to people or invisible social forces. It exists rather in terms of materialized social kinds. Social kinds are made up of power-clusters and the processes that anchor them. Powers belong to a system of relations, not a specific entity on its own. Focusing on similarities and ignoring the causal processes that have produced those similarities has historically undermined scholarly generalizations and theorizing of all sorts.

Many social scientists have also postulated an unhelpful opposition between agent and structure. But now we know that social kinds are produced in feedback loops with sentient beings producing and being produced by them in turn. Instead of presuming a tension between agency and structure, we should think of strength and weakness of anchoring as a continuum in which an individual has less or more capacity to alter (consciously or unconsciously) a specific social kind and its properties.

Many scholars also continue regularly to argue from the presumption that the social is not "real"—for instance, that hysteria was somehow not real even to those who experienced it. In response, other scholars often want to say everything people experience is "real" to them without explaining what that means. We can be more sophisticated in our account of what it means to be real (see also chapter 1). We can say what a social kind is *real* in relation to and now we know that the usefulness of a given social kind term depends on the purpose to which it is put and its capacity to capture relevant power-clusters. This is true of both ordinary language and scholarly research.

For all the reasons I've been discussing, social kinds do not have necessary and sufficient condition definitions. But neither are they merely the *ad hoc* invention of a particular theorist. To give an account of a social kind would be to elucidate the cluster of powers to which the term refers and then examine the anchoring processes that produce those clusters. In some cases, the terms under which something is classified are likely to have a role in stabilizing its properties (e.g., being hired as a "professor"), but in other cases the terms are going to be largely irrelevant as the kind in question either emerged functionally or describes a cluster of powers produced secondarily by the formation of other kinds (e.g., traffic jams are not dependent on being named as such, but emerge necessarily alongside the history of the automobile). Some social kinds cannot exist without the culture in question having a term for them, while other social kinds require a version of the term to be in place. Part of the duty of scholars is to learn to differentiate between these.

For a social kind to be useful it will have to identify an actual causal process that produces actual property-clusters. A complication is that the social world is fundamentally disjointed. It is woven from overlapping processes that are difficult to disaggregate. Social kinds are heavily crisscrossed, are typically nested, and have vague edges. A given ordinary language term may extend to multiple, competing social kinds. Taken together, I think this suggests a limited conventionalism (or, one might say, pragmatism) in how our kind categories are stipulated.

A given process or social kind will appear to be the *same kind* or a *different kind* depending on the level of analysis and the purpose of its deployment. Hence, we have absorbed deconstructive criticisms, since we can both fully grant the critiques of the classical master categories and repudiate notions of their essential natures, all while still doing our work. Except for the anchoring processes discussed above, there is nothing that keeps the powers or properties of a given social kind stable. There is no essential or cross-temporal meaning to categories like "religion" or "art." Nor is it sufficient to just track the uses of the term "art" as we look at different sorts of power-clusters. No definition of a disciplinary master category is possible. There is no definition of religion.

But in detonating the classical notions of concepts, we have gained an insight into what it means to have disjointed and cross-cuttable concepts. Understood in this way, social kinds can function generatively in a host of scholarly projects.

•

Another important implication of the theory of social kinds presented here is that it necessitates a heightened reflexivity in regard to our scholarly categories. As noted previously, people consistently mistakenly assume that their particular local categories or social kinds are freely universalizable. Ordinary thought and language typically presume the transparency of our concepts (we think "Hendrix's 'All Along the Watchtower' is a damn fine rock song," but we don't spend very much time reflecting on what rock music's properties are, or how rock may have changed over time, or what we mean by "song," etcetera). But the research presented in this chapter (and chapters 2 and 5) suggests that terms historically change their meanings and that social kinds vary geographically and alter their properties in ways that might not be immediately available to us. Even kindhood is contextually dependent. We can afford ambiguities and loose talk in much of day-to-day life, but we must hold the primary categories of scholarly analysis differently. We do not generally apprehend a social kind as a totality but rather from a particular vantage. Scholarly methods, although not typically described as such, are basically ways of trying to compensate for the partiality of our viewpoints. But the theory I've been outlining here pushes us to do more. We should suspend the object laid open or disaggregated while simultaneously rejecting the fallacies of both essentialism and brute anti-abstraction.

To put this differently, all too often scholarship proceeds without recognizing the contingency of local conceptual categories. For instance, Anglophone scholarship about "science" in Japan often misses the mark because the scholar is not sufficiently versed in the British history of science and therefore aims to explain Japan in ways that are subtly anachronistic; likewise, some American scholarship on American "religion" has little sense of the actual diversity of ways "religion" functions as a social kind in other cultures and periods and therefore imagines exceptionalism where there isn't any. Errors of similarity and difference can go both ways. Scholars consistently assume other cultures are either more similar to or more different from their own than is actually the case. Comparison is a nearly unavoidable byproduct of translation (e.g., to translate *imani* as *faith* already implies a comparison). In different circumstances, insider accounts that aim to avoid comparison tend to produce their own blind spots or anachronisms (e.g., presuming Johannes Gutenberg invented the movable-type printing press out of ignorance of the pioneering work of CHOE Yun-ui 최윤의). These issues would be partially alleviated if scholars would recognize their categories as historically and culturally conditioned social kinds. Two of the concrete implications of this are that 1) scholars who work on other cultures or periods need to apprehend the contingencies of their own local social kinds; and 2) that scholars who work only on their own culture and period need to know at least some other different historical and cultural contexts.

•

To illustrate what a social kind theory allows us to see, I would like to gesture at a couple of social kinds.

To treat "hammers" as a social kind is to recognize that as an artifact kind, people are unlikely to find the "social construction of hammers" to be a useful de-reifying insight. That said, it can be clarifying to see how they are constructed as a kind. The main functional power of a hammer is its capacity to deliver an impact to a small area, usually that of another smaller object. This means that it is constrained by basic physics, including the hardness of available materials and the functional need to direct force effectively. Hammers in general are an ergonic kind, and it should not be surprising that we have recovered evidence of convergence on the production of hammers by proto–*Homo sapiens* at least 3.3. million years ago. Already in the middle Paleolithic period different people hit on the construction of hammers in terms of a weighted head attached to a handle.[85] Additionally, the notion of social construction in social kind theory lets us distinguish between a rock found on a beach and a hammer insofar as to be a social kind requires that a sentient being has a causal role in giving it powers. So one might use a rock to hammer, but a rock becomes a hammer only when it has been changed or formed according to that use.

While hammers are a generic social kind produced by ergonic convergence anchoring, subtypes of hammers then depart from this broader class. The subtype "claw hammer," for instance, came into being along with the production of forged iron nails by the Romans. Thus, this type of hammer took on further (relational) powers over and beyond those of an ordinary hammer. Subsequent claw hammers were basically produced by mimetic anchoring processes, with the environmental constraint that they were limited by both their capacity to produce focused force and their capacity to pull nails (whose properties were evolving with it). The actual physical composition of hammers changed over time according to developments in other material technologies (including forging techniques, the development of rubber grips, and so on). So as mimetic kinds, claw hammers are descended from a common ancestor. But it is also worth noting that the name for them as tools varies significantly between languages and there are regional variations in specific stylistic features (e.g., German *Zimmermannshammer* means literally "carpenter's hammer," a typical German claw hammer which, rather than having two claws of equal length, tends to have one long and one short claw; but most German and English native speakers would recognize both regional variations as claw hammers).

Furthermore, the physical properties of hammers also lend them representational properties. Someone could write a whole book (and probably has) on hammers as metaphors, but it is worth noting that the metaphorical imagery of hammers, while necessarily varied, is partially constrained by its reference to the functional properties of hammers as well as the depiction of hammers in earlier referenced sources. Thus, for instance, Thor's special weapon *Mjǫllnir* is referred to as a *hamarr* (hammer) in Old Norse texts, which play on the weapon's capacity to deliver a powerful impact like that of a "thunderbolt." But the meaning and powers of Thor's hammer are produced by the expanding canon of literary, filmic, and other artistic depictions of Thor's hammer (which have only minimal consistency).

Finally, before we leave the subject of hammers, a given member of the kind "hammer" might be a functional tool, an art object, a focus of worship, a political symbol, and so on at different times depending on either its creation or different moments of use. All that is to say that the question is not "*is this hammer religious?*" but "*when is this hammer religious?*" and this social kind theory gives us the capacity to answer that. A hammer displayed in an art gallery is going to be read as an art object with some of the attendant attributes of art objects (e.g., people will attribute to it a specific creator, attempt to read it aesthetically or in its broader art historical context, etcetera). If the same hammer is placed on an altar it is then going to take on a different set of attributes (e.g., people will tend to see it in terms of its symbolism, of say Asatru faith, and so on). All that is to say, a specific artifact's membership in a broader set of kinds is situationally and contextually dependent.

•

To return to where this all started, we could begin to look at the disciplinary master categories as social kinds. Again, I have written books (and could write more) about the category "religion" alone. First, because "religion" is a kind that is typically essentialized, we need to begin by de-reifying it. To treat religion as a process social kind is first to grant the critique. Religion is a culturally specific category with a troubling history that displays a set of arbitrary presuppositions. Religion has no core, no necessary and sufficient conditions for membership. Instead of the binaries produced by the naive presupposition of essentialism, we can now talk in degrees—that is, things flagged as "religion" can be both colonial and anti-colonial in different measures in different places. To grant the nominalism, we note that religion is not a universal object but an aggregate of particulars. Accordingly, religion functions differently in different cultures, periods, and discourses. Its distinction from other fields, like the secular, is inconsistent and unstable. Religion is historically contingent. The same is true of "religions."

Having granted this critique, we might observe that while conditioned, the formation of religion is non-arbitrary. It has been reified, but the reification process can be studied. Religion is relational but not nonexistent. It may be a mobile signifier, but it has a particular grammar. It is the product of a historical moment, but cannot be reduced to its origin. It exists as discourse but it contains elements that resist assimilation into discourse. It is the product of hegemonic power, but it is also the site of resistance.

There is a lot more that could be said here. But most things marked as "religions" only share any powers in common with other "religions" because of dynamic-nominalist anchoring processes, which an analysis into this area demonstrates. (They mostly share internal properties in common due to mimetic processes). Various entities become "religions" by being named or classified as such according to internal diplomacy, domestic law, scholars, and so on.[86] This is not a teleological or transhistorical process, but one that came out of a particular logic at a particular moment in Western Christendom, and its globalization was necessarily selective and to some extent arbitrary. Further, it was negotiated rather than effected by unidirectional imposition or hegemony. And, as I demonstrated in my earlier writing, there have to be various incentives or enforcement mechanisms that encourage the classification to take hold.

The goal of religious studies is not to find a better definition for religion. There are no stipulated or otherwise definitions that will capture the category, since the glue that binds it together is that of various dynamic-nominalist processes (with mimetic processes operating at the level of

individual "religions"). This means that the search for the essence of religion is over. There is no more work to be done analyzing a given "concept"
of religion. We cannot merely uncritically repeat what our sources say
about "religion" because they often disagree and because they are wrong
about how "religion" actually functions as a social kind. But it is not true
that nothing can be said about the nature of "religion." Rather, we can
look at and analyze its historical and cross-cultural unfolding, and in so
doing we can learn much about the nature of our social world.

Furthermore, if I am right in my hunch that "religion" and most of the
other disciplinary master categories are basically "historical individuals,"
then we need to tackle them all together. The story of how "art," "religion," "science," and so on came into being as transnational categories is
not multiple histories, but one grand (albeit roughly contemporary) history with a large number of local variations. We do not need a bunch of
autonomous definitional endeavors or siloed disciplines. What we need
instead are more scholars working together to trace the enfolding set of
categories, many of which emerged in their current form alongside the
diffusion of the current version of the university system itself. My hope is
that this monograph will inspire more projects along this line of research.
The results could be illuminating.

·

By way of postscript, I should note that "social kind" is a social kind term
that necessarily captures itself. There is useful work to be done aggregating and disaggregating its usage. We could trace the term's history and explore the advantages and disadvantages of its utility. If it becomes overly
essentialized at any point, it will need to be deconstructed. Eventually,
when it has done its work, it will fade. All things have their time. But if we
are going to change the social world, we first need to understand it.

PART III: HYLOSEMIOTICS

5: Hylosemiotics:
The Discourse of Things

The meaning of the forest is multiplied a thousandfold if one does not limit one-self to its relations to human subjects but also includes animals.

JAKOB VON UEXKÜLL, *A Foray into the Worlds of Animals and Humans*

Imagine this: You are out for a hike in the foothills of Kyoto, Japan in order to visit a Shinto-Buddhist shrine venerating Thomas Edison and Hein-rich Hertz as the "Divine Patriarchs of Electricity and Electro-Magnetic Waves."[1] After speaking with some shrine attendants and collecting some pamphlets, you set off into the bamboo forests that border the shrine, where you find yourself on a footpath that curves gradually up Arashiyama Mountain.

It is a cool spring day, and there is light rain in the forecast, so as you walk you scan the sky for signs of precipitation. The trail markers are all in Japanese, and while you can read the language, you find yourself com-paring the signs to the markers on your map to make sure you are in the right place. You take a few photographs with your phone so that you can later compare them to other images from the same spot.

You have been hiking for just a short time when you find yourself face-to-face with a red-faced snow monkey whose bright white fur stands out in stark contrast to the greenery around you. It is surprisingly close: ten feet away, seated on a branch of a tree just above your head.

The two of you freeze and regard each other. The monkey's eyes meet yours and you glance away to break the gaze, and then back at the monkey surreptitiously to see how it will respond. A light breeze whistles through the bamboo.

All at once the snow monkey looks past you, lets out a high-pitched hooting, and swings off through the branches. You have no trouble recog-nizing its call as one of distress, and you can hear other unseen monkeys also fleeing the area. No sooner has the monkey vanished than you turn around at the sound of an approaching group of Japanese tourists who are hiking with a small dog, which you assume must be the reason the mon-key sounded its alarm call.

•

Why does this matter? For reasons I will explore, this case pushes to its limits much of the inherited philosophy of language common to the contemporary humanities and social sciences. At the very least, if you are steeped in postmodernist philosophy and the attendant poststructuralist account of language (as I had been at the time this happened to me in March 2015), there are several aspects of this encounter that will bother you on closer scrutiny. This is because various features of the account above begin to put pressure on two very different premises about language, which I will explain in greater detail below: namely, 1) the supposition behind much of both analytical and continental philosophy of language that language use is unique to *Homo sapiens*; and 2) the differential account of meaning central to poststructuralism.

In the first case, there are many different ways to define language. But many theorists would agree that if humans did not come to language in a single, grand evolutionary leap, then there must be something like a continuum between nonhuman primate communication and human speech. As one contemporary linguist has observed, anyone who accepts "the theory of evolution . . . must accept also that language is no more than an evolutionary adaptation—one of an unusual kind, perhaps, yet formed by the same processes that have formed countless other adaptations. If that is the case, then language cannot be as novel as it seems, for evolutionary adaptations do not emerge out of the blue."[2]

In this respect, the monkey's "kuan" alarm call in response to the dog also seems to have been an act of communication—one that was intended not for me, but rather for its unseen group members. Indeed, there have now been more than fifty years of work on the calls of snow monkeys (*Macaca fuscata*) and other primates, most of which suggests that their calls have semantic significance.[3] Indeed, a famous set of experiments on vervet monkeys demonstrated that they have different alarm calls for different predators and that when monkeys are exposed to prerecorded calls they respond appropriately.[4]

Furthermore, as I later learned, vocalizations are not the primary way monkeys communicate; if anything, gesture (including eye contact) is even more important. Snow monkeys engage in visual co-orientation by tracking each other's eye movements, and staring directly into the eyes of another monkey (or in this case, a human) is a signal of aggression.[5] So even though I did not fully register it at the time, many animal behaviorists would agree that the monkey was at least provisionally communicating with me.

This suggests, as I explore in this chapter, that taking animal communication seriously might provide an innovative vantage on human language. To avoid confusion at the outset, I am not saying that snow monkey communicative signals are identical to human language in their range or flexibility of producing meaning (especially their capacity for self-reference or producing hierarchically structured syntax).[6] More specifically, I want to demonstrate the value of reorienting our notion of discourse to include a continuum of signs, including the chemical signals trees send to each other through their roots, the scent trails of ants, the dances of bees, the hissing of snakes, and the roaring of lions. This will allow us to see human communication in a new way and to answer a number of puzzling conundrums around the nature of meaning.

Second, this experience also began to put pressure on the linguistic model I had internalized under the sign of the negative. For reasons I will elaborate momentarily, the nearly hegemonic "poststructuralist" account of meaning was wholly inadequate to explain nonhuman communication (many poststructuralists have assumed humans are uniquely imprisoned in linguistic categories); furthermore, it is equally inadequate to explain key aspects of human communication (as explored below). So the encounter with the snow monkey will be a jumping-off point to reevaluate this background account of meaning.

These issues are important because questions of meaning are central to research in the human sciences, even if we do not always recognize them as such. A theory of meaning is vital to translation, as we always have to adjudicate interlinguistic equivalents (e.g., what 神社 means in English). But meaning is also crucial to textual interpretation (e.g., what does "establishment of religion" mean?), the interpretation of actions (why did my Japanese host-father clap twice in front of the statue of the stone fox?), and even understanding more generally (how did he know to bring an umbrella?). Meaning is also important to how we come to apprehend ourselves—in Charles Taylor's memorable formulation, we are "self-interpreting animals."[7] Questions of meaning are thus at the root of almost everything we do in the human sciences. All of which is to say, while the poststructuralist version was largely a failure, a notion of what meaning itself means could not be more important.

For a range of reasons, then, the inherited semiotics common to much of the human sciences will not do. A new semiotics is in order. In the years since my encounter with the monkeys of Arashiyama, I have been working to formulate such a semiotics in dialogue with my brother, Seth Josephson, whose doctorate is in Animal Studies. We have dubbed it "hylosemiotics," drawing the prefix "hylo" from the Greek ὕλη ("matter" or "forest").[8] For reasons that will become clear shortly, hylosemiotics includes much of what is often called hermeneutics, rendering the hermeneutics–

semiotics opposition moot. We hope to publish our more extensive system elsewhere, but this chapter is my version of an outline of our joint project, charting its key commitments and early insights.

Hylosemiotics draws on a range of theorists.[9] It combines their insights with recent findings in animal and plant communication to formulate a panspecies model of signs and meaning itself. But to toss out some positional jargon as fodder for readers already familiar with various forms of semiotics and hermeneutics, it might be best to think of hylosemiotics as an expansion of a C.S. Peirce–influenced biosemiotics to include the semiotics of nonbiological symbolic systems (e.g., robots/computers) combined with an account of meaning drawn from hybridizing Ruth Millikan's teleosemantics, Deirdre Wilson and Dan Sperber's relevance theory, and a repurposed version of Richard Boyd's notion of accommodation to explain reference magnetism. Readers from a continental perspective will also see the influence of Martin Heidegger's hermeneutics, but stripped of its anthropocentrism. After naturalizing philosophy of language around nonhuman models, the project then emphasizes the materialized representations that mediate cognitive processes to produce extended minds.

In broad brushstrokes, the following will provide an account of meaning and its materialization, a description of the relationship between signs and the world, that should be of instant interest to scholars in a range of disciplines.

To provide a little more explicit signposting, section 5.1 will begin by dialectically mediating poststructuralist semiotics and New Materialist ontology. I argue that these two putatively opposed movements both fail in interesting ways, but by recouping the emphasis on semiotics from the first and the turn to matter from the second they can be sublated into something much more interesting. Readers already ready to reject both poststructuralism and New Materialism can skip directly to section 5.2, which begins theorizing meaning by tacking back and forth between a minimal metaontology and a minimal semantics (more fully articulated in section 5.3). A brief excursion makes the case against the impossibility of translation in section 5.4. Then section 5.5 puts forward a specific hylosemiotics of specific signs. The rest of the chapter begins exploring the implications of this sign theory for scholarship in the human sciences.

5.1 Beyond the Linguistic Turn

Postmodernism is consistently identified as part of a broader "linguistic turn." According to the most common account of this turn, it is as though philosophy, having translated all of its problems into problems of language, became nothing more than a language game; or perhaps postmodernism (or poststructuralism) represents the grand finale of an increasing overemphasis on the authority of language that finally abandoned even the notion of linguistic structures and rejected anything outside the free play of unattached linguistic signs.[10]

While there is something to this account, as I noted in the introduction, "poststructuralism" is an American invention largely assembled from a bricolage of French theorists merged with a handful of doctrines drawn from an older stratum of American New Criticism. There was no poststructuralist movement in France and the linguistic turn was much older than the common narrative presumes. Nonetheless, if postmodernism had a specific philosophy of language or semiotics it can be seen in what later Anglo-American scholars canonized as "poststructuralist." (I'll use the term "poststructuralist" in what follows to talk about this subset of postmodernism.) Thus, while analytic philosophers and linguists formulated a very different account of language (see note), a crude poststructuralism gained ground throughout much of the human sciences, where it continues to linger, shaping many scholars' attendant ideas of discourse in general—and, in powerful but often unseen ways, anchoring a set of assumptions about the way language relates to the world.[11]

In this section, I reconstruct this terrain in grand overview. Then, I gesture at a recent putative opposite, New Materialism. I will argue that taking up both movements together, or more precisely drawing the attention to semiotics from the first and the attention to ontology and matter from the second, permits us to turn the linguistic turn inside out and make it do productive work.

·

Many scholars tend to take as given two things about language they inherit from the Swiss linguist Ferdinand de Saussure. First, Saussure is well known for having asserted that *"the linguistic sign is arbitrary."*[12] This statement has gone on to produce significant amounts of criticism and confusion. Indeed, Saussure immediately qualified this statement, and did so again in greater detail in a generally overlooked later section of the same work.[13] Despite how it has sometimes been read, Saussure's doctrine of the arbitrariness of the sign was mainly an attempt to repudiate linguistic theories in which particular sounds were thought to have a natural or organic connection to the thing they represented. But Saussure's original claim was misread and many later interpreters came to think of language more broadly as fundamentally arbitrary in its construal of meaning.

Second, following Saussure, signs are habitually characterized as dyadic in structure. As Saussure put it, "the linguistic sign unites, not a thing and a name, but a concept and a sound-image" or a "signified and signifier."[14] In this Saussure is intentionally suspending the issue of external reference. For example, the meaning of the English word "frog" would be a particular concept FROG, not a particular thing in the world. This was not a denial that signs referred to external objects (as it has often been taken to be); nor was his emphasis on "arbitrariness" meant to suggest that an individual English speaker might be free to use the word "frog" to refer to any old animal they chose. Actually, Saussure recognized that language had conventions and that reference was one function of linguistic utterances. But rather than debating which languages did a better job of describing the world, he suggested that linguistics should focus primarily on variation in linguistic structures and suspend debates around external reference or correspondence.

It is less interesting from this perspective whether the English "frog" captures what one might think of as an actual biological genus (it doesn't) than how it relates to other adjacent concepts such as "toad." The linkage between signifier and signified is maintained by the relationship a given sign has to the whole system of signs in which it exists. A sign must be distinguishable from others in its sign system; and according to Saussure, the meaning of a sign results from its difference with respect to these others. The meaning of the term "man," for example, depends on its exclusion of other meanings such as those of "child," "woman," "animal," and so on.

Saussure promoted what amounted to a kind of semantic holism, in which meaning emerged not from isolated signs, but from the sign system as a whole. In oft-quoted lines, "Language is a system of interdependent terms in which the value of each term results solely from the simultaneous presence of the others . . . concepts are purely differential and defined not by their positive content but negatively by their relations with the other terms of the system."[15] Structuralism explicitly inherited this account of meaning. Claude Lévi-Strauss argued that "the meaning of a word depends on the way in which each language breaks up the realm of meaning to which the word belongs; and it is a function of the presence or absence of other words denoting related meanings."[16] While not completely excluding reference, Lévi-Strauss's structuralist methodology presumed this account of linguistic structures.

Saussurean semiotics became as important as it was because various notions of "linguistic relativity" had already come to dominance. Saussure's inadvertent legacy was therefore an internalist semantics that disconnected words and concepts from anything in the material world. A sign's meaning was thought not to be rooted in its capacity to refer to things, but instead to be determined by its relative position within a system of signs. This claim was frequently amplified in the hands of later interpreters who transformed Saussure's methodological bracketing into the assertion that the whole idea of meaning in terms of linguistic reference was either misguided or downright impossible.[17] As Catherine Belsey has astutely summarized, the central exhortation that defined much of poststructuralism was *"difference, not reference."*[18]

Here is the thing: this whole account of meaning fails. Its fundamental presuppositions are mistaken. To start with, semantic holism comes in different variants, but it often amounts to some version of the idea that the meaning of a term or sentence is merely its relationship to either a subset of a language or a language as a whole. Analytic philosophers often associated holism with Quine and Wittgenstein, and the latter's statement that "understanding a sentence means understanding a language."[19] In the hands of a poststructuralist, it is either the idea that the meaning of a word comes from the structure of the language as a whole, or (in a more modest formulation) the idea that meaning expresses a relationship between concepts and other concepts without external reference.

While I think there is something to be said for localized semantic holism (a.k.a. contextualism), grand semantic holism as a theory of language runs into obvious problems. To toss out a few: First, if you have to understand a complete language (or a complete linguistic structure) to understand a single sentence, then by implication unless you suddenly gained access to a language as a whole, you could never understand even a single sentence—so learning a language would be impossible. Second, if meaning requires the whole linguistic structure of a language, then it might also suggest that since no one knows the meaning of *all* the words in the English language, then no one actually knows the meaning of *any* of the words in the English language.

Third, if semantic holism were true, then the introduction of a single new word into a language should change the meaning of all other terms in the language. But how could the introduction of "youthquake" (Oxford's 2017 "new word of the year") alter the meaning of the otherwise unrelated sentence "What is the relative atomic mass of oxygen"?

Fourth, semantic holism might suggest that translation was impossible, because to translate one English sentence into Japanese would require translating all of English into Japanese. But to translate the sentence "Please pass the salt" into Japanese "塩を渡してください" clearly does not require the complete translation of the entire English language.

Fifth, even modest semantic holism often implies the so-called "hermeneutical circle" that is commonly believed to arise from the contention that to understand part of a text a reader needs to understand a whole text, but to understand the whole text a reader needs to understand a part of the text. The hermeneutical circle is supposed to be a paradoxical circularity rendering interpretation impossible, but it is really just a problem with the broader assumptions of linguistic holism.[20]

Sixth, if meaning is a relationship between concepts without reference, then any two people's versions of a language would be incommensurable as there would be no way to check if two speakers share the same meaning of even one of their terms (without reference). Finally, if meaning is produced only by differences, then the meaning of every concept might seem to require meaning to be deferred from one concept to the next in an infinite chain of differed relations.[21]

Observations like these are sometimes used to challenge the notion of meaning as such, but what they actually suggest are disastrous faults in this broader stratum of theories. Indeed, many poststructuralists knew that the received Saussurean account of meaning was flawed. Derrida and company presented numerous critiques of this model—challenging the value of linguistic structures, repudiating logocentrism, emphasizing the places that they saw language breaking down, and the like. But instead of proposing an alternative account of meaning, these theorists have often left readers thinking that *meaning is impossible*, and to some extent they have bequeathed this view to subsequent scholars in a range of disciplines.[22]

To approach this differently, we might ask: what is a theory of meaning for? Or, more specifically, what kind of work should either a semiotics or theory of meaning be able to do for those of us working in the human sciences?[23]

You might think that a good theory of meaning would be able to do at least some subset of the following: account for what it means to know a language or understand a specific sentence (e.g., to be able to finish the sentence "the meaning of the word 'fish' is . . ." or to be able to explain what a person who understands the meaning of the sentence "that is a fish" is understanding); explain what it is that translations share with the text they purport to be translations of, or provide at least a crude account of when two different terms from different languages mean the same thing; suggest how one might adjudicate different interpretations of a particular linguistic text (e.g., "what Shakespeare really meant by 'malice' was . . ."); elucidate what meaning a particular sign communicates; or more fundamentally, explain in some rudimentary sense how communication, the production of meaning, or translation are possible. (Some philosophers also identify meaning with what determines truth conditions, but I do not, see note.)[24] It would be an added bonus if such a theory could provide some sense of how human language relates to or emerges from animal communication.

On these grounds, poststructuralism was a failed theory. Not only could it not answer any of these questions, but as a received model it often denied that many of them had any answers. Any attempt to pinpoint meaning (or arrest its dissemination) was seen as misguided. Translation was thought to be impossible. Every interpretation was taken to be equally valid. Humans were seen as uniquely imprisoned in linguistic mediation. Hermeneutics was seen as an inescapable circle, and so on. The main point I want to make is that these conundrums are not grand insights into the human condition, but rather evidence of an unsuccessful philosophy of language.

To be fair, poststructuralism made a number of positive contributions. It focused attention on rhetoric and rendered the opacity of language suspect. It reminded scholars that the categories through which we view the world are not fully determined by the world. It also emphasized semiotics (even if, from my vantage, the wrong version of it) and the importance of attention to signs, symbols, and discourse. Moreover, I think Derrida in particular was approximately correct in noting that there are problems with treating spoken language as the paradigmatic exemplar of communication.[25] Despite being hampered by the legacy of Saussurean semiotics, which he presumed even as he repudiated it, Derrida in his gesture toward "arche-writing" suggested the need for a material semiotics capable of troubling the easy binary between "reality" and "representation" and of saying something substantive about *how the world itself represents*. That is what I aim to do in what follows.

In summary, many problems in the human sciences are indeed problems of language. But poststructuralism was uniquely unsuited to solve them. There is a reason for this. As I will explore in greater detail in chapter 6, poststructuralism was basically negative dogmatism masquerading as a (failed) semantics. Much of what scholars were getting out of poststructuralism was that their claims about the meaning of texts (broadly construed) could not be adjudicated. If meaning is impossible and every interpretation is equally valid, then you can't be wrong. In practice, of course, this did not work. We went on judging each other's scholarship, meaning, and interpretations (indeed, paradigmatic poststructuralist works are themselves mostly attempts to stake out particular interpretations), but we did so without the benefit of a theory of language to justify our behavior.

Poststructuralist theories would also have little to contribute to the simian encounter that began this chapter. To see why, we can find a representative example of this kind of theorizing in a book I read as part of the research I was doing in Japan. *The Invented Self: An Anti-Biography, from Documents of Thomas A. Edison*, written by the American historian David Nye on an explicitly poststructuralist model, argues thus:

> This study rejects the existence of its subject, Thomas Alva Edison. . . . He once existed, but neither he nor any other figure can be recreated. The references in these pages lead not to a hero, but to yellowed papers. . . . Only a bumpkin would look for the real Edison in this semiotic shell game. . . . Such a pattern will avoid the attempt to return to some pre-semantic "reality" behind the documents.[26]

Nye's anti-biography gets most of its energy by denying Edison's relevance as a historical figure. Texts about Edison have no source beyond other texts. Images of Edison have no meaning beyond their relationship to other images in general, and so on. For Nye, all linguistic signs are in some sense supposed to be "arbitrary," by which he mainly seems to have taken to mean that attempts at reference are impossible or at the very least misguided.[27]

To illustrate why this is such a dysfunctional theory of language, we could say about the snow monkey what Nye said about Edison. The encounter in question had no subject. My references were not to a monkey but to other signs. (This is a baffling account of meaning, as it would seem to suggest that where I say "look at that monkey" I would have to be gesturing to other discursive moments, not making reference to a specific creature). Only a "bumpkin" would try to figure out what kind of animal I referred to, or if it really existed. (Maybe I actually saw a bear or a lemur.) To look to any particular extralinguistic "reality" behind my account would be misguided. (I might as well have imagined it.) There are only arbitrary differences between signs—no similarity, no reference, no fixable meaning. (Why am I even telling you this? Because to write would seem to be a misdirected attempt to assert a particular meaning.)

Further, Nye and his fellow poststructuralists would have rejected the possibility of non-arbitrary, isomorphic aspects of maps or photographs. They would have repudiated the possibility of "translating" between Japanese and English, or at least they would have rejected the idea that certain translations might be more accurate than others. (As a preliminary counter-argument, the existence of *inept translations* pushes against this view. For an example, watch the Monty Python sketch "Dirty Hungarian Phrasebook" [episode 25, 1970], which depicts John Cleese pretending to be a Hungarian in a British shop trying to order with the help of a perversely inaccurate Hungarian–English phrase book. While trying to request matches and cigarettes, he winds up saying things like "My hovercraft is full of eels" and "you want to come back to my place, bouncy-bouncy?" This phrasebook is farfetched, but if you grant the existence of inept translation, mistranslation, or bad translation then you have conceded the possibility that translations can be more or less accurate.) Animal communication and natural signs would be necessarily beyond these theorists' typical horizon. Poststructuralist accounts of meaning would do nothing to explain my ability to interpret the rain clouds, Japanese texts, or the call of the snow monkey, much less snow monkeys' ability to understand each other.

One might think that this nonhuman encounter would be ideally suited to analysis by contemporary New Materialism, since New Materialists have often defined their movement in opposition to poststructuralism and they have regularly taken pride in dethroning the human from their ontology. There are many things I like in that movement, but the surprise is that New Materialism would have just as many problems explicating the encounter. Indeed, it will turn out that New Materialists can do nothing to explain the interaction above; they can only describe it. As the following demonstrates, New Materialists have tried to be post-semiotic, but they keep setting up problems that only a semiotics will solve.

·

If there is one thing the diverse collection of theories grouped under the banner of the New Materialisms seem to share, it is that their turn to materiality is motivated by a rejection of the "linguistic turn."[28] Rosi Braidotti—the feminist philosopher generally credited with devising the expression "new materialism"—summarized the birth of the movement thus: it "emerges as a method, a conceptual frame and a political stand, which *refuses* the linguistic paradigm."[29] Their criticism of the linguistic turn mostly boils down to some version of the assertion that—as Karen Barad put it—"Language has been granted too much power."[30] In brief, they argue that "postmodern" or "poststructuralist" theorists have overemphasized words and overlooked things. While this critique has merit, New Materialists tend to be unaware of how indebted they are to the very movements they oppose.

New Materialism's technical vocabulary is largely drawn from poststructuralism and literary theory. The term *actant*, for instance, comes from structuralist literary analysis, where it was used to refer to the "functions or roles occupied by the various characters of a narrative," and it appeared in the writing of canonical poststructuralist thinkers like Roland Barthes and Julia Kristeva.[31] *Assemblage* is another example of this pattern. Indeed, Saussure uses "assemblage" (*l'agencement*)—the same term that many associate with Giles Deleuze—more times than he uses the word "structure."[32] Moreover, despite claims that Actor-Network-Theory is an alternative to structuralism, Lévi-Strauss treated both "network" (*réseau*) and "assemblage" as near synonyms for the now discredited "structure." After all, notwithstanding some misleading metaphors of structures as cages or laws, what the structuralist primarily meant by structure was a system of relations or a network of nodes. The irony is that scholars who would probably not be caught dead using terms like "structure" in a positive sense are in the process of reimporting terms like "network" and "assemblage" to do all the work "structure" did in classical structuralism. Almost without skipping a beat, New Materialists exchanged linguistic networks for material assemblages. It was even possible for some of the same theorists to go from paragons of poststructuralism to paragons of New Materialism, merely by saying about matter what they had previously been framing in terms of discourse.[33] That the New Materialists were often translating into ontology what poststructuralists were doing in terms of language does not make them necessarily mistaken, but begins to hint at the limitations of their project.

Other limitations are clearest in their ordinary operating procedures. A typical scholarly work informed by New Materialism outlines a particular assemblage (or network) that the scholar wants to study and then identifies the actants—both human and nonhuman—that make up that assemblage. There is nothing wrong with this as a first-pass approach. The notion of assemblage is especially useful when it pushes us to consider more than texts and their authors. But this procedure establishes nothing on its own. Everything can be construed as part of an assemblage. Once a case study has enumerated all the particular things that make up an assemblage (say, the person who signs the mortgage, the person who gave them the mortgage, the paper the mortgage has been made out of, the place the mortgage has referred to, the plastic of the chair they were sitting on when they signed the mortgage, and so on), there is little interpretive work that can be done. All we are left with is a jumble of connections that on their own have very little explanatory value. Assemblage does little more than indicate that something is of interest to a researcher.[34]

New Materialists often claim to speak for nonhuman agents, but they do so without registering their own interpretive procedures. This is clear in the Achilles' heel of much of New Materialism: its unbridled admiration for "agency." The problem is that "agency" is largely a vacuous category that gets most of its mileage by being opposed to a strawman.[35] For example, when a New Materialist says that "[a rock] has agency not only in its capacity to excite the human mind, but also in the energy of its atoms that support a mountain overhead,"[36] this amounts to the claim that rocks both exist materially and can be perceived by humans—truisms few people would reject. This notion of material "agency" only makes sense in contrast to the view that mind or discourse produces the world and nothing exists to be perceived. But as noted in chapter 1, almost nobody has ever claimed that the world exists exclusively within mind or language. Poststructuralists did suspend the physical world, but they did not deny its existence. In contrast to the New Materialist account, the rock's "agency" in supporting a mountain could be better elucidated with a theory of causation, while the rock's ability to inspire suggests its function as a sign.

To provide another example: in the opening pages of *Vibrant Matter*, Jane Bennett describes her encounter with an "assemblage" consisting of a glove, some pollen, a dead rat, a bottle cap, and a stick of wood. Instead of seeing these as merely "passive" objects, she is struck by this collection of things and its agency or "ability to make things happen, to produce effects."[37] But Bennett never really tells us what those effects are or what that agency amounts to, nor does she describe any object in detail. They are mere placeholders. There seems to be no interesting way that the "dead rat" is exerting meaningful "agency" on the bottle cap or any of the other artifacts in Bennett's assemblage.[38] But this is typical inasmuch as once the assemblage is traced, there is often no more work that can be done.

Before we move on, I want to reiterate a point from chapter 4—namely, that multiple realizability pushes against the claim by Barad and others that "matter" and "meaning" are identical and "cannot be dissociated."[39] You can make a chisel out of steel or wood or stone. It is equally a chisel. Does it make a difference to an analysis of an assemblage if a mortgage was written on paper made from cotton or from wood-pulp? If it was signed with a black pen or a blue one? Although I can imagine unusual case studies with something at stake in either of these distinctions, in general most of the matter in the "assemblage" does not matter for a given analysis. Not all of the matter that instantiates a given social kind is crucial to the social kind. As I argue here, what is crucial is the part of the matter that has semiotic content or function.[40]

Not to belabor the issue, but New Materialism cannot do much more with the encounter that began this chapter than focus our attention on the nondiscursive features of the environment. If we actually want to understand Bennett's assemblage, or the agency of a rock or even of my snow monkey, we need instead a theory of how things, living and nonliving, act on each other—not merely in their material effects, but in how they take on meaning. In a future book I intend to produce a new theory of causality, but here I provide an account of meaning. New Materialists have largely been unaware of the extent to which their work has been limited by the inheritance of the Saussurean semiotic paradigm they share with poststructuralists, and have overlooked the potential of an alternative approach to language. The very linguistic turn they criticize has the potential to solve the problems with their analyses.

•

In summary, the linguistic turn was valuable insofar as many of the problems endemic to the human sciences are indeed issues of language and interpretation; but especially in its poststructuralist variant, the linguistic turn also ushered in a failed theory of meaning. New Materialism, which aspired to repudiate the turn to language in favor of an emphasis on materiality, merely transposed poststructuralist presuppositions about language into ontology. But its emphasis on materiality at least was well directed. Hence, I will argue that taking up the linguistic turn and its putative antidote together is the key to moving forward.

5.2 A Minimal Metaontology

The two initial insights that make hylosemiotics possible are that: 1) semiotics and ontology have to be done side-by-side, as it is a mistake to try to formulate a theory of language by completely bracketing off meaning from the physical world in which meaning occurs; and 2) we need to naturalize any theory of language to see human semiotic behavior on a continuum with at least that of other animal species.

I want to begin my exploration of the first of these insights by doing something that will look very strange from the vantage of much of contemporary philosophy of language, which has generally gotten quite good at compartmentalizing ontology away from theories of meaning.[41] It will lead to perhaps the two most important implications of hylosemiotics—a minimal ontology and an account of meaning.

We might begin by asking: what are the things that humans and other animals do more or less successfully? We navigate the world in various ways. We feed ourselves. We reproduce. We have expectations. We communicate with each other. The fact that we can do those things more or less successfully is amazing, and it has direct ontological implications. If the world were really a completely incomprehensible place—if it were the unknowable hyper-chaos or mutually non-overlapping linguistic universes anticipated by various postmodernists and poststructuralists—we couldn't do that.

This suggests that the world must have at minimum two basic features: 1) the world must consist in rough property-clusters (see chapter 4; I'm using *properties* here rather than *powers* to emphasize physical actualization); and 2) it must have limited cross-temporal stability or minimal causal regularities. This probably reads as a naturalized version of the basic Kantian question—how must the world be structured such that any kind of sentient being can have any kind of knowledge of it whatsoever? And the answer might appear to be a deflationary restatement of Kant's "forms" of intuition (space, time/causality), but bear with me.

Physical properties are not evenly distributed across the universe, nor do they exist in an undifferentiated confusion. The local environment—at least from the vantage of planet Earth—consists in things that can be apprehended as roughly delineable property-clusters. When I look out my window on a summer's day, I see clusters of green things with a common flexibility and shape that make up the grass; I see a largely undifferentiated cluster of blue that makes up the sky; and so on. I am talking in terms of rough appearance, but one could imagine any set of physical properties (e.g., viscosity, luminance, temperature, material constituents, reflectivity, shape) and note that these properties tend to cluster, with other sorts of things between them (e.g., air or water or earth or space).[42]

This uneven distribution of property-clusters would need to exist for humans and other animals to navigate the world, because there must be at least something like it to differentiate the world into recognizable units. I am not saying that these clusters have to exhibit clearly consistent structures, nor do all members of a particular kind have to share all their properties, nor do the clusters have to be definable by necessary and sufficient conditions. We do not need all the metaphysical baggage associated with classical accounts of natural kinds or invariant natural laws.

These property-clusters do not need to have sharp edges. Indeed, granting at least some fundamental vagueness will be important in what follows. It is worth noting that vagueness comes in twice here: first, many physical entities (e.g., clouds and mountains) are vague because they lack precise spatial boundaries; and second, many properties themselves (e.g., gray, bald) are vague because of how they are applied (e.g., whether a particular object like a faded once-black shirt is gray can be vague). Put another way, vagueness is exhibited by most predicates (fast, red) and most nouns (child, toy) whose category membership is full of borderline cases.[43] (A third order of vagueness built into linguistic usage will be discussed below.) It does not much matter for my account whether vagueness is ontological, epistemic, or semantic. All I am getting at is that, at minimum, the world must consist in rough clusters, which while they often have vague boundaries can nonetheless at least provisionally be roughly distinguished from one another.[44]

These clusters may also be continually in the process of changing, but they must exhibit at least some cross-temporal stability and they must interact with each other in at least minimally consistent ways. *Contra* Hume and Meillassoux, all we need is relative, local stability. If the world around us were fluctuating at a dizzying speed in unpredictable ways with things popping in and out of existence, then no animals would be able to interact with it effectively. There would be literally nothing to hold on to. While the processual nature of existence is important to recognize, most of the things we encounter change gradually or in generally predictable ways (at least compared to the fairly rapid changes exhibited by some social kinds).[45]

Succinctly put, in order for humans and other animals to have any chance of navigating our environment, the universe must be composed of relatively stable property-clusters, which exhibit local and at least somewhat consistent behaviors or causal regularities.

Crucially (and this is my main point), many different cosmologies would support this minimal ontology. The universe could be just as it has been described by contemporary physics or Immanuel Kant. It could equally be described by pre-conquest Nahua thought as having been woven together in the continual unfolding of *teotl* energy. Either classical Charvakas or contemporary Seventh-day Adventists could be right about the world, but it does not matter for our current purposes which one is correct. There are actually few cosmologies that this minimal ontology excludes, and most of those are either purely hypothetical or completely solipsistic. (If you are truly convinced that I am only a figment of your imagination, you are welcome to stop reading.)[46] Indeed, the main cosmology it excludes is the implicit ontology of a typical (if exaggerated) poststructuralism that has totally rejected the idea of stable reference and argues instead that we live in completely separate, incommensurable, and linguistically (or culturally) determined worlds.

In summary, I am not offering a particular ontology; I'm suggesting a metaontology—that is to say, describing some minimal constraints on any ontology that could be compatible with sentient beings having even limited ability to navigate and have crude knowledge of their environment.

Given this minimal *metaontology*, we might say that humans and other animals come to know the property-clusters that make up their environment by interacting with things (material signs and their affordances, explained below), coming to recognize somewhat consistently some of their properties, their peaks or cores, and roughly how to distinguish them from one another, even if we are not always able to recognize their indistinct edges.

This means we have to be provisionally able to do two different kinds of operations: track property-clusters over time/space and distinguish relevant adjacent property-clusters of the functional sortal class. For example, to be able to consistently recognize "cows" when I see them, I need to have some weak, provisional, but fairly dependable way of tracking the cluster of properties that most cows share, and I need some way of being able to remember the relevant non-cow properties that distinguish cows from bulls or horses.

A key point is that we need not be using the same criteria to identify roughly the same cluster. It is likely that being physically embodied humans with comparable sense-organs, we are similarly constrained in how we interact with our environment and what kind of things we can choose to track.[47] Our judgments of similarity are, after all and as we have been noting, task dependent. But many, if not all, property-clusters are *robust*—that is to say, independently accessible by different senses.[48] Accordingly, other kinds of animals with very different senses are likely to be able to pick out roughly similar clusters at least to the extent that they share with us similar forms of embodiment and interest. For instance, I and the cat may have completely different ways of identifying the bat flying around my ceiling. The cat may be primarily using hearing and I might be primarily using sight. But we are still tracking intersecting bat-property-clusters.[49]

By way of another example, you may know me by sight and identify me best when you see the length of my nose, the shape of my face, and the color of my hair; but the listeners to my podcast might not be able to pick me out of a lineup and instead recognize me by the timbre of my voice, while my neighbor's dog may recognize me primarily by smell. As I age, my properties will change over time: my hair will gray, my voice will get more gravelly, and even the components of my particular scent will shift. But many people and animals will continue to recognize me because we are collectively pretty good at tracking property-clusters and distinguishing them from one another (even if we rarely agree exactly).[50]

Also, to be clear, I am not saying our qualia are identical—your subjective experience of "blue" may be closer to my subjective experience of "red," and so on. As long as most of us generally agree that strawberries and fresh blood are roughly the same color, for the purposes of this theory it does not matter if our subjective experience of that color differs.

What I mainly mean to suggest is that there is a very small set of—we might say "transcendental"—constraints on the kind of possible world we must be living in.[51] If humans and other animals live in an environment we can even crudely navigate fairly successfully, that puts some minimal limitations on what that environment must look like. This implies something about meaning that I will explore in the following section. But the central thing I am getting at is this: *the world being a certain way and its being the thing that our conceptual and linguistic practices need to accommodate* (including the overlapping similarities of these practices across different times and domains) *plays a huge role in our ability to understand one another.*

I want to highlight a few implications of this metaontology before we proceed:

First, I need to say something about the relationship between language and thought. On the one hand, the general consensus of most psychologists and cognitive scientists is that not all thought occurs in language.[52] Even in our day-to-day life, examples of non-linguistic thought includes the common experience of having an idea but not being sure how to put it into words; and the observation that babies and animals seem to exhibit thinking without having the capacity for language.[53] But on the other hand, there is also a good amount of evidence that when we are thinking in a specific language that language does tend to have some impact on how we think. For instance, the way that various languages label hues tend to influence our recall and color-sorting. Nouns that are gendered grammatically differently in various languages have an effect on the associations of those objects. Different languages also force people to specify and pay attention to different features of their environment (such as left or right or north or south). Moreover, rhetorical framing and shared conceptual metaphors (e.g., time is money) do tend to unconsciously shape our thoughts and actions in important ways. But most linguistic categories imply emphasis, salience, and influence rather than worldviews or distinct life-worlds.[54]

This has concrete implications for the way that meaning is conceptualized. A number of philosophers have thought that sharing linguistic meaning is equivalent to sharing *concepts*, understood as mental representations or psychological states.[55] For instance, the English "cow" and the Spanish "vaca" are supposed to have the same meaning insofar as they evoke the same COW concept. But this model is mistaken. Even speakers of the same language do not share identical mental representations. As noted in chapter 3, an influential set of studies provided evidence that native English-speakers disagree over the categorization of basic terms. Other research has shown that speakers of the same language typically differ over how to adjudicate color boundaries; and that the same object maybe seen as members of different categories depending on the task at hand.[56] Alternate ways of thinking of concepts as information stores or ways of recognizing things would also suggest that people do not have identical concepts. For instance, we probably know different things about *forsythia* (I know very little, aside from the fact that it produces lots of yellow flowers) and we presumably have different ways of recognizing it and distinguishing it from other plants when we encounter it. Hence, taken together, there are many reasons to reject the view that meaning (even within a given linguistic community) is shared mental-representations.

Second, because of problems with internalist accounts of meaning, some analytical philosophers—famously Hilary Putnam and Saul Kripke—have gone in the opposite direction from the poststructuralists and rather than rejecting reference argue that (at least for certain classes of words) "meanings just ain't in the head!"[57] These philosophers often portray "meaning as a direct connection between language and world bypassing mind."[58] In parallel to behaviorism in psychology, the mind was seen as unknowable and basically ignored. Reference at least was supposed to consist in a largely unmediated word-world relationship. In this respect, some analytic philosophers came to a position that was nearly diametric opposed to Saussure's account of meaning. Poststructuralists were largely bracketing out the world, while analytic externalists were largely bracketing out the mind. But while both of Putnam and Kripke's externalist accounts of meaning have something to them, they are also flawed for similar reasons.[59]

For instance, in *Naming and Necessity*, Kripke argued proper names and natural kind terms get their meaning from a "historical chain picture" of how naming works, basically that an initial "baptism" attaches a term to a referent, which is historically handed down to later speakers.[60] But there are several arguments against this model, including that there is a tendency for the reference of names to drift (e.g. the name Madagascar for the island comes from a confusion made by European cartographers about references to Mogadishu on the African mainland).[61] More importantly, ostensive reference is often underdetermined.[62] Even proper names generally have vagueness built into them. For instance, the exact boundaries of Mount Greylock are ambiguous and historically disputed. So if proper names were pure reference without descriptive content then it might seem difficult to ascertain what part of the reference to which the term attaches.[63] The types of vagueness I mentioned earlier point us toward the problem: what part of the physical world does Mount Greylock pick out? A particular peak or set of peaks? What are its boundaries? And so on.

Returning to the minimal metaontology above can help us make progress on the issue. It implies that mental-representations do not carve up the world so much as trace property-clusters and learn to recognize their re-occurrence.[64] Neither words nor concepts categorize or subdivide the world as much as they tend to track certain aspects of it. Most human and other animal behavior does not necessitate adjudicating vague edges and borderline cases. We tend to target peaks of mountains or cores of clusters and even then, we probably do so at least slightly differently. For most purposes, even when I am going for a hike, the exact boundary of Mount Greylock does not matter very much to me, and to say that I was hiking on Mount Greylock will satisfy most people with a vague and general sense of my whereabouts that day. More precisely formulated, we both track property-clusters and learn to distinguish between them when necessary. *Contra* Kripke, names do not fix references, rather they can help us coordinate attempts to trace overlapping property-clusters. Indeed, reference itself is task dependent and concepts function as intermediaries.

Third, that said, learning a new word is generally not memorizing a definition but becoming comfortable fixing a reference. For instance, when I was teaching my daughter the meaning of the word "cat" I did so by pointing, not by defining "cat," providing a description of cat-relevant-properties, or telling her which features distinguish cats from other animals. Teaching her the meaning of "cat" therefore is done by directing her attention to a particular core of a property-cluster and assuming that she will infer from context and my ostensive behavior the things I was trying to indicate. There is no reason to think her and I have identical mental-representations of cats, we know different things about cats, and we may adjudicate borderline cases differently. This model of tuition is not just true of household pets or medium size objects. Indeed, most new words enter a language without definitions (e.g., when "hip-hop" was first used to refer to a musical subculture it was done by pointing to a set of DJs and rappers, not by promoting a definition, listing essential features, or articulating a set of differences between hip-hop and neighboring musical styles).[65]

We learn most of our words in context through reference-fixing practices and without being provided with extensive specification of meaning or use. *Contra* Saussure we do not primarily acquire meanings by learning to map signs onto conceptual differences. Concepts are not ways of dividing up the world. It could almost go without saying but when our fellow primates learn how to communicate, it is not by mastering definitions but rather by coming to associate certain signs (calls, symbols, gestures) with particular references.[66] Again, these references are not to natural kinds, but to imprecise and often inconsistently demarcated property-clusters.

Fourth, because we tend to track and distinguish different things, and because we tend to learn most of our words implicitly via context, rather than as a result of explicit definition, if we think of concepts in terms of mental-representations everyone has their own concepts.[67] But inasmuch

as we are capable of tracking overlapping property-clusters, we can coordinate or share what we are talking about. (I will return to this momentarily.)
Against much of analytic semantics, reference is necessarily conceptually
mediated, but meaning is not reducible to shared concepts. Rather, *utterances are used to guide inferences*. I communicate because I want you to
infer something about what I am talking about and ostensive meaning is
just one of the possible things I might be expecting you to infer.

Indeed, one of the direct implications of the metaontology and account
of meaning I am providing here is that reference is not something that
words do in themselves, but rather reference is something that people do
with words (or more precisely, as will be discussed momentarily, reference
emerges from the coordinated voluntary-sign making activities of communities of sentient beings).[68] Talking about "Mount Greylock" is just one
way of coordinating attention toward a particular vague property-cluster
for a particular task. The boundaries evoked by "Mount Greylock" will depend on the task at hand. Mount Greylock means something different for
purposes of Mountain Day festivities, establishing legal property boundaries, geological research, backpacking, etcetera. Nor is reference limited
to speech. I could also signal something similar by pointing, showing you
a photograph, or just leading you on a hike.

5.3 The Meanings of Meaning

We can build on the minimal metaontology described above by actually
granting one of the defining features of the linguistic turn — namely, that
the world is accessed not via unmediated experience, but semiotically or
hermeneutically. This is a crucial insight that oddly enough appears in
the writings of theorists from very different backgrounds — including C.S.
Peirce, Martin Heidegger, Ruth Millikan, and Jakob von Uexküll (a perhaps
lesser known Baltic German biologist whose most influential writings
date from the 1920s). I will discuss Peircean semiotics in more detail in
the next section, but as Peirce put it, "The entire universe is perfused with
signs, if it is not composed exclusively of signs."[69] To clarify, this is not the
claim that language constructs the world; rather, the core of this insight
is that humans — and in the case of Millikan and Uexküll, other biological creatures — encounter the world not as raw sense experience awaiting
categorization, but in terms of its functional relevance or meaning.

Let me elaborate. You do not see the materialized depths of the book
in front of you, nor do you see its constituent atoms. At best you see its
surface, and this surface is brought to you via reflected ambient light. The
quality of light varies significantly depending on illumination. The pages
of the book literally reflect different hues or colors under different lighting

conditions. But your visual processing centers discard information about the illuminant in order to reconstruct a received image of the book as distinct from its background. Your mind is projecting the back of a book as a solid three-dimensional object, even if you have never turned it over in your hands. Your various sensations are being stitched together. We often do not realize this is the case because we are not conscious of our own process of perception. We just think we see a book, when in actuality a varied manifold of visual and tactile sensations are synthesized into a sense of a persistent object.[70] Even that apprehension of a persistent object is already entangled with "meaning" (discussed and defined in greater detail momentarily).

The differences between Heidegger's and Uexküll's versions of this insight are the most important for our purposes. Heidegger argued that "The lived world is present not as a thing or object, but as meaningfulness."[71] While I can force myself to see differently, when I glance at my desk I do not see a set of brown or black colored shapes; I see instead my coffee cup, "always already" imbued with "meaning." For this reason, Heidegger came to see the experience of Being as fundamentally connected to hermeneutics or interpretation. This position contributed to Heidegger's broader assertion that humanity has "fallen away from itself as an authentic potentiality for Being its Self, and has fallen into the world."[72] One common reading of Heidegger is that humans are uniquely exiled into a linguistically, or at least hermeneutically, mediated world. We do not see the fallen branch so much as we see a club with which we might beat our enemies. This exile into linguistic mediation is often taken to be the central claim of the linguistic turn. But while I would agree with Heidegger's emphasis on the importance of hermeneutics and symbolic mediation, I argue that humans are not exceptions, and the fact that other creatures share this state with us means that it is not exile, but home after all.

Here is where Uexküll comes in. His crucial realization was that meaning is vital to all biological organisms, not just humans. Animals do not simply respond to stimuli. Rather, they respond to the *meaning* the stimuli have for them. Animals interpret the data from their senses (e.g., identifying food as opposed to a mating partner) according to different "carriers of significance" (*Bedeutungsträger*), or, we might say, according to their functional relevance or meaning.[73] When a badger smells a particular pungent aroma, it provides the badger with the meaning (or in contemporary language, information) that a tasty earthworm is nearby. Moreover, animals do not just interpret signs, they also produce them. Deliberately or not, living beings leave a mark of themselves, create a vibration, leave a scent, that others can identify and, through interpretation, use to produce meanings.[74] In this respect, animals are situated in rich semiotic environments.

While Heidegger made his argument by appeals to the human condition, Uexküll's heirs in animal etiology and neurobiology have provided a wide range of empirical evidence about the capacity of animals to interpret evidence from their senses as well as to produce signs.[75] (Moreover, subsequent research in animal behavior has demonstrated pretty conclusively, *contra* B.F. Skinner, that animals are not mindlessly responding to stimuli but that they acquire knowledge based on their experiences. They learn about and interpret the world.)[76]

In summary, this broader understanding of signs and meaning suggests that all animals, not only humans, interpret the world.[77] It comes to us in materialized signs.

·

This insight, combined with the minimal ontology described above, lets us begin to specify the meaning of meaning. To get there, I'd like to articulate my departures from the semantics proposed by the British philosopher Paul Grice. Many philosophers have seen meaning purely in terms of language, but Grice helpfully distinguished between two types of meaning: "natural meaning" and "non-natural meaning." As an example of the first, Grice gave "those spots mean measles" (what we refer to as a "symptom" later). In Grice's account, if it turns out that the person in question was not actually sick, then that sentence turns out to be false. The spots did not, in fact, mean that the person in question had measles. In contrast to this type of meaning, we might take the sentence "When Keith uttered *Don es muy inteligente*, he meant that *Don is very smart*" as an example of non-natural meaning.[78] Notice that this sentence can be true even if Don is not, in fact, very smart.[79] In the broadest of brushstrokes, Grice argued that the crucial difference between natural and non-natural meaning was that natural meaning expressed a causal law while non-natural meaning was rooted in the speaker's intentions (combined with linguistic conventions).[80] Thus, Grice's model was what would later be called "intention-based semantics."[81]

Grice's model is an important first step, but his account of meaning can be improved on. In the first instance, what Grice describes as "natural meaning" I would argue is the primary and foundational form of meaning (and it is a shame that Grice focused his attention primarily on the other type). Some of the evidence for its primacy is that sign interpretation is ubiquitous among animals, but various species are more or less social (e.g., adult leopards basically only meet to mate).[82] Moreover, infants learn to observe the world before they learn to understand language. Even more basically, you have to be able to perceive sights, sounds, or tactile sensations before you are able to ascertain which ones are intended to be communicative. Hence, natural meaning has to be prior to "non-natural meaning" (a term I don't much like, for reasons that will become clear).

More importantly, natural meaning and non-natural meaning are more entangled than Grice's typology would suggest. While Grice usefully theorized about what is implied rather than explicitly stated in a given utterance, his account of implicature does not go far enough because it still identifies meaning in intention. But a significant aspect of the meaning of a sign token (or utterance) is what we normally call context. So when Keith says "*Don es muy inteligente*," he might be asserting the meaning "Don is intelligent," in response to someone questioning Don's intelligence. But if he is taking a Spanish test, he might not be intending to make any particular claim about a person called "Don," and instead might be communicating that he can accurately recite a sentence in Spanish. These are analyzable by way of implicature. But if Keith slurred his words while saying the phrase, it might also indicate that Keith is drunk—a "natural sign," but one that might communicate the additional meaning that Keith is not presently clear-headed—a potential negative sign for Don's intelligence or perhaps Keith's grade.

The problem for Grice is that unintended meanings like these are a huge part of communication and how we reconstruct their intended meanings in the first place. People say things all the time that have the potential to provide insights into their thought processes, background assumptions, or moods, and which they did not intend to convey. As any serious poker player will note, we all have "tells," or micro-expressions. One of the things that makes email so fraught is the difficulty of reconstructing the emotional cues and context that provide the necessary background from which the narrow intentional aspect of meaning can be reconstructed.

Another thing that Grice's limited account overlooks is his assertion that natural signs are always related by causal laws. This has led some subsequent philosophers to think of natural signs or natural information as an "objective commodity." But as discussed in greater detail below, many signs do not reflect causal laws. Most physicians will argue spots only mean that it is likely that the patient has measles, and then only when they appear alongside other relevant symptoms.[83] Similarly, despite the ubiquity of the example, smoke doesn't invariably mean fire. Smoke could also mean the presence of a smoke machine, or a combustion source being extinguished; indeed, it might mean something is just hot but not burning, as many materials smoke *before* reaching ignition temperature. Further, a given sign can mean different things to different observers. Two people witnessing the same cloud might infer different information from it (say, wind direction for one and likelihood of rain for the other). Thus, as

Ruth Millikan argues, signs tend to be correlational, and "Nothing will be a natural sign of anything else absolutely. Rather, there will be things that can serve as signs or do serve as signs for a given [individual] or species."[84]

To begin to put Grice and the snow monkeys in dialogue, one might ask: are monkey screams merely naturally meaningful—something that they reliably do in the presence of certain kinds of things? Or is this a case of "non-natural" meaning? If a monkey makes the flying-predator sound, but there is a drone rather than a predator, did this monkey scream *mean* flying predator, or does it now mean "drone"? Our first clue is that the behavioral evidence suggests that monkeys can lie.[85] Moreover, even animal species which seem incapable of intentional deception make choices about whether to produce signals or to remain uncommunicative.[86] All that is to say, animals (and perhaps other species of living organisms) produce voluntary signs for individual purposes. In this regard monkey cries have what Grice would have called "intentional" meaning. This suggests that Grice's typology is in error. It also has two further implications: on the one hand, a trained human should be able to interpret monkey cries and access this intentional meaning if they can reconstruct why the monkey was making a call and what range of sensory inputs give range to similar responses; and on the other hand, monkey cries are still meaningful for even untrained humans insofar as they mean that monkeys are nearby.[87]

.

Instead of a bifurcation between natural and non-natural meaning, we need to think in terms of asymmetries between meaning-making and interpretation, or sign production and sign consumption. More specifically, in the technical vocabulary of hylosemiotics, sentient beings have the capacity to interpret both *voluntary* and *involuntary* signs. (The contrast is scalar rather than binary.)[88] Here we mean to distinguish between a consciously emitted sign and an accidental sign either emitted unconsciously or produced by the non-sentient world. For instance, the smell given off by my skin, while of semiotic interest to my cat, is involuntary as it is not a sign I am normally intentionally emitting. Voluntary signs have both intentional and unintentional meaning, while involuntary signs typically have only unintentional meaning.[89]

Although typically noted only in passing, this asymmetry fits research in animal communication. For instance, the German primatologist Julia Fischer has observed that various "studies [suggest that there is a] deep divide between sound production and sound processing in animals. Genetics strongly determine sound patterns that are susceptible to very small modifications at best. By contrast, acoustic processing is a flexible and open system: almost everything can and must be learned."[90] As I would put it, while humans and a few other animal species are capable of extensive modification of our voluntary sign production apparatuses (calls, scents, gestures, etcetera), most animal species lack this control and instead of making totally new signs, typically refunction or modify preexisting sign behaviors in response to novel stimuli.[91] Put differently, many animals adapt their communicative signals to changing environments (e.g., developing warning calls for newly introduced species), but they do so by learning new responses to preexisting or subtly modified signals. For that reason, much of the shifting meaning of animal communications happens in sign interpretation, not sign production.

So why do animals produce voluntary signs in the first place? I would argue that broadly speaking, animals typically produce voluntary signs in order to get perceivers to infer something about the animal in question or its environment.[92] My cat meows because it wants me to infer that it is hungry and to prompt me to get it more kibble. Its meow also communicates to me that it is right next to my head, even if I didn't know it was there before. In that respect, the cat's particular utterance both carries information and communicates intention inasmuch as it is an attempt to influence my behavior.

I want to emphasize that voluntary sign production is the imposition on a material form of a function that makes it into a representation (e.g., soundwaves, chemical trails, written words). In this respect, voluntary signs are causally mind-dependent, but humans are not the only animals with minds. (Crucially, voluntary signs are social kinds, discussed below.)

Differentiating between voluntary and involuntary sign helps us interpret the example of the monkey. Insofar as the monkey was engaged in voluntary communication, the intended meaning of the monkey's voluntary sign was something like "run, there is a flying predator," whether or not there was a flying predator (presuming that was the meaning the monkey was trying to communicate, even if it was either wrong or deceptive). From the vantage of a particular meaning-interpreter, though, the monkey's call carries both its voluntary meaning (as a clue to the monkey's intentions or purpose in producing the sign filtered through the sign's function as a social kind) and its involuntary meaning (which would be more or less accurate depending on how often cries of this sort reliably indicated a flying predator).

•

Voluntary signs are social kinds. One of the larger interventions of hylosemiotics is building on the theory of social kinds elaborated in chapter 4.

As I argued, "Social kinds are 1) socially constructed, 2) dynamic clusters of powers, 3) which are demarcated by the causal processes that anchor the relevant clusters." This describes both the kind to which a given voluntary sign (e.g., word) refers and the mechanisms that stabilize the sign itself. Again, a sign is distinct from its reference. Social kinds and their terms are like wheels within wheels. To explain, we might ask what powers (or properties) the English word "house" has as distinct from the social kind to which it typically refers. "House" is spelled in a particular way. English speakers have to be able to distinguish it from orthographically similar words, such as "horse." It has a characteristic pronunciation (with regional variation). It typically functions as a noun in the grammatical system of the English language. These are not properties of houses as social kinds—houses aren't spelled in a particular way; the term "house" is. The processes that anchor shared property-clusters in house construction are independent from the processes that anchor the spelling and pronunciation of the word "house" (e.g., similar methods and material constraints have affected house building in contemporary Germany and France despite different words for houses). The social kinds model would draw our attention to all the various anchoring processes that work to standardize spelling, pronunciation, and so on. It would also remind us that negotiation and asymmetries between powers (and differing capacities to recruit anchoring processes) are part and parcel of determining a sign's properties. And it would encourage us to track the sign's changing history and regional variation. Voluntary signs are necessarily dynamic and relational rather than fixed and comparatively stable. It could almost go without saying, but as social kinds, voluntary sign meaning is at least partially a product of negotiation and asymmetries of power.

Thinking of voluntary signs as social kinds also reminds us that the question of whether a given token of the sign is the same or different is to some extent task-dependent. For instance, house, HOUSE, and *house* could count as three different tokens of the English word "House," or as two or three different signs, depending on my purpose and which features of the social kind I am tracking.

Putting Deirdre Wilson and Dan Sperber's "relevance theory" into the vocabulary of hylosemiotics, I would suggest that voluntary signs do not encode meaning so much as provide clues to a sign-producer's meaning.[93] Recast, voluntary signs are "ostensive signals" that function to attract a perceiver's attention and focus it on a particular meaning. The word "house" can be used to refer to specific houses, to pick them out from the background of the world. But reference use is necessarily weakly anchored, as natural languages tend to be very flexible. So I can can see a friend arrive at a pub and say, "Zot Quixote is in the house!" and my friends can recognize that with "house" I am not suggesting that Zot lives in the pub or that the pub is a house, but rather enthusiastically greeting him. Even when used non-euphemistically, "house" takes the conjunction of other indexicals (that house/this house), possessives (my house), or gestures to complete the sign and do the work of establishing meaning.

·

Classical philosophers of language have often taken as their model of meaning declarative truth-conditional sentences (e.g., "Socrates is a man"). But if snow-monkey calls are taken as a point of departure for an account of intentional meaning, then it encourages us to see different features of language as paradigmatic (arguably, it encourages us to focus on the pragmatic rather than the semantic features of language). This has several concrete implications.

First, voluntary signs, as the snow-monkey example illustrates, are better analyzed in terms of their purpose, function, or "intention" than in terms of binary truth conditions. Restated, when analyzing animal calls, we are dealing not precisely with truth, but with some form of success. The monkey successfully communicated "flying predator!" insofar as it caused other monkeys to run, which presumably was what the monkey emitting the cry was intending to do, but it was inaccurate in its description because the drone was not a flying predator or a threat. It was both a successful example of communication and an inaccurate one. Many human natural language sentences aren't strictly speaking true or false either. For instance, the sentence "It is raining" is neither true nor false on its own. It requires a context (place/time) in order to be interpreted. Even then, whether it is raining or not can be vague. Are a few drops sufficient to say that it is raining? What if they are infrequent? How many droplets make it count as raining? What if we subtract a droplet? What is the maximum delay between droplets to qualify as rain? Thus, a given utterance is better analyzed in terms of the pragmatic purpose behind the communication (which, of course, is typically related to a state of affairs in the world).

Vagueness is not just fundamental to the world—it is built into language. As noted above, basic predicates like "tall" and "bald" are vague; even the word "borderline" is vague. Our reasons for speaking also have vagueness built in because our interests change over time. When I say I want "some beer," the meaning of "some" is vague (exactly how much beer) and will likely change over the course of an evening of drinking.[94] Although not all context-sensitive terms are vague (e.g., "I"), vague terms tend also to be context sensitive (e.g., Keith is tall for an American philosopher, but short for a basketball player). Vagueness is typically all the way down, so to speak, as we don't always know ourselves exactly what we mean with a given thought or utterance. What we mean by "tasty" (or "beautiful") will likely vary over time and can change based on introspection, new experiences, context, etc. All of this variation and vagueness might be more or less consciously available to us. All that is to say, vagueness is endemic, and much of what we think of as context is part of the meaning of a sign.

To clarify further, the theory of meaning I am outlining here is a broadly inferential one. Sentient beings use inferences to interpret our environment (see chapter 6), including both voluntary and involuntary signs. Communication is inference, not decoding. Part of the evidence for this is that two utterances of the same sentence in the same language can mean different things (e.g., "yeah, right" could mean "yes, correct" or "no way"). Miscommunication typically occurs not from misunderstanding a specific word's typical usages, but from presuming different premises or contexts. Similarly, mistranslation arises not from problems of coding equivalences (e.g., the problem is not finding the equivalent word for "right" in Korean), but from different contextual premises.

Any given utterance could produce a wide range of inferences. Some of these are things the communicator is trying to get the perceiver to infer (a.k.a. intentional meaning), and others are unintended. Moreover, figurative "loose talk" is *the norm* and not the exception.[95] For instance, we regularly say things like "Iowa is flat" or "John is a monster when he's drunk," but we do not mean literally that Iowa completely lacks hills or that John changes shape when he drinks. So how does a sign consumer know what the intended meaning is? A lot more could be said about this, but if Wilson and Sperber are correct, "Every utterance conveys a presumption of its own optimal relevance."[96] The perceiver assumes that the utterance is worth communicating and relevant to shared context.

•

We can supplement our account of how reference is coordinated by returning to Richard Boyd's account of accommodation, described in chapter 4. The core of Boyd's account is his claim that the "naturalness" of a natural kind emerges from an "accommodation" between actual causal structures and the classificatory practices of a specific "disciplinary matrix." To paraphrase, he claims that what he calls "natural kinds" emerge from a dialectical process in which specific disciplines come to modify their conceptual categories by reference to the actual causal structures of the world. Many attempts at generalizations fail, he says, or succeed only partially. But he goes on to say that "disciplines" attempt to formulate reliable inductive and explanatory practices, and in the process gradually come to either reject or refine their conceptual categories.

I'm going to take Boyd's skeleton and hang on it a rather different flesh. I will drop the term "naturalness," as I think it is confusing, and I am in this section interested not so much in "kinds" or the taxonomic processes of scientific disciplines as in reference as such. As I argued above, conceptual categories are less about determining sharp edges around concepts than about focusing attention on particular relevant features of the environment. Accordingly, while Boyd's account of accommodation relies on a correspondence theory of truth, I am more concerned with the success of a voluntary sign in communicating its intended meaning; but as I said above, while both voluntary and involuntary signs may be "inaccurate," only a voluntary sign can be both "successful" and "inaccurate." This is because only a mind can be mistaken or intentionally deceptive (e.g., presumably a dark cloud that only looks like a rain cloud isn't doing so on the basis of having a mind). So what does Boyd's accommodation thesis look like when this work is done? As provisional shorthand, this is what I have in mind:

1) Voluntary sign reference emerges dialectically from a community of signaling organisms' use of signals to navigate their environment successfully; and 2) the signs' reproduction is motivated by success, here explained in terms of its "accommodation" or accuracy in picking out the relevant features of the world.

By this point, we have roamed so far from the anatomy of Boyd's accommodation that it is likely to look like a different kind of monster completely.

The fundamental question is: why is a given voluntary sign (or set of signs) being reproduced in a particular community? In other words, why do monkeys repeat specific calls? The short answer is that it is because they fulfill a function within a particular signaling community.[97] Signaling suggests a stake in the practical success—that is, success in action. What is important to Boyd is the idea that the practical success is explained in terms of the way practices are accommodated to causal structures. The practices work because the signaling is generally approximately correct. We also need to expand this to consider not just causal structures, but the rough property-clusters discussed in the preceding section. In doing this, however, we should remember that we can reference both social kinds and other property-clusters in the physical world.

Again, voluntary signs themselves are social kinds, so their meaning tends to drift, but signs are capable of reference insofar as they are weakly constrained by an accommodation between signaling, their reason for being reproduced, and the relevant features of the world.

To provide a hypothetical example: a monkey using the system of signals that includes what we could call the "flying predator" leads to success because the call is typically used in response to aerial predators and leads to behaviors that do diminish the chance of a monkey getting snatched by hawks. Furthermore, this leads to a notion in which the correctness of "flying predator" is dependent on whether there really is an aerial predator nearby. Thus, we might describe it in terms of the signal system's accommodation to relevant features of the monkey's environment.

Moreover, to treat monkey calls as metaphysically compromised or *merely* social constructs because they relate to the snow monkey's needs, desires, and discursive structures would seem to be a grand error. We also seem to be able to figure out what the monkeys have in mind (different predators), even if this discovery does not tell us what features of the predators they are tracking. Nor can we be sure whether all the monkeys in the troop treat the calls in the same way. I doubt it; even native English speakers disagree about the edges of the color blue.

What does this mean for our theory of meaning? Terms in different languages have different typical extensions, but reference is typically rooted in *task dependent* judgments of similarity and difference (perhaps something like a Neo-Fregian intension > extension and, perhaps, co-referring expressions). Insofar as we think that meaning is determined by extension, if group A at one time uses a term that has one extension, and group B at another time uses a term that has another extension, then the terms can't mean the same thing in terms of reference, even if the word used is identical. Nevertheless, we can roughly understand things that were said by earlier groups, and they can roughly understand us. Why? In part because the aspects of the world that we are using different languages to talk about overlap in a systematic way.[98] When early Linnaeans use "pisces," a fish-word that encompasses fish and aquatic mammals, and contemporary English speakers use a fish-word that excludes mammals, the degree to which we can understand each other derives from an overlap in the inductively relevant features of the world that we tracked by using our various terms. Recast, both linguistic communities are getting at overlapping property-clusters and communicating inferences about them. But we can reconstruct differences in meaning (or sources of potential translation error) between linguistic communities by charting the dissimilarities of their background premises. In another historical example, some of Joseph Priestley's references to dephlogisticated air overlap with what contemporary chemists would call oxygen, and some do not. (From Priestley's writings on the subject, we can also infer many things about his background beliefs including both those that he intended to communicate and those which he did not.) *Contra* Kuhn, I would argue that to the extent that intersecting property-clusters are being referenced, these different paradigms are in fact roughly commensurable.[99]

This is true not just for us, but also for nonhuman animals like the snow monkeys. We can interpret (or translate) the calls of the snow monkey to the extent to which we can discover the features of the world they are tracking and the function of the signals they are producing about those aspects of the world. This highlights one of the main themes of this chapter: namely, that signs are not the sole province of humans. Rather, the distinction between human and nonhuman semiotic behavior has been overdrawn, as I have shown. This suggests a relationship between language and the world that is not the mere imposition of language on a passive nonhuman environment.

In a later section, I will get even more specific about different sign types and other semiotic processes. But before I do so, I want to show how the theory I am promoting here does the work a theory of meaning should do, as discussed earlier. In brief, I think it can account for what it means to understand a specific sentence. It can tell us what (at least in principle) translations share (overlapping property-clusters or power-clusters). It provides a vantage to interpret signs of all sorts in the next section. In sum, it tells us how meaning, communication, and translation are possible.

To provide an example that will let us explain this efficiently: when someone is trying to understand the meaning of the sentence "that is a fish," part of what they are looking for is the reference. In this case, the reference is not to a "natural kind" (as Saul Kripke and others have argued), but rather to a fuzzy-edged property-cluster. In abstract terms, the similarity between the Japanese sentence "それは魚です" and "that is a fish" will depend on the overlap between the property-clusters typically captured by "魚" versus "fish" in each language at a particular historical moment. The particular terms are themselves social kinds with their own histories, variations, implicit inferential premises, and anchoring processes. Moreover, part of the meaning of the sentence—the non-voluntary part—depends on inferences extracted from the context in which it is used. When stated in person, the pointing finger is part of the sign and is doing some of the work of identifying the "that" of the sentence, but the fish is also doing part of the work by being the thing referred to. The perceiver assumes that the communicator is typically trying to maximize relevance. The context of expression may also be meaningful to the interpreter in other ways—it may communicate an emotional state, a set of beliefs, an identification of a previously unknown species, and so on.

For scholars in the human sciences, the theory of meaning here also suggests a preliminary response to a particular dilemma about interpretation. One of the things closely associated with poststructuralist (and earlier New Critical) textual criticism was the "death of the author" that rejected the claim that a text could be read in terms of authorial intent, and accordingly sometimes rejected the notion of "valid" interpretations altogether.[100] Barthes and company were right to observe that texts have multiple layers of possible meanings. Texts exceed what their authors intended for them. A careful reader of Barthes's *L'Empire des signes*, for instance, will learn much more about Barthes's Orientalism (and his exoticization of Japan) than the author necessarily meant to reveal. To understand a text, a reader typically relies on premises or information that is not explicitly conveyed in the text. The wider the range of "potential implications," the greater what Wilson and Sperber call the "poetic effect" or breadth of possible meanings.[101] There is plenty of room for psychoanalytic readings and unconscious meanings. We are also sometimes inspired by the way a text "speaks to us" to come to ideas that the original author could never have conceived. We often ask of a text questions that are basically normative or extrapolative (e.g., what should "the right to bear arms" mean today, or what does the *Dhammapada* mean to me personally?). There is nothing wrong with that. Reader reception often differs from what an author intended, texts can inspire in different ways, and so on.

I will also argue that we should use abductive inferences to reconstruct meaning/intention (see chapter 6), but even then discovering authorial intentions can be difficult and occasionally impossible. Authors are not necessarily consistent in their word usage.[102] Sometimes authors are also intentionally ambiguous or multivalent. Multiply authored texts suggest authors can miscommunicate or have competing purposes. Meanings can be obscure for a range of reasons. (Thinking in terms of property-clusters and anchoring processes makes it analytically clear both why there is no "objective" meaning and why there can be really bad subjective readings.) But none of this implies that any reading is equally good, nor does it mean that reconstructing authorial intent is misguided or impossible.

Indeed, reading in terms of authorial intent continues to be the main operating procedure today, even by scholars who think they have rejected it. When scholars want to know what Barthes meant by "death of the author," for instance, they look at all the different things he said about "the author," either published or unpublished, and then square the different accounts with each other or show how they changed over time. (Also, if you are tempted to disagree with me by denying that we have the capacity to discover authorial meaning, I want to note that to do so is self-refuting because it already presumes that I am an author whose intended argument you have accurately understood.) Again, we have to recognize that language does not *encode* intent so much as provide evidence for it. That is why authorial meaning can be so maddeningly hard to reconstruct.

All told, a text is not limited to its authorial meaning (though that is one important part of it). Voluntary sign production is only one kind of meaning a text can possess and by which we can analyze it, but there are other kinds of meaning available, and even intentional signs can have unintended meanings.

·

This is a long chapter so I'd like to summarize what we have established so far. Sign-consumers interpret both voluntary and involuntary signs. We read the world. The meaning of a sign is the inferences (or we might say information) that a sign-consumer draws from it. It necessarily appears in the context of previous background premises. Utterances (or specific sign tokens) have both voluntary and involuntary meaning. Involuntary signs tend to be correlational in different respects; they are not objective information so much as they can produce different kinds of inferences in different contexts. Voluntary signs are ostensive inferential signals intended to influence the behavior of perceivers and to attract attention and fix it on the inferences the sign producer wants to communicate. Sign-consumers both tend to focus on the parts of their environment that are most relevant to them and they tend to assume the interpretation of voluntary signs that maximizes relevance.

Voluntary signs are social kinds, which vary and change over time depending on anchoring processes. Part of reconstructing the meaning of a voluntary sign involves reconstructing the intentions behind its production and reproduction. One of the main things that voluntary signs are used for is reference. Put differently, reference is just one part of intention we might want to figure out. But reference is typically directed toward social kinds or loose property clusters, not clearly demarcated natural kinds. At best reference is overlapping not identical. Co-referring expressions have different anchors even if the result is often the same (e.g. referring to "animals with hearts" or "animals with kidneys" will pick out the same set of animals but the references will be differently focused). Misunderstandings often come from different background premises or assumptions that are being brought to bear on the utterance in question.

Before moving on, I want to underscore (and return to later) one more implication of my semiotics—namely, that communication does not take place in some abstract linguistic horizon. A sign has to be physicalized in order to be interpreted. Signs must become sound waves, scent trails, printed letters, and so on before they can be meaningful. *Meaning is of the world*, not separate from it. This should not be a surprise, it should be rather obvious, but it has tended to be lost in philosophies of language that are exclusively focused on the arbitrariness of signs or the limitations of words. A later section explores this in greater detail, but here a brief digression is in order. Presenting this material in draft form, I have noticed that some scholars get caught up in the idea that translation is impossible. This is important, because if it is, then much of what we do in the human sciences would have to be ruled out as unfeasible. So I want to counter that argument briefly below. (If you already grant the possibility of translation, you are welcome to skip ahead to section 5.5.)

5.4 The Lion's Roar: A Brief Excursion on the Possibilities of Translation

If a lion could talk, we could not understand him.

LUDWIG WITTGENSTEIN, *Philosophische Untersuchungen*
(translated by G.E.M. Anscombe)

In a sense, nothing is untranslatable; but in another *sense, everything is untranslatable; translation is another name for the impossible.*

JACQUES DERRIDA, *Le Monolinguisme de l'autre*
(translated by Patrick Mensah)

To declare its impossibility is not an argument against the possible splendor of the translator's task.

JOSÉ ORTEGA Y GASSET, *La Miseria y el esplendor de la traducción*
(translated by Elizabeth Miller)

In 2014, two dictionaries of supposedly "untranslatable" words were published in English. As measured by sales, the more popular of the two was *Lost in Translation: An Illustrated Compendium of Untranslatable Words from Around the World*, by the British author Ella Frances Sanders. Anyone picking up *Lost in Translation* hoping for some discussion of the limits of translation will instead find terminology from diverse languages translated into English and sometimes juxtaposed with small illustrations. For instance, the Tagalog *kilig* is defined as "The feeling of butterflies in your stomach usually when something romantic or cute takes places" and illuminated with a trio of butterflies.[103] While there seems to be no single-word translation of *kilig*, a single Tagalog term has nonetheless been rendered into English by producing a sentence as an equivalence. Despite the book's title, this translation by expansion is what professional translators have long been referring to as an "additive translation." *Kilig* does not seem to be an untranslatable word. Rather, Sanders seems to have breezily bypassed the issue of untranslatability and the meaning of the book's subtitle is only explained in the publisher's gloss as referring to "foreign words that have no direct translation into English." Difficult to translate is a far cry from untranslatable.

The parallel *Dictionary of Untranslatables: A Philosophical Lexicon* is itself a translation of *Vocabulaire européen des philosophies: Dictionnaire des intraduisibles*, edited by the French philosopher and classicist Barbara Cassin. While Cassin's work is much longer and includes both a more extensive list of terminology and lengthier definitions, its translation strategy is roughly similar. It selects a term, often lists translations in different languages, and appends an English definition. For example, the Romanian term *Dor* is glossed "ENGLISH: melancholy, homesickness, spleen, loneliness/ FRENCH: *désir, douloureux, deuil, tristesse, nostalgie*," and the entry that follows then goes on to explain the meaning of *Dor* in greater detail.[104] Sadly, it lacks illustrations.

Since any term designated as "untranslatable" is given (if anything) more translations into more languages, a reader might understandably regard this dictionary with suspicion. But Cassin (and her English translators) at least addresses the basic paradox of a dictionary of translated untranslatables. Cassin suggests an alternate definition of "untranslatable":

> untranslatables in no way implies that the terms in question, or the expressions, the syntactical or grammatical turns, are not and cannot be translated. . . . It is a sign of the way in which, from one language to another, neither the words nor the conceptual networks can simply be superimposed.[105]

Insofar as "untranslatable" has again been redefined as merely "difficult to translate," one might suspect that something has been lost in translation. But it is my contention that Cassin has been caught in a larger impasse common to many critiques of the impossibility of translation.

These examples might sound flippant. But they are emblematic of a widespread claim—in many sectors of the academy, translation is said to be "impossible."[106] This claim matters because it is often taken to threaten ethnography, to undercut comparative religion or literature, to rule out empathy across cultures; and, in one significant reading of Thomas Kuhn, this is what renders scientific paradigms incommensurable.[107] But as this section's opening examples illustrate, it is far from clear what "the impossibility of translation" actually means. This section, which is an abridged version of a much longer essay, will suggest how many accounts of the impossibility of translation run aground.[108] Consider it a digression, but an important one for readers who presume that translation is impossible.

The most straightforward argument against the impossibility of translation is hinted at in the untranslatable dictionaries discussed above. Here is the problem: the impossibility of translation is generally communicated by way of examples that are nothing so much as translations themselves. We could start from the obvious ironies signaled in the section epigraphs above, in which I have juxtaposed some of the most famous texts on the impossibility of translation with their respective translators. Most of the important arguments against translation have been translated into multiple languages; indeed, many Anglophone readers only ever encounter them in translation.

Not only have all of Jacques Derrida's writings on the impossibility of translation been repeatedly translated; his very justifications for translation's impossibility are themselves translations. The examples Derrida uses to explain untranslatability—such as the Greek word *pharmakon* or the phrases "he war" in James Joyce's *Finnegans Wake* or "mercy seasons justice" from *The Merchant of Venice*—he provides only to translate the supposedly untranslatable aspects of their meaning.[109] Similarly, when Benjamin Whorf wanted to argue that Hopi ideas were impossible to translate into the conceptual apparatus of English, he did so by translating Hopi sentences into English. Again, Whorf was translating the very thing he claimed was impossible to translate.[110] These thinkers are far from alone; as the philosopher Donald Davidson observed, this contradiction is rife throughout arguments for the impossibility or incommensurability of translation.[111] Every attempt to explain an unstranslatable word is itself a translation of that word.

Here is the heart of the paradox: to give a specific example of untranslatability requires being able to communicate to readers what has been lost in translation; but if you can communicate to readers what has been lost in translation, then the language in question is not in fact untranslatable. One cannot make a clear case for the impossibility of translation without undercutting one's own case. Most of the works arguing for the impossibility of translation are full of translations, and the more evidence they provide, the more it weakens their argument.

Space prohibits a full exploration of Derrida's many discussions of translation, which generally exhibit this contradiction. But in *"Qu'est-ce qu'une traduction 'relevante'?"* (1998), however, Derrida tellingly observes:

> If you give someone who is competent an entire book, filled with translators' notes, in order to explain everything that a phrase of two or three

words can mean in its particular form (for example, the *he war* from *Finnegans Wake*) . . . there is really no reason, in principle, for him to fail to render—without any remainder—the intentions, meaning, denotations, connotations and semantic overdeterminations, the formal effects of what is called the original.[112]

This pushes against the impossibility of translation, but I think Derrida is right that translation is a question of economy. If you are willing to devote sufficient time and energy to it, anything can be translated.

This evokes one of the most common misunderstandings non-translators have about the enterprise of translation—namely, the assumption that translation is the production of one-to-one lexical equivalence. As noted above, claims that a word is untranslatable often amount to the observation that there is not a *single* equivalent term in another language. But this lack of word-to-word correspondence is trivially true. For instance, in French there is a single word *borgne* meaning "one-eyed," but no one would seriously argue that *borgne* is untranslatable. Translation often involves more or fewer words in the source or target language.[113]

In the quotation above, Derrida is referring to a well-known (if inelegant) approach to translation by way of amplification. Particularly complex ideas may take a significant amount of text to explain and translate. For instance, one could easily dedicate a whole book to explaining the Japanese term *wabi-sabi* 侘寂, but that book would amount to a very long amplifying translation.

What does it mean for translation and meaning as such?

Languages do focus attention on different features of the world (e.g., different color terms, as discussed above). Part of what makes the search for equivalences so hard is that not only are words social kinds, but they often also refer to social kinds, which are typically exceptionally varied both cross-culturally and temporally. Every metalanguage is also an object language (and grues are endemic).[114] Furthermore, whether different languages or periods have the "same" or "different" social kinds is both task dependent and a question of whether they share relevant power-clusters and anchoring processes. But whether a translator bothers to highlight these differences is going to depend on how much is resting on this sameness and the purposes for which the translation is being produced. We have to be careful not to assume that our particular language's linguistic terms correspond in a robust way to the structure of the world. This does not mean that we are trapped in "prison houses" of language. If we see the world partially filtered through categories influenced by language and culture, then it should be possible for poets, philosophers, and scientists to let us to see the world in new ways by promoting new concepts and terms.

And indeed, this might seem to be one of the functions of translation it-self—not just to expand any given language, but to expand the world that is there to be perceived.[115]

Translation is interpretation. That does not mean that it is fully sub-jective. Rather, it means that translation requires not just knowledge of words, but also knowledge of context, cultural norms, and so on. Trans-lating some particularly rich concepts might require whole books' worth of effort. Similarly, as Kwame Anthony Appiah has observed, to translate meaning fully, such as an Akan proverb into English, often requires a "thick translation" that with annotations and glosses seeks to locate the proverb in its cultural context.[116] My hope is that a greater awareness of particular social kinds and their histories will come to inform how things are translated (both encouraging us to be more careful in translating and also presuming more difference in social kinds between periods, cultures, etcetera). Again, these suggest certain translation strategies, not transla-tion's impossibility. As noted above, miscommunication typically origi-nates not in a problem of decoding, but from different shared premises or changing contexts. So Wittgenstein would be right that to formulate a good translation often requires knowledge beyond the language itself.

Instead of demonstrating the impossibility of translation, many cri-tiques of translation really imply that translation is difficult and that there are often multiple good ways of translating something. This is because both source and target languages are regularly changing. Not to keep re-peating myself, but social kinds tend to be heterogenous both geographi-cally and temporally. Connotation is also highly varied both within a lan-guage and between languages. Even speakers of the same language from the same cultural background often do not precisely share meanings around gray areas and category hierarchies. We often have different asso-ciations with particular words or phrases. All this means that linguistic terms are social kinds (as I argued in chapter 4).

Communication is both vague and fallible. We often have unacknowl-edged differences in our background assumptions. But while miscommu-nications are always possible, language mostly gets the job done. If we follow Jakobson and include intralingual translation or rewording as a core example of translation (e.g., an intralingual translation of "bache-lor" within English might be "an unmarried man"), then translation itself is less an obstacle than it is central to the metalinguistic signal-checking that facilitates communication. At the least, translation is not any more impossible than communication in general.

By and large the philosophers I have consulted considered human language to be the paradigmatic form of communication. The lion speaks, in the quote from Wittgenstein above, rather than baring its teeth. But one implication of hylosemiotics is that we can reconceptualize translation in semiotic terms. If we think of translation as the transposition of one sign into another, then translation is ubiquitous and frequently ekphrastic. It is often the translation or the transposition of a sign from one medium into another (most conventionally, think of "translating" a novel into a film). Looked at this way, we can see ekphrastic translation everywhere. This is often how we attempt to get around linguistic limitations. It is hard to describe Rodin's famous "The Thinker" in words alone. A photograph can do a better job—and a photo of a sculpture is a form of translation. Moreover, if someone has never tasted one, it can be extremely hard to communicate verbally what a pineapple tastes like. But the pineapple's taste can be "translated" by mixing together another set of flavors that approximate its flavor. The synthetic food industry in America provides plenty of examples of attempts to translate or approximate the flavor of some natural ingredient in terms of other flavors. Look at this way, ekphrastic translations are widespread.

Before leaving the subject of translation, I want to emphasize that once both the impossibility of translation and notions of simple lexical correspondence are discarded, the question becomes not *how* translation is possible, but *why* a given translation has been produced. For this reason, I find it helpful to turn to what Lydia Liu has referred to as "translingual practices"—viz., "the process by which new words, meanings, discourses, and modes of representation arise, circulate, and acquire legitimacy within the host language due to, or in spite of, the latter's contact/collision with the guest language."[117] The enterprise of translation itself needs to be historicized and treated from a higher (might we say meta-?) perspective. Hence, we need to think of words—necessarily including those produced in translation—as social kinds that reflect the systems of power and anchoring processes that give them their meaning.

My main aims in this section have been modest. I have primarily been focused on shifting the burden of proof. After decades of scholars taking for granted the impossibility of translation (while often reading arguments it in translation), we have come to be rightly suspicious of the limits of translation and to emphasize the ways in which languages differ. Idealized notions of the universality of European linguistic categories and quests for natural equivalences have often run aground. Translation is frequently fraught and misunderstandings are all too common. The impossibility of translation has thus become a dogmatic position in across many disciplines and it anchors a whole host of theorizing. But translation is not impossible and every piece of evidence marshalled for the impossibility of translation is itself a translation. So what I want to suggest here is that the limits of translation are roughly equivalent to the limits of language itself.

5.5 A Hylosemiotics of Sign-Aspects

This section is an attempt to provide hylosemiotics with a theory of signs. Building on the notion of meaning above, we can now specify the functions of signs and produce a typology of distinct sign-aspects. Thus, what follows clarifies how various types of signs warrant distinct sorts of inferences or meanings.[118]

As referenced earlier, much of what we think of as postmodernist theory inherited a faulty semantics inspired by Saussure. Usefully, another paradigm for semiotics was developed by Charles Sanders Peirce.[119] Peirce's work provides us with three crucial advantages over the Saussurean tradition of semiotics that help connect sign-making to its material instantiation.

First, while Saussure saw the sign as composed of two parts, a signifier and a signified, Peirce observed that such a connection is only possible if it is made by an individual or process that operates as an "interpretant." Peirce's understanding of the sign is thus triadic (rather than dyadic). He argued that a sign is not just "something which stands for something," but "something which stands for something to somebody in some respect or capacity."[120] A Peircean sign is triadic because it consists in a relationship between a signifier, its signified meaning or reference, and its interpretant. It is this crucial "to somebody" that makes the relationship between the signifier and the signified possible. In this respect, meaning does not exist on its own but is always dependent on an interpreter. In the language of Donna Haraway, meaning is always "situated."[121] But this does not mean that every sign is equally open to all interpretations; rather, Peirce argued that a sign typically has a definitive meaning within a particular interpretive frame. (Hence my distinction between voluntary and involuntary meaning above.)

Second, Peirce developed his triadic model of semiotics as a rejection of the then prevalent "communication" model. In a communication model, language is best understood in terms of a sender who emits a signal (or sign) with the purpose of communicating a message to a receiver. Communication is successful if an interpreter decodes the intended meaning of the sender.[122] The communication model makes fidelity between intended message and interpretation the primary concern, but often (as I have mentioned earlier) unintended meanings are more useful for the purposes of the one doing the interpretation. The striking of the one o'clock bell may help me navigate my way across campus or tell me that the person ringing the bell has shown up for work. Neither of these is an intended meaning, but both are nevertheless examples of semiotic processes.

Third, and most importantly, what Saussure took as the entirety of semiosis, Pierce considered one of several overlapping ways for signifier and signified to be linked.[123] While Saussure's focus was on linguistic meaning, Peirce had a broader notion of semiotics that included all human communicative activity, from painting to gesture; and from these inspirations he articulated an elaborate and evolving theory of different kinds of signs. Ultimately his systemization implied sixty-six classes of signs (although he never described most of them), but subsequent semioticians have generally emphasized three key sign types drawn from his early writings.[124]

The three sign types of classical Peircean semiotics are as follows: 1) *The symbol* is a sign in which the relationship between the signifier and the signified is arbitrary. Although Peirce emphasized external reference rather than concept as the source of meaning, this notion of the sign roughly parallels the standard Saussurean version. But his other two sign types are more interesting. 2) *The icon* (or what he called a "likeness") is a sign in which the signifier and the signified share "a mere community in some quality." Hence, an icon's form is non-arbitrary in relation to what it represents. Photos are typically thought to be a sign of this type. 3) *The index* is a sign in which the relationship between the signifier and the signified is "a correspondence of fact" or "thisness." Indices, for Peirce, include both what we may call ostensive reference (indicating its position in space and time) and signs that indicate a causal correlation (smoke is an indexical sign indicating the presence of fire).[125]

Although we will adapt and alter his model—including refining and suggesting new sign-aspects—Peirce's theory of semiosis is a starting point for hylosemiotics. The inclusion of the interpretant as an essential element of semiosis indicates how meaning—even knowledge—is always situated. A sign does not indicate anything if it doesn't enter into the experience of an interpreter. A tree that falls in a forest when no one is around may make sound waves, but those waves would be meaningless without someone (or something sentient) to interpret them.[126] In this way, the proximity of the interpretant to the sign, the method through which the sign appears, the perceptual system that makes it available, and the conditions that allow for the sign to appear against its background are all essential concerns in understanding any given example of semiosis. Poststructuralist theory invited scholars to imagine a system of meaning apart from the conditions of its instantiation. A situated approach reminds us that the "for whom" question cannot be overlooked (even if materialized signs travel and so have the potential to be read differently in different situations).

Taken together, this gives us a much better starting point for our semiotics. It was not that poststructuralists were ignorant of Peirce. They sometimes granted that there were icons and indexes; they were just rarely interested in them. Instead, they were mostly absorbed by the particular ways in which we are "condemned" to communicate in symbolic language. But, as I have been arguing, we are not so condemned. Not that there is a way out of hermeneutic mediation, but symbolic language is not our only interaction with the world, it is not even our only semiotic interaction with the world, nor are we the only creatures engaged in semiotic communication—the natural world is vibrantly semiotic.

.

Hylosemiotics reformulates Peirce's basic insight in terms of "sentient beings," which we will provisionally describe as beings capable of perceiving and thus capable of acting as interpretants of signs.[127] Historically, the European philosophical tradition has generally seen humans as the sole entities with sentience or consciousness. But recent work in philosophy, biology, and cognitive science has increasingly provided reasons we might want to think of sentience as a continuum that includes at least all biological entities and perhaps more.[128] To be clear, we do not want to say that all beings have the same kind of consciousness or degree of subjectivity.

"Sentient beings" are any beings that have the capacity to respond to signs. This includes not just animals but also plants, bacteria, fungi, enzymes, and perhaps even some information-processing machines like computers. At minimum, I agree with Daniel Dennett's assertion that it is explanatorily valuable to reconstruct the behavior of certain entities (including, in his account, software) *as if* they had minds capable of making decisions and formulating intentions.[129] In the metamodernist lingo, this means treating animals and some machines as if they were sign-processing or semiotic entities.[130] While my brother and I are actually committed to a more robust ontological claim about the diversity of sentience, readers skeptical of nonhuman or animal consciousness are welcome to take our reference to sentient beings as a practical postulate on the level of Dennett's "intentional stance." The following pages will show the value of including sentient beings in our discussion of semiotics.

To underscore how hylosemiotics is different from New Materialism,

I want to make sure that you know the following. Hylosemiotics departs from the New Materialist account of agency. If all that it means for a stone to have "agency" is that it exists, then the statement is empty. Some entities have the capacity to make choices and others do not. We also do not mean semiotics as a metaphor. Not every interaction is an interpretation. To be sure, causation and meaning are related, but they are not identical. The mountain doesn't interpret the rock if the mountain has no ability to choose how to react.

Expanding Peirce's typology to include sentient beings necessitates a fundamental alteration in his basic taxonomy of signs. At the outset, rather than thinking in terms of different classifications or types of signs, it is better to think in terms of "aspects of signs" insofar as a given sign may exhibit more than one aspect.[131] Certain kinds of signs might even be thought of as on a continuum or gradient between different sign-aspects. That said, as a preliminary set of sign-aspects we'd like to propose, on a higher level, voluntary vs. involuntary signs, followed by: 1) *symbol*, 2) *icon*, 3) *index* (with subtype *self-sign*), and 4) *correlation* (with *symptom* as a subtype). This section explores these different sign-aspects and shows how they are relevant to more than human communication.

First, on a higher level (as noted repeatedly above), it is useful to make an initial distinction between *voluntary* and *involuntary* signs. This represents a scalar spectrum between signs consciously emitted by a sentient being and accidental signs either emitted unconsciously by a sentient being or produced by the non-sentient world. Panpsychists, monists, and New Materialists invested in the consciousness of matter might want to think of this as a distinction between consciously and unconsciously sent signs. Even if crystals are conscious (which I doubt), they presumably emit some sparkles by accident. The upshot is that voluntary signs can also be analyzed in terms of intention. In this respect they are different from involuntary signs, but as will be argued, the reception of both voluntary and involuntary signs can be approached in Peircean terms.

·

Symbol. Insofar as the symbol, as an arbitrarily embodied sign, is the only sign-aspect shared by both Saussurean and Peircean semiotics, it might be surprising that symbols are not the sole providence of the human world. A cat twitching its tail to communicate hostility is an example of a symbol because, as in a Saussurean sign, the connection between tail movement and emotion is purely conventional.[132] The motion itself does not bear any direct relationship to the emotion expressed. Likewise, when acacia trees are in the process of being eaten by giraffes, they release a warning blast of ethylene gas that causes neighboring trees of the same species to push animal-specific toxins into their leaves to deter further grazing, thereby protecting the local tree population.[133] Ethylene gas has no specific relationship to foraging herbivores, so its connection is arbitrary. When early automated guided vehicles used red magnetic tape embedded in the floor or attached to objects as location cues, they were translating arbitrary magnetic codes into information about their current position. Japanese snow monkeys issue different alarm calls for different kinds of predators such as snakes or ravens, but the calls themselves are arbitrary and not imitative of those predators.

Icon. As noted above, many signs share a likeness with the thing they represent. To be clear, I have been arguing throughout this book that similarity is not absolute but task dependent (e.g., sorting blocks by color the red ones are more similar; sorting blocks by shape the round ones are more similar). Hence, likeness or similarity exists on a sliding scale and according to particular task or interpretive frame. But it is not mere convention.

For instance, on one extreme of likeness, a forged copy of van Gogh's "Starry Night" gains its meaning by way of fidelity to the colors and textures of the original. But we could imagine this on a sliding scale leading through poster copies of "Starry Night" to parody sketches of "Starry Night." In each case, the object in question gains some of its meaning by way of specific sorts of similarity as well as specific kinds of difference. Icons suggest problems for a thoroughly arbitrary account of signs. For example, photography, even when highly conventionalized, still suggests that photographs are capable of exhibiting at least some non-arbitrary relationship to the subject they depict. Indeed, research suggests that one need not be socialized to be able to identify particular people from their photographs. Even pigeons recognize photographs of familiar human faces.[134]

Iconic relationships do not have to be visual. A recorded voice bears an iconic relationship to the original utterance. Likewise, we might think of maps, anatomical diagrams, and so on as examples of dominantly iconic signs. By way of another example, think of a continuum between a three-dimensional photographic and topographic representation of a landscape (say, produced by a drone) leading through increasing abstraction or stylization until it becomes a conventional road map. Again, there are aspects of convention or symbolization in maps and diagrams, but they gain much of their meaning from task dependent relations of likeness.

The human world is not alone in producing icons. A chameleon changing its skin color and patterning to match that of the leaf on which it is perched is an *icon* because it has a non-arbitrary resemblance to the leaf depicted. It is also clearly communicative since chameleons change their colors to respond to the visual capabilities of the predator they are worried about at a given moment. As signs go, a chameleon changing its color might be thought of as a type of lie because it is an attempt to mislead predators.[135] But the lie only works if the chameleon is capable of adopting a similarity vis-à-vis the predator's perceptual sorting process. Much of camouflage functions this way. Think of Batesian mimicry, in which an animal evolves to copy the color patterns of another toxic species, as another example of iconicity. The coloring of *Papilio polytes* butterflies is iconic insofar as they have evolved to copy the aposematic warning coloring of *Byasa alcinous* butterflies in order to deter predators.[136] Smells can also be iconic. There are orchids that are capable of emitting a fragrance that mimics a female fly's sexual scent in order to attract male flies searching for mates and trick them into coming into contact with the orchid's pollen.[137] Again, this is an example of iconic or non-arbitrary signage.

Peirce's account of index included both signs indicating location and those indicating a causal correlation or conjunction. Although location-indicating and causally correlated signs often co-occur, there are plenty of reasons we might want to distinguish them, and this has caused subsequent confusion among later semioticians who use the term "index" for both functions. For that reason, we will parse this notion into two different sign-aspects—indexical and correlational.

Indexical refers to sign-aspects that reference, point to, or indicate location in space and/or time. Already in his famous *Confessions*, Augustine proposed that early childhood language acquisition involved indexical reference, suggesting that we learn the meaning of words when adults make a sound and point to something in the world.[138] Although that model has been criticized by some later philosophers, contemporary research in developmental psychology has emphasized the importance of pointing for early language, so perhaps Augustine was on to something.[139] Looking at all of this from the vantage of hylosemiotics, we want to emphasize that there are ways in which an act of indexical reference includes multiple sign components—the pointing gesture itself and whatever is being pointed at. If I tap your chest and say "you," then my finger, my words, and your physical body make up the sign insofar as they are all components that need to be observed in order to recognize the sign's meaning.[140]

Other examples of indexical semiosis would include the howl of a wolf, which communicates an animal's current location to packmates and rivals; and also the "waggle dance" of honeybees, which is used to indicate the direction and distance from the hive to a particular food source.[141] Equally, the *beep* of a microwave that indicates that it has finished heating something is an indexical, even though we normally think of its meaning differently. Computer programming languages make use of indexing all the time.[142] For example, arrays in C store data together under a particular variable name that can be retrieved by a pointer. A stop sign gets some of its meaning by suggesting the location at which one is supposed to stop.

Self-signs (the term comes from Millikan) might be thought of as a subtype of the index. These are aspects of signs whose primary function is self-reference.[143] Self-signs function like names or identifiers. For instance, the label on a coffee mug that says "coffee mug" or the outside packaging color of a highlighter that indicates the color of the ink are also self-signs. When I introduce myself, especially if you have already heard of me, by saying "I am 'Professor Storm,'" I am producing a self-sign; or if you humorously reenact how you knocked over my coffee mug, then you are standing in for your previous self as a self-sign. One central component of humpback whale songs seems to be signature information that identifies the individual whale.[144] Male great tit birds (*Parus major*) also seem to emit self-identification information as part of their tunes.[145]

Correlational is meant to capture the aspect of signs which suggest a non-accidental, causal correlation between the signifier and the signified.[146] (Here we are departing from Peirce's conflation of both cause and reference under index.) Correlational signs have degrees of strength depending on the strength of the correlation they indicate.[147] By way of example, dark clouds are correlated with precipitation because clouds get denser and more opaque the more water and ice droplets they accumulate. When you see a dark cloud, it means that it might rain soon. Knowledge of the actual causal mechanism in question is not necessary for a sign to suggest a correlation, but understanding causation permits a better appraisal of signal strength. Correlational signs do not have to be future-oriented. If you step out of a café and see that the ground is covered in droplets of water, those droplets function as a correlational sign that indicates that it has probably just rained (admittedly with weak strength, however, as a storeowner may just have washed down the sidewalk).

Humans are not the only animals that track correlational signs. The odor of butyric acid is a correlational sign ticks use to detect the likely presence of a mammal—information that they use in combination with their sensitivity to temperature as part of how they decide to attach themselves to a host.[148] As these examples illustrate (and as will be discussed in greater detail in the account in chapter 6 of abductive inference), such correlational signs can reinforce each other, and in that respect can be mutually strengthening.

Correlational signs are necessarily situated. Hence, their meaning emerges in relationship to their *indexical* sign-aspects. A certain kind of tracks might be correlated with the presence of gophers in one geographic range, while roughly the same type of tracks might indicate ground squirrels in another region.[149] In this respect, a correlational sign needs to be interpreted contextually in order to make sense. It will turn out that much of meaning actually includes and requires the specification of context. A friend looking out the window and saying "it's raining" might be a correlational sign insofar as my friend mostly says it is raining only when it is in fact raining. But crucially, a particular utterance of "it is raining" takes its meaning in part from the physical context of a place and time where it is supposed to be precipitating. To reference another sign-aspect, it should be noted that even conventional symbols like the name "Athena" indicate a particular person only once the proper local context has been specified.

The *symptom* is a subclass of correlational signs that indicate the presence of a disorder. The inclusion of the symptom is a gesture to the very beginnings of semiotics. The Greek physician Hippocrates first articulated "semeiotics" as a medical specialization focused on uncovering symptoms *sēmeion* (σημεῖον), literally "marks, signs, or tokens" that stand for something other than themselves.[150] For instance, a bull's-eye rash is a symptom or correlational sign that indicates a likelihood of Lyme disease, while excessive salivation combined with abnormal aggression are signs that together correlate with the presence of rabies. Nor are biological entities the only things that exhibit symptoms. The presence of unexpected pop-up windows and slow performance of a computer are symptoms of a computer virus, while a grinding noise in a vehicle might be evidence of worn brakes.[151]

This list of sign-aspects is not meant to be exhaustive. Again I want to remind us, against the partisans of "natural information," that a given token is only a particular sign for a particular interpretant and for a particular purpose. The same chirping cricket might cause one listener to infer external temperature (correlational sign) while another listener might merely have the idea that there are crickets about (indexical sign). Future work will also expand on the notion of sign-vehicles and trace the way that different sense faculties and media affect the transmission or interpretation of different sign-aspects. But they suggest different ways in which meaning can be inferred from the environment and provide a preliminary set of tools for hylosemiotics.

5.6 The Mind Turned Inside Out

The picture of human beings as having . . . both an "inside" and an "outside" is so commonplace, so (as it may seem to us) commonsensical, that we find it hard to realize how strikingly modern it is.

GARETH MATTHEWS, "Consciousness and Life"

Richard Rorty argued in *Philosophy and the Mirror of Nature* that much of the history of post-Cartesian philosophy has presumed a binary opposition between an immaterial mind and a material world, which has often been transposed onto a mind-and-body dualism. Rorty suggests that given this presumptive framework, the thinking subject is typically portrayed as a phantasmal homunculus looking outward from inside the cave of the brain toward an external world. Philosophy has hence been trapped in a particular orientation to the problem of knowledge which assumes: "To know is to represent accurately what is outside the mind; so to understand the possibility and nature of knowledge is to understand the way in which the mind is able to construct such representations."[152]

Rorty criticizes this philosophical orientation, asking: What makes us think that consciousness, thoughts, emotions, and pains all belong in the mind and not the body? Why do we think that mental events lack extension and are immaterial? For instance, why do we treat a stomach-ache as a physical bodily sensation, while imagining that dreams and beliefs are purely mental phenomena?

There is not space here to evaluate Rorty's arguments fully. In general, my sense is that he leaves out numerous counterexamples, and the critique is more worthwhile than the proposed alternatives. But he gets at least one important thing right: many philosophers have taken for granted an opposition between the mental and the physical, and consequently have imagined representation as a product of human minds. Not that these philosophers have historically been ignorant of the representational function of art or language; rather, they have presumed that "aboutness" requires the activity of a conscious human subject. Thus, as discussed in an earlier chapter, they have often given unwarranted weight to half-skeptical thought experiments that sow doubt about an external world without doubting their own presuppositions. Even more significantly, most poststructuralism is basically a retooling of this dualism in a skeptical key, with language taking the place of thought.

Hylosemiotics has suggested that there is something misleading about a dualism between object and representation, or mind and external world. This section explores some of the implications of overturning this dualism in the latter formulation and inverting standard notions of a mental inside and a physical outside. In brief, we argue that subject and object, mind and body, are interdependent.

At first pass it is worth emphasizing that the universe—or at least the sentient constituents of it—comes to know itself through hermeneutic mediation. Put more personally, we come to know—and even become— ourselves through interacting with the world.[153] You would not be able to recognize your own face if you had never seen it mirrored in a reflective surface or photographed. We come to self-consciousness in part by being mirrored literally or in the eyes of others.[154] When we clasp our own hands together we experience ourselves as both subject and object. We learn what it is like to both touch and be touched. [155] Moreover, in very basic ways, we are permeable, such that with every breath and every meal we are constantly exchanging matter with our surroundings.[156] All of this should begin to put pressure on the commonsense bifurcation between mental inside and physical outside.

To follow this thread further, thinking relies on the physical world. Philosophers, cognitive scientists, and anthropologists working on subfields known variously as extended cognition, active externalism, cognition in the wild, a materialist epidemiology of beliefs, ecological psychology, the embodied mind, or social ontology have in their own respective idioms often converged on a set of three main insights about human thought processes that I'd like to discuss in relationship to the rest of the sentient world.

First, *knowledge emerges from the exploratory manipulation of the physical world*. We come into being not as disembodied consciousnesses or homunculi looking outward through a window onto existence, but as actively embodied and situated agents.[157] This can be illustrated with a widely repeated anecdote about artificial intelligence research. Early programmers assumed that they could get a computer to model its environment by feeding it data from a video camera. But raw visual data turned out to be nearly impossible for the computer to process usefully. Vision alone was too ambiguous. A model of the world seemed to be required *before* the computer could interpret what it saw. This was known as the "problem of underdetermination."[158] But humans process exceptionally complex visual data effortlessly. At first, the response to this disconnect was to assume that we come preloaded with something like a world-model; but research from developmental psychology suggested that while infants are not completely blank slates, most of their early knowledge of the world comes from dynamically interacting with it.[159] This led a group of cognitive scientists to replace the notion that learning occurs by building models abstracted from sense-data with a model of learning that presupposes a direct connection between sensing and acting. In their metaphor "the brain [functions primarily] as a controller, not as a model-builder."[160] In sum, knowledge and action are fundamentally intertwined.

As Rodney Brooks famously put it, "the world is its own best model."[161] We learn by going into the world and interacting with it, rather than passively spectating it. An infant learns about a wooden block by touching it, tasting it, banging it onto the desk to see what sound it makes, and looking at it from all different sides. Through thousands of interactions like these, a child begins to develop a sense of her world and an awareness of herself as part of it. (Much of what we call animal play seems to be exploratory manipulation in a similar sense.)[162]

We also do not choose our perceptions. We cannot choose what we see, only how we interpret it. There are myriad limitations on interpretation, too. In the vocabulary of environmental psychology, perception is about producing an agent–world "coupling" with the purpose of discovering "affordances," namely "the possibilities for action that a particular object permits a particular agent."[163] Sometimes this coupling is sufficiently robust that we come to have a phenomenological sense of the object, as if it were part of us. For example: when a skilled surgeon comes to feel that a knife is like a secondary finger; when an expert driver comes to identify with their automobile such that it feels like an extension of their own body; or when a person with a prosthetic limb develops extended proprioception or the ability to perceive what the limb touches.[164] This coupling is a bidirectional, interdependent relationship between agent and object. It functions rather like a feedback loop in which a sentient agent interacts with their environment and is shaped by it in turn.

In another legendary example from the early days of cybernetics, Herbert Simon suggested that an ant takes a complex path across a sandy beach not because the ant is plotting a complex course in its head, but because the environment it is traversing is itself complicated. In this account the world itself contains complex information.[165] This means that much of the physical world does not have to be modeled inside the cognitive structures of a sentient being because the world is already there to be interacted with.

To put it in terms of meaning, I cannot properly distinguish between beech trees and birch trees, but nonetheless I can have a totally coherent conversation about both species. A sailor could mistakenly think a whale was a coldblooded fish and still have no problem tracking it. As Hilary Putnam observed, this is partially about the way meaning functions indexically.[166] We can refer to things without understanding them. As noted above, I have disagreements with Putnam, but I think he is right that we can get by not really understanding our references because the world is doing some of the work for us. A sailor does not need to know very much about a whale in order to be able to interact with it, because the whale itself necessarily has at least a limited role in that interaction.

Second, *matter (and energy) are used to store information and alter cognitive complexity*. For our purposes, one of the key insights of early Soviet psychology was that memory is not only stored in our brains, but that humans are capable of extending "the operation of memory beyond the biological dimensions of the human nervous system and permit[ing] it to incorporate artificial, or self-generated, stimuli," namely in the production of "signs."[167] Early shepherds made tally marks on sticks to keep track of the number of sheep in their flocks. An older generation tied strings around their fingers as a way to jog memory. Desk calendars help administrators keep track of appointments. Pill boxes remind people to take their medications and help them keep track of how many tablets to take. Ants leave scent trails that they use to find their way back to the nest and to lead others to a food source. All of these are examples of externalized memory produced via material signs.[168]

The most obvious example of this phenomenon is writing itself. More than two thousand years ago, Plato's *Phaedrus* provided an account of the invention of writing and suggested that people "will not practice using their memory because they will put their trust in writing, which is external and depends on signs that belong to others, instead of trying to remember from the inside, completely on their own."[169] For Plato it would seem that the externalization of memory is a kind of forgetting or loss of knowledge. He would be disturbed to know that this trend has continued in the age of the machine. We no longer remember telephone numbers; we have our phones remember them for us.[170] We don't just offload information to objects. Our conscious mind offloads (or perhaps embeds) habits, which then no longer require conscious attention (e.g., playing guitar, learning to walk or drive). That said, however, for as far back as we can reconstruct, humans have been externalizing our memory; and rather than thinking of them exclusively in terms of new forms of cognitive alienation, we might best imagine writing and attendant computer technologies as distinct phases in offloading particular memory functions.

But it is not merely memory that we externalize; we use our external world to alter the cognitive complexity of specific tasks.[171] For instance, to reduce the complexity of a mathematical problem we count on our fingers or write out a formula on the blackboard. A nautical slide rule makes navigation easier because much of the computation is actually being done by the artifact itself.[172] Airports have developed intricate physical systems to reduce the cognitive demands of air traffic control.[173] Submarines are designed to divide cognitive labor by assigning different measurement gauges and controls to different individuals. In this respect, materialized signs can permit solutions to more demanding cognitive problems by facilitating coordinated and distributed cognition.

Third, *public semiosis permits collective representations*. As noted above, perception can be thought of as interactive, dynamical feedback that results in the coupling of agent and environment. But it is not just non-humans we encounter in this manner. By producing public representations—which necessitate their materialization even if only in terms of sound waves—individuals can engage in "dialogical coupling."[174] Succinctly put, we learn to "think together" by bouncing ideas off of each other, commenting on each other's writing, working together on a blackboard, or grabbing our guitars and jamming together. For humans, like other social animals, the production and consumption of signs is part of a process of coordination or synchronization between different individuals. Although there are many reasons to be cautious about the interpretation of fMRI data, preliminary neuroscience research suggests that telling stories can produce coupling or mirrored brain activity in speakers and listeners.[175] All that is to say, while we rarely perfectly converge on shared collective representations, much of the anxiety about the impossibility of communication seems overblown.

This has important implications for how we conventionally construe the relationship between private and public concepts. For instance, many scholars tend toward presumptions about the formation of concepts that echo the classical empiricism of John Locke. Basically, they assume that we come to form concepts based on our experiences, and that our experiences of simple objects lead toward our understanding of increasingly complex concepts. We learn what an "orange" is, then we learn what "juice" is, and eventually we can combine them into a reliable concept of "orange juice" and other fruit juices. This contributes to the sense that the most basic level of concepts occurs in the form of private thoughts. This idea has something going for it insofar as thinking seems to precede language and many of our individually experienced memories and ideas are never communicated.[176] But there are reasons to think of public concepts or public representations as the more basic level.[177]

From the very moment a child is born, she is bombarded with public concepts as materialized signs. An infant's first contact with orange juice is likely to be accompanied by parental explanations, even if she is too young to comprehend them fully. Instead of being isolated thinkers who come to acquire concepts through a process of philosophical meditation, we gain our categories and even our basic understandings of the world through the consumption and interpretation of already materialized signs (both human and nonhuman in origin).

This has straightforward implications for disciplines in the human sciences, because we are often interested in understanding the homogeneity or heterogeneity of macro-human phenomena—a.k.a. culture or society. One might ask: what is it that members of a given "culture" share? We have to avoid two different extremes. On the one hand, as the example above suggests, our ideas of the world are not formed in isolation and thus are not completely idiosyncratic (insofar as we are both using the expression "orange juice" and we don't mean completely different things).

On the other hand, it would be an equally grave error to become trapped in an immaterial approach to the subject and assume that everyone in a given culture shares identical concepts. A naive version of this is Richard Dawkins's notion of "memes" as idea viruses that copy themselves from mind to mind. As noted in chapter 3, cultural transmission is a process that involves not perfect copying, but rather constant change. The hylo-semiotic approach, on the other hand, permits us to see that members of a "culture" do not share identical concepts, but they often formulate their private concepts in reference to similar or shared materialized signs. This recognition permits much greater specificity for an analysis of culture, which is no longer constructed in terms of diffuse shared representations, but can be reconceived as the result of concrete interactions and material vectors.

Public representations have more than a communicative function. Material objects necessarily play a role in mediating social relations, for instance by marshalling powerful emotions (think propaganda), inspiring desires (think advertising), enforcing power (think guns), and establishing dominance hierarchies (think commodity accumulation).[178] This is true of both human and many nonhuman social worlds. When we think of human collectives, we need to not overlook the material objects that form part of their ligature (e.g., Starbucks is not just a group of people but a collective that includes financial capital, buildings, espresso machines, pounds of roasted coffee, and so on). As discussed in chapter 4, material signs are part of our social life and indeed might be thought of as key components of the social. [179] You can find this insight communicated with sophistication and force in the writings of Arjun Appudarai and company, and it can easily come across as one of the key benefits of a New Materialist analysis.[180] But you can also find it in Marx, where it counted as a central claim of the old-fashioned dialectical materialism; and indeed, the social function of objects can be found in the classical sociological theorist Emile Durkheim.[181] I say this not to knock the broader insight in any way, but merely to locate it in its longer historical trajectory. Also, it is worth underscoring the intervention I made above that not all matter is relevant to a given social relation—what is relevant is the semiotic component or materialized sign-aspect.

In summary, hylosemiotics permits us to turn the mind inside out, and in so doing to see three broad and concrete ways in which what has previously been understood as private mental life is externally realized. First, knowledge does not come primarily from introspection, nor is the mind like some kind of homunculus looking outward from the windows of the eyes; rather, knowledge emerges from the exploratory manipulation of the physical world. Body and mind co-arise interdependently. We learn by going into the world and interacting with it. This means we can rely on the complexities of the world to do some of the work for us, including (to some extent) problems of reference and complexity. This will be discussed in more detail in chapter 6. Second, we use matter to store information and alter cognitive complexity. We physically encode memory in writing and images. We make marks on objects to keep track of them or to count better. We build tools so that the objects themselves do some of the thinking for us. Digital computers are only the latest phase in a long history of humans offloading different kinds mental processes into our built environment. Third, the public creation of signs is part of what makes collective representations possible. The social world is composed of materialized signs. We share concepts to the extent that we do in good part because of common reference to public representations.

5.7 Conclusion: A Light in the Abyss

If I were as eloquent as Demosthenes I would need to do nothing more than repeat a single phrase three times: reason is language, λόγος. *I gnaw at this marrow-bone and I will gnaw myself to death over it. There still remains a darkness over this depth for me. I am still waiting for an apocalyptic angel with a key to this abyss.*

J.G. HAMANN, Letter to J.G. Herder, August 6, 1784

Reason is language—this was Johann Hamann's provocative and prescient suspicion. Although it comes from a letter written by Kant's famous "frenemy" more than two hundred years ago, it seems no less relevant today. According to some accounts, postmodernism, by reducing philosophy to the level of language and then disrupting the old economy of the sign and the possibility of linguistic structure, has hastened the disintegration of meaning itself. Knowledge is nothing more than language games and the production of power, while words have been unmoored from their referents and texts have vanished behind a maze of infinite interpretations.[182]

But this chapter has been working to turn inside out the linguistic skepticism that defined much of poststructuralist thought. The problem with the "linguistic turn" was that it did not go far enough. In secondhand formulations, scholars imagined that the world was constructed out of discourse, but they overlooked the conjoining insight that discourse was constructed out of the world.

Hamann too got things backward. It is not that reason is merely language, but rather that language is "reason." Or at least language is one of our ways of coming to understand and interpret our environment. Language is imperfect, fallible, flawed. Different languages focus attention on different features of the world. We all must cultivate a greater reflexivity about the limitations and biases of linguistic categories. But we are not imprisoned in our grammars. We are capable of nonlinguistic thought. Language is a tool. It is like a net to catch fish. We should not mistake it for the fish, but we do not need to jettison the net. Heidegger was right that Being is hermeneutics, but he was wrong about what that implied. Humans do not possess an inborn lack necessitating a search for meaning and exiling us from nature to a dark abyss. Rather, to be a sentient being is to be interwoven with an environment. We are all part of a cosmos that attempts to know itself.

In sum, we live in a world of signs—and humans (and other animals) respond to those signs in manifold ways, semiotically but not just symbolically. We need to move past a postmodern semiotics that sees us imprisoned in our linguistic categories. Instead, I have been arguing, there is significant benefit to be gained from embracing what amounts to a metamodern semiotics or hylosemiotics.

To frame the project differently, in linguistics and philosophy of language there has been a strong incentive to treat meaning as separate from metaphysics or ontology. Disciplinary specialization has often encouraged theorists to bracket out the world when coming up with their theories of language. Although extensional semantics tried to do something different by way of conjoined notions of reference and natural kinds, even philosophers of such were still generally stuck on a notion of the autonomy of language as a specifically human endeavor. While I am sure there is a lot of work to be done by specialists in modifying the insights articulated here, I hope that this chapter demonstrates the value of nonspecialists attempting to take up language, metaphysics, and the findings of biology (especially animal ethology) together. That humans can read, something we cannot have been selected for evolutionarily, suggests that our ability to apprehend and interpret signs is rooted in something more fundamental. As I have been arguing, sentient beings are semiotic beings.

I have also been arguing that many of the functions classical empiricists suggested were the sole province of the human mind are better thought of as emerging in dynamical relationship to our environment or as a materialized semiotics. We come to know ourselves via interaction with the world. We store memories outside our bodies. Much of our mental capacity, since at least the earliest proto-human began marking its environment, has been aided by our ability to offload cognitive complexity. We come to at least partially share public concepts, sentiments, and social presumptions. Rather than conceiving of epistemology in terms of an isolated thinker coming to know the universe, we might instead think of the universe coming to know us.

Thus far I have been aiming to show that there are more productive notions of discourse than those inherited from Saussure. My brother and I agree that a Peircean semiotics is a better starting point for understanding the relationship between discourse and the world. It is possible to formulate a nonhuman semiotics that includes a wider notion of sign-producing and -receiving entities. If we focus on the materialization of the mental, we are able to turn the mind inside out. I hope we have also suggested some productive tools for an analysis of culture and sign relations.

This directly benefits those of us in the human sciences, because the mind turned inside out is amenable to study. Moreover, although they are often interwoven, we can distinguish between meaning-producing *semiosis* and meaning-receiving *semiotics* or *hermeneutics*. As I argued in chapter 1, while the first is social construction, the second need not be (meaning can come from something that was not produced to provide meaning).

To reiterate other insights from this chapter, speech is evanescent, and if you think of discourse in terms of the spoken word, then language might seem to be immaterial and perhaps even outside of or separate from the world. But looked at from the vantage of monkey calls and indications of rain, we can see that the world is richly semiotic. We are constantly reading or interpreting the world. Every sign is only available to us because it has been materialized, even if only in the eardrum's vibrations from incoming sound waves. Indeed, even dualists must grant that we can only get to the physical by way of the mental, and we can only get to the mental by way of the physical. Moreover, many of the questions we want to ask in the human sciences are about the beliefs and attitudes of other people, but we only get to access these beliefs when they have been externalized in the physical world.

Translation is possible. Every argument for the impossibility of translation has to either forgo examples or undermine its own ambitions. Although future generations may find it hard to reconstruct why translation was thought to be beyond the bounds of possibility, this self-defeating dogma has underpinned vast swathes of human sciences—from anthropology to literary studies to skeptical philosophy of science. To provide one last example, when Thomas Kuhn wanted to demonstrate the incommensurability of scientific paradigms, he did so by comparing accounts of *phlogiston* and oxygen and in that respect rendering them commensurable.[183] Kuhn thus undercuts his grand argument that one paradigm cannot be translated either into another one or into a neutral third point of view. Paradigms can be and often are compared, even by the same theo-

206 : CHAPTER 5

rists who reject their commensurability.[184] In summary, while every translation is an interpretation, not every interpretation is equally valid.

Meaning is inference. We interpret both voluntary and involuntary signs. To be interpretable, signs have to be physically instantiated. Our ability to process language evolved from our ability to perceive the environment. Sentient beings apprehend the world and each other semiotically. There is no such thing as objective information, because involuntary signs generate different kinds of interferences in different contexts. Words are tools, but they don't function (or mean) on their own. Voluntary signs are ostensive inferential signals meant to affect perceivers' actions and to focus their attention on the inferences the producer of the sign wishes to express. Apprehending the meaning of an utterance often requires reconstructing the purposes behind its creation. Although there is more to meaning than reference, coordinating reference is a crucial part of communication in part because we do not share mental representations, nor do we share ways of tracking property-clusters. In that respect, references are at best functionally overlapping (or co-referring), but are rarely identical. Perceivers tend to assume the interpretation of voluntary signs that maximizes relevance. Voluntary signs are social kinds. Miscommunications often derive from differing background presuppositions and the high entropic nature of social kinds. Intentional meaning is crucial to communication, but we perceive much more than intentional meaning.

•

If this were merely a work of social science the whole monograph might have ended here. But it would have left unaddressed the thorniest knot of postmodernism—namely, the relationship between knowledge and value, skepticism and cynicism. It seemed less useful to me to articulate an entire system of social kinds and semiotics, only to have it scoffed at on the grounds that all knowledge itself is merely a mask thrown over domination, or the like. What follows sets us up to explore the value of knowledge and then advance our knowledge of value.

PART IV: KNOWLEDGE AND VALUE

6: Zetetic Knowledge

The game of doubting itself presupposes certainty. . . . A doubt that doubted everything would not be a doubt.

WITTGENSTEIN, *On Certainty*

Postmodernism is regularly identified with the claim that nothing can be known.[1] The association between postmodernism and deep-seated skepticism goes back in part to Jean-François Lyotard, who characterized the postmodern condition in terms of "an internal erosion of the legitimacy principle of knowledge."[2] But similar views have been expounded by other theorists.[3] Indeed, critic after critic has accused postmodernism of being a corrosive form of indiscriminate doubt.[4] Although occasionally particular types of skepticism heave into view, time and again postmodernism is equated with a generalized "loss of certainty."[5] These charges have if anything been amplified in recent years, and one now routinely comes across the assertion that postmodern skeptics ruined the humanities and ushered in post-truth politics.[6]

But the actual history is rather different. To sketch its broad trajectory, the first wave of postmodernism was indeed imported into the Anglo-American academy as a type of skepticism, as various interpreters mobilized the most skeptical elements of the canon of postmodern thinkers to the exclusion of their non-skeptical positions. In the second wave, experts—sometimes including the canonized thinkers themselves—attempted to correct the caricature of a postmodernism that rejected all knowledge. Nonetheless, because it was these very interlocking negative doxa that many scholars and students found most evocative, postmodernism continued to live on precisely as a cognomen for the skepticism and anti-truth cynicism its original authors and importers had repudiated.

The end result is that while theorist after theorist deploys the most skeptical pieces of Foucault and company, we also have quote after quote of these same theorists explicitly and repeatedly denying that they are skeptics. Let me provide a few examples.

Michel Foucault's critical genealogies and writings on the relationship between power and knowledge were often mobilized toward skeptical ends. Aware of his reputation, Foucault commented that "as far as the general public is concerned, I am the guy who said that knowledge merged with power, that it was no more than a thin mask thrown over the structures of domination," and he has often been read on these grounds.[7] But Foucault also repudiated this misunderstanding, which he characterized as "so absurd as to be laughable," adding that "if I had said, or meant, that knowledge was power, I would have said so."[8] At the very least, this suggests Foucault's account of power-knowledge was not supposed to terminate in the particular skeptical positions with which he is regularly misidentified.[9]

Early in Jacques Derrida's Anglo-American reception he was characterized as a "pure enough skeptic to make no positive [truth] claims at all," and thus deconstruction was widely identified with a cynical rejection of the possibility of truth.[10] But Derrida himself also explicitly rejected this view, stating that "deconstruction" does not amount to "skepticism, empiricism, [or] even nihilism" and that "the value of truth . . . is never contested or destroyed in my writings, but only reinscribed in more powerful, larger, more stratified contexts."[11] Nonetheless, even today some scholars continue to suggest that Derrida argued that knowledge is impossible because there is always room for potential doubt.[12] Hence, in much of the secondary literature, deconstruction is treated as the universalized skepticism that Derrida would seem to have repudiated.

By way of a last example, Bruno Latour's writings have undergone a significant shift in emphasis, if not view. Early in his career, Latour called for a "new skepticism" and argued that "there is no scale of knowledge and, in the end, no knowledge at all."[13] But starting in the early 2000s, Latour began asking if "critique had run out of steam" and arguing "that a certain form of critical spirit has sent us down the wrong path. . . . The question was never to get *away* from facts but *closer* to them, not fighting empiricism but, on the contrary, renewing empiricism."[14] Thus, one can find in his writings (and among his followers) both skeptical and anti-skeptical positions.

All that is to say, if postmodernism was not primarily generalized skepticism, there was nevertheless a reality to the appearance. Rampant forms of cynicism are on display throughout the academy, if often in decontextualized excerpts, the writing of lesser-known scholars, and echoed in classrooms across the country. Looked at this way, the human sciences include both the partisans of "cynical reason" and their putative enemies, who rarely engage in depth with the actual philosophical problematics of the "postmodernism" they criticize.[15] But Enlightenment-boosters do this at their peril. Unaddressed skepticisms become buried landmines waiting to explode. So here I will aim to defuse them.

As noted in the introduction to this book, epistemology is often conflated with ethics and vice versa. This in turn encourages smuggling in value criticisms masked as appraisals of knowledge. While ethics and epistemology are clearly related when they become entangled, the problems they suggest can become knotted together to the point of indecipherability. Accordingly, this chapter begins from the suspicion that we need to provisionally separate purely epistemological issues from their normative variants and address the issues evoked by epistemological concerns independently. Values will return later.

On the epistemological register, I argue that the problem with postmodern (and, as it turns out, "enlightenment") skepticism is that it is not sufficiently radical. The issue is not that we doubt too much, but that we do not doubt enough. We fail to be skeptical about skepticism itself, when this is exactly where skeptical thought should lead us. The core philosophical confusion that generates both contemporary forms of skepticism and positivism is a mistaken notion of knowledge and an unproductive fixation on certainty. More concretely, in the pages that follow I argue that we should be skeptical of precisely those various forms of negative dogmatism that masquerade as skepticism, and that if we can bring ourselves to doubt the possibility of indubitable certainty and irrefutable epistemic foundations, many of the quandaries of skepticism will melt away, and we will be left with a new form of humble knowledge, which I call "Zeteticism."

But we will go further still. After establishing a foundation in antifoundationalist Zeteticism, the rest of the chapter takes us one step further and argues that a specific type of inference is particularly well-suited to the human sciences. It used to be thought that knowledge had to be produced either on the model of mathematics, by *deductively* reasoning from foundational premises, or by generalizing *inductively* from specific empirical examples, which was often supposed to be the model of the natural sciences. But as grand epistemological strategies, both deduction and induction have run aground in different ways. In contrast, this chapter argues for *abduction*, or inference to the best explanation, which provides a better model for both the human sciences and scientific inquiry in general.

6.1 Doubting Doubt

Nothing is completely immune from doubt. Any given sense impression could be distrusted as perhaps being the result of a dream, a mirage, a magical trick, a visual distortion, an optical illusion, a hallucination, a digital simulation, or a deception produced by a deceiving deity or an evil spirit.[16] You could even be a brain in a vat experiencing convincing phantom perceptions produced by means of cortex stimulations.[17] Thus, the senses can always be doubted.

Nor is *a priori* knowledge completely immune from skepticism. Your assumptions about basic mathematical statements such as "68+57=125" could also be wrong—a deceiving god could have warped your calculation; or you might be mistaken about the concept of addition or the meaning of the "+" sign; or, even if you are correct about the arithmetic, mathematics itself could turn out to be incomplete or inaccurate in some way we have not yet anticipated.[18] Logic itself might be inconsistent. Analytical truths could rest on unjustified presuppositions of synonymy.[19] Every argument for first principles must be based on prior principles, potentially either rendering those principles suspect or leading to infinite regress. Thus, at least in theory, no mathematical proof can be totally and unquestionably certain. In sum, both *a priori* axiomatic deduction and *a posteriori* empirical evidence are susceptible to doubt.

Despite his arguments to the contrary, even René Descartes's famous *cogito* "I think, therefore I am" can be doubted on several different grounds.[20] That thoughts necessitate a thinker can be questioned. That there *was* a thought is far from proving that there *will be* future thoughts, much less that there is a unitary mind thinking those thoughts. The existence of the "I" is not guaranteed. The more modest statement, "a thought happened," could even be doubted insofar as concepts of "thinking" or "occurring" might be muddled.[21] All in all, if you decided to doubt absolutely everything, you could not be certain about the meaning of the very concepts through which you thought those doubts into existence. As I'll elaborate, "doubt" itself can be doubted.[22]

So how can we avoid paralyzing doubt? It is not uncommon to blame Descartes for his incorrigible skepticism. But the truth is the exact opposite. Descartes was not a skeptic. The problem with his philosophy is *certainty*, not doubt. Although Descartes begins his famous *Meditations* with a discussion of "things that may be called into doubt," this skepticism was only a preparation for the grand quest for certitude. He was explicit about this. Descartes identified "all knowledge" with "certain and evident cognition" and he explained that "I was not imitating the skeptics, who doubt only for the sake of doubting . . . on the contrary, *my whole aim was towards certainty*."[23] Descartes's goal was not to encourage us to distrust our senses, but rather to produce rigorous and undeniable knowledge about an external world.[24] Indeed, except for a few brief pages at the start of *Meditations* and *Principles of Philosophy*, the vast bulk of his oeuvre aimed at describing the composition of the universe.[25] Descartes argued that certain knowledge was the only true form of knowledge, and alleged that he had found it in innate ideas. Yet, the more he wrote and dialogued with other philosophers, the more potential doubts Descartes had to address.

Insofar as they allowed Descartes to equate knowledge with indubitable certainty, subsequent philosophers have been repeatedly drawn back into doubt. Descartes set the standard for knowledge too high. Generations of philosophers' best efforts to ground knowledge only amplified potential doubts. In all fairness, there has been a lot of epistemology since — lots of other skepticisms and quasi-skepticisms: Pascal's, Bayle's, Hume's, Jacobi's, Hamann's, Schlegel's, Kant's unwitting skepticism (according to some), Nietzsche's, and the like. But many of these mobilize their doubt by showing that *certain* knowledge is impossible. This is because the search for irrefutable foundations is a misguided quest, doomed to failure. Many contemporary skepticisms are the inadvertent product of lost Cartesian certainty.

·

All that said, "postmodern skepticisms" have had a distinctive profile. For the last several decades, to be a skeptical academic has generally meant agreement with some subset of the following propositions: Essentialism is a kind of violence. Science is illegitimate or suspect. Scientific facts are constructed by extratheoretical interests. Knowledge is just an expression of power. Power is domination. No truth claims can be grounded. There are no facts, only interpretations. Every perspective is equally legitimate. All knowledge is relative to an individual's standpoint. If a term or concept was formulated in a colonial context, it must be false, and deploying it is a kind of violence. Classification is a form of conceptual imperialism. All binaries are violent hierarchies. Every system or structure is established on the grounds of something that it both excludes and presupposes. Concepts are fundamentally fraught. Every abstraction is a loss. Everything is discourse. Meaning is differential. Meaning is constantly deferred and can never be stabilized. Language determines thought. Being is always already before language. Philosophy is phallocentric or logocentric. Logic is merely the codification of heteronormative, white, male thinking. There are no more metanarratives. History is over. Knowledge is impossible.

A lot could be said about these claims. Some of them have more merit, others much less. Many of them are incompatible with each other. Some are in direct contradiction with themselves ("no truth claim can be grounded" is itself a truth claim). Different scholars assent to differing subsets of these claims, more or less self-consciously. Despite their fundamental incongruities, the way they are typically presented together makes them harder rather than easier to challenge. And so on. But my main point is something more basic—namely that, strictly speaking, none of these statements are in fact doubts. They are *declarations*, not uncertainties. This makes a difference because it suggests that the skeptical doxa of postmodernism we have come to believe in are themselves *not actually skepticisms*.

To elaborate, Sextus Empiricus begins *Outlines of Pyrrhonism*—the most important surviving work of classical Greek and Roman skepticism—by distinguishing between three groups of philosophers: Dogmatists (like Aristotle) who think they have discovered the truth, Negative Dogmatists (like the Academic Skeptics) who think that knowledge is impossible, and true Skeptics (such as Pyrrho) who suspend judgment and keep on investigating and doubting.[26] From Sextus' vantage, the problem with the Academic Skeptics is that those who confidently reject the possibility of knowledge are just as dogmatic as those who confidently assert that they have discovered the truth.[27] If a philosopher says that nothing can be known, then we can ask them whether they think they know this. Here is where negative dogmatists and profound doubters part ways. Incomplete skeptics say that the only thing we can know is that we cannot know, while thoroughgoing skeptics doubt even that. Consequently, self-referential skepticism leads not to the impossibility of knowledge, but to doubts about whether knowledge is possible.[28] In this respect, postmodern skeptical academics—like the Academic Skeptics Sextus criticized—are devoted to the various doxa of their incomplete skepticisms.

Sometimes, however, postmodernist skepticisms are articulated not as dogmas, but rather as methods—e.g., the hermeneutics of suspicion or genealogy.[29] These too can be made to double back on themselves. To hint at what this might look like: The hermeneutics of suspicion is directed at exposing a text's hidden agendas or unmasking its political unconscious. The central features of this hermeneutics' self-description are its novel insights and its rejection of easy answers. But as a hermeneutic it relies on rote strategies and prepackaged rhetoric, and its insights are anything but novel insofar as they typically presume the things they are looking to unmask (racism, sexism, neo-liberalism, etcetera) behind every text. Thus, we should be suspicious that the hermeneutics of suspicion is not sufficiently suspicious of itself.[30]

Similarly, one could perform a genealogy of genealogy (as indeed I do in greater detail elsewhere).[31] But in a nutshell, the striking thing about Foucault's account of genealogy is that it consistently emphasizes Nietzsche's *Zur Genealogie der Moral* as the source of this "genealogical" method. By privileging the origins of his attack on origins, Foucault might seem to be undermining his own efforts. But the real problem is that Foucault is not just giving his method a source, but effacing one insofar as the term "genealogy" itself had a long history of meaning—something like "pedigree or descent," often in the context of family or race, and later evoking Darwinian notions of evolution. Nietzsche himself seemed to have used it in this basically racializing sense. Moreover, as I demonstrate elsewhere, Foucault embraced "genealogy" as a term to obscure his own debt to structuralism, which he concealed by erasing positive references to structuralism in later editions of his own published works. So if by "genealogy" scholars are intending to evoke a kind of historiography specializing in tracing the changing "significations" and meanings of concepts, then in that respect Foucault's "genealogy" is suppressing its own genealogy.

.

So where does all this leave us? At the outset, we can, and even need to, overcome positive dogmatism and epistemic overconfidence by doubting the certainty of various claims to certain knowledge. This turns out to be easy, as certitude is quite simply an impossibly high bar. Having done that, we can reject the paralyzing cynicism of incomplete skepticisms by either deploying them against each other or turning them onto themselves. Self-referential skepticism doubts itself and becomes something new.

We need not become Pyrrhonists like Sextus. The Pyrrhonists proceeded by way of a practice of equipollence, which meant that—like a contemporary television journalist—they would collect arguments for and against any given position until the matter in question became undecidable. They thought that by extending this undecidability to everything they could achieve tranquility (*ataraxia*).[32] This is clearly not what we need today. On an ethical level, many skepticisms have been consistently allied with pragmatic authoritarianisms.[33] Skepticism in practice often leads to the formation of ideologies that don't even have to bother to justify themselves as anything more than ideological (e.g., Mussolini's *Diuturna*).[34] On an epistemological level, Pyrrhonic skepticism is not in fact a useful stance for scholars, who after all are professionally required to adjudicate knowledge claims. We need humble, emancipatory knowledge—not all-consuming doubt. Succinctly put, we need a form of knowledge that has learned the lesson from critiques of both dogmatism and negative dogmatism alike.

Furthermore, today self-described skeptics are often dogmatists, insisting that some particular position or genre of belief is not the case. Many contemporary skeptics are closeminded materialists who are fully committed to rejecting the possibility of anything that would challenge this outlook. Rather than doubting their own knowledge, they doubt other people's. All this suggests the need for a fresh term for a philosophical orientation that has jettisoned skeptical dogmatism without becoming Pyrrhonism. To refer to this epistemological stance I have revived an archaic English word that had largely fallen out of use: namely, Zeteticism, which was once defined as follows:

> Zetetic. ze-'tet-ik, adj or n (Greek *zetetikos*, from *zeteein* to seek) Proceeding by inquiry; a search or investigation; a skeptical seeker of knowledge . . . it has come to mean both the process of inquiry and one who so proceeds. A zetetic is thus a sort of intellectual agnostic who, while seeking greater truths, is always wary of falsehood.[35]

With all that I have said above as its starting point, I also mean Zeteticism as a gesture toward the work of the Norwegian philosopher and founder of "deep ecology" Arne Næss, who uses it to refer to a particular attitude toward knowledge I will explore in the following pages.[36] Succinctly put, as an alternative to modernist certainty and postmodern doubt, I offer metamodern Zeteticism.

6.2 Knowledge without Certainty

I am one of those lifetime seekers that the ancient Greeks called a zetetic. . . . *From my research on scepticism and the foundations of science and logic, it became clear to me that pluralism (every event has many descriptions and possible outcomes) . . . and a healthy scepticism (always seeking the truth but never claiming it) make up the most consistent approach to respecting the perspectives and experiences of others, human and nonhuman.*

ARNE NÆSS, *Scepticism: Wonder and Joy of a Wandering Seeker*

Absolutely certain knowledge is impossible.[37] Everything can be doubted. So we must grant the possibility of uncertain knowledge. Many skepticisms can be avoided if we become skeptical of the presumed link between knowledge and unshakable conviction. Comprehensive certainty is an unreasonable standard for epistemology. We can be skeptical of everything, including skepticism itself, *but*, crucially, that does not mean that everything is equally dubious. Some positions are better supported by the evidence than others. Doubt itself is even parasitic on the possibility of true beliefs (it only makes sense to argue that the world is an illusion in contrast to a non-illusory world).[38] Our goal is not a rejection of critique, but rather an amplification of critique that necessitates that critique become more discriminating and more fine-tuned. Yet we have to recognize that we often do not know when we know. Just as we do not always doubt the right doubts.

Næss argued that to be a Zetetic is to grant pluralism (that any given event has multiple possible descriptions), and that we cannot know when we know. Both are important, but I want to focus on the implications of the latter.[39] The Zetetic denies the prospect of certain knowledge, but also rejects the claim that we can know when we know something to be the case. Some things we think we know and we are right about, but we are wrong about others, and in many cases we cannot know which is which. One consequence of this skeptical attitude, Næss argues, is that Zetetics should refrain from using the word "true" or asserting that they "know" something, and should say instead, "I believe that x is the case."[40]

I do not quite agree with this language reform, but Næss has a point because, as David Lewis has observed, most people do not seem to include the possibility of being incorrect in their conception of *knowledge*. A Zetetic, however, who has granted the possibility of doubt, can tolerate statements like "I *know* there is a pine tree outside my window, but I may be mistaken." Lewis has maintained that pronouncements like this just seem to "sound wrong," and on these grounds he has argued for "infallibilism."[41] But many skeptics will argue that all statements Lewis is confident that he knows and has guaranteed to be infallible might also be wrong. So he is always in danger of claiming knowledge for a position that could subsequently be refuted.[42]

All that is to say, a Zetetic goes forward recognizing that we are using the word "knowledge" in a peculiar way. When a Zetetic says we "know x" or that x is "true," we are not making statements about absolute knowledge or infallible knowledge; rather, we are saying that we have contingent, situated reasons for provisionally thinking that "x" is the case. Zeteticism represents a humility toward knowledge. On a deep level, as a Zetetic, I recognize that I can know things but that there is always the possibility that I may be wrong. This conception of knowledge has an innate flexibility built in to it. Because I am not attached to certainty, I should be more able to take in new information and to change my mind to incorporate it in productive ways.

We can be even more specific about where degrees of confidence are warranted. As the ancient Greek skeptic Carneades observed, "in ordinary life, when we are investigating a small matter we question one witness, when it is a greater matter, several witnesses, and when it is an even more essential matter we examine each of the witnesses on the basis of the mutual agreement among the others."[43] To paraphrase: lacking certain knowledge, most of us already tend to adjust our standard of evidence depending on the magnitude of the implications for being right or wrong. This is a good impulse that we can develop further.

Zeteticism, then—like American pragmatism—needs to be a pragmatic stance that connects knowledge to its practical stakes for belief and action. A Zetetic can go further than a skeptic in recognizing when she might be wrong. Zeteticism means that a person can be justified in asserting that they "know x" (in the provisional sense above) if there is not a *significant* chance they are wrong about it (having evaluated a sufficient amount of evidence prior to making a truth claim). What counts as *significant* is directly tied to the practical consequences of being wrong. More significant consequences lead toward higher practical standards of confidence. This seems to be the way it usually works in scholarship as well, although we tend to be more or less conscious of this.[44] It makes sense that we get more cautious as the stakes get higher. We should. Ideally, if the entire argument of a monograph rests on a specific claim, then the evidence for that claim should be as solid as it can possibly be. In contrast, the chance that I am being deceived by an evil spirit is unlikely to be a factor in my evaluation of a manuscript, unless I have some further reason to think that I might be haunted. Depending on the risks of a given task, we can determine what degree of doubt is warranted.

Zeteticism is not anti-critique. Rather, it is a deepening of criticism that necessitates more precisely crafted analysis. From the vantage of Zeteticism, many postmodern skeptical doxa are transformed into cautions. It makes sense to be more skeptical of someone's assertions when they seem to coincide cozily with their self-interests. It makes sense to be more cautious about knowledge claims that seem to benefit those in power. Many of the "postmodern" propositions listed above can be rendered less dogmatic and hence more valuable by making them conditional, more fine-grained, or transforming them into operative suspicions and not blanket statements (e.g., classification *can* be conceptual imperialism; we *should* scrutinize concepts formulated in colonial contexts and see if they actually hold when separated from those contexts/interests; language does not fully determine thought but we should continue to explore how and where it shapes it). But all of these can be addressed by altering the standard of evidence rather than rejecting knowledge as such. We need to be able to separate why someone might be telling us something from an evaluation of the claim's evidence.

We need to be careful not to conflate knowledge with its source. That means not dismissing or accepting particular claims because of their bearer's particular race, gender, or sexual orientation. We have to be especially wary of meaning change, blind spots, and Eurocentric presuppositions (many of these emerge from reifying social kinds—see chapters 2, 3, and 4). We need to be self-critical and reflexive, and to aspire toward an awareness of our own finitude. But we also have to be able to recognize when people we don't like are telling the truth. If an asshole told you your car was being towed, their rude behavior would be of less importance than the veracity of their statement. It's important to be able to recognize when this is the case. Sometimes people in power are actually telling the truth. Zeteticism encourages us to treat our knowledge as always only provisional and approximate. The Zetetic can remind us that knowledge and doubt are not incompatible. Just because we can doubt does not mean that we do not know. This is all very different from rejecting knowledge as such.

Zeteticism also needs to reject the popular assertion that everyone has their own truths. Although the idea that everyone has their own truths sounds positively ecumenical, it leads toward contradictions. If everything that I believe is "true for me," then saying that something is "true for me" doesn't add anything. It is merely an emphatic restatement that I believe something. Unless we think that mistaken beliefs are impossible, then everything I believe *cannot* be true (even for me). Indeed, the Zetetic is committed to the view that I am probably wrong about some of the things I believe in (I just don't know which ones). The only way to make sense of truth being relative to any individual's standpoint is to allow for the possibility of people being wrong about what is true for them. Commitment to humble knowledge means recognizing that people do not automatically possess their own truths. In precis, we all have the capacity to be wrong and we may even be wrong about ourselves.

Zeteticism is a position that holds lightly to knowledge itself, knowing that even the very standards of knowledge are in a constant process of change. In effect, Zeteticism recognizes that knowledge itself is an unfolding social kind (albeit an ergonic kind). Many academic practices (e.g., double-blind peer review, replication studies, book reviews) can be thought of as anchoring processes intended to safeguard or verify knowledge claims. Whether they are successful or not, many of these institutional norms were intended to stabilize knowledge or confer specific properties on it. But we also have to recognize the inevitable drift shared by all social kinds. Thus, recognizing it as a social kind means appreciating that knowledge is a process, not a final terminus. Zeteticism is a way of reframing knowing in terms of its impermanence.

Finally, for all his ecological thinking, Næss's vision of the Zetetic project still tends to overemphasize the autonomy of the autonomous thinking subject. As an alternative, I want to take a brief detour through the Japanese philosopher TANABE Hajime (田辺元)'s crucial work, *Zangedō to shite no tetsugaku* (Philosophy as a Method [lit. Way] of Repentance). Our key to unlocking its relevance is in the central term in the title—*Zange* 懺悔—which in Japanese Jōdo Shinshū Buddhism referred to "repentance" and even more specifically to the turn or moment in which we recognize that we are an incomplete, limited, finite being who cannot achieve liberation by means of Self-Power (*jiriki* 自力) but instead must proceed by relying on Other-Power (*tariki* 他力). When we apply this method of thinking to the discipline of philosophy itself, it will have illuminating consequences. Tanabe further glosses *zange* as "metanoetics" μετανόησις ("thinking-afterward," or "repentance"), which he imagines as a pivot toward finitude that applies not just to the individual striving toward liberation but to philosophy as a whole.[45]

In broad strokes, Tanabe argues that philosophy is broken, but that it is not enough to repudiate all of the work philosophy has done and can do, since the act of philosophizing is both flawed and necessary. This means that what we need is a philosophy in spite of itself, a philosophy of "other-power" which can only appear when it relinquishes its own autonomy or investment in "autonomous reason." This is a philosophy for the "unknowing."[46] These are not people who don't know (or worse, who are willfully ignorant), but people who like Socrates recognize that knowledge is limited. This community of the unknowing consists of people who have given up on the autonomy of their individualistic and egotistical forms of reason to work together in pursuit of limited reason and humble knowledge. I think this is an admirable mission that serves to counterbalance the egotistical tendencies of many intellectual projects and to remind us of the importance of humble, collective endeavors.

I want to take something from Tanabe that is not found in Næss—namely, the importance of renouncing self-power in the pursuit of knowledge. To refashion the phrase typically misattributed to Francis Bacon, *knowledge is other-power*. One of the main upshots of several independent trends in philosophy (including feminist epistemology, science studies, and the sociology of knowledge) has been the recognition that it is a mistake to conceive of knowledge in terms of the autonomous individual knower.[47] As noted in chapter 5, the mind is not a solitary ego peering out from our eyes. The classical "liberal subject" is a myth. We come to consciousness not through self-reflection, but via a dynamical process of engagement with the physical world and with a community of other knowing subjects. There are no private languages. What makes the discovery of "facts," limited truths, and even provisional knowledge possible is the disposition of a particular "thought-collective" or epistemic community. This should not be paralyzing. Every scholarly work is an intervention in an ongoing conversation with other people. To make progress is to make progress relative to and within our communities. This is not a rejection of knowledge but an acknowledgment that it is always in some sense relational. Part of the value of a community of inquiry is its capacity to check individual biases and blind spots. We often learn best from our mistakes. Knowledge is socially constructed. Theories are social kinds, but their utility is based on accommodation to our community and the relevant causal structures of our environment.

To take a step-back: "relativism" has a bad reputation and what I've just said in this chapter so far may have raised red-flags for some readers. But, contextual relativism is trivially true. "The salt shaker is on my left" is a true statement relative to one's seat at the table. More importantly, many statements would seem to be true relative to their circumstances (or context) of assertion. For example, as noted earlier, the validity of statements like "the population of my town is 7,754 people" is relative to both the context (my town is Williamstown, MA) and the time at which the statement is made. So assuming that statements about "the population of my town" are completely non-relative would be a mistake. Similarly, the truth of statements like "Francis Bacon was a scientist" would seem to be relative to which Francis Bacon we are talking about as well as the (changing and) richly contextual meaning of the word "scientist" and the possible social kinds toward which it could refer. In sum, while space prohibits a fuller elaboration, at the very least relativism is not necessarily the bugbear it is often made out to be. Epistemic progress means solving local problems in context, but the context is continually shifting.[48] What we think of as established facts are in constant flux (e.g., the consensus about how many planets are in the solar system, whether diamonds are nature's hardest material, the value of Planck's constant, the total population of Germany, and the exact length of a meter have all changed in recent decades). There are no eternal facts.[49] Neither are there brute facts.[50] In a manner of speaking, facts have a "half-life" like radioactive materials, giving off flashes of energy before they decay.[51] Some of these facts have changed because of vicissitudes in the property-clusters they track, while others have changed because of shifting meanings.[52] Even standards for knowledge itself have undergone significant transformations over the *longue durée*. These are all direct consequences of the theory of social kinds I have been outlining in this monograph. A Zetetic recognizes that everything—except perhaps Zeteticism itself—will eventually become obsolete, but that does not render it valueless.[53]

Thought that terminates in skepticism and then seeks no further is not liberating. Thought that transcends skeptical dogmatism to achieve Zeteticism is. One might think of it as a dialectical process in the Hegelian sense: limited abstraction is followed by negation, which is then followed by a pivot that suspends them both. The methodology articulated in chapter 4 can be read in this sense. Instead of choosing between false certainty and incomplete skepticism, we need emancipatory, humble, Zetetic knowledge. The next section demonstrates how to put this into practice; how to produce Zetetic knowledge practically. In essence, we are asking: what should we doubt? What should we take to be knowledge? How should a Zetetic seek? How should we hold our minds? What should our practice be as Zetetic scholars in the humanities today?

6.3 Zetetic Abduction and Prediction: Inference beyond Pattern Recognition

Most of what we do in the human sciences is pattern recognition, and we are very good at it.[54] We identify the role of religion in the writings of Langston Hughes, chart the figure of the refugee in French philosophy of the 1930s, or trace how nurses preserve forensic evidence in Baltimore hospitals. Occasionally, we make grand pronouncements about secularization, scientific discovery, or imperialism, based on what we have observed. Much of what we think of as theories or scholarly arguments in the human sciences are in fact descriptions of patterns. We are in the habit of making generalizations, hedged or sweeping, based on themes we have extracted from our source material. As I have said before, generalizations are not bad in themselves and are actually necessary in both scholarship and ordinary life. But scholarly generalizations open up a particular problem that has been the bane of many theoretical programs across the disciplines—specifically, that practicing pattern recognition on its own does not tell us how and where patterns apply. Restated, identifying patterns does not help us to anticipate future patterns or understand why patterns arise in the first place.

Individual case studies are judged mostly on their internal coherence. But without a better metatheory of what makes a good theory or generalization, we don't have a clue about which generalizations will hold beyond a particular example. We don't know if Hughes's notion of religion was exceptional, if the refugee figured differently in French philosophers a decade later, if Baltimore nurses are representative of nurses elsewhere, or if anything we say about secularization, scientific discovery, or imperialism is really generalizable beyond our cherry-picked set of examples. Without a better metatheory of what makes a good theory, we don't know the value or utility of own scholarly efforts.

In what follows, I aspire to remedy that. To do so, I show how metamodern Zeteticism enables us to understand, practically, how we should structure our thought, how we should evaluate evidence, how we should formulate generalizations or theories, and what status they should have once they have been produced. I will argue that we should think of our scholarly knowledge production in terms of abduction or inference to the best explanation. Further, I will propose that Zeteticism and abduction can be combined in ways that benefit both. In sum, what follows is the key to the production of Zetetic knowledge.

.

Many philosophers have followed Aristotle in bifurcating evidential inference into two modes—deduction and induction. *Deduction* is the classical model of logical analysis that starts from an established premise and arrives at what are supposed to be its rationally necessary conclusions. While there is less consensus about *induction*, it is often described as "an inference from the particular to the universal" or "a generalization from a sample to a whole population." Case in point: after witnessing a large group of black crows, a person might generalize by means of induction that "all crows are black"—or perhaps more modestly, "most crows are black." Although induction is often presented as the core of the scientific enterprise, it has been severely criticized on a range of grounds.

Following David Hume, several philosophers have observed that one of the central problems with induction is that some kinds of inductive inferences are indeed not very well supported and may even be irrational, while others are much more trustworthy.[55] In an oft-repeated anecdote, a man falls from a fifty-story building. As he passes each floor he says to himself, "so far so good, so far so good . . . so far so good."[56] Of course, the joke is that falling forty-nine out of fifty floors without injury does not warrant confidence in a safe landing, and to conclude that a safe landing is likely is thus a bad inference. Not all inductive generalizations from an observation will be reasonable, and why this is the case cannot be established from within the framework of induction itself. Induction can only be justified circularly; it has trouble distinguishing between good and bad generalizations (or weak versus strong inductions); and it cannot produce knowledge about unobservable entities. We can see part of the problem if we ask ourselves why the inductive inference "my last cat was white, my current cat is white, therefore all cats are white" fails, whereas the inference "my last cat was warm-blooded, my current cat is warm-blooded, therefore all cats are warm-blooded" succeeds.

To use a more relevant example, what makes you think that any generalization about "religion" extracted from a particular case study is going to apply to anything beyond the study itself? This is not just a problem for religious studies—you could substitute almost any other category for "religion." Most scholarship runs into the same problem. We can see this if we recognize that most academic generalizations can be formalized as the inductive projection "all observed As are Bs," therefore "all unobserved As will be Bs." This is a weak induction because it does not express any theory about *why* unobserved As will be Bs. We have no evidence that the pattern will hold beyond the weak reasoning that seeing as how falling forty-nine stories hasn't hurt us, falling fifty won't either. The upshot of this is that all the descriptions of observed "religion" don't tell us anything about unobserved examples of "religion." We could grant any definition of "religion" and work out an infinite number of case studies and on their own they still won't help us make generalizations about "religion" as such, given that, either in the past, present, or future, there will always be cases that we haven't observed.

•

Fortunately, induction is not the only way to account for patterns or formulate generalizations. There is an alternative account of inference sometimes referred to as *abduction, inference to the best explanation*, or, in Classical Indian philosophy, as *arthāpatti*. I will treat all of these terms as synonyms (terminology discussed in note).[57] At a first order of approximation, an abductive inference is an inference which goes from an observation to a hypothesis that provides the best explanation or account for that observation. Abduction involves what are sometimes considered two steps: 1) generating a hypothesis which works backward from the presented phenomena to their cause (basically a reverse *modus ponens*); and 2) discrediting or ruling out alternate hypotheses.

Non-philosophers likely associate abductive-style inferences primarily with medical diagnosis or the reasoning of fictional detectives. If you've read a mystery novel, you can imagine how this goes. A detective steps into a room and sees a bloody knife and a dead body. The detective infers that the person whose fingerprints are on the knife is the murderer. The detective's confidence in their conclusion grows the more evidence they find that connects the suspect to the killing (establishing time of death, evidence of motive) and the more they can eliminate alternative suspects. The sleuth's conclusion is fallible and could be revised based on fresh evidence.

We frequently make use of this mode of reasoning in everyday life. Indeed, psychologists have argued that abduction is cognitively basic, cross-cultural, and closely connected to how children learn.[58] To be clear, abduction is not the only kind of reasoning people use, nor are people necessarily rational in all circumstances. Indeed, there are a number of very good reasons to reject the rational choice model that has dominated sociology and economics.[59] That said, a mass of psychological evidence has largely refuted the claim that people in different cultures have fundamentally different modes of reasoning.[60] But there is also evidence that individuals use different cognitive strategies in different circumstances.[61] So it is not the case that we think abductively or even rationally all the time; rather, we are capable of adopting specific inferential modes in diverse contexts. Even in our scholarly disciplines, we often make use of different reasoning styles. Yet scholars and scientists in different disciplines do make abductions all the time, often without realizing it.[62] This is a good thing.

Bluntly put, *induction* has trouble providing any proof that the next time we encounter snow it will also be cold, but we can use *abduction* to discover the causes behind particular patterns of evidence. For instance, the reasoning processes by which scholars came to theorize the Q source gospel were abductive. For those unfamiliar with this, one of the most fascinating findings of nineteenth-century biblical scholarship was Christian Hermann Weisse's discovery that the gospels of Matthew and Luke share references to the sayings of Jesus that they could not have gotten from Mark. Moreover, because Weisse was able to rule out (on a range of philological grounds) that the authors of Matthew and Luke read each other, he hypothesized that the two gospels shared a third source, the postulated Quelle or Q sayings gospel.[63] While the issue is still considered unproven, Weisse and subsequent scholars discovered Q abductively. Since none of them had encountered Q firsthand, its existence could not be established by direct experience much less inductive generalization. But that it existed can be hypothesized based on the ability of the hypothesis to explain the historical evidence, especially insofar as we can rule out counter-hypotheses.

In summary, just as we use inductive reasoning without realizing it, we also sometimes use abductive inferences regularly without knowing it. But becoming conscious of the role of abduction in our research can produce a better appraisal of its strengths and weaknesses. This is because many scholarly oversights and errors are based on a failure to consider contrastive alternatives.[64] We fight for or against particular arguments without considering, much less ruling out, alternative explanations for the evidence. Moreover, many basic scholarly generalizations are weak because of overlooked assumptions in their selection of possible theories or unconscious biases in their sampling methods. Consider the ways a sampling method or perspective may be biased even in the basic statistical sense (for example, being non-random or non-representative, rather than merely the result of biases in the sense of dangerous stereotypes or impure motives). Indeed, thinking of the work we do in terms of abductions directs our attention to how we might be wrong. For all these reasons, we need a better sense of abduction and its strengths and weaknesses.

•

In more formal terms, the pattern of reasoning behind abduction is:

> D is a collection of data (evidence, observations, givens)
> Hypothesis H explains D
> No other available hypothesis explains D as well as H does
> Therefore, H is probably correct.[65]

There are a number of different things to consider when deciding on the probability of a given hypothesis, including: How reliable is the evidence? How well does the hypothesis stand on its own (e.g., is it internally consistent)? How decisively does the leading hypothesis outweigh other contenders (e.g., does it have greater explanatory power, simplicity, plausibility, or productive promise, and so on)? How conclusively have we ruled out the alternatives? How thoroughly have we considered the full range of possible alternative explanations?[66]

Abductive reasoning also has several distinct advantages over classical induction, and in that respect addresses many of the philosophical worries about induction. As the example of "Q" suggests, abduction seems to be able to provide us with information about entities that are not observable directly. A lot of academic philosophy has worried about the status of "unobservables," as most of our scholarship involves forming hypotheses about things we cannot observe directly, including everything from the existence of black holes to the historical reconstructions of archeological sites.[67] Sexist attitudes, for example, are not something that can be observed directly, but they are something we can infer abductively from actions or words when we have eliminated other alternative explanations. All of these examples pose problems for philosophers who presume that enumerative induction is the source of empirical knowledge, but these become less perplexing if we see them in terms of abduction rather than induction. The hunt for explanatory "unobservables" has been incredibly fruitful. All the academic disciplines regularly produce evidence for causes that are not perceivable without mediation. Rather than seeing this as evidence that we know nothing, however, we may more productively conclude that abductive inferential structures are ubiquitous in scholarly research.

This allows us to see how abduction has a distinct advantage over deduction as well. Deductions are best understood as producing conclusions by extracting implicit information from their premises. In that respect, deductions are tautological, or "truth preserving." But abduction is a type of ampliative inference that transcends its premises to produce new information. The end result of an abduction may actually give us more information than we started with.[68] For example, we might abduce that the only way to explain the perturbations in the orbit of Uranus is by positing a previously undiscovered planet (Neptune), which was only much later observed using a telescope. In this respect, abduction enables movement from observation to theory and back.

Another problem that has long bothered traditional empiricists is that an inductive generalization is generally weaker than the initial sense experience. The observation "all tigers have stripes" is necessarily less reliable than the claim that "this tiger has stripes." This has led some philosophers to conceive of knowledge as starting out from a relatively solid foundation of basic sense impressions, but getting progressively flimsier as we subsequently abstract or generalize. Taken to extremes, presuming induction from observations as the only source of knowledge about the external world can lead toward philosophies — such as a transcendental phenomenology or a skeptical empiricism of the sort associated with Hume — in which only raw sense experience is taken as genuine and the existence of the external world is either suspended or regarded as rationally unjustifiable. When all is said and done, inductive generalization seems inescapably to reduce certainty (and worse, as we can always doubt even our preliminary sense impressions).

Abductions, by contrast, frequently exhibit what has been called *emergent certainty*, namely that "the conclusion of an abduction can have, and be deserving of, more certainty than any of its premises."[69] This is because of two different features of abduction. First, abductive inferences can synthesize multiple points of evidence that are not equally robust on their own. We can accumulate clues that make us more confident in our identification of the murderer even if each piece of evidence is inconclusive in isolation. A silhouette or a familiar voice might not mean much on its own, but piecing both of them together might let us to be more confident in identifying Alfred Hitchcock in a particular film. As the saying goes: "If it looks like a duck, swims like a duck, and quacks like a duck, then it probably *is* a duck." I might not be fully certain about how to interpret an animal's coloration, movement patterns, or vocalization taken separately, but taken together these data points can provide evidence for the hypothesis "that we have a small aquatic bird of the family Anatidae on our hands."[70] In this respect, further investigation can contribute to the verification of a particular hypothesis, increasing our confidence over time.

Second, abductive inferences often increase certainty by eliminating contrastive alternatives. An abduction is weak if we have only selected from a "bad lot" of possibilities.[71] This is why assembling a good contrastive set that does its best to exhaust the full spectrum of plausible hypotheses is one of the most important and most overlooked aspects of abductive inference. Alternatives in a contrastive set do not need to be mutually exclusive. It may be the case that both the butler *and* the wife committed the murder together. The French Revolution may have been caused by the deregulation of the grain market leading to rising bread prices and food scarcity *as well as* by a political crisis conditioned by Louis XVI's breakdown of relations with provincial parliamentarians.[72]

In most cases, however, contrasting explanations are incompatible, and by eliminating alternatives we can arrive at more robust conclusions.[73] Identifying negative evidence for one hypothesis can strengthen our evidence for another hypothesis insofar as the two are part of the same contrastive set. If we think only two people were in a position to have murdered Frankie, then discovering Charlie could not have committed the crime makes Sam a more likely suspect. Inductive generalizations cannot gain strength by means of either further investigation or negative evidence, but abductions can. To sum up, while inductive generalizations reduce confidence, abductive inferences can increase confidence.

•

Zeteticism can be combined with abduction to the benefit of both. If we do so it suggests that we need to also attend to a set of pragmatic considerations. A lot of ink has been spilled arguing about what counts as "the best" explanation. Abduction has been accused of being flawed because what is meant by "best" is not uniformly specified. But this is actually an advantage, as from a Zetetic perspective it makes a lot of sense to maximize epistemic pluralism and consider different possible "best" explanations based on the purposes behind seeking an explanation in the first place.

Another advantage of combining Zeteticism with abduction is that it allows for the goodness of a hypothesis to be judged by multiple criteria, so that explanatory power, plausibility, simplicity, etcetera may be evaluated separately, and the judgment of a single "best" might be based on a hypothesis standing out in more than one dimension, or trade-offs between dimensions of comparison can be considered explicitly (e.g., likelihood verses generalizability). What counts as the best explanation of the cause of a devastating office fire would be different for a structural engineer who wants to know why the building material ignited than for the fire marshal who might be more interested in whether it was caused by negligence or arson. Even in these cases, not all explanations will be equally good and some hypotheses will be rejected by both engineers and fire marshals (e.g., that the blaze was caused by fire-breathing mice). Explanation can happen on different levels and in response to different questions. Thus, alternative explanations need not be incompatible, or even explanatory rivals, and different explanations might simultaneously be accepted as "best" if they explain different aspects or are useful for different purposes.

But—and this is important—as scholars we need to be explicit about our criteria. If two explanations seem equally to elucidate the observations, but one is preferable on particular moral or pragmatic grounds, then we need to be clear about that part of our decision-making. You might choose to invest your energies in testing a particular hypothesis because if it is correct it will help more people or because you judge it to be more likely based on other extra-theoretical commitments. This is not necessarily misguided. I am not opposed to norms in scholarship, but I want to emphasize the importance of making norms explicit so as to avoid value-smuggling and talking past each other.

It is especially appropriate here to add a set of postmodern skeptical doctrines transformed into cautions; or recast, to make abduction more Zetetic. As numerous thinkers have observed, there has been a long history of skepticism in various prejudicial modes that presumed very limited notions of what kinds of knowledge are possible. There has also been a long history of testimonial injustice in which evidence was dismissed because of the race, gender, sexual orientation, age, religion, or what have you of the person providing the evidence. Abductive inferences are strengthened by enlarging the set of considered hypotheses. Hence, all of these types of pre-judgments work to erode the strength of relevant inferences. But we can do better.

As the contemporary postcolonial thinker Boaventura de Sousa Santos argues, the point of decolonizing knowledge "is not to ascribe the same validity to every kind of knowledge but rather to allow for a pragmatic discussion among alternative, valid criteria without immediately disqualifying whatever does not fit the epistemological canon of modern science."[74] I agree with de Sousa Santos's noble aspirations for a broader form of emancipatory knowledge, and I think Zetetic Abduction is the ideal inference model for the decolonized, humble knowledge he is calling for.

·

I also want to argue that the widespread philosophical despair over induction can be addressed by changing our basic typology of inference.

The common bifurcation of inferences into deduction and induction is itself a problem. Instead, I think it is better to understand inference on a spectrum between abduction and prediction (see below). Inductions are really a subtype of abductions, and at the opposite extreme, abductions can become deductions. Restated, abduction should be thought of as the principal inference type.[75] With this model in hand, we can judge better and worse inductive generalizations on abductive grounds. This is the key to answering the problem of the falling man mentioned above. From the vantage of induction itself there is no principled way to adjudicate *a priori* between better and worse inductive generalizations (all should be equally valid as inductions, hence the weaknesses of induction identified by multiple philosophers above). But we can judge inductions based on the standards of abduction. Good inductive generalizations are really "abductions wherein the frequency in a statistical sample is best explained by a causal story that proposes the frequency in a parent population along with the method of drawing the sample."[76] That is, stronger inductive generalizations are those that present a hypothesis about the relationship between the observations and the cause of those observations, which in turn necessitates a theory about the degree to which the sample is representative. Evaluating inductions with abductive principles permits us to reject generalizations promoted by overly optimistic falling men and people who obsessively collect white cats.

Further, as noted previously, scholars who follow Hume have often argued that induction can only be justified in terms of induction, thus producing a vicious circle. By way of a preliminary counter-argument, deduction itself—or at least the core syllogistic structure of *modus ponens*—can also only be justified circularly. Given that Hume thought deduction produced valid and certain knowledge, this might suggest either that deduction is in fact equally useless, or that circularity is not the problem it has been made out to be.[77] But I'll take another tack. Insofar as abduction allows us to differentiate between better and worse inductions, an abductive justification of a robust induction is not itself circular. The best explanation for the hypothesis that a particular induction is reasonable could be that it is good at discerning actual causal patterns in the world. Although this does not justify all inductions, it suggests that *good* inductions, at least, can be justified non-circularly by means of abduction.[78]

All that is to say, our basic philosophical typology is inadequate. As we have seen, good inductions are best thought of as a subtype of abductions. This means that classical induction is not in fact central to either perception of the external world, or scientific knowledge. So criticisms about induction are miscalibrated if they are taken to authorize grand skepticisms.

But a further insight is that abductions can be deductive in the limit, because if you can establish all logically possible hypotheses, and completely exclude the alternatives, then an abduction can be put in a deductively valid form as a disjunctive syllogism (*modus tollendo ponens*). Put in more formal terms:

Some explanation must be true.
All possible explanations are considered.
All except one are ruled out.
_____
That one must be true.

Although there will only be a very small number of situations in which all possible explanations can be considered, this means that both induction and deduction can be seen as falling under the category of abduction. Thus, it would seem that abduction is more central and provides more insightful terms of analysis for the way we acquire knowledge about the world than induction or deduction.

Instead of seeing inference in terms of the classical induction-deduction split, a better way to conceptualize inference types is on a spectrum between *abduction* and *prediction* (with mixed types in between). In many respects, abduction and prediction are symmetrical inference patterns: abductions go from observation to explanatory hypothesis; predictions go from hypothesis to expected observation.[79] Fragile predictions are basically weak inductive predictions which lack a theory about why the pattern will hold. To be sure, we often make generalizations of this sort, especially in areas of which we have little knowledge (e.g., why will the sun rise in the east? Because it has always risen in the east). But as we begin to formulate more refined knowledge of the world, predictions can take the form of hypotheses (e.g., why will the sun rise in the east? Because of the direction of the Earth's rotation).

Just as an abductive inference attempts to explain a set of observations by means of a hypothesis, a prediction takes a hypothesis and attempts to project the likely observations into the future. While abductions tend to describe causal relations, predictions tend to project causal outcomes. Just as abductions can be falsified by counter-evidence, predictions can be falsified by counter-evidence when the anticipated outcome fails to occur. But there are also significant differences between abductions and predictions. Some things you can explain without being able to predict beyond the formulation of a probabilistic hypothesis (I can explain the roll of the dice without being able to predict what a given throw will look like). But we also often make predictions without explanations—for example, as a result of reliance on secondhand knowledge. I am predicting it will likely snow later today because my iPhone app tells me that it will likely snow later today. The prediction is fragile insofar as it isn't grounded in a specific hypothesis on my part, but it is likely to be accurate assuming that my weather app is good at its job (i.e., the scientists who created it formulated accurate hypotheses). Abduction and prediction are mirrored yet inferentially distinct patterns. That said, they are often entangled. We often use abductive inference to establish a hypothesis that then authorizes us to predict future outcomes, or we use failed prediction to rule out a rival hypothesis.

This points us to a further implication about the way inference to the best explanation works: abduction is best thought of as a dynamical exchange between a sentient being and its environment that complements the hylosemiotics outlined in chapter 5 (some thinkers have argued that even nonhuman animals engage in abduction).[80] We see patterns in our sense-data. We generate explanations for those patterns. We evaluate those explanations, consider alternatives, and decide where to look for more evidence. Those explanations often lead us to predictions. We test those predictions with new observations, and so on.[81] Further, against a skeptical notion of the mind imposing itself on the world, this process occurs by way of interaction with the external environment. We do not simply look at the world outside through the window. We pick things up. We drop them. We taste them. We chew on them for a little bit. We assemble evidence from multiple senses via a process of interaction. We form hypotheses about the external world from our role as situated and embodied agents.[82] All of these are part and parcel of abductive inference as a dynamic process. All that is to say, abduction is the core inference type behind hylosemiotics, as it is part of how we extract meaning from signs.

Finally, I want to underscore that abduction suggests the procedures through which we come to discover social kinds, their power-clusters, and their anchoring mechanisms. It shows us that the discovery of patterns is not by itself sufficient for robust generalizations without an emphasis on the causal origins of their similarity. It also suggests how we might want to adjudicate between different accounts of a specific social kind. We should, when possible, formulate contrasting hypotheses and work toward the account that permits the better explanation of the observed pattern.

In summary, abductive inference is a better way to understand the reasoning that underlies empirical knowledge of all sorts. Abductions are fallible, but rather than leading to extreme skepticism, they reveal the strengths and weaknesses of arguments from the basis of empirical evidence and invite improvements through, for instance, showing that rival hypotheses either have not been considered, or have not been sufficiently ruled out.

Finally, conjoining Zeteticism with abduction suggests that pragmatic considerations should also be taken into account when considering the importance of concluding at all.[83] It is often the case that we need to suspend our decision between some set of rival hypotheses until we have gathered more evidence. It often makes sense to continue to consider seemingly less likely but still possible explanations. Even if we have identified the fingerprints on the murder weapon, we should not prematurely rule out the possibility that the suspect might have been framed. On the level of disciplines, it can be useful to keep around a range of rival theories rather than throwing all our weight behind a particular one prematurely.[84] Theories that have fallen out of vogue occasionally turn out to better explain later findings, and sometimes seemingly rival theories turn out to be complementary. Thus, it makes sense to encourage explanatory pluralism, if only to retain alternatives so that they may be argued against, thus strengthening the argument for the leading theory. Even when we have concluded, we have to recognize that our knowledge is provisional and should be held lightly.

6.4 Conclusion: From Skeptical Dogmatism to Emancipatory Zeteticism

"Postmodern" skepticisms grew because many people thought that doubt was liberating and even progressive. This may be the hardest part of the cynical zeitgeist for later generations to reconstruct. While postmodernism was typically situated on the political Left, one of the more interesting developments of the last few years has been the sense that the old postmodernism now lives on the Right. This should not have been a surprise. A broader view of history shows that philosophical skepticisms have generally been either de-politicizing or used to justify conservatism and authoritarianism.[85] "Fox News" is not exceptional in this respect. Examples abound. This was no less true in the "postmodern" moment. We spent too long letting our politics determine our epistemology. As a result, we ended up with both an incoherent epistemology and a failed politics. Under the shadow of incomplete skepticisms, speaking truth to power became doubting the power of truth; and often the structures of power were left in place.

Incompatible skepticisms gained purchase because doubt is always possible. But many skepticisms fade once we allow space for uncertainty. Skeptics often gain the most mileage by presenting fairly dubious skeptical arguments (e.g., your senses may be deceptive because of the machinations of an evil spirit), which, while unlikely, cannot be definitively ruled out. A Zetetic, however, can always doubt these skeptical arguments. The *practical stakes* of the doubt can be reasserted (if you really thought you were being deceived by an evil spirit, then why are you arguing with me, since I'm presumably an illusion?). Indeed, most skepticisms seem to have little practical effect, as the most avowed skeptics typically go about their day in the same manner as their non-skeptical peers.

Inevitably, postmodern skeptical positions suggest latent epistemological commitments; their very uncertainty is motivated by a craving for absent certainties and a resultant investment in their own doxa and dogmas. When skepticism learns to doubt itself, it ceases to be skepticism and becomes metamodern Zeteticism.

Zeteticism grants that disbelief and doubt are always possible. We might always be wrong. Any given statement might be debunked. But dubitability alone is not particularly noteworthy. The human mind is limited and the world is fundamentally complicated and enigmatic, so uncertainty is endemic and the best we can hope for is a form of knowledge with limited precision and confidence. We can say that we know something even while knowing that we may not know it absolutely. Some claims are rightly judged more dubious than others. We still need to guard against epistemic overconfidence and false presuppositions about the autonomous capacity of our own rationality. People, scholars included, often want to believe comfortable falsehoods. We need to be wary of these. All the same, even provisional knowledge is vastly superior to paralyzing doubt.

In this respect, analytical philosophers might see Zeteticism as a species of pragmatic fallibilism.[86] This is not an outlandish project since versions of fallibilism have been comparatively common across the globe (including in contemporary analytic philosophy), while claims to produce undeniable knowledge or generalized skepticism have been rare and often self-defeating outliers.[87] That said, many contemporary self-identified "fallibilists" are too optimistic in their appraisals of the status of current truth and knowledge claims. They often suggest that they basically have everything figured out, but just cannot prove it. Yet many of the things they were confident about have since been overturned.[88] Thus, from a Zetetic vantage, many optimistic fallibilists are just dogmatists who've agreed not to be jerks. In contrast, Zeteticism would remind us that many robust philosophical positions and empirically successful theories have been shown to be false by later theories, thus demonstrating that excessive confidence in the status of current knowledge is unjustified. We need the right admixture of self-assurance and doubt.

Metamodern Zeteticism enables us to move past cynical reason and toward emancipatory knowledge. In this chapter, I have been attempting to demonstrate concretely how coming to think of our scholarship in terms of abduction or inference to the best explanation can sharpen our thought and make us better theorists. Zeteticism fused with abduction can help us ascertain where to better apply skepticisms and how better to formulate generalizations. Further, unlike other forms of reasoning, abductive inferences exhibit emergent certainty, since both accumulating evidence and excluding alternate hypotheses make abductive generalizations more robust. While we will never reach complete certainty, Zetetic abduction thus demonstrates that intellectual progress is possible and shows us how we might work to achieve humble knowledge.

This chapter does not stand on its own, because for theories in the human sciences to move beyond weak inductive inference to more robust abductive explanation we need to be able to specify the common properties of the entity we are talking about *and* the causal, anchoring processes that have produced those properties. We need to not just identify patterns, but explain why they hold. Yet we have historically been missing the right account of the basic structuring entities addressed by our scholarship. This is a problem my theory of social kinds aims to solve.

Finally, having provisionally (and perhaps only partially) distinguished epistemology from ethics, I will in chapter 7 look again at different legitimate ways of moving from fact to value and back again. We need a reevaluation of values, including those concerning knowledge itself.

7: The Revaluation of Values

The postmoralist society characterizes an epoch in which duty is watered down and weakened, the idea of self-sacrifice is socially delegitimized, morality does not demand devotion to ends higher than one's self, subjective rights overpower imperative commands, and [what passes for] moral lessons are conveyed by [television] commercials about better living, sunny vacations, and coming entertainments.

GILLES LIPOVETSKY, *Le Crépuscule du devoir*

Out of the pressures of plentitude . . . [comes] a revaluation of values by means of which the accumulated forces are shown a path, a direction, so that they explode in lightning and deeds.

NIETZSCHE, *Writing from the Late Notebooks*

Postmodernism used to be regularly accused of having engineered the demise of collective values and thus having ushered in moral relativism or ethical nihilism.[1] In the writings of influential theorists—like Lipovetsky, quoted above—postmodernism coincided with a self-centered and postmoral age.[2] According to this well-worn line of criticism, widespread moral relativism has set people "adrift on an uncharted sea, left to find [their] moral bearings with no compass and no pole star."[3] According to other philosophers, "postmodern emotivism" has won the day, and ethics has been reduced to merely personal preference, perhaps chosen the same way we select our shoes, as a matter of fashion and convenience.[4] Indeed, one used to frequently hear remarks to the effect that "Nietzsche's declaration *'Nothing is true; everything is permitted'*—[is] the battle-cry of postmodernism in six words."[5] These charges were false.

It was often said that postmodernism was a failed politics or a debilitating form of cynicism and political disillusionment.[6] Unable to justify ethical or political commitments, postmodernism was supposed to have opened the door to global capitalism.[7] Values were coopted by the financial markets, and the dollar and the stock derivative have pulled down the cross and shattered the picket lines. Perhaps with the advent of postmodernity, we came to find ourselves gasping for air in a deepening moral vacuum.

But if not too long ago a host of thinkers argued that postmodernism was going to destroy ethics, that same scene has produced what its enemies, often the same people, now denounce for its overzealous ethical commitments. Postmodernism is today criticized both for being a cynical repudiation of ideals and for being a hotbed of activism.[8] Postmodernism is often taken to be both depoliticizing and politically correct. Anti-postmodernists who have noted the seeming inconsistency of these charges often suggest that it was postmodernism itself that underwent a change of epic proportion. For instance, in the eyes of one scholar, "At the moment postmodern theory lay dying in the academy, it bore a child, namely, 'social justice.'"[9] Other theorists similarly argue that "Postmodernism has, depending upon your view, either become or given rise to one of the least tolerant and most authoritarian ideologies that the world has had to deal with since the widespread decline of communism. . . . [It] refers to [this] ideology simply as 'Social Justice.'"[10] Accounts such as these purport to explain how in the mid-2010s postmodernism supposedly exchanged moral relativism for rigid moralism.

Here is the problem: postmodernism, as an academic model, was nearly always moralizing but often also simultaneously either ethically relativist or actively value neutral. This is the contradiction I aim to explain at the outset of this chapter. I show how scholars under the sign of the negative promoted values, but typically values that they themselves did not recognize as such. Recast, I explain how value neutrality and moral relativism proliferated alongside negative ethical absolutes. I then turn this seeming contradiction inside out to reevaluate the role of epistemic values in scholarly inquiry and to provide a vision of a pluralistic, positive ethical goal for the human sciences.

There is a long history of describing various epochs in terms of the radical atomization of ethical norms. But different theorists place the blame differently. In some sectors, the disappearance of values is still believed to have been exacerbated by the advance of science. In Max Weber's paraphrasing of Leo Tolstoy, "Science is meaningless because it gives no answer to our question, the only question important for us: 'What shall we do and how shall we live?'"[11] It is widely held that it is a "naturalistic fallacy" to extrapolate from "is" to "ought" or from "fact" to "value." Insofar as facts are understood to be the sole legitimate subject of science, it is often asserted that science cannot legitimately provide values and thus scientific progress is supposed to lead to values being increasingly exiled from the world.

The critique of activist or ethically motivated scholarship is not new. Along this line, and again in reference to Weber, scholars regularly hold up value neutrality or value-free science as ideals. Scientific and scholarly objectivity are widely supposed to be incompatible with ethical or political commitments. In Religious Studies in particular, theorists like Donald Wiebe have spent decades ferreting out "crypto-theology" and berating other scholars for importing values into their scholarship and teaching.[12] Ethical ideals are routinely portrayed as obstacles to objectivity and are blamed for Religious Studies' failure to properly cohere as a secular "scientific discipline."[13] Value-driven approaches are often presented as antithetical to serious research in the field.[14]

Religious Studies is not alone in this respect. For instance, economics was established as a discipline along an internal split between "positive" and "normative" economics, the former associated with "fact" and the latter associated with "values" (although these distinctions have since become controversial).[15] Across the academy there have been many decades' worth of scholars arguing that social scientific disciplines can only make themselves truly scientific by expunging moral commitments and banishing values. It would seem that attacking social justice as incompatible with scientific objectivity has been going on for a very long time.

Taken together, it might seem that the diffusion of postmodern skepticism and the advancement of modern science have both contributed to the delegitimization of values. It is as though cultural relativism and value-free science have conspired to produce a vapid and postmoral society. By all rights we should be living in an amoral age—yet (as I argue in this chapter) these commonplace truisms are wrong. But they are wrong in an interesting way.

Various forms of ethics have always prospered in the humanities and social sciences. For evidence one has only to look through our journals and other scholarly publications, which have a long history of frequently employing value-laden terminology. That said, much of this moralizing language has been resolutely negative or critical in tone. But we were never lacking in ethics; we just drove ethics underground (though not that far). Indeed, as I argue here, it is the very discourse of value neutrality that has caused us to embrace values that we do not name as such and perhaps do not even know to be values.

The central contentions of this chapter are that our aim for value-free human sciences is largely misguided; that to make progress we need to bring our values to the surface and submit them to further scrutiny and refinement; and, crucially, that it is possible to imagine (and I want to call for) an alternate and fully normative purpose for the human sciences. I will make the case in five parts. First, I briefly gesture at the moral climate of peak postmodernism, which, far from being a vacuum, was full of ethical language—but with a peculiar asymmetry: advocacy has historically been rejected as overly moralizing while at the same time scholars continue to castigate immoralities under the guise of doing legitimate factual criticism.

Second, I show how the human sciences were at the center of an illusion about the relationship between science and values. Third, I focus in the core of the chapter on a set of legitimate ways philosophers have identified for moving from *is* to *ought*, and touch upon the case for the ubiquity of epistemic norms or values. This section is the analogue to chapter 2's deconstructive dojo. It shows various valid strategies for relating facts to values and vice versa. For fellow scholar-activists, however, it also provides a cautionary note about the limits of normative advocacy as currently undertaken in many sectors of the academy.

Fourth, once we transcend the failed project of value neutrality, I put forth a proposal not about what the humanities and social sciences have been, but about what they should be: a means toward *making us better people*. Restated, I provide a normative argument for human flourishing or well-being (that even goes beyond the human to include multispecies flourishing, for humans, after all, do not exist in a world disconnected from that of other creatures). I'll begin this section by making the case for eudaimonic or virtue ethics, with a weight toward classical Greek, Indian, and Chinese contributions to that topic. Finally, I amend virtue ethics by introducing a little critical theory. I propose a reformulation of the virtue ethical goal away from individual satisfaction or happiness and onto "Revolutionary Happiness," which I argue should be our main collective project in the human sciences; further, I argue that future scholarship should be evaluated at least partly in terms of its contribution toward this shared goal.

7.1 The Values of Postmodernism

You asked me before if I was not a nihilist who rejected morality. I say: No! . . . In a sense, I am a moralist.

MICHEL FOUCAULT IN CONVERSATION WITH MICHAEL BESS, 1980

"Postmodernism" did not coincide with a departure of values, but rather a proliferation of negative lodestars.[16] Think of the terms—racism, sexism, anti-semitism, homophobia, patriarchy—that proliferated as morally inflected condemnations in the very time period the theorists referenced above described as an ethical vacuum.[17] Of course, this language evoked moral wrongs rather than positive ideals, but it was no less ethically motivated. These terms and their more recent siblings (such as transphobia, ableism, anti-blackness, toxic masculinity, and more) are all a significant part of the public conversation, where they often meet with other morally loaded terms from elsewhere on the political spectrum—like anti-Christian, disrespectful, unpatriotic, un-American, and elitist. To this, scholars have contributed a further set of concepts that signal intertwined moral and intellectual castigation—such as ethnocentrism, Eurocentrism, logocentrism, anthropocentrism, androcentrism (why do we have a problem with centers?), Otherizing, totalizing, stereotyping, linguistic violence, and so on, as well as adapting terms that originally lacked moral registers, such as privilege, appropriation, essentialism, and problematic, which have now also become foci of ethical censure.

I do not think there is anything wrong with much of this vocabulary, and it is incredibly valuable to draw attention to suffering and deprivation. I merely want to make two simple points: first, it is all moral language; and second, most of this is not new. (It could almost go without mentioning, but almost all of this moralizing language was fully in place long before the period when critics imagine postmodernism shed its moral relativism.) Scholars have a long history of fiercely policing moral wrongs—then as now. We scholars have never been lacking a morality, but we have also been calling out "activist scholars" in the name of objectivity since at least the 1970s and pointing out failures to adhere to "value neutrality" since at least the 1950s.[18] There has been for at least half a century a consistent back-and-forth or perhaps necessary tension between ethically motivated and avowedly ethically neutral scholars. In this respect, the attempt to expunge values might seem both failed and unnecessary. It is often our inherent sense of justice and righteousness or pursuit of things like truth and knowledge, that motivates most of us to enter the academy in the first place. Why, therefore, pretend that our work must be free of ethics, when ethics is often central to our choice to do the work we do?

The postmodern canon is equally full of normative accounts. Already from *L'écriture et la différence* (1967), Derrida had been expounding on an "ethical imperative" of openness to the Other drawn from Levinas. Irigaray had been criticizing phallocentrism and the marginalization of women in psychoanalytic theory since *Speculum de l'autre femme* (1974). Barthes's early essays are full of musings on Marxism and political commentary; as he put it, "Political knowledge is therefore the first object of political action."[19] I could keep going. Indeed, as the quotation above illustrates, Foucault and company were not immoralists but ethical or political theorists, and they often saw themselves as such. "Postmodern skepticism" gained ground not because it rejected norms, but precisely because people thought it could advance what amounted to a progressive, ethically motivated politics. We did not pass through an epoch where everything was permitted.

That said, except for some anodyne references to "diversity," most of our contemporary moral language is, and has been, *negative*, as if we imagine that if we can merely eradicate the *im*moral, we will be left with what we think of as the moral, but we won't need to call it such. The hypocrisy of this position ought to be clear. Scholars are trying to sneak ethics in without telling anyone by framing their scholarship in a negative register and by (consciously or not) implying that it is value neutral to anyone who might question the project's ethics.[20] The truth is that we live not in a post-moralist society, but in a richly moralizing one. There is nothing wrong with this; in truth it can become the very thing that helps us to advance our scholarship productively and fruitfully. Once we bring our suppressed morals to the surface and allow them to expand beyond mere negativity, we will be able to communicate more clearly across disciplinary lines.

Again, as noted in chapter 6, a pervasive feature of the academy under the sign of the negative has been a confusion of ethics with epistemology. This results in common but fallacious smuggling operations in which, on the one hand, epistemological assertions are overruled based on ethical or political motives, and on the other, epistemological skepticisms are marshalled against optimistic ethical or political initiatives. This confusion should be ameliorated once we recognize the role ethics plays in our work.

Instead of presenting fully articulated epistemological criticisms, scholars regularly invalidate various claims to knowledge on political/moral grounds (e.g., sexist metaphors can be found in Newtonian physics, therefore we should think twice about accepting a mathematized astrophysics).[21] We police most strongly the citational practices of those we think of as ethically misguided (e.g., Michael Bellesiles's citations in *Arming America* were intensely criticized by gun enthusiasts who disagreed with its thesis and ultimately forced the press to retract it).[22] The phrase "poor scholarship" is often used to signal an ethical rather than an epistemological failing. We were cancelling each other (left and right) long before cancelling became a buzzword.[23]

Often this form of criticism gets its mileage by conflating the personal character or identity position of the thinker with his or her thought.[24] Indeed, it may seem that instead of the death of the author we have become experts in the *ad hominem*. But even when it does not take the form of character assassination, this mode of theorizing often smuggles ethical or political arguments in under the guise of empirical criticism or research. Less frequently, this confusion runs the other way. Positive political or ethical projects are also undercut by skeptical challenges to their epistemology (e.g., the charge that progressive politics is worthless because it is rooted in a naive essentialism). Even today, when various theorists have exchanged epistemology for ontology, the problem remains, as moralized ontology has taken over from moralized epistemology.

In very broad terms, this smuggling has had two negative consequences: First, by continually denying the role of ethics in a given work, it has largely exempted contemporary ethical positions from serious engagement and direct criticism. Normative ethics is cordoned off in its own specialized subdisciplines; alas readers in other fields are not expected to take it seriously. The majority of scholarship is put into the service of inconsistent value positions and undertheorized ethical norms, and even sophisticated analysis regularly terminates in simplistic Manichean binaries.

Second, the articulation of these ethical strategies has been largely negative. The main affective modes on which critical scholarship builds are guilt, melancholy, and condemnation.[25] The issue is not that we began focusing on "race, gender, and identity" (all of these are important, especially when studied together), but that we have come to do so predominantly in a key of scorn.[26] Theorists have become primarily apostles of gloom, despair, and outrage. This pessimism is paralyzing. Rather than promoting positive values or envisioning better worlds, we regularly tear each other down. Everything is "problematic" and little is "praiseworthy" (except perhaps the most abject of suffering).[27] We often see ourselves as speakers of difficult truths, but positive cultural or political change can be hard to motivate when almost all we do is critique. Above all, we need to move past our negative line of critique not by abandoning it altogether, but by shifting our focus, acknowledging our own ethics at play, and arguing for what we *do* want to see rather than only for what we want to destroy.

Finally, I want to suggest a basic insight: all these negative critiques and scornful moralisms actually presuppose various forms of flourishing, even if these are typically unarticulated. To criticize racism is effectively to hold on to the hope (no matter how fleeting) of racial justice; to call out patriarchy suggests an alternative, no longer male-dominated society; to critique anthropocentrism has often been to encourage, no matter how faintly, the possibility of ecotopia, and so on. Dialectically put, we need to negate the ethical negations of postmodernism and construct a world in which these various negative lodestars have been overcome. All we need to do is recognize what we are arguing for and then argue for it unapologetically and with our ethics in plain view.

One clue to this positive project is the work of Michel Foucault. If there is one theorist in the postmodern canon who is most resolutely identified

with a challenge to ethics, it is Foucault. He came to international promi-
nence in good part through his critique of the role of the normative function of discipline, corrective punishment, and bodily control in everyday
life. Foucault was interested in tracing, or perhaps exposing, the formation of a notion of "morality as obedience to a system of rules."[28] In his
later life, however, Foucault shifted his attention to articulating a positive
form of ethics founded not in obedience or rules, but in "care for self, both
in order to know one's self . . . and to improve oneself."[29] Thus in Foucault's project we can see glimmers of something that looks like a search
for philosophy as a way or life or perhaps even virtue ethics. I will explore
those in a later section of this chapter.

But first we need to ask: if scholars frequently engage in value criticism without getting in trouble for promoting values, why do we not recognize our work as ethical? Why have so many scholars simultaneously promoted moral or cultural relativism while also criticizing things like racism
and sexism? And why do most scholars seemingly lack positive ethical
projects? Perhaps it is because we have internalized a false dichotomy between fact and value.

7.2 The Value of Value-Free Social Science

Max Weber is frequently described as the central figure in the call for
value-free social science. The famous sociologist is portrayed as having
risen above the political partisanship of his day to pave the way for an objective and impartial analysis of society and culture. Indeed, in Weber's
name scholars have been taught to equate "objectivity" and valueless-
ness, such that the existence of value-laden concepts might seem to challenge the independence and validity of the human sciences. Elsewhere
I have already aimed to clear up a pervasive misreading of his notion of
rationalization, but here I want to clarify another pernicious set of confu-
sions around his notion of value neutrality.[30]

Weber did indeed argue that *Wertfreiheit*—usually translated "value-
freedom" or "value neutrality"—was crucial to the social sciences.[31] In
part this was motivated by his desire to protect professors from being excluded from jobs based on their political convictions.[32] But on a philosophical level, Weber explicitly embraced a common reading of Hume
(discussed momentarily) in granting a "logical distinction between 'existential knowledge,' i.e., knowledge of what 'is,' and 'normative knowledge,'
i.e., knowledge of what '*should be*.' "[33] Weber argued that because science,
even social science, could describe only what is and not what should be,
researchers needed to make clear the distinction between "empirical factual assertions on the one hand" and political "ethical or philosophical

value-judgments on the other."[34] To this opposition, Weber added a characteristic emphasis on the difference between means and ends in which he presumed that the role of social sciences was to interrogate means, but that the determination of ends was outside the realm of scientific inquiry.[35]

Later critics have often seen the turn toward value neutrality as part of an attempt to make sociology more like a natural science; while that is probably true of many theorists, Weber's project was actually different.[36] Weber argued that value neutrality was important in the human sciences because the disciplines' typical form of knowledge production was different from the natural sciences. Weber granted the conceptual dichotomy, popularized by Wilhelm Dilthey, between two modes of knowledge— *Erklären*, the predictive or reductive explanation associated with the natural sciences; and *Verstehen*, the interpretation or sympathetic understanding associated with the human sciences.[37] Weber's sociology was focused on *Verstehen* because he thought that sympathetic understanding of sociological research subjects was crucial to interpreting their motivations and attitudes more generally. Interpretive sociology should provide an interpretation of actions and what makes those actions meaningful. Value neutrality comes in here because Weber argued that this mode of understanding required the researcher to suspend their own beliefs and values so as to be better able to interpret those of the people they are studying.[38]

But in addition to calling for value neutrality, Weber argued that social sciences should also acknowledge the importance of *Wertbeziehung* or value relevance in the composition of research agendas and their subsequent interpretation. In brief, Weber was acknowledging that evaluative interests and subjective values give scholars the passion for their topics. Moreover, a research topic's cultural relevance and value produces its broader impact.[39] Hence, social scientists need values and they need to be aware of the value relevance of their particular subjects. Some later interpreters have argued that Weber thought values belonged only in the "discovery phase" of scientific research.[40] But in his methodological writings, Weber actually argued that values are unavoidably entangled in scholarship in the human sciences. The very objects of study are constituted by values, both of researchers and of their subjects.[41] Perhaps the phrase "value agnosticism" or even "empathy" would better capture what Weber meant, because he argued that it was not the researcher's place to either praise or condemn their objects of study as right or wrong, good or bad. But clearly we have fallen far from his intended model.

Weber's argument was not, as it is often misunderstood to be, that all values should be expunged from social sciences, but instead that social scientists need to clearly distinguish between value judgments and factual statements. Naturally, Weber granted the importance of values in selecting the subject of research, but he also warned scholars against allowing subjective values to determine scholarly conclusions. Nonetheless, being value neutral did not mean being value-less. Rather, it meant a clarity about one's own values and their role in one's choice of research projects, and this clarity was meant to allow a researcher to look at their subject with an awareness of the factors influencing the scholar's own perception.

·

In parallel to the construction of value neutrality in sociology, notions of cultural and moral relativism arose as methodological premises in anthropology.[42] Franz Boas, the so-called "father of anthropology," is often credited with inventing cultural and moral relativism.[43] But when read more closely, Boas's early formulations do not fit the received view. In the influential works in question, he observed that there was a strong tendency for the anthropologists of his day to criticize various cultures on moral grounds (e.g., moral condemnations of nomadic societies for abandoning the elderly and infirm).[44] Yet, as Boas argued, these criticisms were often rooted in misunderstandings of the motives and contexts of the people being judged (e.g., in nomadic societies it is often the elderly themselves who want to be abandoned, to allow more vigorous people to have the food and other resources they need). Accordingly, Boas cautioned against assuming the inherent superiority of one's own culture and against adjudicating other cultures' ethics before we actually understand them. But he added the proviso that once scholars really understand another culture, they can then criticize it if need be.

Despite being retroactively reconstructed as the promotion of indiscriminate cultural relativism, Boas actually provided something like a plea for tolerance, a rejection of ethnocentrism, and an argument for methodological suspension of judgment until understanding could be reached.[45] (Rather than focusing on inter-cultural comparison, some theorists also interpreted ethical relativism historically—observing that moral norms have a tendency to shift over time, such that each generation typically thinks of itself as more moral than its predecessors. This suggested that any attempt to judge historical figures was doomed to failure.) Although space prohibits a full exposition of the philosophical implications of and problems with ethical relativism, my main point is that the original formulations were in many respects analogous to Weber's account of value neutrality as a precondition for social scientific inquiry.

•

All told, the contemporary ideal of scientific value neutrality largely emerged from a controversy in German sociology in the early twentieth century, but it took hold in the United States in the Cold War era, where it came to meet with and amplify an earlier anthropological emphasis on cultural relativism that originally functioned as a similar suspension of ethics in the service of scholarly detachment.[46] Hence, scholars across a range of academic disciplines came to assume that ethics and values were incompatible with objective inquiry. In the same Cold War context, US American politicians began accusing social scientists of advocating communism and atheism. Thus, internal calls to depoliticize the human sciences were also an attempt to defend the value of academic endeavor from political pressure by emphasizing its ethical neutrality.[47]

Nonetheless, contemporary philosophers often attribute the main argument for the impartiality of science to one very famous paragraph in David Hume's *A Treatise of Human Nature* (1739). In the passage in question, Hume observes that moralists are quick to make surreptitious movements from "the being of a God" or "observations concerning human affairs" to a series of normative claims, which are generally illustrated by an unexplained transition from "usual copulations of propositions, *is*, and *is not*," to those of "*ought*, or an *ought not*." Yet Hume saw this move as illegitimate: since "this *ought*, or *ought not*, expresses some new relation or affirmation, 'tis necessary that it should be observed and explained; and at the same time that a reason should be given, for what seems altogether inconceivable, how this new relation can be a deduction from others, which are entirely different from it."[48]

Subsequent theorists have assumed that Hume had demonstrated that no ethical or value judgments can be drawn from purely factual premises, thus severing value from fact. For this reason the separation of fact and value is widely taken for granted. By way of example, many people would assume that there is a fundamental difference between stating *the fact* that a Subaru Impreza is a car and making the *value judgment* that a Subaru Impreza is a good car. Seemingly by implication, science can describe the world but not evaluate it. Permitting values in a scholarly discipline would therefore seem to open a Pandora's box of subjective preferences, coloring the results of any research undertaken. Thus, normative claims by scholars are supposed to be examples of "breaking Hume's law" or committing "the naturalistic fallacy" or unreasonably extrapolating "ought" from "is."[49]

Yet, Hume was not in fact an advocate of "Hume's Law"; and, more importantly, as several philosophers have argued, the whole bifurcation of "is" and "ought" is actually incoherent.[50] This is important because many of us who work in the human sciences have been persuaded to engage our work in value-neutral ways. But we have been convinced to do so on what amount to false premises.

The key passages from Hume's oeuvre have been read out of context. The whole point of the relevant chapter of Hume's *Treatise* is that traits are virtues if they give rise to certain sentiments. Hume goes on to argue that breaking promises makes us feel bad, hence he himself deduces from an *is* about human nature that we *ought* to keep promises. Indeed, Hume makes is-to-ought generalizations repeatedly in his philosophical writings.[51] It seems likely that in the famous passage in question, Hume was either a) reformulating the implications of his skepticism about inductive inferences; or b) restating a famous eighteenth-century meta-logical principle that logical arguments are by definition tautological because they only restate conclusions that are already built into the premises (hence, a moral conclusion can only be deductively demonstrated from moral premises).[52] But regardless of the correct interpretation of the original passage, Hume did not follow what is today called "Hume's Law," and it is unlikely that he meant to promote anything like it.

7.3 Illusions of Fact and Value: Overcoming the Is–Ought Distinction

The whole idea that one cannot legitimately move from an "is" to an "ought" is fundamentally mistaken in ways that are easy to reconstruct. Indeed, while in some sectors of the academy the is–ought bifurcation and the call for value neutrality are taken as givens, a number of theorists (many working independently) have either explicitly attacked the fact–value distinction or argued for legitimate ways to move from a descriptive to a prescriptive statement (list in note).[53] In what follows, I want to catalog some of the different ways this can work. In that respect, I want to suggest different, potentially successful strategies for producing these kinds of statements.

But before I do so, I want to emphasize that this does not mean that all attempts to generalize from a fact to a value are equally worthwhile. Scholarship is full of bad is–ought arguments (e.g., "x is natural, so x is good" is erroneous). Many scholars also presume shared but undertheorized values that are worth criticizing. Furthermore, as Weber noted, the distortion of evidence to fit prejudged conclusions makes for sloppy research; and Boas would also remind us to practice ethical humility and not to presume the superiority of our own moral high ground. But with caveats such as these in the background, let me suggest some legitimate moves.

Correct belief. In most cases, it would seem that we *ought* to have accurate beliefs about the world. For instance, the statement "this glass contains arsenic" is the epitome of a non-normative descriptive statement of fact. But if "this glass contains arsenic," then it would also seem that I *ought* to believe "this glass contains arsenic," especially if I am feeling thirsty. This could be extended to most correct statements about the world. If "it is snowing," then I ought to believe it is snowing (especially when picking a jacket); if "smoking causes cancer," then I ought to believe that smoking causes cancer, and so on. These examples pose problems for the conventional account of the relationship between fact and value because they all represent a direct movement from a description (fact or "is") to an ought. Restated, they all provide clear evidence that non-normative descriptions can reasonably lead to normative conclusions. Indeed, all this suggests that correct belief itself is a value-laden or normative concept, that we *should* have accurate beliefs about facts or non-normative aspects of the world, and for very functional purposes.[54]

Epistemic values. Value judgments or at least is-to-ought statements are also a regular part of how various academic disciplines, including the natural sciences, operate. A lot of basic academic vocabulary is evaluative and even necessitates going from fact to value or description to norm. For instance, the word "valid" itself is clearly evaluative. To say someone "has a valid argument" is a judgment that said argument has a positive value. Moreover, the logical notion of validity is rooted in a set of descriptive criteria (to be valid, the conclusion must follow from the premise, and so on). So in their use of the word "valid" philosophers are moving from a description of the argument to an evaluation of it, and they seem to do so frequently and with little difficulty. Indeed, philosophers often argue that we ought to make valid arguments and often see their pedagogical mission at least as teaching students how to do so. To assert that committing the naturalistic fallacy of moving from is to ought renders an argument invalid is itself an evaluative judgment that does the very thing it prohibits. To belabor the point, every time a philosopher says that we need to reject value judgments because "Hume's law is valid," they are doing the very thing they are criticizing. Hence, as commonly construed, the naturalistic fallacy is itself a fallacy.[55]

But philosophers are not the only ones to routinely deploy evaluative language. Academic disciplines spend significant time and energy appraising the quality of research. To do so, they have historically evoked a set of "epistemic values."[56] These can be seen most clearly in book reviews, in synthetic review essays, and during disciplinary controversies, which tend to judge work with reference to such criteria as coherence, plausibility, novelty, significance, accessibility, clarity of organization, thoroughness, and so on. All of these are normative judgments. Moreover, values such as these have often been used to adjudicate between rival theories or research programs or to settle theoretical debates.[57] Calling out plagiarism, praising originality, and emphasizing explanatory breadth are all value judgments. But we should feel good about this. No discipline could function without normative principles to differentiate between good and bad research. These judgments help us to advance the state of scholarship and ourselves, to mutual benefit.

The scientific spirit.[58] While scholars calling for value neutrality in the human sciences often describe their opponents as forfeiting scientific impartiality, a number of influential philosophers of science have argued that collective norms are the key to the scientific enterprise. Although one could be skeptical about the ubiquity of these ideals, it has been argued that what makes "science" successful as a collaborative project is a commitment to shared values—such as the value of sharing ideas, evaluating truth claims based on impersonal criteria, trust in accurately reporting research, and the virtue of rigorous testing—that govern the professional life of the scientific community. A limited form of value-neutrality appears in this context not as a precondition for "objective" knowledge, but rather as itself an aspirational scientific ideal.[59]

More importantly, value judgments about evidence are what produce facts in the first place. For something to be labeled a "scientific fact" it has to have achieved collective recognition by the scientific community.[60] This should not make one doubt all facts as metaphysically compromised; rather, we should acknowledge that the collective recognition is necessarily value-laden because it requires judgments according to some of the epistemic values discussed above.

Values are based on facts. If the last few paragraphs gestured toward ways that facts are dependent on values, another straightforward breaking of the fact–value dichotomy is based in the parallel observation that many values are dependent on factual evidence (and often relate to "correct beliefs" as mentioned above).[61] The statement "the government should raise the minimum wage to provide a minimal living standard and spur the economy" is a clear expression of a value in the ought sense, but it rests on factual claims about the relationship between the minimum wage and both living standards and economic growth. Many differences between political parties are dissimilarities of particular values, but those values are themselves based on evidential claims. Even if the evidence itself is disputed (e.g., number of deaths in school shootings or whether climate change is anthropogenic), there is factual evidence at stake in such dis-agreements. Moreover, although value conflicts are often portrayed as in-tractable, people do change their values based on new understandings of facts. (For example, some Irish Catholics became disillusioned with the Catholic Church when sexual abuse scandals became public knowledge in the 1990s. Factual evidence about the institution's response to the behav-ior of certain priests led some people to change their fundamental values and even their religious identification.[62]) In sum, many of the values we hold are based on our assessment of particular evidential claims.

Thick ethical concepts. The human sciences in particular often make use of "thick ethical concepts" (or "normative-descriptive terms") that in-clude both descriptive and evaluative elements.[63] To call an individual a "sexist" is both a normative repudiation and a descriptive evaluation of their attitudes as evidenced in their words or deeds. A scholar's notion of what counts as sexism is likely to be rooted in their sensitivity to gender relations and their judgments about what counts as appropriate behav-ior in context. The scholar's own values likely have an impact on their as-sessment of what amounts to sexism or how sexism should be measured. Thus, identifying sexism is value relative, but scholarly (rather than flip-pant) charges of sexism are also a matter of marshalling evidence and can be the subject of reasoned debate based on that evidence. Different scholars may not have the same criteria for judging sexism, but (at least in principle) those criteria can be articulated, and the values behind the judgment can be discussed rationally.

Adjudicating sexism might sound especially fraught, but many of our basic concepts — including terms like healthy, egalitarian, oligarchy, tyran-nical, racist, dictator, repressive, terrorist, kind, and authentic — express similar entanglements of description and evaluation.[64] Again, this means that we can actually evaluate how to apply them even if their application involves both normative and factual elements (and even if scholars often end up disagreeing).

Bridging notions. There are a number of specific "bridging notions" which allow one to infer an entailment from a description. Basically, a particular subject's expression of an intention or goal allows for the for-mulation of both a logical and a normative conclusion from that initial ex-pression. To quote one summary of the general formula of such: "You want to achieve E. Doing M is the one and only way to achieve E. Therefore, 'you should do M' must be held to be analytic, in the sense of being guaranteed correct by virtue of the meanings or functions of the terms it contains."[65] Norms can be argued for by framing them in terms of their implicit goals, which are also often related to specific facts about the world. Terms like "want" or "need" often function this way. For instance, the statement "if you want to avoid getting cancer, you need to eat fewer processed foods" requires you to agree with the original value (not getting cancer), but then leads to impartial and factual, yet nonetheless normative, recommendations about what you should do. As I argue below, aspirations toward "health," "happiness," and "well-being" permit bridges of this sort and indeed even suggest the logical entailment implicit in an Aristotelian or eudaimonic ethics (e.g., formulas such as "if you want to be happy, then you should do x, as x is conducive to happiness" are sufficient grounds on which to build a whole system of ethics).[66]

Values masked as facts. There is also a persistent line of criticism especially associated with Marxism, but also found in critical race and gender theory, that there is a problem with the whole framing of the fact–value dichotomy.[67] This critique takes different forms, but its predominant form is generally to expose the value-laden presuppositions about some set of established "facts."[68] Recast, it often amounts to the claim that the values of dominant groups don't read as values and that "social facts" are often a defense of the status quo. For example, the success of capitalism is presented as an accomplished fact not a value, but success can only be measured according to a set of (presumably already capitalistic) values. Similarly, early primatology was full of sexist presumptions that prevented scientists from even considering possible theories that would have better explained the data they were collecting.[69] Some supposedly proven or established "facts" are just the conventional assumptions of a discipline at a given moment. For instance, the idea that there is a unitary form of intelligence that can be measured in a numerical "IQ" produced a bunch of "facts" about different IQ measurements for different populations, but this has been criticized as rooted in the racial and social prejudices (or, one might say, values) of the specific researchers who established the grounding assumptions of this whole line of research.[70]

It should be noted that most accounts of this sort *do not reject all facts* because the very unmasking operation of demonstrating that some specific factual claims are covertly values is itself typically rooted in factual claims. Thus, in one influential account, calling out hidden values like these is part of how disciplines become more rather than less "objective" (see problems with the term "objective" below).[71] To reiterate, this does not mean that there are no "facts," or that facts and values are identical; rather, it means that we have to be able to hold established claims up to careful scrutiny in order to discern biases of different sorts.

It has similarly been argued that the whole fact–value distinction is itself value-laden, works to frame certain projects as "too subjective," and is part of policing the boundaries of certain disciplines (often in prejudicial ways). For instance, in Religious Studies, the assertion that theological values can be clearly distinguished from non-theological values turns out to be hard to defend because the very distinction often amounts to a theological claim in its own right. Similarly, appeals to scholarly distance and value-free research have historically been used to discourage researchers from minoritized backgrounds from working on the issues that are most valuable to their own communities.[72] At the very least, calls for value neutrality are often rooted in naive notions of the fact–value distinction itself and are regularly applied selectively.

●

All told, there are many legitimate ways to bridge the fact–value distinction and thus the call to eliminate values from scholarship in the human sciences is destined for failure. This cuts two ways. Theorists only interested in the political or ethical value of their scholarship should know that distorting one's scholarly conclusions in the service of political goals is ultimately self-defeating. It does no one a service to let politics run roughshod over evidence or to reverse-engineer scholarship based on predetermined ethical commitments or according to simplistic moral binaries. Part of the function of good scholarship is to unmask those errors. But similarly, scholars who think that they can expel all values from their scholarship are merely hiding their true ambitions and agendas in ways that should equally be available to debunking. Scholarship regularly appeals to evidence, but we need to recognize that we all have values inextricably entangled with that evidence.

To some readers this might sound dire. Part of the problem is that the word "value" covers both subjective preferences and epistemic, political, or ethical evaluations. These subjective preferences are not what I or most of the philosophers cited above have in mind. Nor am I asserting the naive view that all facts are values (or value-laden) as a way to discredit them. The presence of values does not mean that a discipline is "unscientific" or that it has been contaminated by ideology; even natural sciences use values as a basis for choosing topics, judging the value of research, and so on. Much of the anxiety about "scientific relativism" and extra-theoretical influences on theory adoption is misguided. As I have been arguing, the presumed incompatibility between logical "objectivity" and social values is mistaken.[73] Logic encodes epistemic norms. Theory adoption is often determined by scientific values (like internal consistency, ability to make correct predictions, and explanatory power).[74] None of this, however, means that knowledge has been fundamentally undermined. Again, the goal is not to render all scholarship subservient to values, but rather to become more aware of values' guiding role in our research and, more importantly, our lives.

I also agree with Amartya Sen and others that when values are openly stated, they are more amenable to rational inquiry and debate. In this respect, we need to be much more explicit about our values. It might go without saying, but in order for values to have traction, they probably should be justified in broad terms. This is part of what John Rawls referred to as "public reason." Much of mainstream ethical vocabulary is resolutely negative and rests on a set of implicit moral assumptions that have rarely been subjected to serious scrutiny. (Put differently, much of popular ethical discourse across the contemporary political spectrum is anemic and rests on under-analyzed ethical presuppositions.) Focusing more on constructive projects and thinking more deeply about public justifications for values would hopefully have a positive impact on this popular stratum of discourse.

The academy is not in much better shape. Because ethical arguments across the disciplines have routinely had to mask themselves as criticism and to assume only negative lodestars rather than positive goals, a lot of scholarly moralizing has been produced via guilt by association with a widely recognized injustice, such as slavery, colonialism, racism, or Nazism.[75] Calling out oppression is vital, but there is a tendency for condemnations to expand indefinitely.[76] Given the ubiquity of systematic injustices, it has been only too easy to find a connection between them and any given position or thinker. Nuanced readings are vastly outnumbered by simplistic, sweeping condemnations of various individuals. Naive moral binaries predominate. For all these reasons, many of the negative lodestars associated with postmodernism were under-justified (e.g., logocentrism became a bad word for academics who had never read a lick of Derrida, much less Ludwig Klages, and had only a vague sense of what it implied).[77] As several studies have shown, people are often more than willing to adopt (and even internalize) made-up social rules to join new groups.[78] Moreover, norms have a tendency to shift and in less than a decade behaviors that were once seen as morally neutral can become widely castigated (or the reverse). So it has often been enough to slap an "-ism" on the end of a word to rally people against those associated with it. But weakly grounded ethical norms have a tendency to melt away during generational or cultural shifts.

It also worth emphasizing that facts are also relevant to most moral issues because values often rest on specific claims of an empirical nature. This should be reassuring for scholars because, if a value is part of a theory, then that value can be tested as part of that theory. In summary, making values and their justifications explicit allows us to hold the values up for scrutiny and to determine which are most useful for our shared purposes. In the worst case, we can always agree to disagree.

There is also a lot more work to be done in discerning the distinctions between epistemic and non-epistemic values. Although some of the philosophers cited above have begun doing this, we need more conversations about specific values and their role (positive and negative) in our teaching and research. Many scholarly negative lodestars could use reappraising or formalizing. We might ask—what epistemic values should we have? And we might join various domain-specific ethicists in asking—what are the ethical commitments or moral hazards of our specific areas of research? I hope this chapter will spur more such conversations.

But I also have something more ambitious in mind. I have been asking scholars to put their cards on the table, and I want to hold myself to the same. Accordingly, in the next section, I begin to argue for not just the goal of my research, but more broadly what I think the goal of research in the human sciences should be.

7.4 The Human Sciences as a Way of Life

Philosophy was a mode of existing-in-the-world . . . the goal of which was to transform the whole of the individual's life.

PIERRE HADOT, *Philosophy as a Way of Life*

In the current academy, the central mission of many educational institutions seems to be preparing students to enter the job market—albeit one that probably no longer exists. In this context, it might seem hard to ask the question "what does it mean to make progress in the human sciences?" After all, in the era of "big science," progress in STEM disciplines is routinely depicted as technological advancement and is largely measured in terms of military or capitalist interests, grant money, investments, or quantity of publications. So long as these goals are being met, the idea of "progress" goes more or less unquestioned, and the underlying assumption seems to be that as long as engineers are producing new fighter jets and iPhones and medical researchers are producing more types of pharmaceuticals and therapeutic treatments, the natural sciences are progressing just fine. To be fair, some institutions pay lip service to the importance of pure research for its own sake, but in practice, productivity is increasingly measured in terms of sheer volume rather than quality of publications. Despite these quibbles, it seems to be generally assumed that the natural sciences, at least, are making regular and steady progress.[79]

In contrast to uncritical depictions of progress in the natural sciences, the dominant narrative among most of my colleagues in the humanities is (rightly or wrongly) one of decline. Scholars often resist the idea that the humanities could be said to be advancing at all, and even when they grant the possibility of such an idea, they also tend to describe progress merely in terms of quantity of publications.[80] As one contemporary theorist put it: "Progress in the humanities, one instinctively assumes, must have occurred, as there has been progress in the other areas of culture. . . . The nearly commensurate effort in the humanities—all the books, editions, scholarly journals, research grants, institutes, and symposia—must have accomplished something."[81] So if it has accomplished something, what is the accomplishment? We often say that a work is "making a contribution" or "advancing the state of the discipline." But to make progress toward something would seemingly require a goal, even if only so we can know how to evaluate our contributions to a collective scholarly effort. So, I ask you, what should be our shared goal?

In the last two sections of this chapter, I put forth a proposal not about what the human sciences have been, but about what they should be: a way of life directed *toward human flourishing*. What would this mean? I have a sense of what it might entail, which I describe as the pursuit of Revolutionary Happiness. Having said that, my broadest ambition is to encourage openness and reflection about our goals. I envision a space in which there is room for new ideas, debate, and also pure research for its own sake. Moreover, I think both ontological and teleological differences are valuable. Yet it is important to note that scholarship in the human sciences is going to have normative implications and motivations whether we acknowledge them or not. The very thing driving the negative tone of much of scholarly moralizing is the suppression of positive values in the name of objectivity. So, it is time to move past the era that necessitates that scholars hide or defer a discussion of their deepest commitments.

In what follows, I bring some of my own most deeply held convictions to the surface and allow them to attract critical scrutiny in the hope that this will shape them into something better and stronger. In the world of scholarship, we have gotten very good at a hermeneutic of suspicion—so good that even works calling for an end to such critique (such as Rita Felski's *Limits of Critique*) often refrain from advocating detailed positive projects out of, I can only imagine, a fear of the resultant critique. This whole book has been an attempt to argue for a positive project, and I want to begin to resolve it with an exploration of the project's ethical and political aims. That said, in many respects, these next two sections are a gesture toward what I imagine will be a future monograph. So consider this part of the chapter on the order of a promissory note, a first pass at what may be expanded to become a fuller work of normative ethics and political theory.

And I want to note that if you have been reading this with a mind turned only toward critique and without a conscious and thought-out alternative, I would like you to think about the following question: if not this, then what?

•

Here we go. As the French philosopher Pierre Hadot accurately observed, before the contemporary disciplining process, philosophy was understood as a way of life. Philosophy was not the mere accumulation of facts, abstract theorizing, or a merely scholarly career, but a pursuit of knowledge that was supposed to be transformative on a personal and cultural level. Philosophy was a method for learning how to live and how to die well.[82] It is time we brought this purpose back, not just for philosophy—for the human sciences as such.

To get us there, we can take inspiration from what I think is the single most exciting movement in philosophy of ethics in the last hundred years: namely, the revival of "virtue ethics," inaugurated by the British philosopher Elizabeth Anscombe.[83] Although virtue ethics is a diverse movement, it aims to recover a way of life or account of moral character with the potential to return ethics from the heights of abstract speculation to the realm of practice.[84] Moreover, proponents of virtue ethics claim to have renaturalized moral theorizing in such a way that it can be held up for social scientific scrutiny. They argue that the good life, if there is such a thing, can be studied empirically. Furthermore, while the other dominant approaches in normative ethics—deontological ethics and utilitarianism—have few analogues to "ethics" outside of modern Europe, efforts to characterize a life well lived (and its attendant virtues) are evident throughout the ancient world, and can be seen prominently in South and East Asian thought.[85]

Those who are already familiar with the philosophical subdiscipline of virtue ethics will observe that in the rest of this section I depict an inclusive version of the field, leaving many of its internal debates unresolved. This is intentional because I mainly want to promote the value of virtue ethics in general, so the particular version of virtue ethics matters less. Readers familiar with Classical Greek, Indian, and Chinese philosophy will also recognize many of the moves made here. The sources in this case are less relevant than the argument itself, since many of the moves being made are shared, or blended, and I am favoring no particular tradition over any other. But I want to put the argument not in terms of authority, but in a normative key. I want to persuade you.

My primary aim in this section is to convince you that *it is possible to live a life worth having lived* and to begin to build from that a set of ethical/political norms. As noted above, a movement from a descriptive *is* to a normative *ought* is justified once a goal has been identified. For example, "If your goal is to win the chess game, and the board is set so that only one checkmate is possible (queen f1 to a6), then you should move your queen from f1 to a6" is a rather straightforward assertion. Thus, goals allow legitimate, objective transitions from fact to value. In what follows, I am not so much advocating one particular goal as suggesting that if you haven't already, you should find a goal that permits a discussion of the quality of your life as well as the introduction of various prescriptions toward bettering it.

•

I think there is a common set of fundamental reasons we get up every morning. I do not mean the proximate causes, such as alarm clocks, crying toddlers, or overly impatient canines. Nor do I mean the short-term goals, like getting to work or class. I mean the ultimate reasons. Succinctly put, we do a lot of things as means, not ends. We work as a means to earn money. We earn money to pay rent, buy food, and for various luxuries. We pay rent so as to have a place to live, and so on. But there is a basic end or goal behind all these daily ambitions, even if we have forgotten it. There is at least one thing we do for its own sake, not because it fills other goals but because it is the thing that is behind them. Aristotle referred to that goal as *Eudaimonia* εὐδαιμονία (literally to be in good spirits, happy, prosperous, or flourishing), but we might translate it as "Happiness."[86] There are other ways that this goal could be described. To make the case differently:

1. Most of us want to be happy.
2. Most of us want psychological and physical well-being.
3. Most of us do not want to suffer unnecessarily.
4. Most of us also want to live a life worth having lived, a meaningful life.[87]

These frequently amount to different ways of referring to the same goal. It is hard to be happy when you lack well-being or you feel you are suffering deeply or unnecessarily. It is hard to have well-being when you are deprived of happiness or are suffering too much. Number four, a meaningful life, seems to require an intersection of the three items that precede it. We could name the intersection of these positive traits in many differ-

ent ways: eudaimonia, nirvana, *lekil kuxlejal*, flourishing, meaningful existence, happiness, or well-being. I'm not saying these goals are identical;
but for my grander purposes here, the differences are less important than
the similarities.

I am committed only to the modest claim that it is possible to live a life
worth having lived. Everything else follows from that. If someone chooses
consciously to embrace this goal, then we can move from is to ought and
begin to establish a normative system for them. To take this on will require an assent to at least *one* of four claims—either that you want to be
fundamentally happy, that you want to live a meaningful life, that you
want to minimize suffering, or that you want to achieve psychological and
physical well-being. Even if you are aspiring toward salvation in heaven
or some other postmortem existence, I suspect you'll want to have lived a
meaningful life on earth. It is enough for current purposes for the reader
to embrace some combination of the four, but I'll call the intersection of
some measure of these goals "Happiness" with a capital "H." (For reasons
of simplicity, I am using capitalization here rather than subscript—see
chapter 4. But happiness$_1$ might be thought of as an emotional state characterized by a hedonistic if typically transient feeling of joy that is likely
partially anchored by neurological responses to pleasure. Happiness$_2$ or
Happiness is a thicker ethical concept, which the following pages will illuminate.)[88]

There are many ways that Happiness needs to be distinguished from its
lowercase sibling. First, Happiness is not something that one achieves *in
totum*, like being perfected or saved; rather, it is something one achieves
by working toward it over the span of a whole life. Flourishing is a process,
not a product. Happiness is impossible to attain as a fixed state. Indeed, it
has been argued that flourishing is incompatible with stasis or even being
only one thing.[89] Flourishing is rather the ability to change or to become
something else. To be Happy on this account would seem to necessitate at
least the possibility of personal growth.

Second, "Happiness" is not primarily an emotion. It is not sensual
pleasure, the chemical numbness of Prozac, a feeling of merely physical
satiation, or passing euphoria. Rather, it represents a more robust (and
pluralistic) conception of flourishing. Unlike an emotion, Happiness is
something you can be wrong about. You can think you are "Happy" when
you are just fleetingly "happy" (happy$_1$). If Happiness is experiential or
empirical (with a range of significant variations and definitions), how to
live your life is a question of practical knowledge.

Third, embracing Happiness does not mean constantly being cheer-
ful, much less never being unhappy or discontented. I'm not asking you
to lighten up. Happiness means that suffering when encountered can be

learned from or surmounted, and it means that negative emotions can be fully experienced without our also feeling broken, bitter, or despairing, because we know that we are working toward a fulfilled life. As I elaborate below, in contrast to how we ordinarily use the word happiness, capitalized "Happiness" is a political and ethical demand to have lived a good life.

Fourth, I find it helpful to interpret this goal alongside the injunction attributed to Solon the Wise: "I count no man happy until his death."[90] I take this to mean that we need to be able to ask ourselves at regular intervals, what kind of life would you like to have lived? This is to imagine ourselves in the future at the end of our life reflecting back on the course of our life (hence the convoluted verb tense). We should aspire to live the kind of life our future selves can regard positively and affirm.[91] This way of seeing ourselves can facilitate self-judgment in the present moment. Most of us will want to be able to say that we were good people. But this also requires the capacity and maturity to be able to imagine your future self, looking backward. We also have to be conscious that we could be entirely wrong about who we will become and what we will value (see chapter 6). But humility about the limits of foresight should not deter us in our aspirations to live a life our future selves could regard highly; rather, it should remind us of the need for changes in direction and help us illuminate a fuller picture of our life choices. We need to practice imagining our obituaries before our lives have passed us by. This looking backward is part of what differentiates Happiness from chemically induced euphoria. We might in a given moment feel happy on some bliss-inducing substance, but I think if we looked back on a life spent in a narcotic coma, most of us would not think of that as a life well lived. It would not be a Happy life in the sense that I am discussing here.

Finally, Happiness is an aspiration to develop fully as a human being. Aristotle described *Eudaimonia* as the telos or purpose of all human existence. We could debate whether humans have a species-wide common purpose or type of flourishing, and I would caution us against universalizing this notion of humanness at the expense of the diversity of human experience.[92] But many thinkers have framed their projects in similar terms. As Molefi Asante argues (building on Afrocentric thought): "One must understand that to become human, to realize the promise of becoming human, is the only important task of the person."[93] Similarly, TU Weiming 杜维明 observes that in the Confucian philosophical tradition, "from childhood to old age learning to be human never ceases."[94] We find analogous sentiments in everything from Classical Greek philosophy to Renaissance humanism to Ojibwa folk traditions. All of which is to say, numerous thinkers from diverse cultural backgrounds have evoked the praxis of working to maximize humanness or full human potential as a grand goal.[95]

So the question becomes, how can we achieve Happiness? The first thing to note is that it is different for different people. We aspire to and imagine different things. We have disparate aspirations. But that does not mean Happiness is fully subjective or reducible to what each person imagines Happiness to be. If Happiness is actually possible (with a range of significant variations), how you should live your life becomes a practical question. Happiness won't be exactly the same for everyone, but it will share common features and there are common mistakes insofar as there are many things that people imagine will make them happy that, when attained, will not do so. Part of the point of education should be to facilitate self-discovery, to focus on people finding for themselves their idea of a meaningful life.

We can make some generalizations about what probably will not be sufficient for Happiness. Happiness does not come from fortune (within certain limiting cases), because some people can be happy or unhappy no matter what happens to them. Likewise, pursuit of fame itself does not lead to Happiness because fame is fragile, fleeting, and easily taken away. Succinctly put, meaningfulness should not depend on things out of your control.

Happiness also cannot be found in the pursuit of mere sensual pleasure. Some kinds of sensual pleasure might contribute to Happiness, but sensual pleasure alone cannot be the sum of a meaningful life because pleasure is transitory and easily lost. The more we attach to sensual pleasure, the more painfully we feel its removal. Again, this does not mean pleasure should be avoided, but that it is insufficient for Happiness. There is also a common Aristotelian and Confucian argument that a key function of education is learning to take pleasure in healthy things. Some of the things people ultimately find the most pleasurable and life-affirming are acquired tastes (Sun Ra's cosmic jazz, modern art, whiskey, or even coffee), and one might think that part of the educational process should involve learning to differentiate between healthy and unhealthy (or we might say self-destructive) pleasures or learning how to have certain pleasures in appropriately moderate measure. But while some pleasures might contribute to Happiness, pleasure itself is not sufficient.

Likewise, the pursuit of wealth or power can be means, but they should not be ends in themselves. That said, poverty and deprivation make Happiness harder to achieve (hence the need for Revolutionary versions of Happiness, discussed below), but being wealthy or powerful does not make people happier. Many of the wealthiest and most powerful people

in the world are profoundly unhappy. Indeed, the pursuit of wealth is a significant source of malaise in contemporary capitalist society.

All told, Happiness must be something that happens in and over the
course of a person's life. It is not found in many of the things contemporary consumerist societies tend to describe as sources of happiness (sensual pleasure, fame, wealth). Happiness is possible without these ephem-
era, and even if these are attained, they usually leave unhappiness in their
wake. Again, there was a significant debate among Aristotle's students
and the Stoics about whether there were minimal amounts of health and
wealth required for a person to flourish. But contemporary cross-cultural
research into happiness (with the limitations of its focus on the emotional
category) also provides evidence that beyond a certain minimum level of
material comfort, wealth does not make people happier.[96] I will return to
this minimum below.

Most people do not find Happiness in their jobs. Many people all over
the globe spend their lives engaged in what the anthropologist David
Graeber called "bullshit jobs," jobs that even the employee knows are basically meaningless.[97] Whether it is working at a call center, a fast-food restaurant, a law office, or a bank, or managing a hedge fund, many people
secretly feel their careers are pointless. Moreover, we live in an era of pre-
carious labor and declining workers' protections. While an older generation often felt trapped in a particular job for life, the lack of professional
stability actually makes us more vulnerable, more fragile, and forces us to
make greater compromises in order to cling to temporary employment.
(We can see this in the adjunctification crisis in higher education.)

A confounding effect is that turning an activity into a profession tends
to make it unpleasant. Whatever it is we love most (e.g., playing guitar), we
do not want to do that every minute of every workday or it would become
boring and disagreeable. We typically want to do more than one thing with
ourselves, or at least maintain the freedom of choice. This is part of what
Marx and Engels meant by "alienation" (*Entfremdung*).[98] But you don't
have to be a Marxist or a Weberian to see how professional specialization
transforms potentially well-rounded people — who might want to, for instance, hike sometimes, do carpentry sometimes, play guitar sometimes,
and maybe even write the occasional critical criticism — into specialized
workers whose basic way of being and self-expression has been narrowed
to a small range of activities from which they are increasingly alienated.
This is not universally the case, and there are those lucky few who find
their chosen career to be fully rewarding, but they seem to be the exception rather than the rule. Hence, against some threads in virtue ethics, I do
not think most of us will be lucky enough to find meaningful professional

employment. This might suggest that either we need to find Happiness elsewhere or we ought to make demands to change the system.

•

The core insight of virtue ethics is that morality is not primarily about conformity to a set of preestablished rules, but about becoming a better person. Many ethical systems tend to overemphasize individual, rational choices. Normative depictions in both popular and scholarly forums all too frequently sort people into innately good or evil, law-abiding or criminal, saint or sinner—as though individual human nature was fixed or immutable. Virtue ethics by contrast is a broad moral theory rooted in the importance of good habits and self-cultivation.

Most virtue ethicists agree that there are certain character traits or dispositional capacities that will help us fulfill our human potential.[99] Aristotle referred to these traits as *arete* ἀρετή, "forms of excellence." We will call them "virtues." Virtues are the qualities that make up a good (or Happy) person's character, such as perhaps wisdom, courage, honesty, generosity, fairness, and so on. There is significant cultural and historical variation in what traits count as virtues.[100] But a crucial point is that virtues are not something that one possesses full stop—rather, they represent a propensity to act in a certain way when one encounters a particular set of circumstances. Brave people are those that act with bravery. Some people might have a natural tendency to be brave, but even then, this tendency has to be nurtured. This means that virtues are not held so much as cultivated, practiced, and exercised.

This leads toward the predictable follow-up question—how do you learn virtues? There are a few different ways to cultivate virtue. First, virtues can be learned explicitly from the teachings of parents, educators, pastoral counselors, and the like. Second, another way to cultivate virtues is through critical self-reflection. For instance, Marcus Aurelius' *Meditations* often amounted to spiritual exercises intended to keep track of his successes and failings in following a virtuous life.[101] (I keep a diary for the same purposes.) A third route toward the cultivation of virtue is meditative practices intended to develop particular character traits (e.g., Mettā or loving-kindness meditation).[102] For this latter reason, I see various contemplative practices as important to Revolutionary Happiness insofar as they permit the cultivation of greater reflexivity and particular virtues.

But one of the most significant ways to learn virtues and flourishing more broadly is to model oneself on the behavior of others. Consider for example the statement attributed to Confucius in the *Analects* 論語 "When walking with two other people, I will always find a teacher among them.

I focus on those who are good and seek to emulate them, and focus on those who are bad in order to be reminded of what needs to be changed in myself."[103] In this respect, *Imitatio Christi* or "WWJD" is on the right track. Many influential Confucian theorists argued for the importance of emulating the positive behaviors of other people, and believed that even outwardly imitating various traits can cause them to become internalized responses.[104] You perform a role until you become the role. You act brave until bravery becomes second nature to you.

A lot more could be said about this, but I want to call those that we aspire to emulate "heroes" (with a non-gendered use of the term). Heroes can be good models in spite of their flaws and regardless of whether they exist or not. For instance, someone could take inspiration for bravery from the example of Wonder Woman just as easily as they could model their bravery on Mother Teresa. This modeling is possible even when we recognize the flaws of our heroes. Indeed, knowing how Mother Teresa's particular egoism got in the way of her ability to help others makes her a better model of a hero, because we can learn from her failings what we need to watch out for even as we emulate her.

Thus far I have been articulating a fairly generic form of virtue ethics (with perhaps a little bit more East Asian influence than typical). A point of departure is that many of the classical theorists of virtue ethics imagined that there was a single model for the good life. Aristotle basically encouraged his followers to become philosophers; Confucius urged people to become civil servants (君子, *junzi* or "exemplary persons"); the Buddha suggested that they be monks and nuns, and so on. But I think there are many possible ways to live the good life. For some people it is contemplation, for others it is political action, for others it is devotion to their family, etcetera. Again, we can make the wrong choice if we fail to understand ourselves. Moreover, when combined with the epistemology I discussed in chapter 6, the challenge becomes how to live a good life when we can't be certain we know what the good life is. This means that pursuit of the good cannot be handed to us and takes personal experimentation, practice, and growth. Simply put, I am suggesting a pluralistic account of virtue ethics.

But a more significant point of departure from mainstream virtue ethics is that I agree with the Indian philosopher Śāntideva (and others) that compassion is the central and most important virtue.[105] Part of this amounts to the claim that even people who cultivate other virtues (e.g., bravery, wisdom) will not be ultimately Happy if those character traits are held selfishly or if they are expressed without care for others. Moreover, the activities that cause us to feel the most deeply happy are those that benefit other people. Again, with all the necessary caveats, empirical happiness research also suggests that people often report feeling happier if they have been helping others.[106] The Happiness I get from eating even a very tasty bowl of soup is likely to be minor and fleeting at best, but helping serve soup at a soup kitchen can be profoundly moving. Working for the benefit of others also lessens the experience of our own suffering. If I inadvertently hurt my back helping my daughter climb a tree, her pleasure in her accomplishment renders my minor suffering insignificant. (But note that compassion is not excessive altruism or self-martyrdom. It is not intentionally harming ourselves or allowing ourselves to be harmed merely for others' benefit.)[107] Our lives are deeply intertwined with others; so helping out in our community benefits not just our own life but those who are entangled with us.

One of the persistent critiques of virtue ethics in general is that it has often provided self-centered models for the ethical path; but there is a long history, especially in Buddhist philosophical circles, of emphasizing compassion as a core component of a fulfilled and meaningful life. This is not a claim located exclusively in Buddhism. Significant theorists in feminist ethics such as Annette Baier and Patricia Hill Collins have come to similar conclusions, although their preferred terminology often refers to empathy and "an ethics of care."[108] All that is to say, an emphasis on the importance of compassion, solidarity, and mutualism in a life well lived appears in a number of very different ethical systems.

Compassion in this account cannot be mere sympathy. As will be elaborated in the next section, it too is not just an emotion; rather, it means a mindset dedicated towards working for the benefit of others. The argument for the centrality of this virtue is that our lives are relational. In some significant sense we thrive or fail to thrive together. If you want yourself to flourish, you have to focus on the flourishing of others as well.

Human flourishing as a goal is in many respects a recovery of the early roots of the humanistic disciplines. I am not saying that studying the human sciences inherently makes people more ethical; rather, I see the potential within each discipline for the recovery of specific goals or functions that would be directed toward different aspects of human flourishing. While I aim to smash disciplinary silos in favor of a broader human sciences, we can imagine existing disciplines recovering the value of their objects (perhaps now held more fragilely, given the critique I made in earlier chapters) for the purposes of Happiness.

To reiterate, once a collective (even polyvalent) goal is embraced, it permits fully objective discussions of what it would take to reach those goals. This would mean, for instance, sociology about building a better society, political theory about formulating more equitable politics, literary studies and aesthetics about both teaching enjoyment and recovering representation as a font of ethical models, religious studies as recuperating specific sources for ethically motivated ways of life, and history for how these various projects have succeeded or failed. Psychology has already begun making some promising steps in this regard in the subfield of happiness studies (even if researchers in this domain as it currently exists often lack a sufficiently thick account of Happiness); and if other disciplines followed suit, philosophy of human sciences might be reimagined as an attempt to explore how these fit together to generate a fully flourishing life. Part of pedagogy would be about teaching students how to put into practice in their own lives the discoveries of the various disciplines. Again, this would not be a return to a particular political project or a regression toward an idealized golden age, but a recovery of some of the concerns that motivated early humanists and social theorists. Taken together, the effect of this would be to refocus the human sciences as a way of life.

To clarify, just as I believe there needs to be room for some hyperspecialized research, there is also value in projects undertaken as ends in themselves. Not every research program automatically needs an answer to how it would make the world a better place. For instance, a scholar may just want to excel at reading Akkadian for its own sake. There is nothing wrong with that. Moreover, for some people Happiness might mean striving to be the best scholar of Akkadian they can be. This is even praiseworthy, and especially so if it emerges from personal introspection on the meaning of life. Nonetheless, because scholarship for scholarship's sake and scholarship for reasons of professional advancement are probably the dominant modes of the current moment, I want to encourage us instead to reflect more fundamentally on grand purposes and to reappraise the broader value of our collective endeavor for promoting flourishing.

Finally, if it has not already been made clear, I imagine the human sciences as a study of not just humans but also the multispecies environment in which we live. The Vietnamese thinker Thích Nhất Hạnh argues that *tiep hien* 接現 or "interbeing" is the heart of compassion. Interbeing suggests that because we are profoundly entangled not just with other people, but also with our nonhuman environment; our Happiness is dependent on not just ourselves doing well, but our human and nonhuman community all doing well together.[109] Although space prohibits a full argument, I think Thích Nhất Hạnh is correct, and indeed I believe we need a commitment to not just human flourishing, but multispecies flourishing. This takes on greater urgency in the face of anthropogenic climate change and global pandemics. The hylosemiotics articulated in chapter 5 is part of a contribution to that broader panspecies project. All that is to say, Happiness depends on compassion not just for other people, but for all sentient beings.

7.5 Revolutionary Happiness: Critical Virtue Ethics

The goal of the revolution had become the happiness of the people.

HANNAH ARENDT, *On Revolution*

In this short section, I want to put the *revolutionary* in Revolutionary Happiness. In the preceding section, I imagined what it would look like if the human sciences were reoriented toward human flourishing. This alone would be a massive step forward, but working toward Happiness alone is not sufficient. Virtue Ethics itself needs to be modified. Why?

The feminist theorist Sara Ahmed provides an influential critique of happiness. Ahmed is responding to a range of psychological studies that suggested that being a feminist does not necessarily make individual women happier. As a rebuttal, Ahmed criticizes the pursuit of happiness in general, which she sees as contributing to an environment in which minoritized groups are asked to make due with less, stop complaining, and just cheer up. I find her critique useful, especially because it shows us that psychological studies about "happiness" can potentially lead to a ridiculous conclusion if their concept of happiness is not sufficiently interrogated. It additionally highlights something I have to clarify. What I am referring to by Happiness is human flourishing, which is no *mere* feeling of something like pleasure or satisfaction, but something much more. Revolutionary Happiness arises from the feeling of living a life worth having lived. As noted above, Happiness is thus not incompatible with other basic sense feelings, like outrage, fear, or sadness, so long as our actions continue to be motivated by a desire to pursue a live worth having lived. To merely pretend to be happy and sit down and shut up when we are suffering as part of minoritized, subjugated communities would be an egregious mistake, and not something for which Revolutionary Happiness is advocating.

I am not saying that we should be content with the current state of things—in fact, quite the opposite. We should pursue that which brings us Happiness, or perhaps we should pursue a meaningful life itself, doing everything we can in order to bring about a world in which the minoritized people who share our form of suffering can be Happy. In addition to this, I argue that we can enlarge our sphere of consideration to include all of humanity and more—all sentient beings. So if someone argues that you can't pursue Revolutionary Happiness if you are a feminist "killjoy," they've got it wrong. Sometimes being a "killjoy" is a way of claiming Happiness for yourself and for others, not rejecting it.[110]

This brings us to an exploration of collective flourishing as a politics. The call for Happiness itself and on its own is clearly no good if it becomes a pacifying demand to accommodate to the status quo. Moreover, if carelessly formulated, the focus on Happiness would not necessarily address the negative lodestars and vices scorned by postmodernism that I discussed at the outset of this chapter.

By way of reminder, our current moment has been a font of well-intentioned moralizing in a mode that is both melancholy and outraged—two feelings which, again, are not necessarily incompatible with Revolutionary Happiness. They bring our attention to the realities of victimization and suffering, and as such they are helpful. Now, however, I'd like to ask: what would it look like if we inverted this mode of critique? What would it look like to embrace positive rather than negative lodestars? What if we negate negative moralizing?

I need to clear up a potential misreading: this is not an attempt to distract from the real suffering of victimhood! Do not make the mistake of thinking I am saying that we must only focus on the positive aspects of subjugation. What I am arguing for is a better and stronger method for transforming victimhood into empowerment and for broadening scholarship beyond merely tallying various forms of suppression to include promoting liberation. If we allow our wounds to fester, they weaken us, but once healed, they can make us stronger. So let me ask again: what would it look like if, instead of focusing the majority of our scholarship on the critique of negative models, we turned more of our attention toward actively promoting various kinds of liberating, compassionate thinking?

If one of the main things many of us see ourselves dedicated to in the human sciences is overcoming various intersectional forms of oppression, including necessarily racism, sexism, homophobia, anti-Semitism, and religious prejudice, then we might start by reorienting ourselves toward the goal of Happiness. But we can't stop there. In order for this move to be as transformative as I want it to be, we need both critical theory and virtue ethics. A new normative ethics implies at least the *possibility* of a new normative politics, which could dramatically transform our current social sphere.

Integrating critical theory into virtue ethics has two concrete implications. First, to be fully actualized, Happiness needs to become capable of making demands on the existing political order (hence Revolutionary); and second, the thing that holds everything together is the fundamentally important turn toward compassion. Remember that you can be compassionate and still be angry about injustices—and you should be. Anyone who tells you that you need to let go of your anger as a means of calming you down before your needs have been addressed is operating out of self-interest rather than compassion. Nevertheless, we can extend compassion even to those people by recognizing that they are suffering individuals like

ourselves, even if they are unable to understand fully the extent of our particular suffering. We need to center compassion in our account of Happiness because it is to our ultimate benefit. Succinctly put, if flourishing is
truly interconnected, *none of us* can completely thrive in an unjust society.
That includes the oppressors, though they may not know it yet. So when
we are fighting for justice, it is for their sake as well. Therefore, when we
fight for justice for all, it is necessarily motivated by compassion for those
who are different from ourselves, although we don't often think about it
that way. We have to recognize the radicalness of a politics of compassion,
because it goes against many of the dominant political discourses of our
current moment.

To explain further, the choice of the term "revolution" in "Revolutionary
Happiness" was primarily inspired by Hannah Arendt's *On Revolution*.[111]
Although I think as an explanatory model her account of the French and
American revolutions is not terribly persuasive, Arendt does recover a key
insight from the Declaration of Independence and its famous evocation of
"Life, Liberty, and the Pursuit of Happiness"—namely, "that no one could
be called happy without his share in public happiness, that no one could
be called free without his experience in public freedom, and that no one
could be called either happy or free without participating, and having a
share, in public power."[112] She argues that public happiness is a higher
goal than personal happiness. It necessitates a public freedom to create
lasting community with others.

We can see a similar impetus in the writings of Max Horkheimer. In
his famous "Postscript" to *Critical Theory*, Horkheimer argued against the
merely individual or egoistic happiness of bourgeois society, adding that
"critical theory, on the contrary, having the happiness of all individuals as
its goal, does not compromise with continued misery."[113] To paraphrase:
like Ahmed and Arendt, Horkheimer reminds us that aspiring toward
atomized individual happiness is insufficient. We need to work toward
the Happiness of the society as a whole, and doing so necessitates working to alleviate collective misery.

Building on Arendt and Horkheimer, I suggest that we should aspire
toward Revolutionary Happiness, which would be the capacity to lead a
meaningful life with others, which requires the recognition of your voice
and status as an agent (not a mere thing). It is hard for people to find Happiness when their basic humanity or dignity is being systematically denied or when they are prevented from having input on the political fate of
their social worlds. Flourishing typically requires the capacity to be able
to make decisions about one's own community and to be heard. In other
words, to make history. We need to work to abolish financial exploitation,

human trafficking, debt bondage, incarcerated labor, and other forms of contemporary enslavement and injustice. But even this is not enough.

There has already been significant political theorizing about the importance of recognition, political agency, and various forms of communal dis-alienation. These are all worthy goals and, as Arendt notes, important minimal foundations for a meaningful life. But here is where putting political theory in dialogue with the account of Happiness above can push us further to the benefit of both. The word *Happiness* asks for more. It calls our attention to the possibility that people can be recognized and exercise agency *and still be unhappy*.

To explain: neo-liberal theorists often suggest that basic democratic reforms combined with free markets are equivalent to freedom and even the good life.[114] This amounts to suggesting that if they could get rid of the world's poorest slums and produce a lifestyle equivalent to that in the metropolitan middle class, we would all be living in paradise.[115] I do not want to undercut the importance of working to overcome global poverty and other inequalities, but I think this whole line of theorizing is misguided. In many countries the middle class seems to be dwindling; and before we eulogize this vanishing bourgeois world and invest it with nostalgia, I want to suggest that (in its current form, at least) it may not be something toward which we all want to aspire. Bluntly put, a lot of rich white people are profoundly unhappy.

This all has concrete implications for the kind of state or community we need to call into being. We are used to thinking of the state in terms of its capacity to monopolize violence or to secure a set of rights or to facilitate a particular kind of economic growth. Classical liberal economics is famous for arguing that human nature is basically selfish, but that the greater good emerges from selfish pursuits. Yet not only is a policy of selfishness self-sabotaging, but the evidence pushes against egoism as an account of human motivations.[116] So I want to try to imagine a nation dedicated not toward GDP, but toward national Happiness and toward facilitating its citizens' pursuit of meaningful lives. I want to imagine a form of good government that works for the people instead of commanding them and that not only functions as a guarantor of democratic self-governance and collective autonomy, but also works for the promotion of virtue and deeper psychological flourishing. I want to call for a politics dedicated toward compassion, so that injustice can truly be overcome.

I have some significant points of disagreement with "Hanzi Freinacht" and what he refers to as "political metamodernism." But I agree with the central mission of his metamodern politics, which is a call for a "deeper kind of welfare system that includes the psychological, social and emotional aspects of human beings, so that the average person, over the length of her lifespan, becomes much more secure, authentic and happy (in a deep, meaningful sense of the word)."[117] The quest for Happiness therefore serves the common good. In other words, a metamodern politics calls for a political order dedicated not to material comforts, democratic reform, or free labor rights, but toward human (and multispecies) flourishing.

•

All this illustrates the importance of compassion as the foundation of Revolutionary Happiness. The realization that compassion is key to human flourishing is what directs us outward from selfish pursuit of personal gain toward engagement with those around us. This is not mere posturing. A life dedicated to helping of others is ultimately going to be more fulfilling. Moreover, once we take seriously the claim that true compassion necessitates not just feeling the pain of others but working to alleviate it, compassion becomes a politics dedicated toward producing a just society.

To further develop something mentioned above, a politics of compassion is particularly radical in our current historical moment. This is because many sectors of the society have rejected the very possibility of empathy. There are good reasons for this. There have now been several decades of work wrestling with what kinds of voices, bodies, and subjectivities emerge as capable of being seen or heard.[118] The French political theorist Jacques Rancière argued in *Dissensus* that those who speak substantial difference into the reigning distribution of the logical and sensible are literally not heard: they register as babble. Similarly, the Black critical theorists Saidiya Hartman, Fred Moten, and George Yancy write that Black bodies are created to be invisible, that the end of slavery is *not* freedom but a life of being refused the rights of the subject.[119] Even though there is a rudimentary commitment to the belief that everyone must be allowed to speak and be heard in most democratic societies, this has not always been the case. The problem is that even today all are *not* seen and heard.

This line of argumentation is valuable. A lot of people are suffering today and they feel that no one can understand their pain. It might seem hubristic after centuries of ignored or silenced voices to say that compassion is possible; yet a lot of people are in fact empathizing with those who are denying the possibility of empathy, and in so doing are agreeing that empathy is impossible. This is a version of the paradox of untranslatability that I discussed in chapter 5. Rancière, for instance, translates the political demands that cannot be heard into ten theses on politics, and in so doing makes them heard (if not acted on). Similarly, Hartman, Moten, and Yancy make the case that Black bodies are impossible to see by rendering them visible in their prose. Similarly, Gayatri Spivak argues that the subaltern cannot speak basically by speaking for the subaltern.[120] In summary, arguments that empathy is impossible generally rely on appeals to the empathetic capacity of their readers. They work insofar as they can communicate the suffering of those who have not historically received empathy. This whole literature assumes empathy even as it denies it. All this is to say, the critics are right and even righteous to point us to those places in which subjectivities are being denied and voices are being silenced. But they overstate their case when they suggest that compassion or pluralistic solidarity are impossible.

The other point I want to make before moving on is that (*contra* Plato) similarity does not beget friendship. Indeed, I have written two monographs already providing evidence that the most intense animosity is frequently directed toward the proximate other, not the truly other. Of course, people can be callously indifferent to the needs of those they perceive as radically different. Many tragedies have resulted from treating other humans as nonhuman or ignoring the capacity of other sentient beings to suffer. But as Howard Adelman has argued, "Genocide is always and only committed against the proximate other."[121] While Adelman's claim is perhaps an overstatement, the Nazis, for example, often saw more assimilated German Jews as more threatening and more dangerous than their unassimilated peers. The problem was not radical alterity or fundamental incomprehension, but hatred directed toward proximate others and perceived competition over supposedly similar desires.

Furthermore, as historians of Germany have observed, architects of the Holocaust like Himmler and Rudolf Höss regularly "stressed that destroying human lives was an unpleasant task that ran contrary to their 'humane' instincts. But . . . unpleasant acts were necessary and [it was] the will to carry out those acts *in defiance* of feelings of human sympathy" that made genocide possible.[122] Paraphrased, the Nazis were able to carry out horrific atrocities in part because they were able to persuade themselves to overcome innate feelings of empathy for their victims. Similar arguments have been made about the genocide in Rwanda.[123] At the very least, the tragic history of genocides, witchcraft persecutions, heresy trials, and civil wars demonstrates how quickly and savagely people can turn on their neighbors.[124] We can come up with plenty of examples where the victims were seen and their suffering was registered, but in which their persecutions nonetheless continued.

That said, while compassion is not impossible, it can be exceedingly difficult. On a personal level, as someone who has experienced racist physical violence firsthand, I know that one of the hardest forms of compassion to mobilize is compassion for those who have done us harm. Compassion is not the same thing as forgiveness. To feel compassion for the oppressor is not to ignore oppression or even to work less hard to overturn it; rather, it is to recognize that oppression originates in damaged mind-states like greed, hatred, and ignorance. Compassion in this context means working to overcome systemic injustice without hating people; it means working to educate the ignorant and to seek reconciliation. We can hate racism but not the racist who we must work to educate and transform. It is a harder path than merely abhorring and otherizing one's oppressors. Thus, we should take as its inspiration figures like Nelson Mandela, who remarked: "Our human compassion binds us to one another—not in pity or patronizingly, but as human beings who have learned how to turn our common suffering into hope for the future."[125] Moreover, for the reasons noted above I think we need compassion not only for our fellow human beings, but for all sentient beings. We need to become aware of how much ordinary activities rest on environmental degradation as well as exploitation and cruelty toward our fellow nonhuman animals.

Finally, to avoid becoming paternalizing or patronizing, we need to combine Revolutionary Happiness with the Zeteticism or humble knowledge I discussed in chapter 6. Part of TANABE Hajime's "philosophy as metanoetics" was an ethical commitment to finitude he referred to as "great compassion" through "great negation" (*daihi daihi* 大否大悲).[126] He argued that recognizing that we are all limited, damaged, and blameworthy permits us to connect with the finitude in others. The problem is not that we condemn others, but that we fail to condemn ourselves and thus moralize without humility. We are all "problematic." It is the nature of finite beings to mess up. We must, therefore, set out from the mutual recognition of our all too human faults and failings. It is our shared weaknesses that serve as the source for our mutual compassion. We are united in our shared failings and shared suffering. Some people are suffering more, some less; some people are more or less damaged; and we could fight about who is worse off or who is suffering most until we all die. But everyone is imperfect and everyone is suffering. Part of the way we achieve compassion is by recognizing our own limitations and our own suffering, and from that place coming to respond to the suffering of others. This mutual recognition, Tanabe argued, is what permits us to work to together to coproduce a better world.

There is no more fundamental task. As Cornel West memorably paraphrased Theodor Adorno, "The quest for truth, the quest for the good, the quest for the beautiful, all require us to let suffering speak."[127]

7.6 Conclusion

In general, I have been using this chapter as a way to begin a preliminary revaluation of the role of values in the human sciences. Its most straightforward conclusion is that the call to banish values from our research is misguided. Neither stressing the fact–value dichotomy nor emphasizing ethical relativism actually gets rid of values. For instance, even the appeal to expunge theology from Religious Studies itself relies on values—such as secularism or *laïcité*. But I want to reiterate that this is not singular to Religious Studies. It reflects in microcosm the problems with putatively value-free social sciences. Most research relies on epistemic values or thick ethical concepts. So the call for value freedom is not going to be sustainable.

This need not be the threat to "objectivity" that it appears. My sense is that "objectivity" is an unhelpful term caught in too many phantom oppositions. As several theorists have observed, "objectivity" has very different senses, including: impartiality or lack of personal attachment; non-subjectivity; or being directed at producing reliable evidence.[128] Complete lack of personal attachments can be incompatible with values (epistemic and otherwise), but values do not threaten other forms of objectivity. Just because values are being brought to bear on framing research does not mean the result is just the scholar's personal subjective opinion. An intense interest in climate change might lead someone to study a rain forest, but that interest does not render the rainfall information they collect invalid. A personal experience of racism, poverty, or sexism can inspire a scholar's research project, but this should not call its results into question. The same may be said about most research in the human sciences.

But against those who do think primarily in terms of value and have largely abandoned notions of "facts," I want to reiterate that it does no one a service when scholars misrepresent evidence in terms of predetermined political or ethical goals. In this respect, proponents of value neutrality have a point—scholars are sometimes guilty of distorting their source material in the service of unstated values. The critical work of uncovering these biases should continue. But it is not the presence of values themselves that is a problem; the problem is the falsification of evidence. Indeed, a key consequence of appeals to value-free social science in general is that they drive various motivations underground. It is the very assertion that social science should be apolitical that causes scholars to disguise their politics as factual claims, scornful condemnations, or disguised moral judgments. It is the notion that social scientific scholarship should be value-free or ethically relativistic that pressures scholars into hiding their ethical ideals, political interests, and theological commitments. In summary, it is these selfsame appeals to value neutrality that produce crypto-theologies and crypto-ethics.

As an alternative, scholars should work to become conscious of their own values and to make their motivations explicit. The problem is not that we make normative or value judgments, but we still need to excavate the unstated or undertheorized normative commitments that undergird specific subfields. I agree with Max Weber that values are of vital importance in setting research agendas, and that we also need prevent our hopes and fears from warping our conclusions. Likewise, I agree with Franz Boas that we need to reject notions of cultural superiority and, in that sense, make sure that we have comprehended another culture or historical epoch before we claim to judge it. (It can be a useful exercise in humility to imagine what moral failings past or future generations might condemn us for.) We need to be humbler and less judgmental of others.

I have also been arguing against the smuggling of values disguised as epistemological criticisms. But I have also tried to demonstrate some of the many possible legitimate ways to move from a fact to a value and vice versa. To reiterate, the problem is not the combination of ethics and epistemology but muddled accounts of their relationship, which can be clarified once we stop trying to ban ethics altogether and allow for the free and unrestrained analysis of its role in our work. Once they are brought to the surface ethical norms can be subject to scrutiny and debate. (Although the best way to change people's minds is probably through stories, accounts of personal experience, and especially sympathetic anecdotes.)

Along those lines, I have been arguing that the human sciences should embrace a particular value goal—human flourishing. The call for Revolutionary Happiness has concrete implications for scholars. The humanities should be about helping us to flourish as human beings. This is in many respects a return to an early notion of the purpose of the humanities, and of liberal arts more specifically. That said, part of the revolutionary nature of the goal commits us to recognizing that many people on this planet are not in a position to work toward their own full flourishing because they literally are not seen or heard, or because their economic straits pin them to a series of very bad "choices."

For this reason, we need a politics of compassion and uplift. Critical virtue ethics has resonances with what Paulo Freire referred to in *Pedagogy of the Oppressed* as liberating pedagogy directed toward critical consciousness, which enables one to see social and economic contradictions and hence to overturn obstacles to becoming more fully human.[129] It also evokes some of what Horkheimer took as the distinctive feature of the difference between "traditional" and "critical" theory—namely, that traditional theory primarily understands itself as merely describing society, while critical theory is about changing it. Although space prohibits a fuller exposition of the concrete political projects this might suggest, I personally have in mind an emphasis on dignity, egalitarian direct democracy, dis-alienated government, and finally, what indigenous Tzotzil activists have called *ichbail ta muk'* or to help one another to greatness in service of *lekil kuxlejal* or a "life that is good for everyone" founded in a "communal connection to the earth" and our non-human environment.[130] My account of Revolutionary Happiness is a preliminary gesture toward what this might look like.

This also leads directly into the work I have been promoting in this book. We keep trying (and failing) to solve systematic problems by targeting individuals or by policing terms. Yet, in order to actually produce meaningful change, we need to know how social kinds come into being and how their properties are glued together. A common refrain of contemporary cultural criticism is that we often feel trapped in social categories or unjust classifications. We often mistake historically contingent and variable categories for universal or unchanging realities—in effect confusing social for natural kinds. Given that we live in a perpetually unfolding, processual social order, we need to embrace subjectivities that facilitate continual self-transformation. For these reasons, I have been trying to work out a human science that allows us clear-eyed insights into how the social world is currently being produced, but also into how we might produce it otherwise.

8: Conclusion: Becoming Metamodern

Once a [person] travelled far and wide to learn fear. In the time that has just passed, it came easier and closer, the art was mastered in a terrible fashion. But now that the creators of fear have been dealt with, a feeling that suits us better is overdue. It is a question of learning hope.

ERNST BLOCH, *The Principle of Hope*, Vol. 1

There were no metamodernist philosophers, so it became necessary to become one. I have been conceiving of this whole monograph as an intimate philosophical exercise of sorts, over the course of which the reader learns how to disintegrate concepts, how to practice deconstructive vigilance, and then how to achieve a new kind of reconstructive capability. This grants partial freedom from social kinds, allowing for the construction of new, as yet unimagined conceptual building blocks for theory and for society as a whole. In this sense, metamodernism is a kind of Wittgensteinian therapy. But while Wittgenstein was trying to cure the pathologies of philosophy in order to return us to the everyday, everyday ways of being also exhibit their own pathologies. So metamodernism differentiates itself from various anti-philosophies by ameliorating ordinary conceptions as well, making metamodernism a kind of "existential therapy" that applies both to the philosophical realm and to the everyday.

Let us say that having undergone this therapeutic, having thoroughly apprehended this movement of thought, one becomes metamodern. Again, the "meta" prefix primarily indicates a higher position of abstraction, a view from above—or, to use a different metaphor, a self-awareness of how we are entangled in the temporal horizon of our research. As an immanent critique, this has necessarily been a critique of myself and my own philosophical formations. But, having taken this journey together, dear reader, if you are with me, we can now both be *metamodernistas*; which is to say allies in the collective project of advancement. Metamodernism is not fixed. It is growing and evolving. And because it is aware of its own position and limitations, it is capable of expanding beyond those limits.

·

From the vantage of modernism, metamodernism may look like postmodernism: because it rejects table-slapping appeals to objectivity; because it rejects the purifying of values from facts; because it undermines Eurocentrism; because it is so skeptical that it has even become skeptical of skepticism. It may also look like postmodernism because it grants anti-essentialism, discards realism, radicalizes doubt, and deepens the linguistic turn. And most fundamentally, it may look like postmodernism because it actually takes postmodernism seriously, trying to articulate and work through postmodern philosophical claims instead of rejecting them as mere obscurantism. This practice is a necessary first step to working through postmodernism's failings.

From the vantage of postmodernism, metamodernism may look like modernism: because it doubts the skeptical doxa and negative dogmatisms of postmodernism; because it returns evidence to the appraisal of values; because it undermines Eurocentrist universalism without altogether rejecting generalizations. It may look like modernism because of its attempt to articulate a system, grant the possibility of translation, and provide productive theories, and because of its call for compassion and emancipatory (if humble) knowledge. Most fundamentally, it may look like modernism because it articulates itself clearly and with a minimum of jargon—a communication style that is necessary for cutting through bullshit and finding a path forward out of the trap of the endless, eternal (re)turns and superficial re-brandings.

As we should know now, however, metamodernism works through both postmodernism and modernism and is in fact reducible to neither. Indeed, postmodernism was primarily apprehended as a negation of modernism. These limits inhered in its basic formulation. This past is *merely* prologue. Going forward, metamodernism stands on its own.

.

This book opened with a postmortem of postmodernism, and I would like to take a moment to make sure we are clear about what this means. There was a general turn toward negation that was condensed for a generation into a quasi-movement its enemies called "postmodernism" but whose trajectories and timelines were rather longer than those usually ascribed to that movement. Most of the positions associated with postmodernism were articulated by theorists who saw themselves as antagonists with incompatible philosophical commitments. Indeed, many of the theorists most strongly associated with postmodernism were themselves criticizing postmodernism. While it would not be hard to argue that "real postmodernism" has never been tried, there was nevertheless a reality to the appearance. Scholars in a range of fields treated postmodernism as a coherent movement, and they either adopted some of the insights popularly attributed to it or they defined their work in polemical opposition to what they imagined postmodernism to be. It was this which actually gave birth to postmodernism as a scholarly paradigm.

The theory of social kinds lets us be more specific. If postmodernism$_1$ was a mimetically grounded architectural movement, postmodernism$_2$ was a loose cluster of skeptical doxa in a specific set of humanistic and social scientific disciplines, which was weakly anchored by a combination of dynamic nominalist and mimetic processes. Its shared properties were produced by being classified together, edited, and compiled under the heading "postmodernism," especially in a set of Anglo-American secondary literature. It then developed by imitation of the bricolage thus provided. Postmodernism$_2$ was primarily an academic paradigm that fulfilled the needs of a university in the process of refashioning itself, and it found purchase by reframing various skeptical conundrums and yoking them to a liberatory politics. Its properties were stable only insofar as the negative doxa attributed to it were policed by scholars in a range of disciplines.

It is also worth remarking that many of the key thinkers whose writings were reassembled into what amounted to the postmodern canon—such as Baudrillard, Deleuze, Derrida, Foucault, Irigaray, and Rorty—were born in the 1920s and 1930s. They weren't even Boomers, but the generation of Elvis Presley and James Dean. To be fair, there has been a somewhat desperate attempt to find the last living European philosophers who remember May '68 and to make either a trend or a strawman out of them, but these thinkers nevertheless represent the intellectual struggles of an older generation. The scholarly model they provided was useful, but it is now outdated. It is time we consolidated their insights, identified their failings, and moved on.

Put differently, there are various possible ways of defining postmodernism or scholarship under the sign of the negative. But from the heterogeneous array of phenomena referred to as postmodern, I unearthed a particular strand—the auto-critique of philosophy itself as expressed in a small set of fundamental quandaries. Accordingly, this book set out from five "postmodern" problematics: *1) antirealism; 2) disciplinary auto-critiques; 3) the linguistic turn; 4) a broad climate of skepticism; and 5) ethical nihilism*; and by working through each of them seriously and dialectically, we produced something new which has value regardless of its inspirations. The surprise is that the result is a new model for scholarship in the humanities and social sciences that works by granting or inverting all the things that are supposed to make such scholarship impossible. By starting out from a place of not just "postmodern skepticisms," but frequently their most virulent formulations, and by accepting them or turning them inside out, we have transformed them into the groundwork for a new path forward.

.

This has been a prolegomenon toward any future metamodernism. This is a hard book to summarize. I have often felt that each chapter could be its own monograph. (It could almost go without saying, but to get the most out of this project requires actually reading the chapters themselves not just the provided summaries.) Yet, the following will retread its components *in reverse order*. To get us there, I will prepare the ground by doing a final bit of scene-setting.

Metamodernism is a postapocalyptic philosophy of the human sciences and it was conceived in the long shadow of many a disciplinary eulogy. But if the humanities are dying, it has been a slow-progressing illness and long anticipated. Indeed, scholars have been lamenting a "crisis" in the humanities and forecasting their demise for over eighty years.[1] The contemporary structure of the humanistic and social-scientific disciplines seems to have been barely established before there were predictions of immanent collapse. These jeremiads were both right and wrong insofar as by some measures (such as undergraduate enrollments) suggest only a modest decline, but others imply the humanities and social sciences have experienced a massive loss of cultural prestige.[2] Nor are enrollments the best measure of health. We should also not ignore all the economic factors—the defunding of public education, the assault on tenure and rise of adjunct faculty, the corporatization of the university, the ascent of a new administrative middle management, the prioritization of STEM and business degrees—that has led to understandable distress.

Yet, as I have observed several times, the plight of the human sciences has been made worse inasmuch as we have experienced a particular legitimation crisis brought on by the dominance of postmodern *affect* as manifested in paradigmatic forms of theorizing across a range of disciplines. Many of us exchanged solving problems for problematizing. Turned critical thinking inward until it became a circular firing squad. Rejected the possibility of intellectual progress for narratives of decline. Mastered suspicion until suspicion mastered us. Many professors became experts at souring students on the very enthusiasms that drew them to the humanities and social sciences in the first place. Some of these were necessary correctives, but many were corrosive. Sadly, even as this intellectual climate wanes, it threatens to entrench some of its most unproductive habits of thought. We can imagine why postmodern-influenced academic departments found it difficult to justify their positions in the university as a whole (e.g., why fund poststructuralist literary analysis over engineering, especially if the former tells us that every interpretation is equally valid). There are reasons that after a generation of autocritique, the typical privilege of a humanities professor is to be ignored by the society at large. Although there were many good things about the academy under the sign of the negative, it contributed to the caricature of navel-gazing, ivory tower intellectuals endlessly deconstructing themselves.

In response to this legitimation crisis, this book has been an attempt to provide an ambitious defense and systematic reappraisal of the human sciences. I have argued that we must decolonize and dismantle our academic silos because the conventional structure of the disciplines and their domains of inquiry is outdated, redundant, and produces various unnecessary deadlocks. We must also improve on the best parts of postmodernism without succumbing to its pitfalls. We cannot solve everything at the level of scholarly abstractions. Organizing too will be important in the days ahead. But engaging in this collaborative labor could see a plethora of beneficial results.

I have thus provided a new scholarly model we can take to the streets and refurbished a vision of the human sciences as a way of life directed toward pluralistic forms of human, and necessarily multispecies, flourishing. One thing that the classical humanists and contemporary antihumanists actually shared was a notion that to be human is in a certain sense to be essence-less. We are in fundamental respects self-fashioning entities. Our brains are "plastic." Our bodies can be trained. Our minds expanded. Our virtues can be cultivated. We can become better people. We can learn to live more meaningful lives. We can build more just societies and more cohesive communities. We are always evolving, and thus our work is never done. We can make progress toward humble knowledge of ourselves and others. The human sciences can help us get there. Let me try one final time to tell you how.

Metamodern Ethics: Revolutionary Happiness. Postmodernism took hold in the academy primarily as a species of moralizing yoked to a set of skeptical doxa. Under the sign of negative lodestars like logocentrism, essentialism, racism, phallocentrism, and the like, it provided a powerful set of ethical norms. But these were typically not recognized as ethics because they were articulated in a negative key. Proponents of value neutrality and ethical relativism shamed scholars into the notion that displaying commitments was akin to confessing failings. So scholars forced their values underground, only to have them emerge in simplistic condemnations or as ethical judgments smuggled in as epistemological critique.

Preaching a scornful version of value neutrality only perpetuates the problem it is trying to address. What we need—rather than suppressing our values—is to bring them to the surface and make them work for us, because only if they are acknowledged can we address them honestly and openly. Besides, our fear of values is unnecessary. There are many ways to move from an "is" to an "ought." Indeed, once these moves are recognized, we can see various legitimate means through which facts and values can be related. This does not mean that only values are important, but instead that empirical evidence turns out to bear a relation to some value claims, just as some value claims turn out to bear a relation to how we present empirical evidence. Furthermore, one of the most important ways to move from fact to value follows from the recognition of a stated goal. This permits impartial judgments vis-à-vis that goal.

I therefore proposed as a goal for the human sciences negating the negative ethics of postmodern criticism, and in so doing, unearthing a critical virtue ethics directed toward human and multispecies flourishing. Revolutionary Happiness says that if you want to live a life worth having lived, and if you can recognize that others want to do the same, this will transform your view of not only your personal habits, but the whole scholarly enterprise. There are pluralistic ways in which one might conceive eudaimonia, but I argued for engaged compassion as the central virtue. So one of our starting points—postmodernism's putative "ethical nihilism"—has given way to the more productive form of Revolutionary Happiness, which requires not only a reorientation toward ethics, but also a reorientation toward knowledge. For the human sciences to fulfill their potential, they need an epistemological stance that does not default into epistemological overconfidence or immature skepticism.

Metamodern Epistemology: Zeteticism. Postmodernism is identified with universal skepticism, but as we have seen, its skepticism didn't go far enough. It remained attached to the negative dogmas that drove its distrust into prejudged areas. We needed to be skeptical of such prepackaged skepticism. By universalizing doubt, we learned to doubt our own doubts. This led to a revised epistemological stance—Zeteticism—which represents a commitment to non-dogmatic, humble knowledge. Zetetic knowledge is knowledge as a social kind or process, not a final terminus.

Politicized skepticism has failed as both politics and epistemology, and it is now time for emancipatory knowledge. Metamodern Zeteticism combined with abduction helps us to understand, concretely, how theories (and other scholarly generalizations) should be constructed and evaluated. It shows us how we can make *progress* in both positive and negative knowledge (increasing evidence and refuting alternative hypotheses). Rejecting the search for certainty and simultaneously avoiding the philosophical neuroses that come from imagining ourselves to be disembodied consciousnesses, Zeteticism suggests that we can make more philosophical progress by (tentatively) postulating the interdependent co-arising of body and mind. With abductive inference in hand, we also now know how the world serves as its own model and how abduction directs our attention toward discovering its correlations and signs. For this we need a semiotics.

Metamodern Semiotics: Hylosemiotics. Postmodernism is regularly associated with the linguistic turn. The way to untangle the linguistic turn is in certain respects to intensify it rather than reject it. We approach the world semiotically, but like our fellow animals we are not imprisoned in language. Hylosemiotics—a naturalized, material semiotics—explores not only how the world functions in signs but also how sign-making and interpreting activities function across the animal and plant world.

Beyond addressing a number of philosophical problems, hylosemiotics has practical significance on its own. Faced with the unfolding crises of climate change, mass extinction, economic upheaval, and the potential end of the Anthropocene Era of human ascendancy, there have been numerous calls to embrace multispecies coexistence. As valuable as these calls are, they frequently run into trouble when pushing an ill-defined notion of "agency" out of the realm of humans and uncritically onto animals or objects. Hylosemiotics addresses the need to better interpret agency by providing a philosophical framework for cross-species communication that engages with ongoing research in animal ethology and related fields. Thus, hylosemiotics is only the first step, but it has implications for multispecies flourishing.

Hylosemiotics also provides an account of meaning that will be valuable to research across the disciplines. Meaning is inference. We need to think in terms of an asymmetry between sign production and sign consumption, voluntary and involuntary signs, or meaning-making and interpretation. We need to lift up a minimal ontology and a basic semantics together; to show how sentient beings interpret their environment and how communities of signaling organisms accommodate their sign systems to it. This account of meaning thus permits us to see the way in which humans have woven a rich semiosphere around ourselves in terms of social kinds.

Metamodern Social Ontology: Social Kinds. This monograph began with the recognition that many academic disciplines have been in crisis about their disciplinary objects. The answer offered here is not to reject the critique, but to grant it. This was for two reasons. First, we need to accept these strategies for demolition because the disintegration of concepts is in itself a valuable corrective to the reification and misplaced concreteness of the ordinary modes of approach in the human sciences. We have built our scholarship on shaky foundations. Often, we need to know that we are not imprisoned in the categories that have been used to define us. Destructive criticism is therefore necessary—not just for the discipline but for individual scholars—to clear the ground and shatter our old preconceptions, before we can achieve the simultaneous deconstructive vigilance and reconstructive ability our work requires.

Second, granting these deconstructive critiques enabled us to uncover the fundamental nature of the categories themselves as well as the mechanisms that produce and maintain them. In place of fixed and reified notions of our disciplinary objects, we can now see the social world in terms of a process social ontology with temporary zones of stability I have been calling "social kinds."

I described social kinds as *1) socially constructed 2) dynamic clusters of powers, 3) which are demarcated by the causal processes that anchor the relevant clusters.* Social kinds tend to be high-entropic and *niḥsvabhāva* (interdependent), and to cross-cut each other. Moreover, I argued against the standard oppositions between socially constructed and real, culture and nature, and social and physical properties. The core of this monograph has been an attempt to articulate the implications of this social ontology for scholarship in the humanities and social sciences.

This process social ontology provides new models for comparison, a focus on anchoring processes as opposed to pattern recognition, and an attention to how social kinds populate the worlds of humans and other creatures. It suggests a new research paradigm that, by granting diversity and change, focuses attention on stabilization and homogenization processes. It bifurcates language and social kinds so that we can study both. It also implies that we should give up on conceptual analysis as a scholarly mode. We should instead investigate the disciplinary master categories as historically entangled, unfolding power-clusters with a finite set of anchoring processes. From the rubble of the disciplinary objects I have aimed to build a new model for inquiry, but this social kinds theory necessitates, if anything, a heightened reflexivity toward our categories of analysis. Follow-up volumes by myself and (I hope) others will demonstrate the value of this mode of analysis.

My emphasis on power-clusters and the causal processes anchoring social kinds points toward important (and intertwined) issues about causation and power that I cut from the manuscript, not because I had nothing to say, but because I had too much. To explain: much academic theorizing and moralizing presumes asymmetries of power. But there has been remarkably little consensus as to what power is or how it should be theorized. To the extent that there is any consensus across disciplines, power is either conceived in terms of domination/subjection (à la Foucault plus

or minus Gramsci) or it is presumed to be something like a causal relation—an individual's power is supposed to equal their capacity to produce a change in someone else's behavior.[3] Although much in need of
refinement, this suggests that the better we can understand the nature
of cause and effect, the better we can understand power, and vice versa.
Meanwhile, in recent decades, there has been a set of fundamental re-
theorizations of causation in the natural sciences. Standing in the way of
anything comparable in the human sciences is the lack of a fundamental
theory of causation appropriate to our subject matter. (The human sciences aren't physics, but there is much that could be learned from philosophy of medicine.) What I am imagining as the next project will address this on both fronts—providing a new theory of causation for the
human sciences (that necessarily builds on the process social ontology
articulated in this manuscript) and exploring its implications for a new
theory of power.

Metarealism. Finally, I began this book by arguing that the conflict between realism and antirealism is primarily a phantom opposition—just
as is the putative dualism between real and socially constructed. Real is a
contrastive term that requires the specification of a particular converse to
be useful (e.g., references to "the real Napoleon" are misleading without
further specification about which other possible Napoleons are being excluded). To be "real" is often taken to mean mind-independent, but social
kinds are mind-dependent and also real. This led to a theory of various
kinds of mind-dependence and different modes of being real that allows
us to transcend the unhelpful opposition between realists and antirealists
and cures us of that particular philosophical neurosis.

Many controversies between realism and antirealism are about degrees
of confidence in whatever the philosopher in question takes to be the current "scientific paradigm." But now that we know that science is itself a
social kind, we can demystify ourselves of the idea that it holds to a single
paradigm or that its theories and postulated entities rise and fall together.
This is not "anti-science." We can take pride in scientific discoveries, embrace various scientific methods, and praise individual scientists without
portraying a false coherence or reifying "science" as such. Denying the
unity of science as a category means that many debates about the social
construction of specific scientific "facts" (e.g., discussion of the "social
construction" of the peptide TRF) are local problems primarily of importance to the scientific fields in which they arise, which have empirical ways
of trying to answer questions of that sort.

Rejecting scientism-masquerading-as-realism implies the need for
a better epistemology and social metaphysics, which metamodernism
aimed to provide. In sum, to do so required formulating a post-Kuhnian

philosophy of the human sciences grounded in a process social ontology that is capable of tracing the unfolding of de-essentialized master categories in their full complexity. It provides a set of tangible methods for producing a humble, emancipatory knowledge. This is Zetetic knowledge within the horizon of finitude. I neither expect nor want to be the last word on any of these subjects, and some of my ideas will evolve. Metamodernism is not a dogmatism. It neither desires nor imagines an orthodoxy. The problem with systems arises when they present themselves as being completely self-sufficient or all-inclusive. Metamodernism has pretensions to neither.

Metamodernism aspires to be a flash of illumination on a cloudy night. It is the beginning of a conversation, not an end to one. It encapsulates potent forces both destructive and ameliorative that will need to be worked through. This entire project represents a scattering of seeds. If metamodernism is to come to fruition, a few people must choose to grow some of these seeds into something I cannot imagine.

Notes

OPENING

1. I use "deconstruction" throughout to refer to a form of scholarly praxis that has long since escaped Jacques Derrida's more technical usage. For deconstruction beyond Derrida, see Mark Currie, *The Invention of Deconstruction* (New York: Palgrave Macmillan, 2013).

2. To clarify, I find intersectionality useful, but both class and race reductionisms are typically misguided. For a critique of the latter, see Touré Reed, *Toward Freedom: The Case Against Race Reductionism* (New York: Verso Books, 2020).

3. Examples, in order: James Daniel Collins, *Interpreting Modern Philosophy* (Princeton, NJ: Princeton University Press, 1972); Fredric Jameson, *The Cultural Turn: Selected Writings on the Postmodern 1983–1998* (London: Verso, 2009); Victoria E. Bonnell and Lynn Avery Hunt, eds., *Beyond the Cultural Turn: New Directions in the Study of Society and Culture* (Berkeley: University of California Press, 1999); Paul Rabinow and William M. Sullivan, eds., *Interpretive Social Sciences* (Berkeley: University of California Press, 1987); Jürgen Habermas, *Moralbewußtsein und kommunikatives Handeln* (Frankfurt am Main: Suhrkamp, 1983); and David R. Hiley, James Bohman, and Richard Shusterman, *The Interpretive Turn: Philosophy, Science, Culture* (Ithaca, NY: Cornell University Press, 1991).

4. Steve Fuller, Marc de Mey, Terry Shinn, and Steve Woolgar, *The Cognitive Turn: Sociological and Psychological Perspectives on Science* (Dordrecht: Springer Netherlands, 1989).

5. Steven Seidman, ed., *The Postmodern Turn: New Perspectives on Social Theory* (Cambridge: Cambridge University Press, 1995); and Steven Best and Douglas Kellner, *The Postmodern Turn* (New York: Guilford Press, 1997).

6. Terrence McDonald, *The Historic Turn in the Human Sciences* (Ann Arbor: University of Michigan Press, 1996).

7. For various turns to religion, see Hent de Vries, *Philosophy and the Turn to Religion* (Baltimore, MD: Johns Hopkins University Press, 1999); Dominique Janicaud, *Phenomenology and the "Theological Turn"* (New York: Fordham University Press, 2000); Ken Jackson and Arthur Marotti. "The Turn to Religion in Early Modern English Studies," *Criticism* 46, no. 1 (2004): 167–90; Bruce Holsinger, "Literary History and the Religious Turn," *English Language Notes* 44, no. 1 (2006): 1–3; and Philip Gorski et al., eds., *The Post-secular in Question* (New York: New York University Press, 2012). For the corporeal turn, see John Tambornino, *The Corporeal Turn*

(Lanham, MD: Rowman & Littlefield, 2002); and Maxine Sheets-Johnstone, *The Corporeal Turn* (Exeter: Imprint Academic, 2009).

8. Manuel DeLanda, *Intensive Science and Virtual Philosophy*, 3rd ed. (New York: Bloomsbury Academic, 2013), vi; Angela Dalle Vacche, *The Visual Turn: Classical Film Theory and Art History* (New Brunswick, NJ: Rutgers University Press, 2002); Jorge Ferrer and Jacob Sherman, eds., *The Participatory Turn: Spirituality, Mysticism, Religious Studies* (Albany, NY: SUNY Press, 2008); Patricia Ticineto Clough and Jean Halley, eds., *The Affective Turn: Theorizing the Social* (Durham, NC: Duke University Press, 2008); Tony Bennett and Patrick Joyce, eds., *Material Powers Cultural Studies, History and the Material Turn* (London: Routledge, 2010); Paul Jay, *Global Matters: The Transnational Turn in Literary Studies* (Ithaca, NY: Cornell University Press, 2010); Richard Bernstein, *The Pragmatic Turn* (Cambridge: Polity, 2010); Samson Okoth Opondo and Michael Shapiro, *The New Violent Cartography: Geo-Analysis After the Aesthetic Turn* (Milton Park, Abingdon, Oxon: Routledge, 2012); Nikolas Kompridis, ed., *The Aesthetic Turn in Political Thought* (New York: Bloomsbury Academic, 2014); David Howes, "The Social Life of the Senses" *Ars Vivendi Journal* 3 (February 2013): 4–23; Sheryl N. Hamilton et al., *Sensing Law* (New York: Routledge, 2017); Erich Reck, *The Historical Turn in Analytic Philosophy* (New York: Palgrave Macmillan, 2013); Thomas Faist, "The Mobility Turn: A New Paradigm for the Social Sciences?," Ethnic and Racial Studies 36, no. 11 (2013), 1637–46; Fujii Hikaru, *Outside, America: The Temporal Turn in Contemporary American Fiction* (New York: Bloomsbury, 2013); Christine Ross, *The Past Is the Present, It's the Future Too: The Temporal Turn in Contemporary Art* (New York: Bloomsbury, 2014); Barney Warf and Santa Arias, eds., *The Spatial Turn: Interdisciplinary Perspectives* (London: Routledge, 2014); Robyn Wiegman, "The Times We're In: Queer Feminist Criticism and the Reparative 'Turn,'" *Feminist Theory* 15, no. 1 (2014): 4–25; Erika Andersson Cederholm, ed., *Exploring the Animal Turn: Human-Animal Relations in Science, Society and Culture* (Lund, Sweden: Pufendorfinstitutet, 2014); Richard Arthur Grusin, *The Nonhuman Turn* (Minneapolis: University of Minnesota Press, 2015); Sverre Raffnsøe, *Philosophy of the Anthropocene: The Human Turn* (Basingstoke, Hampshire: Palgrave Macmillan, 2016); Martin Holbraad and Morten Axel Pedersen, *The Ontological Turn: An Anthropological Exposition* (New York: Cambridge University Press, 2017). For a meta-study of some of these, see Hester Blum, ed., *Turns of Event: Nineteenth-Century American Literary Studies in Motion* (Philadelphia: University of Pennsylvania Press, 2016).

9. Nadine Kalin, "(de)Fending Art Education through the Pedagogical Turn," *Journal of Social Theory in Art Education* 32 (2012): 42–55; Léna Soler et al., *Science after the Practice Turn in the Philosophy, History, and Social Studies of Science* (London: Routledge, 2014); Thomas A. Tweed, "After the Quotidian Turn: Interpretive Categories and Scholarly Trajectories in the Study of Religion since the 1960s," *Journal of Religion* 95, no. 3 (July 2015): 361–85; and Maarten Franssen et al., *Philosophy of Technology after the Empirical Turn* (Cham, Switzerland: Springer, 2016).

10. ISOMAE Jun'ichi and KAWAMURA Satofumi, eds., *Tasharonteki Tenkai: Shūkyō to Kōkyō Kūkan* (Kyoto: Nakanishiya Shuppan, 2016); Mark Seltzer, *Official World* (Durham, NC: Duke University Press, 2016).

11. For example, William Connolly provides page after page of complexity theory only to tell the reader that we should eat local and buy a Prius. William Connolly, *A World of Becoming* (Durham, NC: Duke University Press, 2010), 91.

12. I critique New Materialism in chapter 5 and speculative realism in chapter 1. For the critique of affect theory, see Ruth Leys, *The Ascent of Affect: Genealogy and Critique* (Chicago: University of Chicago Press, 2017).

13. Why lightning? Lightning illuminates while shattering or destroying that which it strikes; it is both a force of destruction and an energizing source of clarifying radiance. To take a leaf from the Indian philosopher Śāntideva: on a dark night a sudden flash of lightning illuminates everything, likewise this project aspires to be a brief and transient spark of illumination. I also have a love-hate relationship with Nietzsche. But for part of why I, and others in groups Nietzsche might have had problems with (such as the Black Panther Party) have been drawn to his work, see Huey P. Newton, *Revolutionary Suicide* (London: Penguin Classics, 2009), 319–23.

14. I wanted an inspirational project name, and I also wanted to avoid being ideological or promoting another new "-ism." But, in sharing this work with colleagues, people kept referring to the project as an example of "post-postmodernism," which frankly made me nauseous.

15. Michael Harris and Moyo Okediji, *Transatlantic Dialogue: Contemporary Art in and out of Africa* (Seattle: University of Washington Press, 1999); and Moyo Okediji, "Black Skin, White Kins: Metamodern Masks, Multiple Mimesis," in *Diaspora and Visual Culture: Representing Africans and Jews*, ed. Nicholas Mirzoeff (London: Routledge, 1999), 143–62.

16. "Metamodernism" appeared first in the 1970s as a near synonym to postmodernism. See Mas'ud Zavarzadeh, "The Apocalyptic Fact and the Eclipse of Fiction in Recent American Prose Narratives," *Journal of American Studies* 9, no. 1 (1975): 69–83.

In 2010 Timotheus Vermeulen and Robin van den Akker began using metamodernism to refer to "a range of aesthetic and cultural predilections and as a notion to periodise these preferences." Timotheus Vermeulen and Robin van den Akker, "Notes on Metamodernism," *Journal of Aesthetics & Culture* 2, no. 1 (2010): 5677; and Robin van den Akker, Alison Gibbons, and Timotheus Vermeulen, *Metamodernism: Historicity, Affect, Depth, after Postmodernism* (New York: Rowman and Littlefield, 2017). The British artist Luke Turner authored a "Metamodernist Manifesto" in 2011. My account has certain affective resonances with theirs. But I do not mean metamodernism in that way. (Nor do I mean "metamodern" as a kind of oscillation between modern and postmodern.) I am not trying to describe cultural modes or similarities across our current cultural moment; and for reasons that this book will make clear I am not trying to describe a new zeitgeist or periodization.

Postmodernism, as I use the term, is not a periodization or a cultural episteme but a particular scholarly model or paradigm. I am using metamodernism similarly to propose a new one.

Linda Ceriello uses the term "metamodern" to describe an epistemic and aesthetic shift she locates in the 2000s and connects to secular spiritualities and mystical experiences. See especially Linda C. Ceriello, "Toward a Metamodern Reading of Spiritual but not Religious Mysticisms," in *Being Spiritual but not Religious* (New York: Routledge, 2018), 200–218; and "Metamodern Mysticisms: Narrative Encounters with Contemporary Western Secular Spiritualities" (PhD diss, Rice University, 2018). Although not necessarily incompatible with my account, this is not what I am trying to do. Similarly, Seth Abramson has called for an American metamodernism that "reconstructs that which was deconstructed while also acknowledging all that we learned by deconstructing." (Seth Abramson, "Metamodernism in Five Terrible Diagrams," Medium.com (blog), July 26, 2017, http://medium.com/@Seth_Abramson/metamodernism-in-five-terrible-diagrams-5b43 0d681f7c). I broadly agree with Abramson's call but my way of bringing it about is very different.

Finally, a pair of Danish activists have been promoting a kind of metamodern politics under the name Hanzi Freinacht. This political metamodernism will be discussed in chapter 7.

In brief, if the thinkers above are the first significant theorists about metamodernist culture and art, I aspire to be the first significant metamodern philosopher. The scholars listed in this note are doing incredibly import work describing what they see as our current cultural episteme, and I have found their discussions of metamodernism useful inspiration. But they are mostly doing scholarship according to older models; I aim to provide a new one.

17. See Slavoj Žižek, *The Sublime Object of Ideology* (New York: Verso, 2008), 199.

18. Hegel argued: "philosophy returns into itself and reaches the point with which it began. In this manner philosophy exhibits the appearance of a circle which closes with itself." Georg Wilhelm Friedrich Hegel, *Hegel's Logic: Being Part One of the Encyclopaedia of the Philosophical Sciences* (New York: Oxford University Press, 1975), 27–28.

19. Sinan Kadir Çelik, "Postmodernism," in *Encyclopedia of Activism and Social Justice*, ed. Gary Anderson and Kathryn Herr (London: Sage Publications, 2007), 1155.

20. Çelik, "Postmodernism," 1154.

21. See Marc Orlitzky, "Ethical Nihilism," in *The Sage Encyclopedia of Business Ethics and Society*, ed. Robert Kolb (London: Sage, 2018), esp. 1233.

22. See David Foster Wallace, *A Supposedly Fun Thing I'll Never Do Again* (New York: Back Bay Books, 1998), 140; Charlene Spretnak, *The Resurgence of the Real* (London: Routledge, 1999), 64–65; Ken Wilber, *The Marriage of Sense and Soul: Integrating Science and Religion* (New York: Broadway Books, 1999); and Ian Aitken, "European Film Scholarship," in *The Sage Handbook of Film Studies*, ed. James Donald and Michael Renov (London: Sage, 2008), 25–53.

23. For invasion, Camille Paglia, *Sex, Art, and American Culture: Essays* (New York: Vintage Books, 1992), 210. For deconstruction, see François Cusset, *French theory: Foucault, Derrida, Deleuze & Cie et les mutations de la vie intellectuelle aux États-Unis* (Paris: Éditions la Découverte, 2003), 131–32; Mark Currie, *The Invention of Deconstruction* (New York: Palgrave Macmillan, 2013); Susanne Lüde-

mann, *Jacques Derrida zur Einführung* (Hamburg: Junius-Verl, 2011); James K.A. Smith, *Jacques Derrida: Live Theory* (New York: Continuum, 2005); and especially Rodolphe Gasché, *The Tain of the Mirror: Derrida and the Philosophy of Reflection* (Cambridge: Harvard University Press, 1997), 2–3. For poststructuralism or French theory, see Slavoj Žižek, *Looking Awry* (Cambridge: MIT Press, 1991), 142; Johannes Angermuller, *Why There is No Poststructuralism in France: The Making of an Intellectual Generation* (London: Bloomsbury Academic, 2015); Joëlle Bahloul, "France-USA: Ethnographie d'une migration intellectuelle," *Ethnologie Française* 21, no. 1 (1991): 49–55; Cusset, *French Theory*; and François Dosse, *Histoire du Structuralisme* (Paris: Éditions la Découverte, 1991). Angermuller has shown by tracking citations that the reputation of a range of theorists—including Foucault, Derrida, Kristeva, and Irigaray—is largely a product of English language scholarship. Angermuller, *Why There Is No Poststructuralism in France*, 5–6.

24. For further examples, see Claire Goldberg Moses, "Made in America: 'French Feminism' in Academia," *Feminist Studies* 24, no. 2 (1998): 241–74; and Antoine Compagnon, *The Five Paradoxes of Modernity* (New York: Columbia University Press, 1994), ix-x.

25. Kerwin Lee Klein, *From History to Theory* (Berkeley: University of California Press, 2011).

26. Cusset, *French Theory*.

27. John Watkins Chapman is typically identified as the first person to use "*post-modern.*" For this, scholars usually cite Steven Best and Douglas Kellner, *Postmodern Theory* (New York: Guilford Press, 1991), 5. But the source they cite is Dick Higgins, *A Dialectic of Centuries* (New York: Printed Editions, 1978), 7, which only refers to "Chapman" and provides no reference. So barring further evidence, I think this attribution is likely specious. The first Anglophone source I've verified is: J.M. Thompson, "Post-Modernism," *Hibbert Journal* 12, no. 4 (1914): 733–45. In the Spanish-speaking world, Federico de Onís is often credited with coining "*postmodernismo*" in 1934. See Michael Köhler, "Postmodernismus: ein begriffsgeschichtlicher Überblick," *Amerikastudien* 22, no. 1 (1977): 8–18. But there are provocative appearances of *postmodernista* in the Uruguayan poetry scene in 1931. Carlos Reyles, *Historia sintética de la literatura Uruguaya*, vol. 2 (Montevideo: A. Vila, 1931), 1.

28. Rudolf Pannwitz, *Die Krisis der europäischen Kultur* (Nuremberg: Hans Carl, 1917), 64, 226. Also discussed in Jason Ā. Josephson-Storm, *The Myth of Disenchantment: Magic, Modernity, and the Birth of the Human Sciences* (Chicago: University of Chicago Press, 2017), 307.

29. Bernard Bell, *Postmodernism, and Other Essays* (Milwaukee: Morehouse, 1926).

30. Jean-François Lyotard, *La condition postmoderne* (Paris: Minuit, 1979); Charles Jencks, *The Language of Post-Modern Architecture* (New York: Rizzoli, 1977); David Harvey, *The Condition of Postmodernity: An Enquiry into the Origins of Cultural Change* (Oxford: Blackwell, 1989); and Fredric Jameson, *Postmodernism, or, The Cultural Logic of Late Capitalism* (Durham, NC: Duke University Press, 1991).

31. See Dan Schiller, *Digital Capitalism* (Cambridge: MIT Press, 2000); Rich-

ard Sennett, *The Culture of the New Capitalism* (New Haven: Yale University Press, 2007); Guy Standing, *The Precariat* (London: Bloomsbury, 2011); and Shoshana Zuboff, *The Age of Surveillance Capitalism* (New York: Profile Books, 2019).

32. For examples, see Adeshina Afolayan, "We Are All Postmodernists Now! African Philosophy and the Postmodern Agenda," in *Ka Osi Sọ Onye: African Philosophy in the Postmodern Era*, ed. Jonathan Chimakonam and Edwin Etieyibo (Malaga, Spain: Vernon Press, 2018), 207–27; and Arif Dirlik and Zhang Xudong, eds., *Postmodernism & China* (Durham, NC: Duke University Press, 2000).

33. bell hooks, "Postmodern blackness," in *Yearning: Race, Gender, and Cultural Politics* (Boston: South End, 1990), 23–31; and Cornel West, "Postmodernism and Black America," *Zeta Magazine* 1, no. 6 (1987): 27–29.

34. See Josephson-Storm, *The Myth of Disenchantment.*

35. Charles Jencks, *What Is Post-modernism?* (New York: St. Martin's Press, 1986), 6 (omitted from later editions); Ben Agger, "Critical Theory, Poststructuralism, Postmodernism: Their Sociological Relevance," *Annual Review of Sociology* 17 (1991): 105–31; Richard Kearney, "Introduction," in *Continental Philosophy in the 20th Century*, ed. Richard Kearney (London: Routledge, 2003), 2; and Dominick LaCapra, "Criticism Today," in *Jean François Lyotard: Critical Evaluations in Cultural Theory*, vol. 2, ed. Victor E. Taylor and Gregg Lambert (London: Routledge, 2006), 279. See also Michael LeMahieu, *Fictions of Fact and Value: The Erasure of Logical Positivism in American Literature, 1945–1975* (London: Oxford University Press, 2013), 195. For more on logical positivism, see Josephson-Storm, *The Myth of Disenchantment*, 240–68.

36. Jean-François Lyotard, *The Inhuman: Reflections on Time* (Stanford, CA: Stanford University Press, 1991), 71.

37. For example, Jacques Derrida, *Limited Inc.* (Evanston, IL: Northwestern University Press, 1988), 137. Admittedly, Baudrillard might be productively classed as an anti-realist.

38. Rudolf Carnap, *The Logical Structure of the World; and Pseudoproblems in Philosophy* (Chicago: Open Court, 2003), x–xi.

39. For examples: Gerard Delanty, *Social Science: Beyond Constructivism and Realism* (Minneapolis: University of Minnesota Press, 1997), 99; Christine Jones, "Postmodernism's Linguistic Turn," in *Modern Criticism*, ed. Christopher Rollason and Mittapalli Rajeshwar (New Delhi: Atlantic, 2002), 1–10; Daniel Punday, *Narrative after Deconstruction* (Albany, NY: SUNY Press, 2003), 1–2. See also John E. Toews, "Intellectual History after the Linguistic Turn," *The American Historical Review* 92, no. 4 (1987): 879–907, 881–82, 889; Gabrielle Spiegel, *Practicing History: New Directions in Historical Writing after the Linguistic Turn* (New York: Routledge, 2005), 2; Georg Iggers, *Historiography in the Twentieth Century* (Middletown, CT: Wesleyan University Press), 1997.

40. Gustav Bergmann, "Logical Positivism, Language, and the Reconstruction of Metaphysics," *Rivista critica di storia della filosofia* 8 (1953): 453–81, reprinted in Gustav Bergmann, *The Metaphysics of Logical Positivism* (New York: Longmans Green, 1954), 30–77. In some sectors of analytical philosophy, the linguistic turn

is taken back to Russell's famous essay "On Denoting," *Mind* (New Series) 14, no. 56 (October 1905): 479–93.

41. New Criticism got its name from John Crow Ransom, *The New Criticism* (New York: New Directions, 1941). See Donald J. Childs, *The Birth of New Criticism* (London: McGill-Queen's University Press, 2014). To be fair, we could go back to C.S. Peirce, Wittgenstein, Wilhelm von Humboldt, J.G. Hamann, or Friedrich Nietzsche (or even Plato's Cratylus) for comparable insights.

42. Northrop Frye, *Fearful Symmetry: A Study of William Blake* (Princeton, NJ: Princeton University Press, 1947); and William Wimsatt and Monroe Beardsley, "The Intentional Fallacy," *The Sewanee Review* 54, no. 3 (1946): 468–88. T.S. Elliot was also crucial in this movement. Eric Hirsch, *Validity in Interpretation* (New Haven: Yale University Press, 1967).

43. C.K. Ogden and I.A. Richards, *The Meaning of Meaning*, 8th ed. (London: Kegan Paul, 1946), 1, 26. I do not mean to overplay the importance of *The Meaning of Meaning*. The 1920s–1940s saw multiple works addressing thought and language: e.g., Edward Sapir "The Status of Linguistics as a Science" *Language* 5, no. 4 (1929): 207–14; Alfred Korzybski, *Science and Sanity* (Lancaster, PA: International Non-Aristotelian Library Publishing Company, 1933); I.A. Richards, *The Philosophy of Rhetoric* (New York: Oxford University Press, 1936); Samuel Ichiye Hayakawa, *Language in Thought and Action* (New York: Harcourt, Brace, 1939); and Susanne Langer, *Philosophy in a New Key: A Study in the Symbolism of Reason, Rite and Art* (New York: New American Library, 1941). For why Nietzsche's "prison-house of language" was a mistranslation, see Storm, "Language, Mind, Cosmos," forthcoming.

44. Tobin Siebers, *Cold War Criticism and the Politics of Skepticism* (New York: Oxford University Press, 1993), 3, 29.

45. Karl Popper, *The Open Society and Its Enemies*, vol. 1 (London: Routledge, 1947), 60.

46. See Ayn Rand, *Capitalism: The Unknown Ideal* (New York: Signet, 1967), 281; and Cyril Joad, *A Critique of Logical Positivism* (Chicago: University of Chicago Press, 1950), 152. For a fuller exposition, see LeMahieu, *Fictions of Fact and Value*.

47. Thomas Kuhn, *The Structure of Scientific Revolutions* (Chicago: University of Chicago Press, 1996), 43.

48. Josephson-Storm, *The Myth of Disenchantment*, 306–7.

49. For example, see Robert Pippin, "Nietzsche and the Origin of the Idea of Modernism," *Inquiry* 26 (1983): 151–80, esp. 151.

50. Donald Campbell, "Ethnocentrism of Disciplines and the Fish-Scale Model of Omniscience," in Muzafer Sherif and Carolyn W. Sherif, eds., *Interdisciplinary Relationships in the Social Sciences* (Chicago: Aldine Press, 1969), 328–48; Juan Gilbert, "Silos of Academe Thwart Diversity on Campuses," *Chronicle of Higher Education* 55, no. 5 (2008): 45; Lewis Gordon, *Disciplinary Decadence: Living Thought in Trying Times* (New York: Routledge, 2015), 4–5; and Mark Taylor, *Crisis on Campus: A Bold Plan for Reforming Our Colleges and Universities* (New York: Knopf, 2010). For early research on the subject, see Tony Becher and Paul Trowler, *Academic Tribes and Territories* (London: McGraw-Hill Education, 2001).

51. Rogers Brubaker, "The Uproar Over 'Transracialism,'" *New York Times*, May 18, 2017.

52. Religious studies has long been split over whether scholarly distance requires outsider status or only insiders can really understand the essences of specific religions. Both positions are fraught. See José Cabezón and Sheila Greeve Davaney, eds., *Identity and the Politics of Scholarship in the Study of Religion* (London: Routledge, 2004).

53. For repudiations of this, all too common, misreading of standpoint theory, see: Sandra Harding, "Rethinking Standpoint Epistemology: What Is Strong Objectivity?" *The Centennial Review* 36, no. 3 (1992): 437–70; Donna Haraway, "Situated Knowledges: The Science Question in Feminism and the Privilege of Partial Perspective," *Feminist Studies* 14, no. 3 (1988): 575–99; Miranda Fricker, *Epistemic Injustice: Power and the Ethics of Knowing* (Oxford: Oxford University Press, 2011); and Alison Wylie, "Why Standpoint Matters," in *Science and Other Cultures*, ed. Robert Figueroa and Sandra Harding (New York: Routledge, 2003), 26–48.

54. See George Yancy, ed., *Philosophy in Multiple Voices* (Lanham, MD: Rowman & Littlefield, 2007), esp. 14. I would add, however, that appeals to the universal are ubiquitous in not just Euro-American philosophy, but also classical philosophy in East Asia and South Asia, as well as in the Islamicate world more broadly. Indeed, much of what we have preserved of "pre-modern" sub-Saharan African philosophy also makes claims to the universal. For famously universalizing African philosophers, think Zera Yacob and Anton Wilhelm Amo.

55. Kwasi Wiredu, *Cultural Universals and Particulars: An African Perspective* (Bloomington: Indiana University Press, 1997), 5.

56. Gesturing toward Harding and Haraway above, but epistemology is explored in greater detail in chapter 6.

57. Many people seem to abhor ambiguities of gender and "race," so in this autobiographical note, I want to be more specific for those who are curious.

By "queer" I mean that I am a bisexual man enacting a nonconforming masculinity. I am also married to a bisexual woman.

By "mixed race" I do not mean to imply that there are any pure or unmixed "races," much less that race is a useful biological category. For a critique of the former, see Karen Fields and Barbara Fields, *Racecraft: The Soul of Inequality in American Life* (New York: Verso, 2014). But "race" is a relevant cultural construct, and on a personal level I have been consistently racialized in different respects.

Specifically, I am most identified with my Sephardic (Portuguese/Spanish) Jewish and Hispanic heritages, and in different contexts I code as (and have encountered discrimination for being) Jewish, Hispanic, or ambiguously "ethnic." I have other heritages as well that are significant to me personally. For instance, if family tradition is correct, we are also Romani or gypsy (and I grew up thinking of myself as such), and in the unlikely event that 23andme is correct, we are also one drop West African (which, if that's true, I'm proud of, though I would certainly never claim to be Black, as I do not code that way and did not grow up with that self-understanding). All of these are variously racialized such that at times I have personally experienced anti-Semitism or generalized "not-quite-white" racism while in other settings I have passed for "White." (As the child of an immigrant, I also have a complicated sense of my "americanness" or lack thereof.)

The reasons I prefer "mixed race" to "mixed ethnicity" are: First, although there are exceptions, like many US American Hispanics, I experience my Hispanic heritage as racialized and hence non-white in certain contexts. Romani too are typically construed as "brown" or Asian in both the US and Europe. So, I think reading these heritages as non-white is probably not controversial.

But second, and perhaps more controversially, I also think it is a mistake for us Jews to identify as "white." As Michael Lerner has argued, "calling Jews 'white'" is often "in effect denying the history of oppression" and overlooking the long and ongoing history of anti-Semitism in the United States. Basically, contemporary anti-Semitism is functionally a type of racism. See Michael Lerner and Cornel West, *Jews and Blacks: Let the Healing Begin* (New York: G.P. Putnam's Sons, 1995), 67 and also Melanie Kaye/Kantrowitz, *The Colors of Jews* (Bloomington: Indiana University Press, 2007), esp. 1–32. For a more recent discussion in light of rising anti-Semitic hate crimes, see Micha Danzig, "Anti-Semitism in America Is Nothing New. Don't Deny Jewish History and Culture by Calling Us 'White,'" *The Forward*, December 1, 2016. For a rejection of the claim that Jews can or should be understood within the narrow white/black dichotomy, see Jeffrey Israel, *Living with Hate in American Politics and Religion* (New York: Columbia University Press, 2019).

Further, as specifically a Sephardic Jew it is probably harder for me to pass for "White" than some, and for that (and other reasons) I have experienced secondary othering even within Ashkenazi Jewish communities. See Sergio DellaPergola, "'Sephardic and Oriental': Jews in Israel and Western Countries: Migration, Social Change, and Identification," *Studies in Contemporary Jewry* 22 (2007), 3–44.

58. Boaventura de Sousa Santos, *Another Knowledge Is Possible: Beyond Northern Epistemologies* (London: Verso, 2008), xiv.

CHAPTER ONE

1. See: Caleb Miller, "Realism, Antirealism, and Common Sense," in William Alston, *Realism & Antirealism* (Ithaca, NY: Cornell University Press, 2002), 13–25, 14; Silvia López, Jenaro Taléns, and Darío Villanueva, eds., *Critical Practices in Post-Franco Spain* (Minneapolis: University of Minnesota Press, 1994), 161; George Shields, "A Logical Analysis of Relational Realism," in Timothy Eastman, Michael Epperson, and David Griffin, *Physics and Speculative Philosophy: Potentiality in Modern Science* (Boston: De Gruyter, 2016), 127–40, 129; Susan Napier, *The Fantastic in Modern Japanese Literature* (New York: Routledge, 1996), 58.

2. Kuhn, *The Structure of Scientific Revolutions*, 88.

3. See Edward Slingerland, *What Science Offers the Humanities* (Cambridge: Cambridge University Press, 2008).

4. One way to detect whether the encounter with science is superficial is if the humanist in question is citing not scholarly articles but popular summaries.

5. One of my few points of agreement with Alan Sokal. Alan Sokal and Jean Bricmont, *Impostures intellectuelles* (Paris: Odile Jacob, 1997).

6. For example, see R. Andrew Sayer, *Method in Social Science: A Realist Approach* (London: Routledge, 1992). Some critical realists, especially in sociology, are more sophisticated, e.g., Douglas Porpora, *Reconstructing Sociology: The Critical Realist Approach* (New York: Cambridge University Press, 2015). But space prohibits full engagement.

7. Kevin Schilbrack, "A Realist Social Ontology of Religion," *Religion* 47, no. 2 (2017): 161–78. To be clear, some of Schilbrack's criticisms of other theorists are on point. See also Kevin Schilbrack, "After We Deconstruct 'Religion,' Then What? A Case for Critical Realism," *Method & Theory in the Study of Religion* 25, no. 1 (2013): 107–12.

8. K. Brad Wray, *Resisting Scientific Realism* (New York: Cambridge University Press, 2018). See also: Jerrold Aronson, Rom Harré, and Eileen Cornell Way, *Realism Rescued: How Scientific Progress Is Possible* (Chicago: Open Court Publishing, 1995); Anjan Chakravartty, *A Metaphysics for Scientific Realism* (New York: Cambridge University Press, 2007); Stathis Psillos, *Scientific Realism: How Science Tracks Truth* (New York: Routledge, 2005).

9. Ray Brassier, "I Am a Nihilist Because I Still Believe in Truth," blog post, https://xylem.aegean.gr/~modestos/mo.blog/i-am-a-nihilist-because-i-still-believe-in-truth/; and Quentin Meillassoux, *Après la finitude: Essai sur la nécessité de la contingence* (Paris: Seuil, 2006).

10. See Arthur Fine, *The Shaky Game: Einstein, Realism and the Quantum Theory* (Chicago: University of Chicago Press, 1996), 128; Gary Gutting, *Michel Foucault's Archaeology of Scientific Reason* (Cambridge: Cambridge University Press, 1999); and Christopher Johnson, "Derrida and Science," *Revue Internationale de Philosophie* 52, no. 205 (3) (1998): 477–93.

11. Simon Blackburn, "Realism: Deconstructing the Debate," *Ratio* 15, no. 2 (2002): 111–33, 112.

12. See also Fine, *The Shaky Game*; Wray, *Resisting Scientific Realism*; and Paul Magnus and Craig Callender, "Realist Ennui and the Base Rate Fallacy," *Philosophy of Science* 71, no. 3 (2004): 320–38.

13. The other main difference between putative antirealists and realists is whether they hold an optimistic or a pessimistic attitude about whether our current scientific findings will eventually be overturned by a paradigm shift. See Wray, *Resisting Scientific Realism*.

14. Jason Ānanda Josephson [Storm], *The Invention of Religion in Japan* (Chicago: University of Chicago Press, 2012), 143–47, 241.

15. William Alston, ed., *Realism & Antirealism* (Ithaca, NY: Cornell University Press, 2002), 1. See also Nicholas Rescher, *Scientific Realism: A Critical Reappraisal* (Dordrecht: D. Reidel, 1987), 149.

16. Michael Devitt, *Realism and Truth* (Princeton, NJ: Princeton University Press, 1997), 15–16. See also Lee Braver, *A Thing of This World: A History of Continental Anti-realism* (Chicago: Northwestern University Press, 2007), 15.

17. Bimal Krishna Matilal, "A Realist View of Perception," In *The Philosophy of P.F. Strawson*, ed. Pranab Kumar Sen and Roop Rekha Verma (New Delhi: Indian Council of Philosophical Research, 1995), 305–27.

18. Hilary Putnam, *Representation and Reality* (Cambridge: MIT Press, 1988), 107. See also Catherine Kendig, ed., *Natural Kinds and Classification in Scientific Practice* (New York: Routledge, 2015), esp. 2.

19. For the first two, see Gideon Rosen, "Objectivity and Modern Idealism: What Is the question?" in *Philosophy in Mind*, ed. Michaelis Michael and John Hawthorne (Dordrecht: Kluwer, 1994), 277–319.

20. Sally Haslanger, *Resisting Reality: Social Construction and Social Critique* (New York: Oxford University Press, 2012), esp. 87, 131.

21. One can also find precedents for global forms of mind-dependence in Buddhist thought (e.g., the Dhammapada 1:1, "All experience is preceded by mind, led by mind, made by mind") and elsewhere in classical Indian philosophy.

22. Italics in original. James Boswell, *The Life of Samuel Johnson* (Oxford: Oxford University Press, 1953), 333.

23. Bruno Latour, "Clothing the Naked Truth," In *Dismantling Truth: Reality in the Post-Modern World*, ed. Hilary Lawson and Lisa Appignanesi (New York: St. Martin's Press, 1989), 101–28.

24. Derek Edwards, Malcolm Ashmore, and Jonathan Potter, "Death and Furniture: The Rhetoric, Politics and Theology of Bottom Line Arguments against Relativism," *History of the Human Sciences* 8, no. 2 (1995): 25–49.

25. Karl Marx and Friedrich Engels, *The German Ideology* (London: Lawrence, 1970), 37.

26. For example, Quentin Meillassoux's odd assertion that Kantians would have a problem explaining fossils.

27. Manuel Vásquez, *More than Belief: A Materialist Theory of Religion* (Oxford: Oxford University Press, 2011), 13.

28. Andrew Collier, *Critical Realism: An Introduction to Roy Bhaskar's Philosophy* (London: Verso, 1994), 8.

29. George Berkeley, *Principles of Human Knowledge and Three Dialogues* (New York: Oxford University Press, 1996), 38.

30. See Howard Robinson's introduction to Berkeley, *Principles of Human Knowledge*, xiv.

31. Schopenhauer cited in Bryan Magee, *The Philosophy of Schopenhauer* (Oxford: Clarendon Press, 1997), 82.

32. Friedrich Nietzsche, *Sämtliche Werke*, vol. 6, ed. Giorgio Colli and Mazzino Montinari (Munich: Deutscher Taschenbuch-Verlag, 1999), 79.

33. This was basically a variation on Edmund Husserl's phenomenological "bracketing" (*Einklammerung*) or epoché, but reformulated in terms of language instead of bare perception. See Edmund Husserl, *Cartesian Meditations: An Introduction to Phenomenology* (Boston: Martinus Nijhoff, 1960), esp. 20–27.

34. See Jacques Derrida, "Hospitality, Justice and Responsibility," in *Questioning Ethics: Contemporary Debates in Continental Philosophy*, ed. Mark Dooley and Richard Kearney (New York: Routledge, 2002), 77.

35. Jacques Lacan, *The Seminar of Jacques Lacan*, vol. 1 (London: Norton, 1988), 66.

36. Arjun Appadurai, "The Thing Itself," *Public Culture* 18, no. 1 (2006): 15–22.

37. Richard Rorty, *Objectivity, Relativism, and Truth* (New York: Cambridge University Press, 1991), 2, 148; and Rorty, "Beyond Realism and Anti-Realism," in *Wo steht die Analytische Philosophie heute?* ed. Ludwig Nagl and Richard Heinrich (Vienna: Oldenbourg, 1986), 103–15.

38. Fine, *The Shaky Game*, 112.

39. Meillassoux, *Après la finitude*.

40. Lewis Gordon, *Fanon and the Crisis of European Man* (New York: Routledge, 1995), esp. 47–48.

41. Ashley Montagu, *Man's Most Dangerous Myth: The Fallacy of Race* (Walmut Creek: Altamira Press, 1998), 31.

42. Ian Hacking, *The Social Construction of What?* (Cambridge: Harvard University Press, 1999); and Haslanger, *Resisting Reality*.

43. The deceptively simple Thomas theorem (formulated by William Thomas and Dorothy Thomas) that "If men define situations as real, they are real in their consequences" has underwritten a lot of good empirical work, but it has often been interpreted to claim that meaning is constructed anew with each fresh micro-interaction (see Robert Merton, "The Thomas Theorem and the Matthew Effect," *Social Forces* 74, no. 2 [1995]: 379–422). Peter Berger and Thomas Luckmann, *The Social Construction of Reality* (New York: Penguin, 1966) posit something akin to the process social ontology that I advocate in chapter 3, in part by giving an account of how "definitions of the situation" via "institutionalization" take on a relative degree of stability. I think of my project as allied with Berger and Luckmann but providing a more sophisticated account of how social processes function.

44. See Gordon, *Fanon and the Crisis of European Man*; and Charles Mills, *Blackness Visible: Essays on Philosophy and Race* (Ithaca, NY: Cornell University Press, 1998), esp. 41–66.

45. As has been pointed out to me by a reader, there is a similar argument about *real* as a contrastive term in J.L. Austin, *Sense and Sensibilia* (Oxford: Oxford University Press, 1964).

46. Andrew Pickering, *Constructing Quarks: A Sociological History of Particle Physics* (Chicago: University of Chicago Press, 1999).

47. See Jody Azzouni, *Talking about Nothing* (New York: Oxford University Press, 2010); John Bigelow, *The Reality of Numbers* (Oxford: Clarendon, 1988); Tim Crane, *The Objects of Thought* (Oxford: Oxford University Press, 2013); and Boris Kukso, "The Reality of Absences," *Australasian Journal of Philosophy* 84, no. 1 (2006): 21–37.

48. As a real fictional character Sherlock Holmes has properties such as being more famous than any actual living detective. See Crane, *Objects of Thought*, 13.

49. Alexius Meinong, "The Theory of Objects," in *Realism and the Background of Phenomenology*, ed. Roderick Chisholm (Atascadero, CA: Ridgeview, 1981).

50. Crane, *Objects of Thought*, 25–26.

51. See Roy Sorensen, *Seeing Dark Things: The Philosophy of Shadows* (Oxford: Oxford University Press, 2008), 19; and Nirmalya Guha. "No Black Scorpion Is Fall-

ing: An Onto-Epistemic Analysis of Absence," *Journal of Indian Philosophy* 41, no. 2 (2013): 111–131.

52. Crane, *Objects of Thought*, 69.

53. See Stacie Friend, "Fictional Characters," *Philosophy Compass* 2, no. 2 (2007): 141–56; and Bryan Lowe, "Contingent and Contested: Preliminary Remarks on Buddhist Catalogs and Canons in Early Japan," *Japanese Journal of Religious Studies* 41, no. 2 (2014): 221–53.

CHAPTER TWO

1. Dating from Wilfred Cantwell Smith, *The Meaning and End of Religion*, which was originally published in 1962.

2. Jonathan Z. Smith, *Imagining Religion: From Babylon to Jonestown* (Chicago: University of Chicago Press, 1982), xi.

3. See Slavoj Žižek, *The Sublime Object of Ideology* (New York: Verso, 2008), vii.

4. For a more exhaustive list of deconstructive works, see extended notes 23 and 46 below.

5. Marguerite Deslauriers, *Aristotle on Definition* (Leiden: Brill, 2007).

6. Jerry Fodor, *Hume Variations* (Oxford: Oxford University Press, 2003), 6; and William Lycan, "On the Gettier Problem Problem," in *Epistemology Futures*, ed. Stephen Hetherington (Oxford: Clarendon Press, 2006), 148–68, 150. Both cited in Michael Hannon, *What's the Point of Knowledge? A Function-First Epistemology* (Oxford: Oxford University Press, 2018), 17–18.

7. Paul Elbourne, *Meaning* (Oxford: Oxford University Press, 2011), 1.

8. Edward Craig, *Knowledge and the State of Nature* (Oxford: Clarendon, 1990), esp. 2; Michael Huemer, "The Failure of Analysis and the Nature of Concepts," in *The Palgrave Handbook of Philosophical Method*, ed. Christopher Daly (London: Palgrave Macmillan, 2015), 51–76; Stephen Laurence and Eric Margolis, "Concepts and Conceptual Analysis," *Philosophy and Phenomenological Research* 67, no. 2 (2003): 253–82; Stephen Stich, "What Is a Theory of Mental Representation," *Mind* 101, no. 402 (1992): 243–61; Timothy Williamson, *Knowledge and Its Limits* (Oxford: Oxford University Press, 2000).

9. Gilles Deleuze, *Différence et répétition* (Paris: Presses Universitaires de France, 1968), esp. 20–22; and Gilles Deleuze and Félix Guattari, *Qu'est-ce que la philosophie?* (Paris: Éditions de Minuit, 2005).

10. Jacques Derrida, *Margins of Philosophy* (Chicago: University of Chicago Press, 1982), 3.

11. See Axel Honneth, *Reification: A New Look at an Old Idea* (Oxford: Oxford University Press, 2012) and TAIRAKO Tomonaga, "Versachlichung and Verdinglichung," *Hitotsubashi Journal of Social Studies* 48, no. 1 (2017): 1–26.

12. See F. Max Müller, *Lectures on the Origin and Growth of Religion* (London: Longmans, 1878), 8–10, 20.

13. Wilfred Cantwell Smith, *The Meaning and End of Religion* (Minneapolis: Fortress Press, 1991), 21–22.

14. Smith, *Meaning and End of Religion*, 37.

15. There was not even a Hebrew word for "Judaism" until the Middle Ages.

16. Smith, *Meaning and End of Religion*, 53–60.

17. Smith, *Meaning and End of Religion*, 61–62.

18. Smith, *Meaning and End of Religion*, 51.

19. Smith, *Meaning and End of Religion*, 12.

20. Smith, *Meaning and End of Religion*, 327.

21. Smith's theological critique of the concept of "religion" has parallels in the work of Dietrich Bonhoeffer, Franz Rosenzweig, and Ernst Feil.

22. Wilfred Cantwell Smith, "Retrospective Thoughts on the Meaning and End of Religion," in *Religion in History the Word, the Idea, the Reality*, ed. Michel Despland and Gèrard Vallèe (Waterloo, Ontario: Wilfrid Laurier University Press, 1992), 13–22, 15. See also Smith, *Meaning and End of Religion*, 19.

23. An incomplete list of representative works in the critical turn in religion include the following: Philip Almond, *The British Discovery of Buddhism* (New York: Cambridge University Press, 1988); Talal Asad, *Genealogies of Religion: Discipline and Reasons of Power in Christianity and Islam* (Baltimore: Johns Hopkins University Press, 1993); Talal Asad, *Formations of the Secular: Christianity, Islam, Modernity* (Stanford, CA: Stanford University Press, 2003); S.N. Balagangadhara, *"The Heathen in His Blindness . . .": Asia, the West, and the Dynamic of Religion* (Leiden: Brill, 1994); Leora Batnitzky, *How Judaism Became a Religion* (Princeton, NJ: Princeton University Pres, 2013); Michael Bergunder, "'Religion' and 'Science' within a Global Religious History," *Aries* 16, no. 1 (2016), 86–141; Daniel Boyarin, *Border Lines: The Partition of Judaeo-Christianity* (Philadelphia: University of Pennsylvania Press, 2004); Robert Campany, "On the Very Idea of Religions (in the Modern West and in Early Medieval China)," *History of Religions* 42, no. 4 (2003): 287–319; David Chidester, *Savage Systems: Colonialism and Comparative Religion in Southern Africa* (Charlottesville: University Press of Virginia, 1996); Vasudha Dalmia and Heinrich von Stietencron, eds., *Representing Hinduism: The Construction of Religious Traditions and National Identity* (New Delhi: Sage Publications, 1995); Jacques Derrida and Gianni Vattimo, *La Religion: Séminaire de Capri sous la direction de Jacques Derrida et Gianni Vattimo* (Paris: Éditions du Seuil, 1996); Michel Despland, *Le Religion en occident: Evolution des idées et du vécu* (Montreal: Fides, 1979); Michel Despland, *L'Emergence des sciences de la religion* (Paris: L'Harmattan, 1999); Markus Dressler and Arvind-pal Mandair, *Secularism and Religion-Making* (New York: Oxford University Press, 2011); Daniel Dubuisson, *L'Occident et la religion: Mythes, science et idéologie* (Brussels: Complexe, 1998); Ernst Feil, *Religio: die Geschichte eines neuzeitlichen Grundbegriffs vom Frühchristentum bis zur Reformation* (Göttingen: Vandenhoeck & Ruprecht, 1986); Timothy Fitzgerald, *The Ideology of Religious Studies* (New York: Oxford University Press, 2000); Vincent Goosaert, "Le concept de religion en Chine et l'Occident," *Diogène* 1, no. 2005 (2004): 11–21; Jeffrey Guhin, "Religion as Site rather than Religion as Category: On the Sociology of Religion's Export Problem," *Sociology of Religion* 75, no. 4 (2014): 579–93; Peter Harrison, *"Religion" and the Religions in the English Enlightenment* (New York: Cambridge University Press, 1990); Peter Harrison, *The Territories of Science and Religion* (Chicago: University of Chi-

cago Press, 2015); Adrian Hermann, *Unterscheidungen der Religion* (Göttingen: Vandenhoeck & Ruprecht, 2015); HOSHINO Seiji, *Kindai Nihon no shūkyō gainen: Shūkyōsha no kotoba to kindai* (Tokyo: Yūshisha Press, 2012); Aaron Hughes, *Abrahamic Religions: On the Uses and Abuses of History* (New York: Oxford University Press, 2013); ISOMAE Jun'ichi, *Kindai Nihon no Shūkyō Gensetsu to Sono Keifu* (Tokyo: Iwanami Shoten, 2003); Josephson [Storm], *Invention of Religion in Japan*; Richard King, *Orientalism and Religion: Postcolonial Theory, India and "the Mystic East"* (London: Routledge, 1999); Hans Martin Krämer, *Shimaji Mokurai and the Reconception of Religion and the Secular in Modern Japan* (Honolulu: University of Hawaii Press, 2015); Craig Martin, *Capitalizing Religion* (New York: Bloomsbury Publishing, 2014); Tomoko Masuzawa, *The Invention of World Religions, or, How European Universalism was Preserved in the Language of Pluralism* (Chicago: University of Chicago Press, 2005); Russell McCutcheon, *Manufacturing Religion: The Discourse on Sui Generis Religion and the Politics of Nostalgia* (Oxford: Oxford University Press, 1997); Russell McCutcheon, *The Discipline of Religion: Structure, Meaning, Rhetoric* (London: Routledge, 2003); Russell McCutcheon, "The Category 'Religion' in Recent Publications: Twenty Years Later," *Numen* 62, no. 1 (2015): 119–41; Rebecca Nedostup, *Superstitious Regimes: Religion and the Politics of Chinese Modernity* (Cambridge: Harvard University Asia Center, 2009); Brent Nongbri, *Before Religion: A History of a Modern Concept* (New Haven: Yale University Press, 2013); Harjot Oberoi, *The Construction of Religious Boundaries: Culture, Identity, and Diversity in the Sikh Tradition* (Chicago: University of Chicago Press, 1994); Geoffrey A. Oddie, *Imagined Hinduism: British Protestant Missionary Constructions of Hinduism* (New Delhi: Sage, 2006); Derek Peterson, and Darren Walhof, eds., *The Invention of Religion: Rethinking Belief in Politics and History* (London: Rutgers University Press, 2001); Sharada Sugirtharajah, *Imagining Hinduism: A Postcolonial Perspective* (London: Routledge, 2003); Rosalind Shaw, "The Invention of 'African Traditional Religion,'" *Religion* 20, no. 4 (1990): 339–53; Jonathan Z. Smith, *Imagining Religion: From Babylon to Jonestown* (Chicago: University of Chicago Press, 1982); Jonathan Z. Smith, *Relating Religion: Essays in the Study of Religion* (Chicago: University of Chicago Press, 2004); Anna Sun, *Confucianism as a World Religion: Contested Histories and Contemporary Realities* (Princeton, NJ: Princeton University Press, 2013); Teemu Taira, "The Category of 'Invented Religion': A New Opportunity for Studying Discourses on 'Religion,'" *Culture and Religion* 14, no. 4 (2013): 477–93; Jolyon Baraka Thomas, *Faking Liberties: Religious Freedom in American-occupied Japan* (Chicago: University of Chicago Press, 2019); Judith Weisenfeld, *New World a-Coming: Black Religion and Racial Identity During the Great Migration* (New York: New York University Press, 2019); and Tisa Wenger, *We Have a Religion: The 1920s Pueblo Indian Dance Controversy and American Religious Freedom* (Chapel Hill: University of North Carolina Press, 2009).

24. Josephson [Storm], *Invention of Religion in Japan*, 8–11.

25. Josephson [Storm], *Invention of Religion in Japan*.

26. Gottlob Frege, "Sense and Reference," *The Philosophical Review* 57, no. 3 (1948): 209–230. I provide an alternative account of meaning in chapter 5.

27. See Benjamin Beit-Hallahmi, "Scientology: Religion or Racket?" *Marburg Journal of Religion* 8, no. 1 (2003): 1–56.

28. Nongbri, *Before Religion*, 8. A valuable work, but one with an undertheorized account of meaning.

29. William Shakespeare, *King John: The Arden Shakespeare*, ed. John Tobin and Jesse Lander (London: Bloomsbury, 2018), 230.

30. See Josephson [-Storm], *Invention of Religion in Japan*.

31. See Adrian Hermann, "Distinctions of Religion: The Search for Equivalents of 'Religion' and the Challenge of Theorizing a 'Global Discourse of Religion.'" in *Making Religion* (Leiden: Brill, 2016).

32. Meillassoux, *Après la finitude*, 48.

33. For repeated laments about the end of art, Eva Geulen, *Das Ende der Kunst: Lesarten eines Gerüchts nach Hegel* (Frankfurt: Suhrkamp, 2002).

34. For a firsthand account of Dada see Hans Richter, *Dada, Kunst und Antikunst: Der Beitrag Dadas zur Kunst Des 20. Jahrhunderts* (Cologne: M. DuMont Schauberg, 1973). Dada anti-art was foreshadowed by lesser-known movements like *Les Arts Incohérents* (established 1882).

35. There is an ongoing debate about whether Marcel Duchamp or Elsa von Freytag-Loringhoven created the "Fountain" and ready-made art in general.

36. Morris Weitz, "The Role of Theory in Aesthetics," *The Journal of Aesthetics and Art Criticism* 15, no. 1 (1956): 27–35. He expanded this argument in Morris Weitz, *The Opening Mind: A Philosophical Study of Humanistic Concepts* (Chicago: University of Chicago Press, 1977). For other contemporary works in this line of approach, see William Kennick, "Does Traditional Aesthetics Rest on a Mistake?" *Mind* 67, no. 267 (1958): 317–34, 319; Haig Khatchadourian, "Common Names and 'Family Resemblances,'" *Philosophy and Phenomenological Research* 18, no. 3 (1958): 341–58, and "Art-Names and Aesthetic Judgments," *Philosophy* 36, no. 136 (1961): 30–48.

37. Ludwig Wittgenstein, *Philosophical Investigations* (Oxford: Blackwell, 2009), 27e (I:66). See also Michael Forster, "Wittgenstein on Family Resemblance Concepts," in *Wittgenstein's Philosophical Investigations: A Critical Guide*, ed. Arif Ahmed (Cambridge: Cambridge University Press, 2010), 66–87. For a fascinating if ultimately flawed attempt to recover the category of games, see Bernard Suits, *The Grasshopper: Games, Life and Utopia* (Peterborough, Ontario: Broadview Press, 2014).

38. Weitz, "Role of Theory in Aesthetics," 32.

39. Weitz, "Role of Theory in Aesthetics," 34–35.

40. For different accounts of these debates, see Tiziana Andina, *The Philosophy of Art: The Question of Definition—From Hegel to Post-Dantian Theories* (New York: Bloomsbury, 2013); Noël Carroll, ed., *Theories of Art Today* (Madison: University of Wisconsin Press, 2000); and Stephen Davies, *Definitions of Art* (Ithaca, NY: Cornell University Press, 1991). Perhaps the most influential attempt to recoup the category was George Dickie's "institutional theory of art." George Dickie, *Art and the Aesthetic: An Institutional Analysis* (Ithaca, NY: Cornell University Press, 1974), 34.

41. See Harold Osborne, "Definition and Evaluation in Aesthetics," *The Philosophical Quarterly* 23, no. 90 (1973): 15–27, esp. 16.

42. M.H. Abrams, "Art-as-Such: The Sociology of Modern Aesthetics," *Bulletin*

of the American Academy of Arts and Sciences 38, no. 6 (1985): 8–33. Foreshadowed in some respects by Osborne, "Definition and Evaluation."

43. For a survey, see Denis Dutton, "But They Don't Have Our Concept of Art," in *Theories of Art Today*, ed. Noël Carroll (Madison: University of Wisconsin Press, 2000), 217–38. For a significant example, see David Novitz, "Art by Another Name," *British Journal of Aesthetics* 38, no. 1 (1998): 19–32.

44. For instance, something labeled as art comes to be governed by copyright rather than patent law.

45. Similarly, the category of "religious art" becomes doubly problematic: the difference between an object in a context of worship versus the historical appreciation of it. Think of a ritual mask that has become a museum piece. This was often referred to by way of Walter Benjamin as a disintegration of the aura.

46. For significant critiques (especially early formulations), see:

For Law: H.L.A. Hart, *The Concept of Law* (Oxford: Clarendon Press, 1961); Brian Bix, "H.L.A. Hart and the 'Open Texture' of Language," *Law and Philosophy* 10, no. 1 (1991): 51–72.

The POLITICAL: Walter Ullmann, *Principles of Government and Politics in the Middle Ages* (New York: Barnes & Noble, 1961), and *A History of Political Thought* (Baltimore: Penguin Books, 1965); see also Quentin Skinner, *The Foundations of Modern Political Thought* (Cambridge: Cambridge University Press, 1978); J.P. Canning, "Introduction: Politics, Institutions and Ideas," in *The Cambridge History of Medieval Political Thought c. 350–1450*, ed. J.H. Burns (Cambridge: Cambridge University Press, 1988), 341–66; Maurizio Viroli, *From Politics to Reason of State: The Acquisition and Transformation of the Language of Politics, 1250–1600* (Cambridge: Cambridge University Press, 1992); Jens Bartelson, *The Critique of the State* (Cambridge: Cambridge University Press, 2001).

For HISTORY: Much of the debate around history and its narrative tropes has been related to the reception of Hayden White. But there were earlier debates around the "scientific" nature of historical scholarship, including Edward Hallett Carr, *What Is History?* (New York: Knopf, 1961) and David Cannadine, ed., *What Is History Now?* (Houndmills: Palgrave Macmillan, 2002). See also Hayden White, "The Burden of History," *History and Theory* 5, no 2 (1966): 111–34. Elaborated in Hayden White, *Metahistory: The Historical Imagination in Nineteenth-Century Europe* (Baltimore: Johns Hopkins University Press, 1973); White, *Tropics of Discourse: Essays in Cultural Criticism* (Baltimore: Johns Hopkins University Press, 1978); White, *The Content of the Form: Narrative Discourse and Historical Representation* (Baltimore: Johns Hopkins University Press, 1987). See also Kuisma Korhonen, ed., *Tropes for the Past: Hayden White and the History/Literature Debate* (Amsterdam: Rodopi, 2006); and Robert Doran, ed., *Philosophy of History after Hayden White* (New York: Bloomsbury Academic, 2013). Critical studies fields (e.g., critical race and critical gender studies) tend to gain their coherence by challenging rather than establishing their primary objects of analysis. In that respect, these subfields are predisposed toward some of the discursive strategies outlined in this chapter.

For GENDER: The notion of "gender" as a cultural category is often dated to

Robert J. Stoller, *Sex and Gender: The Development of Masculinity and Femininity* (London: Karnac, 1968). See Jemima Repo, *The Biopolitics of Gender* (New York: Oxford University Press, 2016).

For RACE: Race was attacked much earlier—see Jacques Barzun, *Race: A Study in Modern Superstition* (New York: Harcourt Brace, 1937), although we might see the roots of this critique in the work of W.E.B. Du Bois and Franz Boas, among others. Other influential early examples include Frantz Fanon, *Peau noire, masques blancs* (Paris: Éditions du Seuil, 1952); and Thomas Gossett, *Race: The History of an Idea in America* (Dallas, TX: Southern Methodist University Press, 1963).

For SCIENCE: Norwood Russell Hanson, *Patterns of Discovery* (Cambridge: Cambridge University Press, 1958); and Kuhn, *The Structure of Scientific Revolutions*.

For CULTURE: Alfred Kroeber and Clyde Kluckhohn, *Culture: A Critical Review of Concepts and Definitions* (Cambridge: The Museum, 1952); Alfred Kroeber and Talcott Parsons, "The Concepts of Culture and of Social System" *The American Sociological Review* 23, no. 5 (1958): 582–83; Raymond Williams, *Culture and Society, 1780–1950* (London: Chatto & Windus, 1958); Marc Manganaro, *Culture, 1922: The Emergence of a Concept* (Princeton, NJ: Princeton University Press, 2002); Leon Goldstein, "On Defining Culture," *American Anthropologist*, New Series, 59, no. 6 (1957): 1075–81; George Peter Murdock, "Anthropology's Mythology," *Proceedings of the Royal Anthropological Institute* (1971): 17–24 (Murdock also laid similar charges on the notion of the social); Sherry B. Ortner, "Is Female to Male as Nature Is to Culture?" *Feminist Studies* 1, no. 2 (1972): 5–31; John H. Moore, "The Culture Concept as Ideology," *American Ethnologist* 1, no. 3 (1974): 537–49; Carol MacCormack and Marilyn Strathern, *Nature, Culture, and Gender* (Cambridge: Cambridge University Press, 1980); György Márkus, "Culture: The Making and the Make-Up of a Concept," *Dialectical Anthropology* 18, no. 1 (1993): 3–29; Robert Borofsky, "Rethinking the Cultural," in *Assessing Cultural Anthropology*, ed. Robert Borofsky (New York: McGraw-Hill, 1994), 243–49; Jonathan Friedman, *Cultural Identity and Global Process* (London: Sage, 1994), esp. 206–207; and Arjun Appadurai, *Modernity at Large: Cultural Dimensions of Globalization* (Minneapolis: University of Minnesota Press, 1996), esp. 12; George W. Stocking Jr., "Franz Boas and the Culture Concept in Historical Perspective," *American Anthropologist*, New Series, 68, no. 4 (1966): 867–82. See also James Clifford and George Marcus, eds., *Writing Culture: The Poetics and Politics of Ethnography* (Berkeley: University of California Press, 1986); James Clifford, *The Predicament of Culture* (Cambridge: Harvard University Press, 1988); Lila Abu-Lughod, "Writing against Culture," in *Recapturing Anthropology: Working in the Present*, ed. Richard Fox (Santa Fe, NM: American Research Press, 1991), 137–62; Adam Kuper, *Culture: The Anthropologists' Account* (Cambridge: Harvard University Press, 1999); Scott Michaelsen and David Johnson. *Anthropology's Wake: Attending to the End of Culture* (New York: Fordham University Press, 2008). In this respect, Latour was a latecomer in his challenge to the nature-culture binary—see Bruno Latour, *Nous n'avons jamais été modernes* (Paris: La Découverte, 1991).

For postcolonial critiques, see also Peter Worsley, "The End of Anthropology," in *Transactions of the Sixth World Congress of Sociology* (Belgium: International Sociological Association, 1966), 121–29; David Goddard, "Limits of British Anthropology," *New Left Review* 1, no. 58 (1969): 79–89; Gérard Leclerc, *Anthropologie et colonialisme:Essai sur l'histoire de l'africanisme* (Paris: Fayard, 1972); Talal Asad, ed., *Anthropology & the Colonial Encounter* (New York: Humanities Press, 1973); Diane Lewis, "Anthropology and Colonialism," *Current Anthropology* 14, no. 5 (1973): 581–602, esp. 585; Johannes Fabian, *Time and the Other: How Anthropology Makes Its Object* (New York: Columbia University Press, 1983); George Stocking Jr., *Victorian Anthropology* (New York: Free Press, 1987); V.Y. Mudimbe, *The Invention of Africa* (Bloomington: Indiana University Press, 1988); Henrika Kuklick, *The Savage Within: The Social History of British Anthropology* (New York: Cambridge University Press, 1991); Nicholas Dirks, ed., *Colonialism and Culture* (Ann Arbor: University of Michigan Press, 1992); Nicholas Thomas, *Colonialism's Culture: Anthropology, Travel, and Government* (Princeton, NJ: Princeton University Press, 1994); Peter Pels, "The Anthropology of Colonialism: Culture, History, and the Emergence of Western Governmentality," *Annual Review of Anthropology* 26 (1997): 163–83; Helen Tilley, ed., *Ordering Africa: Anthropology, European Imperialism and the Politics of Knowledge* (Manchester: Manchester University Press, 2010). For critiques of the construction of the primitive, see especially Eric R. Wolf, *Europe and the People without History* (Berkeley: University of California Press, 1997), and Adam Kuper, *The Reinvention of Primitive Society* (New York: Routledge, 2005).

For SOCIETY: Dorothy Emmet, *Function, Purpose and Powers* (London: Macmillan, 1958). Her work in this regard was arguably foreshadowed by John Mabbott, *The State and the Citizen* (London: Hutchinson's University Library, 1948). Michael Mann also largely rejected notions of *society* in favor of multiple overlapping and intersecting networks of power, noting that if he could he "would abolish the concept of 'society' altogether." Michael Mann, *The Sources of Social Power: Volume I* (New York: Cambridge University Press, 1986), esp. 1–2; Tim Ingold, *Key Debates in Anthropology* (London: Routledge, 1996); John Bowers and Kate Iwi, "The Discursive Construction of Society," *Discourse & Society* 4, no. 3 (1993): 357–93; Christina Toren, *Mind, Materiality and History: Explorations in Fijian Ethnography* (London: Routledge, 2006), esp. 3–6; and Bruno Latour, *Reassembling the Social* (New York: Oxford University Press, 2007).

For WORD: Tadeusz Milewski, "The Conception of the Word in the Languages of North American Natives," *Lingua Posnaniensis* 3 (1951): 248–68; Paul L. Garvin, "On the Relative Tractability of Morphological Data," *WORD* 13, no. 1 (1957): 12–22; Charles Bally, *Linguistique générale et linguistique française* (Berne: Francke, 1965), 287–89; Robert Dixon and Alexandra Aikhenvald, *Word: A Cross-Linguistic Typology* (Cambridge: Cambridge University Press, 2007); Martin Haspelmath, "The Indeterminacy of Word Segmentation and the Nature of Morphology and Syntax," *Folia Linguistica* 45, no. 1(2011): 31–80. Perhaps the critique of the "word" as a unit of analysis has the longest pedigree since criticisms of the "word" as an analytical fiction appear in the *Vākyapadīya* (On Words and Sentences) by the fifth century Indian grammarian Bhartṛhari. See John Brough, "Some Indian Theories of Meaning," *Philological Society* 52, no. 1 (1953):161–76.

For ECONOMY: Louis Dumont articulated a critique of economy in 1977 that was almost completely ignored by economists. See Louis Dumont, *Homo aequalis 1, Genèse et épanouissement de l'idéologie économique* (Paris: Gallimard, 1977).

47. Alfred Kroeber and Clyde Kluckhohn, *Culture: A Critical Review of Concepts and Definitions* (Cambridge: The Museum, 1952).

48. See Charles Bazell, *Linguistic Typology* (Oxford: Oxford University Press, 1958), esp. 6.

49. For "open concept" see Weitz, "Role of Theory in Aesthetics." For "open texture" see Hart, *Concept of Law*. For "essentially contested concept" see W.B. Gallie, *Philosophy and the Historical Understanding* (New York: Schocken Books, 1964).

50. For an early 1905 challenge to "society" as a misplaced abstraction, see W.E.B. Du Bois, "Sociology Hesitant," *Boundary 2* 27, no. 3 (2000): 37–44.

51. See John Beattie, "Understanding and Explanation in Social Anthropology," *The British Journal of Sociology* 10, no. 1 (1959): 45–60, esp. 55; Bronisław Malinowski, *The Language of Magic and Gardening* (London: Unwin Ltd., 1935), 11; Jonathan Z. Smith, *Map Is Not Territory* (Chicago: University of Chicago Press, 1993); and Matthew Watson, *Uneconomic Economics and the Crisis of the Model World* (Basingstoke: Palgrave, 2014).

52. See Josephson-Storm, *Myth of Disenchantment*, 59–60.

53. Michel Foucault, *Folie et déraison, histoire de la folie à l'âge classique* (Paris: Librairie Plon, 1961).

54. Frequently, the current usage of the key term is the product of the eighteenth or nineteenth century. Therefore, the disciplinary object can usually be presented as both European and "modern."

55. Josephson [Storm], *Invention of Religion in Japan*.

56. Charles Hockett, "*Linguistic Interludes* Reviewed," *Language* 20, no. 4 (1944): 252–55, emphasis in original. A similar claim is made about polysynthetic languages such as Mapudungung in Balthasar Bickel and Fernando Zúñiga, "The 'Word' in Polysynthetic Languages: Phonological and Syntactic Challenges," in *The Oxford Handbook of Polysynthesis*, ed. Michael Fortescue, Marianne Mithun, and Nicholas Evans (Oxford: Oxford University Press, 2017), 158–85.

57. Marilyn Strathern, *The Gender of the Gift* (Berkeley: University of California Press, 1988).

58. Lynn Hart. "Three Walls: Regional Aesthetics and the International Art World," in *The Traffic in Culture: Refiguring Art and Anthropology*, ed. George Marcus and Fred Myers (Berkeley: University of California Press, 1995), 127–50.

59. Malinowski, *Language of Magic*, esp. 15–17, 70.

60. Kuhn, *Structure of Scientific Revolutions*, 149.

61. Think Hayden White.

62. There is little financial support available for literature departments. Scholars advancing the critique are mostly talking to themselves.

63. See Pierre Bourdieu and Loïc Wacquant, *An Invitation to Reflexive Sociology* (Chicago: University of Chicago Press, 1992).

64. See Sandra Harding, "Is Modern Science an Ethno-Science? Rethinking Epistemological Assumptions," in *Science and Technology in a Developing World*,

ed. Terry Shinn, Jack Spaapen, and Venni Krishna (Dordrecht: Springer, 1997), 37–64.

65. For a non-skeptical Kuhn, see Bojana Mladenović, *Kuhn's Legacy: Epistemology, Metaphilosophy, and Pragmatism* (New York: Columbia University Press, 2017).

66. Kuhn, *Structure of Scientific Revolutions*, 44–45. Indeed, it would be only a slight exaggeration to say that Kuhn's paradigm of paradigms was Wittgenstein's notion of family-resemblance.

67. Paul Feyerabend, *Against Method* (London: Verso, 2010).

68. See Josephson [Storm], *Invention of Religion in Japan*, and Josephson-Storm, *Myth of Disenchantment*.

69. See Larry Laudan, "A Confutation of Convergent Realism," *Philosophy of Science* 48, no. 1 (1981): 19–49; and "The Demise of the Demarcation Problem," in *Physics, Philosophy and Psychoanalysis* (Dordrecht: Springer, 1983), 111–27.

70. Edouard Machery, *Doing Without Concepts* (New York: Oxford University Press, 2009).

71. For disciplines to function, they have had to consistently shunt complexities into areas that exceeded the planes of their own system. As I discuss in chapter 3, it is especially hard for the human sciences to produce analytically closed systems, as one is constantly confronted by open systems that interact with each other in magnified orders of complexity.

72. For histories of the disciplining process of physics, see Daniel J. Kevles, *The Physicists: The History of a Scientific Community in Modern America* (Cambridge: Harvard University Press, 1987); Elizabeth Garber, *The Language of Physics: The Calculus and the Development of Theoretical Physics in Europe, 1750–1914* (Boston: Birkhäuser, 1999); Iwan Rhys Morus, *When Physics Became King* (Chicago: University of Chicago Press, 2005).

73. Nonetheless, disciplines often spar with each other over territory and some have multiple, competing objects.

74. Gerald Graff, *Professing Literature: An Institutional History* (Chicago: University of Chicago Press, 1987).

75. Eleanor Rosch. "Natural Categories," *Cognitive Psychology* 4 (1973): 328–50; Eleanor Rosch, C.B. Mervis, W.D. Gray, D.M. Johnson, and P. Boyes-Braem, "Basic Objects in Natural Categories," *Cognitive Psychology* 8 (1976): 382–439.

76. George Lakoff, *Women, Fire, and Dangerous Things: What Categories Reveal about the Mind* (Chicago: University of Chicago Press, 1987), 41.

77. Jerry A. Fodor, *Concepts: Where Cognitive Science Went Wrong* (New York: Clarendon Press, 1998), 102.

78. Davies, *Definitions of Art*, 12.

79. WATANABE Satoshi, *Knowing and Guessing* (New York: Wiley, 1969), 376. See also Nelson Goodman, *Problems and Projects* (Indianapolis, IN: Bobbs-Merrill, 1972); and W.V.O. Quine, "Natural Kinds," in *Essays in Honor of Carl G. Hempel*, ed. Nicholas Rescher (Dordrecht: Springer Netherlands, 1969), 5–23.

80. Octavio Paz, *The Collected Poems of Octavio Paz, 1957–1987* (New York: New Directions, 1991), 429.

81. Quine, "Natural Kinds"; Watanabe, *Knowing and Guessing*.

82. See Forster, "Wittgenstein on Family Resemblance," 69.

83. Example adapted from Goodman, *Problems and Projects*, 445.

84. See also Quine, "Natural Kinds," esp. 46-47.

85. Example comes from Davies, *Definitions of Art*, 14.

86. Maurice Mandelbaum, "Family Resemblances and Generalization concerning the Arts," *American Philosophical Quarterly* 2, no. 3 (1965): 219-28.

87. See Nelson Goodman, "When is Art," in Nelson Goodman, *Ways of Worldmaking* (Indianapolis, IN: Hackett, 1978), 57-70.

88. See Davies, *Definitions of Art*, 11.

89. Morton Beckner, *The Biological Way of Thought* (New York: Columbia University Press, 1959), 22-23.

90. Robert Sokal and Peter Sneath, *Principles of Numerical Taxonomy* (San Francisco: W.H. Freeman, 1963); and Rodney Needham, "Polythetic Classification: Convergence and Consequences," *Man* 10, no. 3 (1975): 349-69.

91. Alston, cited in Benson Saler, "Cultural Anthropology and the Definition of Religion," in *The Notion of "Religion" in Comparative Research*, ed. Ugo Bianchi (Rome: Bretschneider, 1994), 832-33.

92. Jürgen Habermas, *Legitimation Crisis* (Cambridge: Polity Edition, 1988), 2. Habermas was talking about societies and governments as a whole, but his notion can be extended to other kinds of organizations.

93. The challenge would have happened much earlier if more philosophers were familiar with the classical Indian philosopher Śrīharṣa. See Śrīharṣa, *The Sweets of Refutation: An English Translation of the Khaṇḍanakhaṇḍakhādya of Shrīharṣa* (Allahabad: Indian Thought, 1913). For a survey starting with European thought, see Forster, "Wittgenstein on Family Resemblance," 72. For another survey see Herbert Blumer, "Science without Concepts," *American Journal of Sociology* 36, no. 4 (1931): 515-33. An early critique of concepts also appears in Benedetto Croce, *Logic as the Science of the Pure Concept* (London: Macmillan, 1917), although Croce tries to preserve "pure concepts."

94. For the classical notion of the concept, see Edward Smith and Douglas Medin, *Categories and Concepts* (Cambridge: Harvard University Press, 1981).

CHAPTER THREE

1. Jorge Luis Borges, *Collected Fictions* (New York: Penguin Books, 1999), 73.

2. Thanks to Facebook friends for helping me with this list.

3. See Alison Assiter, *Enlightened Women: Modernist Feminism in a Postmodern Age* (London: Routledge, 2005); Alastair Bonnett, *Anti-Racism* (London: Routledge, 2000), 137-42; Diana Fuss, *Essentially Speaking* (London: Routledge, 1990); Liao Ping-hui, "Postcolonial studies in Taiwan," *Postcolonial Studies* 2, no. 2 (1999), 199-211; Andrew Sayer, "Essentialism, Social Constructionism, and Beyond," *Sociological Review* 45, no. 3 (1997): 453-87; Naomi Schor and Elizabeth Weed, eds., *The Essential Difference* (Bloomington: Indiana University Press, 1994); and Charlotte

Witt, "Anti-Essentialism in Feminist Theory," *Philosophical Topics* 23, no. 2 (1995): 321–44.

4. Kenan Malik, "Universalism and Difference: Race and the Postmodernists," *Race & Class* 37, no. 3 (January 1996): 1–17.

5. Roland Barthes, *Mythologies* (New York: Noonday Press, 1991), 75.

6. Schor and Weed, *Essential Difference*, vii.

7. Fuss, *Essentially Speaking*. She notes that one finds this discourse in both feminist theorists and poststructuralist thinkers like Lacan and Derrida, in whose hands the essential essence-less woman seemed to be almost a sexist notion.

8. Sherene Razack, *Looking White People in the Eye* (Toronto: University of Toronto Press, 1998), esp. 162. Think also of Crenshaw's famous account of inter-sectionality: Kimberlé Crenshaw, "Demarginalizing the Intersection of Race and Sex," *University of Chicago Legal Forum* 1, no. 8 (1989), 139–67.

9. Jane Roland Martin, "Methodological Essentialism, False Difference, and Other Dangerous Traps," *Signs* 19, no. 3 (1994): 630–57.

10. For scientific essentialism, see Brian Ellis, *Scientific Essentialism* (Cambridge: Cambridge University Press, 2001). For attempts to use Locke's nominal essences and other anti-anti-essentialisms, see Fuss, *Essentially Speaking*. To be fair, Gayatri Spivak ultimately repudiated the "strategic essentialism" for which she was famous. See Gayatri Spivak, *Other Asias* (London: Blackwell, 2008), 260.

11. Aristotle's phrase *ti ên einai* "the what it was to be" was sufficiently unclear that Roman translators had to coin a neologism, *essentia*, which became the English "essence." There has been regular disagreement about what it meant to possess an *essence* basically ever since (including whether essences are transhistorical and unchanging, causal patterns, or "nominal" linguistic fictions).

12. For the psychological evidence about essentialism about kinds, see Susan Gelman, *The Essential Child: Origins of Essentialism in Everyday Thought* (Oxford: Oxford University Press, 2003).

13. See Alfred North Whitehead, *Process and Reality* (New York: Macmillan, 1957); Nicholas Rescher, *Process Metaphysics* (Syracuse: SUNY Press, 1996); Isabelle Stengers, *Thinking with Whitehead: A Free and Wild Creation of Concepts* (Cambridge: Harvard University Press, 2014).

14. Heraclitus of Ephesus is perhaps the paradigmatic process thinker. Other process thinkers include: Hegel, Marx, Henri Bergson, C.S. Peirce, William James, John Dewey, and more recently Derrida, Deleuze, Manuel DeLanda, Dorothy Emmet, Édouard Glissant, Isabelle Stengers, Michel Weber, Nicholas Rescher, and Ilya Prigogine, among others. One can also find examples of process thought in both classical Indian and Chinese philosophy (esp. Buddhism and Daoism). For the role of process-thinking in Chinese philosophy, see John Berthrong, *Expanding Process: Exploring Philosophical and Theological Transformations in China and the West* (Albany, NY: State University of New York Press, 2008). Moreover, according to James Maffie process-thinking was crucial to Nahua or "Aztec philosophy," see James Maffie, *Aztec Philosophy: Understanding a World in Motion* (Denver: University Press of Colorado, 2014).

15. Maffie, *Aztec Philosophy*, 27.

16. For an account of how Kachina spirit beings, masks, and dolls function in Hopi ritual life, see George List, "Hopi Kachina Dance Songs: Concepts and Context," *Ethnomusicology* 41, no. 3 (1997): 413-32.

17. Michael Lynch, "Ontography: Investigating the Production of Things, Deflating Ontology," *Social Studies of Science* 43, no. 3 (2013): 444-62.

18. People are often supposed to organize their experience into something called "worldviews" or "ontologies," which are believed to represent the "subjective" part of experience in contrast to an "objective" world. In part I'm skeptical of "worldviews" (or "conceptual schemes") because, like Donald Davidson, I see the distinction between subjective and objective contributions to experience to be incoherent. How could one have a coherent system for subjective experience before experiencing the world?

Furthermore, "worldview" seems to be an incoherent concept. It is hard for me to know what it would mean to share a worldview (how many concepts must two people hold in common? How similar would they have to be? What about changing views? Does a worldview only track a subset of concepts, and if so which ones?). As I note repeatedly in this book, even speakers of the same language regularly disagree about what their "shared" terms mean and how to understand them. On these grounds, it would seem that no two people share a worldview. Worldviews are also often supposed to correlate with languages or general outlooks. But which is it? If there were such a thing as worldviews, it would seem that people can have different worldviews and speak the same language (e.g., American Mormon versus American Neo-Dawkins atheist) or speak different languages and hold basically identical worldviews (American Mormon and German Mormon). Do two quantum physicists—one a native French speaker and the other a native Akan speaker—share a worldview? How could we tell? More recent attempts to suggest that different minoritized populations share worldviews seems to me condescending and dangerously essentializing. There is no unitary "worldview" or "ontology" that all Black Americans share. To say otherwise would be to dismiss the diversity within the Black community itself. See Keeanga-Yamahtta Taylor, *From #BlackLivesMatter to Black Liberation* (New York: Haymarket Books, 2016). Similarly, as Olúfẹ́mi Táíwò has argued, "elite capture" within minoritized populations means that the people who are often tasked with speaking for disadvantaged groups are often those who most share their outlook with people in power. In his example, Black elites who set the political agenda sometimes at the expense of working class Black folk. (See Olúfẹ́mi O. Táíwò, "Being-in-the-Room Privilege: Elite Capture and Epistemic Deference." *The Philosopher* 108, no. 4 [2020]: 61-68.) Reframed, a bunch of Ivy League–educated economists all from the same prep schools are likely going to share more relevant features of their outlook than a superficial assessment of their "ethnic backgrounds" might suggest. In sum, demographic diversity, while incredibly important on its own, does not *necessarily* mean conceptual diversity.

19. Ron Mallon, *The Construction of Human Kinds* (New York: Oxford University Press, 2016), 162.

20. Charles Taylor, "Interpretation and the Sciences of Man," *Review of Metaphysics* 25, no. 1 (1971): 3–51, 49–50.

21. Pascal Boyer, *Religion Explained: The Evolutionary Origins of Religious Thought* (New York: Basic Books, 2007), 38–39.

22. See Pascal Boyer, *Tradition as Truth and Communication* (New York: Cambridge University Press, 1990); and Lauri Honko and Pekka Laaksonen, eds., *Trends in Nordic Tradition Research* (Helsinki: Suomalaisen Kirjallisuuden Seura, 1983), 236.

23. See Brian Joseph and Richard Janda, *The Handbook of Historical Linguistics* (Malden, UK: Blackwell, 2003).

24. Michael McCloskey and Sam Glucksberg, "Natural Categories: Well Defined or Fuzzy Sets?" *Memory & Cognition* 6, no. 4 (1978): 462–72.

25. Tony Lawson, "What is this 'School' called Neoclassical Economics?" *Cambridge Journal of Economics* 37, no. 5 (2013): 947–83. See also Tony Lawson, "Ontology and the Study of Social Reality," *Cambridge Journal of Economics* 36, no. 2 (2012): 345–85.

26. Andrew Abbott, *Processual Sociology* (Chicago: University of Chicago Press, 2012); Ellis, *Scientific Essentialism*, esp. 179–94; Ruth Groff, *Critical Realism, Postpositivism and the Possibility of Knowledge* (New York: Routledge, 2004); Hacking, *Social Construction of What?*, 108; Mallon, *Human Kinds*.

27. Michael Omi and Howard Winant, *Racial Formation in the United States* (New York: Routledge, 2014), 110. Also cited in Mallon, *Human Kinds*.

28. Margaret Archer, ed., *Social Morphogenesis* (Dordrecht: Springer, 2013); and Marshall Berman, *All that Is Solid Melts into Air: The Experience of Modernity* (New York: Verso, 1983).

29. Mallon, *Human Kinds*.

30. See Talcott Parsons, *The Social System* (New York: Free Press, 1951).

31. For history of debates about natural kinds, see Ian Hacking, "A Tradition of Natural Kinds," *Philosophical Studies* 61, no. 1 (1991): 109–26; and Muhammad Ali Khalidi, "Natural Kinds," in *The Oxford Handbook of Philosophy of Science*, ed. Paul Humphreys (New York: Oxford University Press, 2016), 397–416.

32. John Dupré, "Is 'Natural Kind' a Natural Kind Term?" *The Monist* 85, no. 1 (2002): 29–49; Hacking, "Tradition of Natural Kinds"; and Muhammad Ali Khalidi, *Natural Categories and Human Kinds Classification in the Natural and Social Sciences* (New York: Cambridge University Press, 2015).

33. Khalidi, *Natural Categories*, 12.

34. Lisa Barrett, "Are Emotions Natural Kinds?" *Perspectives on Psychological Science* 1, no. 1 (2006): 28–58; Lawrie Reznek, *The Nature of Disease* (London: Routledge & Kegan Paul, 1987); Daniel Sulmasy, "Diseases and Natural Kinds," *Theoretical Medicine and Bioethics* 26, no. 6 (2005): 487–513; and Peter Zachar, "Psychiatric Disorders Are Not Natural Kinds," *Philosophy, Psychiatry, & Psychology* 7, no. 3 (2000): 167–82. Although to be fair, there has been some critique of natural kinds in both physics and chemistry. See Holly VandeWall, "Why Water Is not H$_2$O, and Other Critiques of Essentialist Ontology from the Philosophy of Chemistry," *Philosophy of Science* 74, no. 5 (2007): 906–19. For debates about the *species concept*,

see: Benjamin H. Burma, "The Species Concept: A Semantic Review," *Evolution* 3, no. 4 (1949): 369–70; Ernst Mayr, "The Species Concept: Semantics versus Semantics," *Evolution* 3, no. 4 (1949): 371–72; Robert Sokal and Theodore Crovello, "The Biological Species Concept: A Critical Evaluation," *The American Naturalist* 104, no. 936 (1970): 127–53; Michael Ghiselin, "A Radical Solution to the Species Problem," *Systematic Zoology* 23, no. 4 (1974): 536–44; Marc Ereshefsky, "Species Pluralism and Anti-realism," *Philosophy of Science* 65, no. 1 (1998): 103–20; John Dupré, "On the Impossibility of a Monistic Account of Species," in *Species: New Interdisciplinary Essays*, ed. Robert Wilson (New York: Bradford Books, 1999), 3–22; David Stamos, *The Species Problem: Biological Species, Ontology, and the Metaphysics of Biology* (Lexington, KY: Lexington Books, 2003); and Jody Hey, "On the Failure of Modern Species Concepts," *Trends in Ecology & Evolution* 21, no. 8 (2006): 447–50.

35. Biological species are not generally thought to have "essences." Members of the same species do not always have the same properties (e.g., wolves born without eyes are still wolves). The species boundary between wolves and other related canines (such as dogs or ancestral species such as *canis chihliensis*) permits gray areas. You cannot define wolves based on necessary and sufficient conditions. We can imagine possible worlds in which wolves never evolved. There are no specific laws of nature that apply to wolves and only wolves. So it would seem wolves at least do not fit criteria 1, 3, 5, 6, 7, and 8.

36. See Marc Ereshefsky, "Philosophy of Biological Classification," in *Handbook of Plant Science*, ed. Keith Roberts (London: Wiley, 2007), 8–12.

37. Philosophers of biology have spent a long time theorizing about when an exception necessitates a theory change and when it does not. Lindley Darden, *Reasoning in Biological Discoveries* (Cambridge: Cambridge University Press, 2006).

38. Daniel Nicholson and John Dupré, eds., *Everything Flows: Towards a Processual Philosophy of Biology* (New York: Oxford University Press, 2018).

39. For more on *svabhāva*, see Richard Robinson, "Some Logical Aspects of Nāgārjuna's System," *Philosophy East and West* (1957): 291–308.

40. Bimal Krishna Matilal, *Epistemology, Logic and Grammar in Indian Philosophical Analysis* (Oxford: Oxford University Press, 2015), 118.

41. For psychological evidence about cross-cutting in artifactual kinds, see Barbara Malt and Steven Sloman, "Artifact Categorization," in *Creations of the Mind: Theories of Artifacts and their Representation*, ed. Eric Margolis and Stephen Laurence (Oxford: Oxford University Press, 2007), 85–123. For the art instillation example, see *Causa-Efecto* by the Spanish artist Ana Soler.

42. See Nick Haslam, Louis Rothschild, and Donald Ernst, "Essentialist Beliefs about Social Categories," *British Journal of Social Psychology* 39, no. 1 (2000): 113–27.

43. John Searle, *The Construction of Social Reality* (New York: The Free Press, 1997), 57.

44. Searle, *Social Reality*.

45. See Judith Butler, "Performative Acts and Gender Constitution: An Essay in Phenomenology and Feminist Theory," *Theatre Journal* 40, no. 4 (1988): 519–31.

46. See Nelson Goodman, "When is Art?" in Goodman, *Ways of Worldmaking* (Indianapolis, IN: Hackett, 1978), 57–70.

47. Nicholas Rescher distinguishes between processes that are owned by a specific agent (e.g., a particular wolf's digestion) and those that are unowned or distributed across many different agents (e.g., climate change). Rescher, *Process Metaphysics*, 42.

48. While in other ways I agree with Andrew Abbott, a processual sociology should not reduce everything to events, because events are themselves better understood as brief processes.

49. Rowland Stout, ed., *Process, Action, and Experience* (Oxford: Oxford University Press, 2018), 2.

50. Édouard Glissant, *Poetics of Relation* (Ann Arbor: University of Michigan Press, 1997). See also Alexandre Leupin, *Édouard Glissant: Héraclite et Hegel dans le Tout-Monde* (Paris: Hermann, 2016).

51. Manuel DeLanda, *Intensive Science and Virtual Philosophy* (New York: Bloomsbury Publishing, 2013); see also Nicholson and Dupré, *Everything Flows*. Some philosophers have promoted essentialisms that make room for processes. See Ellis, *Scientific Essentialism*.

52. Kirsty Spalding, Ratan Bhardwaj, Bruce Buchholz, Henrik Druid, and Jonas Frisén, "Retrospective Birth Dating of Cells in Humans," *Cell* 122 (2005): 133–42.

53. See Amie Thomasson, "The Ontology of Social Groups," *Synthèse* (2016): 1–17.

54. *The Questions of King Milinda*, vol. 1 (Oxford: Clarendon Press, 1890), 34–57.

55. Dupré, "Natural Kind.".

56. Dupré, "Natural Kind.".

57. See Paul Griffiths, "Emotions as Natural and Normative kinds," *Philosophy of Science* 71, no. 5 (2004): 901–11.

58. See John Sowa, "Signs, Processes, and Language Games: Foundations for Ontology," in *Proceedings of the 9th International Conference on Conceptual Structures* (Berlin: Springer, 2001), 1–44, 6.

59. See Fuss, *Essentially Speaking*.

60. One of the problems is that networks and assemblages are precisely not processes. Connolly, *A World of Becoming*.

61. Roy Bhaskar, *A Realist Theory of Science* (London: Routledge, 2008), xvi.

62. Bhaskar, cited in Isaac Reed, *Interpretation and Social Knowledge* (Chicago: University of Chicago Press, 2011), 57.

CHAPTER FOUR

1. See Mark Blaug, *The Methodology of Economics* (Cambridge: Cambridge University Press, 1992) 46; Margaret Gilbert, "Walking Together: A Paradigmatic Social Phenomenon," *Midwest Studies in Philosophy* 15, no. 1 (1990): 1–14; Alan Kirman, "The Intrinsic Limits of Modern Economic Theory: The Emperor Has No Clothes," *The Economic Journal* 99, no. 395 (1989): 126–39; Katherine Ritchie, "The Metaphysics of Social Groups," *Philosophy Compass* 10, no. 5 (2015): 310–21; and Lars Udehn, "The Changing Face of Methodological Individualism," *Annual Review of Sociology* 28, no. 1 (2002): 479–507.

2. Dave Elder-Vass, *Causal Power of Social Structures: Emergence, Structure and Agency* (Cambridge: Cambridge University Press, 2011) asks the right questions, although I find more persuasive the answers in Lawson, "Study of Social Reality."

3. Brian Epstein, *The Ant Trap: Rebuilding the Foundations of the Social Sciences* (New York: Oxford University Press, 2015), discussed below.

4. Ásta, "Social Kinds," in *The Routledge Handbook of Collective Intentionality*, ed. Marija Jankovic and Kirk Ludwig (New York: Routledge, 2017), 290–99.

5. Bruno Latour defines the "social" as a "trail of *associations* between heterogeneous elements" from "chemical bonds to legal ties, from atomic forces to corporate bodies, from physiological to political assemblies." This is so broad that it includes every kind of connection. That means it is basically meaningless as a descriptor and cannot do any analytical work. Latour, *Reassembling the Social*, 5.

6. I tend to be suspicious when philosophers toss around "emergence," as it is often undertheorized. Most references to emergence are more evidence of a theory's limits than a theory itself. But there are some bright exceptions, such as William Wimsatt, "The Ontology of Complex Systems," *Canadian Journal of Philosophy* 24, no. 1 (1994): 207–74.

7. Richard Boyd, "Realism, Anti-Foundationalism and the Enthusiasm for Natural Kinds," *Philosophical Studies* 61, nos. 1/2 (1991): 127–48.

8. Richard Boyd, "Kinds as the 'Workmanship of Men': Realism, Constructivism, and Natural Kinds," in *Rationalität, Realismus, Revision*, ed. Julian Nida-Rümelin (Berlin: De Gruyter, 2000), 52–89, 68.

9. Boyd, "Kinds," 57–58.

10. Boyd, "Realism," 139.

11. Boyd, "Kinds," 54.

12. After I finished the initial draft of this chapter, Richard Boyd was kind enough to point me to a new paper in which he more fully articulates his semantics. But, alas, I didn't have time to assimilate it fully. So the differences between it and what I propose here and in chapter 5 will have to be ironed out later. See Richard Boyd, "Rethinking Natural Kinds, Reference and Truth: Towards More Correspondence with Reality, Not Less," *Synthèse* (2019): 1–41.

13. Karen Ho, *Liquidated: An Ethnography of Wall Street* (Durham, NC: Duke University Press, 2009). Haslanger also makes a distinction between the *manifest* concepts ("the concept that users of the term typically take [or took] themselves to be applying") and *operative* concepts (basically how the term actually functions) and she accurately observes that genealogical critique often works by unearthing the gap between the two in practice. See Haslanger, *Resisting Reality*, esp. 92. I find this helpful but for reasons this chapter will make clear, I prefer to distinguish between manifest concepts (the shared terrain of popular usage) and operative social kinds (which track how the things to which the concepts reference actually function).

14. Searle, *Social Reality*, 21.

15. Searle, *Social Reality*.

16. John Searle, *Making the Social World* (New York: Oxford University Press, 2010), 22.

17. Searle, *Making the Social World*, 41.

18. This claim is rehashed in Searle, *Making the Social World*, which complicates the view of "collective intentionality."

19. Think also of J.L. Austin's account of performative utterances.

20. Searle begins to address this in *Making the Social World*. My theory of power has been deferred to a follow-up manuscript.

21. Sydney Shoemaker, *Identity, Cause, and Mind* (Oxford: Oxford University Press, 2003), 207.

22. See Tim Crane, ed., *Dispositions: A Debate* (London: Routledge, 2014); Ruth Groff, ed., *Revitalizing Causality* (London: Routledge, 2007); and Phyllis Illari and Federica Russo, *Causality: Philosophical Theory Meets Scientific Practice* (Oxford: Oxford University Press, 2014).

23. DeLanda, *Intensive Science*, vii.

24. Stephen Mumford and Rani Lill Anjum, *Getting Causes from Powers* (Oxford: Oxford University Press, 2011), 5.

25. Illari and Russo, *Causality*, 159. See also Anjan Chakravartty, *A Metaphysics for Scientific Realism* (Cambridge: Cambridge University Press, 2007).

26. I mean to evoke what biologists call "population thinking." Ernst Mayr, "Typological Versus Population Thinking," in *Conceptual Issues in Evolutionary Biology*, ed. Elliott Sober (Cambridge: MIT Press, 2006), 325–28.

27. See Carl Hempel and Paul Oppenheim, "Studies in the Logic of Explanation," *Philosophy of Science* 15, no. 2 (1948): 135–75.

28. Anjan Chakravartty, "Inessential Aristotle: Powers without Essences," in *Revitalizing Causality*, ed. Ruth Groff (London: Routledge, 2007), 160–61.

29. Marc Ereshefsky and Mohan Matthen, "Taxonomy, Polymorphism, and History: An Introduction to Population Structure Theory," *Philosophy of Science* 72, no. 1 (2005): 1–21; and Manolo Martínez, "Informationally-Connected Property Clusters, and Polymorphism," *Biology & Philosophy* 30, no. 1 (2015): 99–117.

30. See R. G. Swinburne, "Grue," *Analysis* 28, no. 4 (1968): 123–28.

31. Ruth Garrett Millikan, *On Clear and Confused Ideas: An Essay About Substance Concepts* (Cambridge: Cambridge University Press, 2006), 17.

32. Machamer, Darden, and Craver discuss causal mechanisms, which they define as "entities and activities organized such that they are productive of regular changes from start or set-up to finish or termination conditions." Peter Machamer, Lindley Darden, and Carl Craver, "Thinking about Mechanisms," *Philosophy of Science* 67, no. 1 (2000): 1–25. This definition is a good starting point for the kind of foundational causal relations I am interested in exploring. But I agree with John Dupré that the term "mechanism" is less useful to a process ontology insofar as it seems to suggest stable structures rather than regular sources of changes (see Nicholson and Dupré, *Everything Flows*). So, my preference will be for the term "process." For an alternate account of stabilizing processes, see Mallon, *Human Kinds*, 162–181.

33. Epstein, *The Ant Trap*.

34. Ian Hacking, *Historical Ontology* (Cambridge: Harvard University Press, 2002), 26. See also Hacking, *Social Construction of What?*

35. Hacking, *Social Construction of What?*, 32.

36. Kwame Anthony Appiah, *The Ethics of Identity* (Princeton, NJ: Princeton University Press, 2005), 66.

37. Josephson [Storm], *Invention of Religion in Japan*, 76–77. See also Robert Goldstone and Brian Rogosky, "Using Relations within Conceptual Systems to Translate across Conceptual Systems," *Cognition* 84 (2002): 295–320.

38. See Josephson [-Storm], *The Invention of Religion in Japan*, 257–59. But I wasn't yet using the technical terms "dynamic-nominalist" or "social kind."

39. Ruth Millikan, *Beyond Concepts: Unicepts, Language, and Natural Information* (New York: Oxford University Press, 2017), 17.

40. We can see this in internet memes, which are both imitative and regularly changing, and in the evolving meanings of the term "meme" itself—see Limor Shifman, *Memes in Digital Culture* (Cambridge: MIT Press, 2014).

41. David Edmonds and John Eidinow, *Wittgenstein's Poker* (London: Faber & Faber, 2002), 33.

42. Cited in Millikan, *On Clear and Confused Ideas*, 26.

43. Shancen Zhao et al., "Whole-Genome Sequencing of Giant Pandas Provides Insights into Demographic History and Local Adaptation," *Nature Genetics* 45 (16 December 2012): 67.

44. Millikan, *On Clear and Confused Ideas*, 22.

45. The term "mimesis" has proliferated in theory circles to mean a dozen incompatible things, but the basic meaning of Greek μίμησις was to imitate or copy.

46. René Girard, "Mimesis and Violence: Perspectives in Cultural Criticism," *Berkshire Review* 14 (1979): 9–19.

47. See James Mahoney, "Path Dependence in Historical Sociology," *Theory and Society* 29, no. 4 (2000): 507–48; see also Paul David, "Path Dependence, Its Critics and the Quest for 'Historical Economics,'" in *The Evolution of Economic Institutions*, ed. Geoffrey Martin Hodgson (Northampton: Edward Elgar, 2007), 120–42; and Paul Pierson, "Increasing Returns, Path Dependence, and the Study of Politics," *The American Political Science Review* 94, no. 2 (2000): 251–67.

48. Although the issue is still debated, see Paul David, "Clio and the Economics of QWERTY," *The American Economic Review* 75, no. 2 (1985): 332–37.

49. Ergonic, from the Greek ἔργον (érgon) "work" or "function." The term is mainly an attempt to avoid the negative associations of functionalism in anthropology and the implausible account of functionalism in evolutionary psychology.

50. C. Tristan Stayton, "The Definition, Recognition, and Interpretation of Convergent Evolution, and Two New Measures for Quantifying and Assessing the Significance of Convergence," *Evolution* 69, no. 8 (2015): 2140–53.

51. Ogura Atsushi, Ikeo Kazuho, and Gojobori Takashi, "Comparative Analysis of Gene Expression for Convergent Evolution of Camera Eye between Octopus and Human," *Genome Research* 14, no. 8 (2004): 1555–61. Khalidi, *Natural Categories*, 132–33.

52. I find carcinization to be especially striking as at least six independent groups of crustaceans seem to have independently converged on crab-like body plans. So I guess: *viva la crustacean!*

53. Example from David Papineau, "Can Any Sciences Be Special?" In *Emergence in Mind*, ed. Graham Macdonald and Cynthia Macdonald (Oxford: Oxford University Press, 2010), 179–97.

54. Jill Pruetz and Paco Bertolani, "Savanna Chimpanzees, *Pan Troglodytes Verus*, Hunt with Tools," *Current Biology* 17, no. 5 (2007): 412–17.

55. Susan G. Josephson, *From Idolatry to Advertising: Visual Art and Contemporary Culture* (New York: Routledge, 1996).

56. Bread is another good example of ergonic convergence. A range of different cultures have converged on parallel ways of producing similar foodstuffs from wheat.

57. Steven Rose, *The 21st Century Brain: Explaining, Mending and Manipulating the Mind* (London: Vintage, 2006), 83. I also reject the notion that humans are a blank slate with zero innate cognitive predispositions.

58. Alan Garfinkel, *Forms of Explanation: Structures of Inquiry in Social Science* (New Haven: Yale University Press, 1981), 129.

59. See Jon Elster, "Snobs," *London Review of Books* (1981): 10–12.

60. Jon Elster, *Explaining Social Behavior: More Nuts and Bolts for the Social Sciences* (New York: Cambridge University Press, 2007), 5.

61. A social formation can be explained in terms of its consequences only if there is something that amounts to a feedback loop that relates a choice to the consequences involved.

62. Anthony Giddens has persuasively argued that it is a mistake to think about institutions originating in broad societal functions; rather, he says they typically emerge from individual actors and their concrete needs. See Anthony Giddens, *A Contemporary Critique of Historical Materialism* (Berkeley: University of California Press, 1981).

63. For the latter, I have in mind work like Michael Hannon, *What's the Point of Knowledge: A Function-First Epistemology* (Oxford: Oxford University Press, 2018).

64. See Mills, *Blackness Visible*, 51–54 for different contradictory ways racial identities are anchored or constructed in the United States.

65. For my call for reflexive religious studies, see Josephson-Storm, *The Myth of Disenchantment*, 11–16. I model this on the reflexive sociology promoted by theorists such as Ulrich Beck, Pierre Bourdieu, Anthony Giddens, Alvin Gouldner, and others.

66. Space prohibits a fuller explanation of how "reflexive religious studies" relates to the forms of critical religion spearheaded by Russell McCutcheon. Suffice it to say, I think of these as allied projects but with different points of emphasis and techniques. Moreover, my broader end goal is to expand this reflexivity beyond the confines of religious studies (or sociology) and toward the human sciences in general.

67. Michael Ghiselin, "A Radical Solution to the Species Problem," *Systematic Biology* 23, no. 4 (1974): 536–44. See also Ghiselin, *Metaphysics and the Origin of Species* (Ithaca, NY: SUNY Press, 1997).

68. See Myron Rothbart and Marjorie Taylor, "Category Labels and Social Reality: Do We View Social Categories as Natural Kinds?" in *Language, Interaction*

318 : NOTES TO PAGES 130–145

and *Social Cognition*, ed. Klaus Fiedler and Gün Semin (London: Sage, 1992), 11–36; and Susan Gelman, *The Essential Child: Origins of Essentialism in Everyday Thought* (New York: Oxford University Press, 2003).

69. Haslanger, *Resisting Reality.*

70. Karl Marx and Friedrich Engels, *The German Ideology* (New York: International Publishers, 1970), 65–66.

71. Theodor Adorno, *Negative Dialektik* (Frankfurt: Suhrkamp, 1966), 21–22.

72. Kwame Gyekye, *An Essay on African Philosophical Thought* (Philadelphia: Temple University Press, 1995).

73. See Herman Cappelen, *Fixing language: An Essay on Conceptual Engineering* (Oxford: Oxford University Press, 2018).

74. "Taxonomy, Polymorphism, and History," 3.

75. Jonathan Z. Smith, *Imagining Religion* (Chicago: The University of Chicago Press, 1988), 21.

76. Except lacking in the scalar self-similarity that define fractals.

77. F.A. Hayek, "The Theory of Complex Phenomena," in *Critical Approaches to Science & Philosophy*, ed. Mario Augusto Bunge (New Brunswick, NJ: Transaction Publishers, 1999), 332–49.

78. Karl Mannheim, *Ideology and Utopia: An Introduction to the Sociology of Knowledge* (London: Routledge, 201).

79. An outgrowth of Boyd's theory has been the "simple causal theory of natural kinds" proposed as a thought experiment by Carl Craver and developed by Muhammad Ali Khalidi. It drops the notion of property clusters and instead identifies natural kinds solely with causal processes. See Khalidi, *Natural Categories*; and Carl Craver, "Mechanisms and Natural Kinds," *Philosophical Psychology* 22, no. 5 (2009): 575–94. But this is a mistake for social kinds because it misses the distinction between properties and the processes that anchor those properties.

80. Craver, "Mechanisms."

81. This is what Steven Pinker has called a "euphemism treadmill." Steven Pinker, *The Blank Slate* (New York: Penguin, 2003), 212. See also Matthew McGlone, Gary Beck, and Abigail Pfiester, "Contamination and Camouflage in Euphemisms," *Communication Monographs* 73, no. 3 (2006): 261–82.

82. See Matthew Melvin-Koushki, "Is (Islamic) Occult Science Science?" *Theology and Science* 18, no. 2 (2020): 303–24.

83. David Chalmers, "Verbal Disputes," *Philosophical Review* 120, no. 4 (2011): 515–66.

84. It is not uncommon for ethnographic subjects to tell researchers that some particular cultural feature has always been the way it is, when archival research reveals otherwise.

85. Sonia Harmand et al., "3.3-Million-Year-Old Stone Tools from Lomekwi 3, West Turkana, Kenya," *Nature* 521, no. 7552 (2015): 310–15.

86. See Josephson [Storm], *Invention of Religion in Japan*. I hope to revisit this (and other case studies) in subsequent research with a more careful eye to a range of anchoring processes (and I hope others will join me). So please look to my professional blog for follow-ups.

CHAPTER FIVE

1. For a fuller account, see Jason Ānanda Josephson Storm, "Dark Gods in the Age of Light: The Lightbulb, the Japanese 'Deification' of Thomas Edison, and the Entangled Constructions of Religion and Science," in *Critical Approaches to Science and Religion* ed. Myrna Perez Sheldon, Ahmed Ragab, and Terence Keel (Cambridge: Cambridge University Press, forthcoming).

2. Derek Bickerton, *Language and Species* (Chicago: University of Chicago Press, 1990), 7.

3. Masataka Nobuo, "Psycholinguistic Analyses of Alarm Calls of Japanese Monkeys (*Macaca fuscata fuscata*)," *American Journal of Primatology* 5, no. 2 (1983): 111–25; Jean-Baptiste Leca, Michael Huffman, and Paul Vasey, eds., *The Monkeys of Stormy Mountain: 60 Years of Primatological Research on the Japanese Macaques of Arashiyama* (New York: Cambridge University Press, 2012); and Julia Fischer, *Monkeytalk: Inside the Worlds and Minds of Primates* (Chicago: University of Chicago Press, 2017).

4. Robert Seyfarth, Dorothy Cheney, and Peter Marler, "Vervet Monkey Alarm Calls: Semantic Communication in a Free-Ranging Primate," *Animal Behavior* 28, no. 4 (1980): 1070–94.

5. J.R. Anderson and R.W. Mitchell, "Macaques but Not Lemurs Co-Orient Visually with Humans," *Folia Primatologica* 70, no. 1 (1999): 17–22.

6. If one insists on defining language in anthropocentric terms—e.g., Angela Friederici, *Language In Our Brain* (Cambridge: MIT Press, 2017)—then this chapter could be thought of as exploring the shared protolinguistic basis of human and animal communication.

7. Taylor, "Interpretation and the Sciences of Man."

8. The phrase "material semiotics" is sometimes treated as a synonym for actor-network-theory. We do not mean it in that sense.

9. Theorists referred to include centrally Richard Boyd, Ruth Millikan, Donna Haraway, and Jakob von Uexküll. But also Stacy Alaimo, Arjun Appadurai, Karen Barad, David Chalmers, Andy Clark, Marcel Danesi, Daniel Dennett, Umberto Eco, Brian Epstein, Donald Griffin, Martin Heidegger, Edmund Husserl, Edwin Hutchins, ICHIKAWA Hiroshi, Eduardo Kohn, John McGraw, Thomas Nagel, Thomas Sebeok, David Skrbina, Daniel Sperber, Bernard Steigler, TANAKA-ISHII Kumiko, Kristian Tylén, Lev Vygotsky, and Robert Yelle. All are cited in the relevant notes.

10. See Claire Colebrook, "The Linguistic Turn in Continental Philosophy," in *Poststructuralism and Critical Theory's Second Generation*, ed. Alan Schrift (London: Routledge, 2014), 279–309; for the others see below.

11. I am assuming most of my readers are not analytical philosophers. So for space reasons, I have had to cut my fuller reconstruction and arguments against Quine, Wittgenstein, Putnam, and Kripke. I hope to publish them elsewhere. For further details, see my professional website: http://absolute-disruption.com.

12. Ferdinand de Saussure, *Course in General Linguistics* (New York: Philosophical Library, 1959), 67, emphasis in original. [Hereafter cited as *CGL*.]

13. Saussure made it clear that he was not suggesting that a given sign is up to

individual choice; and later, in less read passages, he observed that once a language had committed to particular phonetic conventions this served to constrain possible signifiers. Saussure also qualified this arbitrariness of the sign with reference to onomatopoeias. *CGL*, 69.

14. *CGL*, 66–67.

15. *CGL*, 114–17.

16. Claude Lévi-Strauss, *Structural Anthropology* (New York: Basic Books, 1974), 93.

17. Derrida explicitly rejects this as a common misreading of his work in Richard Kearney, ed., *Dialogues with Contemporary Continental Thinkers* (Manchester: Manchester University Press, 1984), 123–24.

18. Emphasis in original. Catherine Belsey, *Poststructuralism* (Oxford: Oxford University Press, 2002), 10.

19. W.V.O. Quine, *Word & Object*, 2nd ed. (Cambridge: MIT Press, 2013), 69, quoting Wittgenstein's *Blue and Brown Books*.

20. Taylor, "Interpretation and the Sciences of Man." But the problem is far from insoluble. Texts can be read more than once. All we need to know is local context, not the text as a whole. Moreover, we can grant uncertainty in meaning.

21. Here I am recasting part of Derrida's critique. See for example Jacques Derrida, *Margins of Philosophy*, trans. Alan Bass (Chicago: University of Chicago Press, 1982), 3. Although to be fair, Saussure also described meaning in terms of similarity and not just difference.

22. Geoffrey Bennington, *Not Half No End* (Edinburgh: Edinburgh University Press, 2011), 133.

23. For one account of the value of semiotics for Religious Studies specifically, see Robert Yelle, *Semiotics of Religion* (London: Bloomsbury, 2013).

24. For some of these, see Michael Dummett, "What Is a Theory of Meaning?" in *Mind and Language*, ed. Samuel Guttenplan (Oxford: Oxford University Press, 1975). While many linguists have produced theories of meaning in terms of the above, most analytic philosophers identify meaning with what determines truth conditions; but while my account is not incompatible with such, for reasons the next section will make clear I do not aim to provide a theory of truth. From the vantage of analytic philosophy what follows is closer to pragmatics than to semantics.

25. Jacques Derrida, *De la Grammatologie* (Paris: Édtions de Minuit, 1967).

26. David Nye, *The Invented Self: An Anti-Biography from Documents of Thomas A. Edison* (Odense: Odense University Press, 1983), 16–17, 118, 198.

27. Nye, *Invented Self*, 118.

28. For example, Stacy Alaimo and Susan J. Hekman, *Material Feminisms* (Bloomington: Indiana University Press, 2008), 1.

29. Emphasis added. Rick Dolphijn and Iris van der Tuin, eds., *New Materialism: Interviews & Cartographies* (Ann Arbor, MI: Open Humanities Press, 2012), 21.

30. Karen Barad, "Posthumanist Performativity: Toward an Understanding of How Matter Comes to Matter," *Signs* 28, no. 3 (2003): 801–31. For other examples,

see Diana H. Coole and Samantha Frost, *New Materialisms: Ontology, Agency, and Politics* (Durham, NC: Duke University Press, 2010), 6; Tamsin Jones, "Introduction: New Materialism and the Study of Religion," in *Religious Experience and New Materialism: Movement Matters*, ed. Joerg Rieger and Edward Waggoner (Basingstoke: Palgrave Macmillan, 2016), 8; and Sarah Ellenzweig and John H. Zammito, eds., *The New Politics of Materialism: History, Philosophy, Science* (New York: Routledge, 2017), 2.

31. Irena Makaryk, ed., *Encyclopedia of Contemporary Literary Theory* (Toronto: University of Toronto Press, 1997), 505.

32. Jason Ānanda Josephson Storm, "Derrida on the Network," unpublished manuscript, last revised 2014. (Hopefully, I'll polish it and put a version on my professional website). Saussure uses "structure" three times and "assemblage" five times in *Cours de linguistique générale*.

33. For example, Judith Butler and her theory of performativity shifted from discourse and speech acts to mattering. Although to be fair, I find her work highly useful.

34. I have not yet said anything that Latour would disagree with given his own recent repudiation of ANT in Bruno Latour, *An Inquiry into Modes of Existence* (Cambridge: Harvard University Press, 2013).

35. Sometimes material agency is contrasted with a strawman Cartesian mechanism that ignores the history of twentieth-century physics.

36. David Tagnani, "Toward a Material Jeffers: Mysticism and the New Materialism," In *Ecopoetics and the Global Landscape: Critical Essays*, ed. Isabel Sobral Campos (Lanham, MD: Lexington Books, 2019), 218.

37. Jane Bennett, *Vibrant Matter: A Political Ecology of Things* (Durham, NC: Duke University Press, 2010), 5–6.

38. For a parallel critique of New Materialism, see Christian Thorne, "To the Political Ontologists," in Thorne, "Commonplace Book" (blog), posted May 10, 2012. https://sites.williams.edu/cthorne/articles/to-the-political-ontologists/

39. Karen Barad, *Meeting the Universe Halfway* (Durham, NC: Duke University Press, 2007), 3.

40. See John Sowa, "Signs, Processes, and Language Games: Foundations for Ontology," in *ICCS '01: Proceedings of the 9th International Conference on Conceptual Structures, ICCS'01*, ed. Harry S. Delugach and Gerd Stumme (Berlin: Springer Verlag, 2001), 1–44.

41. The main exceptions being, of course, the discussion of natural kinds in the semantics of Putnam, Kripke, and company.

42. Here I am departing from Millikan's articulation of a "clumpy world," although I'm trying to get even more minimal. Ruth Garrett Millikan, *Beyond Concepts: Unicepts, Language, and Natural Information* (Oxford: Oxford University Press, 2017). In this respect, I am trying to describe what Subcomandante Marcos poetically referred to as "a world in which many worlds fit." See Subcomandante Marcos, *Our Word Is Our Weapon: Selected Writings*, ed. Juana Ponce de León (New York: Seven Stories Press, 2002), 80.

43. For theories of vagueness, see Richard Dietz and Sebastiano Moruzzi, eds., *Cuts and Clouds: Vaguenesss, Its Nature and Its Logic* (Oxford: Oxford University Press, 2010).

44. See Millikan, *Beyond Concepts*.

45. Time doesn't even have to flow in one direction.

46. The external world can't be completely illusionary.

47. People with vision impairment or who are hard of hearing (or both) are likely to be prioritize different senses, but the point still stands.

48. For instance, you can at least in principle see, touch, hear, and maybe even taste a sparrow (although as a vegetarian I'll recommend you do so gently). For an account of *robustness*, see Wimsatt, "Ontology of Complex Systems."

49. In Uexküll's technical language, the cat and I may inhabit separate *Umwelten*, but they overlap.

50. Millikan, *Beyond Concepts*, argues for a similar ontology (although more contemporary science and less minimalist).

51. I am neither presuming nor refuting sentient beings' ability to access *Ding an sich*.

52. Steven Pinker, *The Language Instinct* (New York: Morrow, 1994). See also Daniel Casasanto, "Who's Afraid of the Big Bad Whorf?" *Language Learning* 58 (2008): 63–79; and Phillip Wolff and Kevin Holmes, "Linguistic Relativity," *Wiley Interdisciplinary Reviews: Cognitive Science*, no. 3 (2011): 253–65. Donald Davidson has argued that the whole idea of a worldview is incoherent—see below.

53. For animals, see José Luis Bermúdez, *Thinking Without Words* (New York: Oxford University Press, 2003); and James Hurford, *The Origins of Meaning* (New York: Oxford University Press, 2007). Although *contra* Pinker, Noam Chomsky, and the various philosophers who have conceived of a kind of protolinguistic, panhuman language of thought, we actually share much less of a "deep structure" than has commonly been supposed. See Nicholas Evans and Stephen Levinson, "The Myth of Language Universals: Language Diversity and Its Importance for Cognitive Science," *Behavioral and Brain Sciences* 32, no. 5 (2009): 429–48.

54. It is also worth noting that even polemically opposed works such as Guy Deutscher, *Through the Language Glass: Why the World Looks Different in Different Languages* (New York Metropolitan Books, 2010) and John McWhorter, *The Language Hoax: Why the World Looks the Same in Any Language* (New York: Oxford University Press, Oxford) have similar views on the relationship between language and thought, both dismissing strong linguistic determinism and supporting weak linguistic relativity. The power of rhetoric has been discussed at least since the original sophists. But for more recent attempts to theorize the impact of conceptual metaphors, see George Lakoff and Mark Johnson, *Metaphors We Live By* (Chicago: University of Chicago Press, 2008).

55. Ruth Millikan, *Language: A Biological Model* (Oxford: Oxford University Press, 2005), 133–37.

56. Brent Berlin and Paul Kay, *Basic Color Terms: Their Universality and Evolution* (Berkeley: University of California Press, 1991); and Lawrence Barsalou,

"Deriving Categories to Achieve Goals," in *Psychology of Learning and Motivation*, ed. Gordon Bower (New York: Academic Press, 1991), 1–64.

57. Hilary Putnam, "The Meaning of Meaning," in *Mind, Language and Reality* (Cambridge: Cambridge University Press, 1975), 227. Putnam's linguistic division of labor might as well be a fantasy of the Académie Française insofar as people do not defer to experts about the meaning of their words. Experts are not regarded particularly highly in contemporary America. But even in communities where they are, we do not expect botanists to know more about the meaning of the term "elm tree" so much as we expect them to know more about plant biology. We do not defer to them for the meaning of words.

58. Hurford, *Origins of Meaning*, 5.

59. Space prohibits a full exposition. But despite their attempts to reject such, both thinkers ended up smuggling in what amounts to concepts. Kripke, for instance, was careful to suggest that his account of naming did not cover all sorts of language, but was generally confined to proper names and natural kind terms. Even in the process of making the case for externalism, Putnam suggested that competent speakers of a language are required to share at least a concept of the "stereotypical" features of a category to count as having acquired the meaning of a word.

60. Saul Kripke, *Naming and Necessity* (New York: Harvard University Press, 1980). Kripke's model is typically called "the causal theory of reference," but more recently Kripke has rejected this formulation in favor of "the historical chain picture." Saul Kripke, "Naming and Necessity Revisited," lecture, University of London, May 30, 2019.

61. Gareth Evans and J. Altham, "The Causal Theory of Names," *Proceedings of the Aristotelian Society, Supplementary Volumes* 47 (1973): 187–225.

62. Here I am thinking of Quine.

63. We also have the classic problem of what "Mark Twain is Samuel Clemens" communicates in non-descriptivist accounts of reference (see above).

64. See Dan Ryder et al., eds. *Millikan and Her Critics* (London: Wiley, 2012, 219.

65. See Steven Hager, "Afrika Bambaataa's Hip Hop," *Village Voice*, September 21, 1982. Reference (or at least indicating) seems to also be basic in animal signaling, albeit more typically in attached signs. That is to say, while human voluntary-signs frequently exhibit "displacement" or refer to times or places separate from the speech act itself, this displacement is comparatively rare in animal communication. Charles Hockett, "The Origin of Speech," *Scientific American* 203, no. 3 (1960): 88–97. But *contra-* Hockett, bees, crows, and ants at least have been observed to engage in displacement.

66. Some responses (or meanings) are probably instinctive, but learned responses to calls are definitely done by way of reference fixing (see below). (Similarly, humans regularly communicate via non-vocal media, like sign-languages and even the written word. This suggests that our ability to apprehend meaning is independent of our ability to produce or comprehend speech.)

67. In Frege's terms people typically do not share senses. This is also one of the reasons that conceptual analysis is a fraught methodology for philosophy.

68. Marga Reimer, "Donnellan's Distinction/Kripke's Test," *Analysis* 58, no. 2 (1998): 89100.

69. Charles Sanders Peirce, "Issues of Pragmaticism," in *Collected Papers of Charles Sanders Peirce*, ed. Charles Hartshorne (Cambridge: Harvard University Press, 1974), vol. 5:448, note 1, para. 5–6 on p. 302. [Peirce's Collected Papers will hereafter be cited as *CP* followed by volume and page number.].

70. Edmund Husserl, *Logical Investigations*, vol. 2 (New York: Routledge, 2015), 221–22; Dan Zahavi, *Husserl's Phenomenology* (Stanford, CA: Stanford University Press, 2008), 25–27.

71. Martin Heidegger, *"Der Begriff der Zeit,"* in Thomas Sheehan, *Making Sense of Heidegger: A Paradigm Shift* (London: Rowman & Littlefield International, 2014), 122. See also Martin Heidegger, *History of the Concept of Time: Prolegomena* (Bloomington: Indiana University Press, 1992), esp. 200–214.

72. Martin Heidegger, *Being in Time* (London: Blackwell, 1962), 220. I am reading *Dasein* as human existence.

73. Jakob von Uexküll, *A Foray into the Worlds of Animals and Humans* (Minneapolis: University of Minnesota Press, 2010), 42.

74. We follow Eduardo Kohn in bridging Peircean semiotics and the animal world, but we reject his view that humans are the only animal that makes symbols. See Eduardo Kohn, "How Dogs Dream: Amazonian Natures and the Politics of Transspecies Engagement," *American Ethnologist* 34, no. 1 (2007): 3–24; and Eduardo Kohn, *How Forests Think: Toward an Anthropology Beyond the Human* (Berkeley: University of California Press, 2013).

75. Discussed largely in the notes that follow.

76. Dorothy Cheney and Robert Seyfarth, *Baboon Metaphysics: The Evolution of a Social Mind* (Chicago: University of Chicago Press, 2008), 7.

77. See Millikan, *Beyond Concepts*. Even the humble tick, as Jakob von Uexküll classically demonstrates (see below).

78. H. Paul Grice, "Meaning," *The Philosophical Review* 66, no. 3 (1957): 377–88, 377. See also H. Paul Grice, *Studies in the Way of Words* (Cambridge: Harvard University Press, 1991). Similarly, Millikan distinguishes between informational signs (which cannot be wrong) and intentional signs (consciously produced signs which can be either true or false).

79. Thanks to Keith McPartland for this example, and I am indebted to conversations with him for much of the content of this section.

80. See Siobhan Chapman, *Paul Grice, Philosopher and Linguist* (Basingstoke: Palgrave Macmillan, 2008).

81. Christopher Gauker, *Words without Meaning* (Cambridge: MIT Press, 2003), 17.

82. Theodore Bailey, *The African Leopard: Ecology and Behavior of a Solitary Felid* (New York: Columbia University Press, 1993).

83. This is where Grice's emphasis on ordinary English usage of the word "means" led him astray.

84. Ruth Millikan, "Natural Signs," in Barry Cooper, ed., *How the World Com-*

putes (Dordrecht: Springer, 2012), 500. When I argue that meaning is inference, this is basically a way of saying that meaning is information, but it is not information as an objective commodity. Meaning needs to be thought of in terms of the information extracted by a particular meaning consumer (which can include but is never purely identical to the meaning ostensibly signaled by a meaning producer). In this I am building on Milikan. But she has a tendency to reduce meaning to reference. I would argue that reference is only part of the meaning we infer. To evoke the classic example, we infer something different about Mark Twain vs. Samuel Clemens insofar as our assumptions about each is different (even if they refer to the same person).

85. Brandon Wheeler, "Monkeys Crying Wolf? Tufted Capuchin Monkeys Use Anti-Predator Calls to Usurp Resources from Conspecifics," *Proceedings: Biological sciences*, vol. 276, 1669 (2009): 3013-18. See also Cecilia Heyes, "Animal Mindreading: What's the Problem?" *Psychonomic Bulletin & Review* 22, no. 2 (2015): 313-27.

86. Cheney and Seyfarth, *Baboon Metaphysics*, 233.

87. In the first case, exactly what range of inputs triggers what I am calling "flying predator" is an empirical question. But it is far from an unsolvable one. See K.V. Wilkes, "Talking to Cats, Rats and Bats," *Royal Institute of Philosophy Supplement* (1997): 177-96.

88. As James Hurford has argued, "a more voluntary act is one less immediately subject to external stimuli, and correspondingly more determined by hidden inner mental processes." Hurford, *Origins of Meaning*, 29-30.

89. This latter hedge is because the question of which aspect of a sign is being analyzed is task dependent. We might think of a child who gets sick on purpose in order to skip school as analyzable by their doctor in terms of the illness's involuntary sign aspect and by their parents in terms of their sign's voluntarily origins. Moreover, for theists the world has intentional meaning.

90. Julia Fischer, *Monkeytalk: Inside the Worlds and Minds of Primates* (Chicago: University of Chicago Press, 2017), 187. But she largely ignores tactile signaling and gesture, which seems to be more important in ape communication.

91. Cheney and Seyfarth, *Baboon Metaphysics*, esp. 219-20.

92. Much of the relevant literature is divided between two different models: influence and information. But I would argue it is both. For various attempts to reconcile these models, see Ulrich Stegmann, ed., *Animal Communication Theory: Information and Influence* (Cambridge: Cambridge University Press, 2013).

93. Deirdre Wilson and Dan Sperber, "Relevance Theory," in *The Handbook of Pragmatics* (Oxford: Blackwell, 2006): 606-32.

94. Delia Graff, "Shifting Sands: An Interest-Relative Theory of Vagueness," *Philosophical Topics* 28, no. 1 (2000): 45-81.

95. Ernst-August Gutt, *Relevance Theory* (Dallas: Summer Institute of Linguistics, 1992), 47; and Dan Sperber and Deirdre Wilson, *Relevance: Communication and Cognition* (Malden: Blackwell, 2004), 233.

96. Deirdre Wilson and Dan Sperber, *Meaning and Relevance* (Cambridge: Cambridge University Press, 2012), 65.

97. Millikan, *Language*, 57–58.

98. One can also refer to things that aren't physical, like triangles or your own thoughts yesterday.

99. Indeed, in the time period in question, rival scientists were actually able to communicate about phlogiston or at least pinpoint their disagreements. For this, see Philip Kitcher, "Theories, Theorists and Theoretical Change," *The Philosophical Review* 87, no. 4 (1978): 519–47, an excellent and generally overlooked response to Kuhn.

100. See Eric Hirsch, *Validity in Interpretation* (New Haven: Yale University Press, 1975).

101. See Gutt, *Relevance Theory*, 53; Sperber and Wilson, *Relevance*, 236–37.

102. Indeed, a lot of scholarly effort is wasted trying to make a particular conception consistent when the simplest explanation might be that the author in question either changed their mind or was inconsistent in their usage (e.g., maybe Aristotle's notion of *being* cannot be reconciled across his philosophical works because his ideas shifted).

103. Ella Frances Sanders, *Lost in Translation: An Illustrated Compendium of Untranslatable Words from Around the World* (Berkeley, CA: Ten Speed Press, 2014).

104. Barbara Cassin, ed., *Dictionary of Untranslatables*, trans. Steven Rendall et al. (Princeton, NJ: Princeton University Press, 2014), 227.

105. Cassin, *Untranslatables*, xvii.

106. Space prohibits a full explanation, but the descriptive–redescriptive opposition proposed by various scholars as a way to identify untranslatable terms is incoherent. Because social kinds are incredibly varied, strictly applied it would make everything untranslatable.

107. Kuhn argues that "students of literature" have shown that metaphor makes "translation impossible" and he tries to extend that claim to the sciences. See Thomas Kuhn, *The Road since Structure: Philosophical Essays* (Chicago: University of Chicago Press, 2002), 75.

108. For a longer version, see Jason Ānanda Josephson Storm, "Lion's Roar: The (Im)possibility of Translation Revisited," in progress, last revised July 2019. When published a link or reference to it will appear on my professional website.

109. For instance, Jacques Derrida often illustrated the impossibility of translation by reference to the phrase "he war," which suggests one thing in German ("he was") and another in English ("he [engaged in] wars"). This provides two translations rather than none.

110. Technically, Whorf argued that they couldn't be translated into a Standard Average European language of which English was one example. Benjamin Lee Whorf, *Language, Thought, and Reality: Selected Writings of Benjamin Lee Whorf* (Cambridge: MIT Press, 1956).

111. See also Donald Davidson, "On the Very Idea of a Conceptual Scheme," *Proceedings and Addresses of the American Philosophical Association* 47 (1973): 5–20. For another example, see José Ortega y Gasset, "The Misery and the Splendor of Translation," *The Translation Studies Reader*, ed. Lawrence Venuti (New York: Routledge, 2012), 49–63.

112. Jacques Derrida, "What Is a "Relevant" Translation?" trans. Lawrence Venuti, *Critical Inquiry* 27, no. 2 (2001): 174–200, 179.

113. See Jean-Paul Vinay and Jean Darbelnet, *Stylistique comparée du français et de l'anglais: Méthode de traduction* (Paris: Didier, 1972).

114. By this I mean to gesture at Nelson Goodman's famous riddle of induction. I would argue that the meaning of terms changes historically and will change in the future. So, for instance, in at least the English object language the statement "Helen of Troy was a man" would be a false statement today insofar as we believe Helen to have been a woman. But not so long ago, "man" was primarily a gender-neutral term synonymous with "human." So "Helen of Troy was man" would have been a true statement. Projecting from contemporary usage changes in which gender is increasingly understood as a matter of personal identification one could even imagine that in the future the statement "Helen of Troy was a man" might become undecidable on the grounds that we do not know Helen's preferred gender identity. This looks a lot like Goodman's color "grue," which has the following property: "if observed before Jan 1, 2017 it is green, but if observed after Jan 1, 2017 it is blue."

115. This is closer to how Sapir and Whorf actually understood linguistic relativism. See Storm "Language, Mind, Cosmos: The Theosophical Roots of Linguistic Relativism," in *Theosophy and the Study of Religion*, ed. Charles Stang and Jason Ānanda Josephson Storm (Leiden: Brill, under consideration).

116. Kwame Anthony Appiah, "Thick Translation," *Callaloo* 16, no. 4 (1993): 808–19.

117. Lydia Liu, *Translingual Practice: Literature, National Culture, and Translated Modernity—China* (Palo Alto, CA: Stanford University Press. 1995), 26.

118. This subsection is largely drawn from Brothers Josephson (Jason Josephson Storm and Seth Josephson), "Signs Following: Towards a Material Semiotics of Religion," manuscript in progress (last modified 2019) and should be thought of as jointly authored.

119. For an account of the religious genealogy of Peirce's pragmatism, see M. Gail Hamner, *American Pragmatism: A Religious Genealogy* (New York: Oxford University Press, 2003).

120. *CP* 2:135.

121. Donna Haraway, "Situated Knowledges: The Science Question in Feminism and the Privilege of Partial Perspective," *Feminist Studies* 14, no. 3 (1988): 575–99.

122. For an influential version of sender-receiver communication, see Claude Shannon, "A Mathematical Theory of Communication," *Bell System Technical Journal* 27, no. 3 (1948): 379–423.

123. Charles Sanders Peirce, *Peirce on Signs*, ed. James Hoopes (Bloomington: Indiana University Press, 1991), 30.

124. See Tony Jappy, *Peirce's Twenty-Eight Classes of Signs and the Philosophy of Representation: Rhetoric, Interpretation and Hexadic Semiosis* (London: Bloomsbury Publishing, 2016).

125. Peirce, "New List of Categories," in Charles Sanders Peirce, *The Writings of*

Charles S. Peirce: A Chronological Edition, vol. 2, ed. Edward C. Moore (Blooming-ton: Indiana University Press, 1982-), 49-58. Peirce referred to these as the *deictic* and *causal* sorts of indices. He also referred to a third type as a *labeling*. We will alter our vocabulary later. See also James Jakób Liszka, *A General Introduction to the Semeiotic of Charles Sanders Peirce* (Bloomington: Indiana University Press, 1996), 38.

126. Of course, it need not have a *human* observer around to be meaningful.

127. The Brothers Josephson do not fully agree about what counts as a sen-tient being. In using the term "sentient being" we mean to gesture toward the Sanskrit *sattva* and its translation in the Sino-Japanese 衆生 or 有情. Although we give a particular list of examples, we want to leave open different cosmolo-gies including both the traditional lists of sentient beings in different schools of Buddhism and the possibility for various kinds of panpsychism, hylozoism, or pantheism.

128. For animal sentience, see Colin Allen and Marc Bekoff, *Species of Mind: The Philosophy and Biology of Cognitive Ethology* (Cambridge: MIT Press, 1999); and Donald Griffin, *Animal Minds: Beyond Cognition to Consciousness* (Chicago: University of Chicago Press, 2001). For machine consciousness, see Owen Hol-land, ed., *Machine Consciousness* (Charlottesville, VA: Imprint Academic, 2003). For panpsychism, see Thomas Nagel, "Panpsychism," in Nagel, *Mortal Questions* (Cambridge: Cambridge University Press, 1991), 181-95; David Skrbina, *Panpsych-ism in the West* (Cambridge: MIT Press, 2005); Godehard Brüntrup and Ludwig Jaskolla, eds., *Panpsychism: Contemporary Perspectives* (New York: Oxford Univer-sity Press, 2017).

129. Daniel Dennett, *The Intentional Stance* (Cambridge: MIT Press, 1989).

130. KAWADE Yoshimi, "The Two Foci of Biology: Matter and Sign," *Semiotica* 127, nos. 1-4 (1999): 369-84, 373.

131. Thomas Sebeok, *Signs: An Introduction to Semiotics*, 2nd edition (Toronto: University of Toronto Press, 2001), 43; Umberto Eco, *La Struttura assente: La ricerca semiotica e il metodo strutturale* (Milan: Bompiani, 1968), 110.

132. Sebeok, *Signs*; but see also John Haldane, "Animal Communication and the Origin of Human Language," *Science Progress* 43, no. 171 (1955): 385-401.

133. Peter Wohlleben, *The Hidden Life of Trees* (Vancouver, BC: Greystone Books, 2016), 7-8.

134. Claudia Stephan, Anna Wilkinson, and Ludwig Huber, "Have We Met Be-fore? Pigeons Recognise Familiar Human Faces," *Avian Biology Research* 5, no. 2 (June 2012): 75-80.

135. Devi Stuart-Fox, Adnan Moussalli, and Martin J Whiting, "Predator-Specific Camouflage in Chameleons," *Biology Letters* 4, no. 4 (2008): 326-29.

136. KATOH Mitsuho, TATSUTA Haruki, and TSUJI Kazuki, "Rapid Evolution of a Batesian Mimicry Trait in a Butterfly Responding to Arrival of a New Model," *Scientific Reports* 7, no. 1 (2017): 6369.

137. Spencer Barrett, "Mimicry in Plants," *Scientific American* 257, no. 3 (1987): 76-85.

138. Augustine of Hippo, *The Confessions: With an Introduction and Contemporary Criticism*, ed. Maria Boulding, David Vincent Meconi, and Joseph Pearce (San Francisco: Ignatius Press, 2012), 1.8.

139. Cristina Colonnesi, Geert Stams, Irene Koster, and Marc J. Noom, "The Relation between Pointing and Language Development: A Meta-analysis," *Developmental Review* 30, no. 4 (2010): 352–66.

140. As Millikan observes: "The addressee is part of the sign on the assumption that whatever is necessary to observe in relation to a conventional sign in order to grasp its truth conditions, granted of course that one knows all the relevant conventions, must be part of the sign. Without it the sign is incomplete." Millikan, *Beyond Concepts*, 120.

141. Fred Harrington and David Mech, "Wolf Howling and Its Role in Territory Maintenance," *Behaviour* 68, no. 3/4 (1979): 207–49; J. Riley et al., "The Flight Paths of Honeybees Recruited by the Waggle Dance," *Nature* 435, no. 7039 (2005): 205–7.

142. Tanaka-Ishii Kumiko, *Semiotics of Programming* (New York: Cambridge University Press, 2010), 105.

143. Millikan, *Beyond Concepts*, 114–20.

144. Gordon Hafner, Lee Hamilton, William Steiner, Thomas Thompson, and Howard Winn, "Signature Information in the Song of the Humpback Whale," *Journal of the Acoustical Society of America* 66, no. 1 (1979): 1–6.

145. Daniel Weary, Ken Norris, and J. Bruce Falls, "Song Features Birds Use to Identify Individuals," *The Auk* 107, no. 3 (1990): 623–25.

146. By correlational sign, I am meaning in part to capture the insights of Millikan's infosign, but with an emphasis on causal and in that respect non-accidental correlations. Millikan, *Beyond Concepts*.

147. Millikan, *Beyond Concepts*, 222.

148. Uexküll, *A Foray*, 45.

149. François Recanati, "Millikan's Theory of Signs," *Philosophy and Phenomenological Research* 75, no. 3 (2007): 674–81.

150. Marcel Danesi, *The Quest for Meaning* (Toronto: University of Toronto Press, 2007), 6.

151. The parallel between biological and mechanical systems might be overdrawn, but they suggest similar examples of the broader category of correlational signs.

152. Richard Rorty, *Philosophy and the Mirror of Nature* (Princeton, NJ: Princeton University Press, 1979), 3.

153. Barad, *Meeting the Universe*. Barad is right to focus on the emergence of entities through a process of intra-action, or as we might say in a Buddhist idiom, via *Pratītyasamutpāda* "interdependent co-arising." But I disagree with the claim that matter and meaning are identical.

154. Nietzsche makes a similar claim in Friedrich Nietzsche, *The Gay Science* (New York: Cambridge University Press, 2001), 211–15.

155. Ichikawa Hiroshi, *Seishin to shite no shintai* (Tokyo: Kōdansha, 1992).

156. For an insightful exploration of this permeability, see Stacy Alaimo, *Bodily Natures* (Indianapolis: Indiana University Press, 2010).

157. Rodney Brooks, "Intelligence Without Reason," *Artificial Intelligence* 47, no. 1 (1991); Kristian Tylén and John J McGraw, "Materializing Mind: The Role of Objects in Cognition and Culture," in *Perspectives on Social Ontology and Social Cognition*, ed. Mattia Galloti and John Michael (New York: Springer, 2014), 140.

158. Michael Dawson, "Embedded and Situated Cognition," in *The Routledge Handbook of Embodied Cognition*, ed. Lawrence Shapiro (New York: Routledge, 2014), 59.

159. Esther Thelen and Linda B. Smith, *A Dynamic Systems Approach to the Development of Cognition and Action* (Cambridge: MIT Press, 1996).

160. Dawson, "Embedded Cognition," 60.

161. Brooks, "Intelligence Without Reason," 139–59.

162. For a summary of some of the empirical evidence, see P.A. Ferchmin and André Eterović, "Play Stimulated by Environmental Complexity Alters the Brain and Improves Learning Abilities in Rodents, Primates, and Possibly Humans," *Behavioral and Brain Sciences* 5, no. 1 (1982): 164.

163. Dawson, "Embedded Cognition," 62; James Gibson, *The Ecological Approach to Visual Perception* (New York: Psychology Press, 2014).

164. Ichikawa, *Seishin*. For phantom limb, Dick Plettenburg, "Prosthetic Control: A Case for Extended Physiological Proprioception," in *MEC '02 The Next Generation, Proceedings of the 20023 MyoElectric Controls/Powered Prosthetics Symposium* (Fredericton: University of New Brunswick, 2002), 21–23.

165. Herbert Simon, *The Sciences of the Artificial*, 3rd ed. (Cambridge: MIT Press, 2008), 51–52; see also Edwin Hutchins, *Cognition in the Wild* (Cambridge: MIT Press, 1995), xiii.

166. Hilary Putnam, "Meaning and Reference," *Journal of Philosophy* 70, no. 19 (1974): 699–711.

167. Lev Vygotsky, *Mind in Society* (Cambridge: Harvard University Press, 1980), 39.

168. Andy Clark and David Chalmers, "The Extended Mind," *Analysis* 58, no. 1 (1998): 7–19.

169. *Plato: Complete Works*, ed. John Cooper and Douglas Hutchinson, (Indianapolis: Hackett Publishing, 1997), 551–52.

170. Bernard Stiegler, *Pour une nouvelle critique de l'économie politique* (Paris: Galilée, 2009).

171. Tylén and McGraw, "Materializing Mind.".

172. Hutchins, *Cognition in the Wild*, 115.

173. Jonathan Histon, "Mitigating Complexity in Air Traffic Control," PhD diss., MIT Department of Aeronautics, 2008.

174. Tylén and McGraw, "Materializing Mind"; Andy Clark, *Being There: Putting Brain, Body, and World Together Again* (Cambridge: MIT Press, 1998).

175. Greg Stephens, Lauren Silbert, and Uri Hasson, "Speaker–Listener Neural Coupling Underlies Successful Communication," *Proceedings of the National Academy of Sciences* 107, no. 32 (2010): 14425–30.

176. For one account of the primacy of private representations, see Jerry Fodor, *The Language of Thought* (Cambridge: Harvard University Press, 1975).

177. Dan Sperber, *Explaining Culture: A Naturalistic Approach* (Cambridge: Cambridge University Press, 1996), 77–82.

178. By saying that objects mediate social relations, I want to suggest that they are part of the social order, but I want to push back against the overblown version of New Materialism that suggests that they are equal participants in it. A handgun doesn't get to choose who it points at.

179. Epstein, *The Ant Trap*.

180. Arjun Appadurai, ed., *The Social Life of Things* (Cambridge: Cambridge University Press, 1988).

181. See Karl Marx, *Das Kapital: A Critique of Political Economy* (Chicago: H. Regnery, 1965); and Emile Durkheim, *The Division of Labor in Society*, trans. W.D. Halls (New York: Free Press, 1984).

182. See for example John Betz, *After Enlightenment: The Post-Secular vision of JG Hamann* (Malden, MA: Wiley-Blackwell, 2012).

183. Kuhn, *Structure of Scientific Revolutions*, 99–100.

184. See Larry Laudan, *Beyond Positivism and Relativism* (Boulder, CO: Westview Press, 1997), 9.

CHAPTER SIX

1. See: Eric Carlton, *Poleteia: Visions of the Just Society* (Madison, NJ: Fairleigh Dickinson University Press, 2006), 191.

2. Lyotard, *The Inhuman*, 39.

3. Christopher Norris, *What's Wrong with Postmodernism* (Baltimore: Johns Hopkins University Press, 1990), 185.

4. See: Alan Sokal and Jean Bricmont, *Fashionable Nonsense: Postmodern Intellectuals' Abuse of Science* (New York: Picador, 1998); Paul Gross and Norman Levitt, *Higher Superstition: The Academic Left and Its Quarrels with Science* (Baltimore: Johns Hopkins University Press, 2003), esp. 11; Stuart Sim, *Empires of Belief* (Edinburgh: Edinburgh University Press, 2006), esp. 53. For a more sophisticated critique, see Susan Haack, *Evidence and Inquiry: A Pragmatist Reconstruction of Epistemology* (Amherst, MA: Prometheus Books, 2009), 12.

5. Examples: Seidman, *Postmodern Turn*, 5–6; Judith Butler, "Contingent Foundations: Feminism and the Question of 'Postmodernism,'" in *Feminist Contentions a Philosophical Exchange*, ed. Seyla Benhabib (New York: Routledge, 1995), 35–58; Maggie MacLure, "Theoretical Resources," *Educational Action Research* 3, no. 1 (1995): 106–16; K.M. Newton, *Modern Literature and the Tragic* (Edinburgh: Edinburgh University Press, 2008), 159; and Kang Dae Joong, "Rhizoactivity: Toward a Postmodern Theory of Lifelong Learning," *Adult Education Quarterly* 57, no. 3 (2007): 205–20.

6. Examples: Jeet Heer, "America's First Postmodern President," *The New Republic*, July 8, 2018; and Helen Pluckrose, "How French 'Intellectuals' Ruined the West: Postmodernism and Its Impact Explained," *Areo Magazine*, March 27, 2017.

For a summary and critique, Michael Peters, Sharon Rider, Mats Hyvönen, and Tina Besley, eds., *Post-Truth, Fake News: Viral Modernity & Higher Education* (New York: Springer, 2018).

7. For readings of Foucault as a skeptic, see Lois MacNay, *Foucault and Feminism: Power, Gender and the Self* (Cambridge: Polity, 1992), 5.

8. Michel Foucault, *Politics, Philosophy, Culture: Interviews and Other Writings* (New York: Routledge, 2013), 264.

9. Gutting, *Foucault's Archaeology*, esp. 273; Linda Martín Alcoff, "Foucault's Normative Epistemology," in *A Companion to Foucault*, ed. Christopher Falzon, Timothy O'Leary, and Jana Sawicki (Malden, MA: Wiley-Blackwell, 2013), 205–25.

10. Charles Altieri, "Presence and Reference in a Literary Text," *Critical Inquiry* 5, no. 3 (1979): 489–510, 490; for an argument against the common misreading of Derrida as a skeptic, see Joshua Kates, *Fielding Derrida: Philosophy, Literary Criticism, History, and the Work of Deconstruction* (New York: Fordham University Press, 2008).

11. Jacques Derrida, *Limited Inc.* (Evanston, IL: Northwestern University Press, 1988), 146. Cited in Peters et al., *Post-Truth*, 220.

12. See Marko Zlomislić. *Jacques Derrida's Aporetic Ethics* (New York: Lexington Books, 2007), esp. 241; Jack Reynolds, "Jacques Derrida," in *Internet Encyclopedia of Philosophy*, https://iep.utm.edu/, 2013; and David Bates, "Crisis between the Wars: Derrida and the Origins of Undecidability" *Representations* 90, no. 1 (2005): 1–27.

13. Bruno Latour, *The Pasteurization of France* (Cambridge: Harvard University Press, 1993), 232.

14. Bruno Latour, "Why Has Critique Run Out of Steam?" *Critical Inquiry* 30, no. 2 (2004): 225–48, 231.

15. For "cynical reason" see Peter Sloterdijk, *Kritik der zynischen Vernunft* (Frankfurt: Suhrkamp, 1983).

16. Combining the eighteenth-century Tibetan scholar Könchog Jigme Wangpo's list of illusions alongside Descartes and others. See Jan Westerhoff, *Twelve Examples of Illusion* (Oxford: Oxford University Press, 2010).

17. Gilbert Harman, *Thought* (Princeton, NJ: Princeton University Press, 1973).

18. Saul A. Kripke, *Wittgenstein on Rules and Private Language* (Cambridge: Harvard University Press, 1982); and Hermann von Helmholtz, *Epistemological Writings* (Dordrecht, Holland: D. Reidel, 1977).

19. W.V.O. Quine, "Two Dogmas of Empiricism," *The Philosophical Review* 60 (1951): 20–43.

20. In the *Principia*, Descartes's preferred formulation was actually "*ego cogito, ergo sum*," but it is often misquoted as "*cogito, ergo sum.*"

21. Even the claim that at least "I think I am seeing a red-triangle" could be doubted, as I might be wrong about the meanings of "red" and "triangle."

22. I take Wittgenstein to be arguing mainly that universalizing doubt is incoherent because the very act of doubting presupposes by contrast some local certainty (such as even the notion that things can be rationally evaluated), which is required to get doubting off the ground. So for that reason universalized doubt

would have to doubt itself and thus be rendered incoherent. See Ludwig Wittgenstein, *On Certainty/Uber gewissheit* (New York: Harper Torchbooks, 2001).

23. Emphasis added. René Descartes, *The Philosophical Writings of Descartes*, vol. 1 (New York: Cambridge University Press, 1985), 10, 125.

24. As Descartes put it in his famous *Meditations*, "that there really is a world, and that human beings have bodies . . . no sane person has ever seriously doubted these things." Descartes, *Philosophical Writings*, vol. 2, 16. See also Stephen Gaukroger, *Descartes: An Intellectual Biography* (Oxford: Clarendon Press, 2003); and Richard Popkin, *The History of Scepticism: from Savonarola to Bayle* (Oxford: Oxford University Press, 2003), 143.

25. See René Descartes, *Oeuvres de Descartes*, ed. Charles Adam and Paul Tannery, 12 vols. (Paris: Léopold Cerf, 1897–1910).

26. Sextus Empiricus, *Outlines of Pyrrhonism*, vol. 1 (Cambridge: Harvard University Press, 1933), 3.

27. Harald Thorsrud, *Ancient Scepticism* (London: Routledge, 2014), 3.

28. Arne Næss, *Scepticism* (London: Routledge, 2005), 3.

29. As deconstruction is typically presented not as skepticism, but as a mode of textual interpretation, I have cut my discussion of it here for space reasons.

30. Eve Sedgwick, "Paranoid Reading and Reparative Reading," in *Novel Gazing: Queer Readings in Fiction*, ed. Eve Sedgwick (Durham, NC: Duke University Press, 1997), 1–37; and Rita Felski, *The Limits of Critique* (Chicago: University of Chicago Press, 2015).

31. Storm, "A Genealogy of Genealogy: Foucault, Nietzsche, History, and Race," unpublished manuscript, presented at the American Academy of Religion conference, 2017. I'll post a link on my professional blog.

32. Against classical skeptics, the Zetetic's aim is not ataraxia, but a lively eudaimonia, and to get there we need to seek as urgently as if our head were on fire.

33. Thorne, "To the Political Ontologists," 11.

34. In a famous section of Benito Mussolini's *Diuturna* titled "Relativismo e Fascismo," he argues that "From the equipollence [lit. equivalence] of all views, the ancient skeptics deduced that the only thing that could be done was to give up on all judging and acting. From the equipollence of all ideologies—the recognition that they are all equally fictions—the modern [fascist] relativist deduces, therefore, that everyone has the right to create his own [ideology] and impose it on others with all the energy of which he is capable." Mussolini's fascism was an ideology that knew itself to be merely ideological. Benito Mussolini, *Diuturna : Scritti Politici 1914–1922*, ed. Arnaldo Mussolini and Dino Grandi (Milan: Casa Editrice Imperia del Partito Nazionale Fascista, 1924), 377.

35. Source: http://phrontistery.info/favourite.html. Zetetic has sometimes been associated with Flat Earthers. I don't mean it in that sense. For the classical Greek, see Sextus Empiricus, "*Pyrrhoniae Hypotyposes*," in *Sexti Empirici Opera*, ed. Hermann Mutschmann (Leipzig: Teubner, 1984), vol. 1, esp. 7. Also, references to a "zetetic" method appear in Kant and Schelling.

36. See Arne Næss, *Selected Works of Arne Næss* (Dordrecht: Springer, 2005).

37. John R. Josephson, "Explanation and Induction," PhD diss, Ohio State Uni-

versity, 1982; Charles S. Peirce, *Philosophical Writings of Peirce* (New York: Dover, 1955), 58.

38. Here I have in mind the Indian philosopher Uddyotakara, who argued in the *Nyāya-vārttika* that false cognitions can only be called *false* in contrast to true cognitions.

39. Næss, *Selected Works of Arne Næss*, vol. 2, lix. I disagree with his possibilism, but space prohibits a full discussion,

40. Næss, *Selected Works*, vol. 8: 125–37.

41. David Lewis, "Elusive Knowledge," *Australasian Journal of Philosophy* 74, no. 4 (1996): 549–67.

42. See Jessica Brown, *Fallibilism: Evidence and Knowledge* (Oxford: Oxford University Press, 2018). You might think you are certain about what penguins eat (Lewis's example), but you could have only dreamed the flightless birds into existence.

43. Cited in Thorsrud, *Ancient Scepticism*, 76.

44. This helps us address the so-called threshold problem of fallibilism. Jeremy Fantl and Matthew McGrath, "Advice for Fallibilists: Put Knowledge to Work," *Philosophical Studies* 142 (2009): 55–66.

45. Tanabe Hajime, *Zangedō to shite no tetsugaku* (Tokyo: Iwanamishoten, 1950).

46. 無知 literally "ignorant." Tanabe, *Zangedō*, 17.

47. See David Bloor, *Wittgenstein: A Social Theory of Knowledge* (New York: Macmillan, 1983); Ludwik Fleck, *Genesis and Development of a Scientific Fact* (Chicago: University of Chicago Press, 1981); Sandra Harding, *Whose Science? Whose Knowledge?* (Ithaca, NY: Cornell University Press, 2016); and Barbara Herrnstein Smith, *Scandalous Knowledge: Science, Truth and the Human* (Durham, NC: Duke University Press, 2006).

48. Larry Laudan, *Progress and Its Problem* (London: Routledge, 1977).

49. See Friedrich Nietzsche, *Human, All Too Human* (Cambridge: Cambridge University Press, 1996), 13.

50. Evoking the principle of sufficient reason.

51. Samuel Arbesman, *The Half-Life of Facts* (New York: Penguin, 2012).

52. Evoking Gottlob Frege, *Posthumous Writings* (Chicago: University of Chicago Press, 1979), esp. 135.

53. Zeteticism will avoid obsolescence if it can continue to recognize that knowledge is transient and tends to become obsolete. I cannot imagine a point at which humility toward knowledge will become totally unnecessary. So Zeteticism can persist by embracing impermanence.

54. Rens Bod, *A New History of the Humanities: The Search for Principles and Patterns from Antiquity to the Present* (Oxford: Oxford University Press, 2014).

55. Hume had other critiques of induction as well. Marc Lange, "Hume and the Problem of Induction," in *Handbook of the History of Logic, Volume 10 Inductive Logic*, ed. Dov Mabbay (Waltham, MA: Elsevier, 2011), 43–91; John Stuart Mill, *A System of Logic*, vol. 1 (London: J.W. Parker, 1851), esp. 324; Georges Dicker,

Hume's Epistemology and Metaphysics (London: Routledge, 1998); and Alfred North Whitehead, *Science and the Modern World* (New York: Free Press, 1967), esp. 30.

56. Appears in the French film *La Haine* (1995).

57. Abduction is most associated with Peirce, but other significant proponents include: Richard Boyd, Umberto Eco, Fann Kuang Tih, Elizabeth Fricker, N.R. Hanson, Gilbert Harman, Ali Hasan, Peter Lipton, Lorenzo Magnani, Cheryl Misak, Ilkka Niiniluoto, and my parents John and Susan Josephson, as well as perhaps the Classical Indian philosophers Kumārila Bhaṭṭa (~660 CE) and Vācaspatimiśra (~900 CE). In treating abduction as synonymous with inference to the best explanation, I don't mean to suggest that Peirce would have understood "abduction" as IBE. See Gilbert Harman, "The Inference to the Best Explanation," *Philosophical Review* 74, no. 1 (1965): 88–95; Fann Kuang Tih, *Peirce's Theory of Abduction* (The Hague: Martinus Nijhoff, 1970); and William McAuliffe, "How did Abduction get Confused with Inference to the Best Explanation?" *Transactions of the Charles S. Peirce Society* 51, no. 3 (2015): 300–319. For *arthāpatti* (literally "presumption" or necessary conclusion) as IBE see Akṣapāda Gautama, *The Nyāya-sūtra: Selections with Early Commentaries*, ed. and trans. Matthew Dasti and Stephen Phillips (Indianapolis: Hackett, 2017); Kisor Kumar Chakrabarti, *Classical Indian Philosophy of Induction: The Nyāya Viewpoint* (Lanham, MD: Lexington Book, 2010); and Daniel Arnold, "Kumārila," *The Stanford Encyclopedia of Philosophy*, Winter 2014, https://plato.stanford.edu. See also Richard Boyd, "The Current Status of Scientific Realism," in *Scientific Realism*, ed. Jarrett Leplin (Berkeley: University of California Press, 1984), 41–82; Umberto Eco, *Semiotics and the Theory of Language* (Bloomington: Indiana University Press, 1986); Norwood Russell Hanson, *Patterns of Discovery* (Cambridge: Cambridge University Press, 1958); Ilkka Niiniluoto, *Truth-Seeking by Abduction* (Cham: Springer, 2018). For Ali Hasan, Cheryl Misak, and Elizabeth Fricker, see their essays in *Best Explanations: New Essays on Inference to the Best Explanation*, ed. Kevin McCain and Ted Poston (New York: Oxford University Press, 2017).

58. See Morag L. Donaldson, *Children's Explanations: A Psycholinguistic Study* (Cambridge: Cambridge University Press, 2006); Igor Douven, "Inference to the Best Explanation: What Is It? And Why Should We Care?" in *Best Explanations*, ed. McCain and Poston; Stephen J. Read and Amy Marcus-Newhall, "Explanatory Coherence in Social Explanations: A Parallel Distributed Processing Account," *Journal of Personality and Social Psychology* 65, no. 3 (1993): 429–47; and Tania Lombrozo, "Explanation and Abductive Inference," in *The Oxford Handbook of Thinking and Reasoning*, ed. Keith Holyoak and Robert Morrison (New York: Oxford University Press, 2013), 260–76.

59. See Warren S. Goldstein, ed., *Marx, Critical Theory, and Religion: A Critique of Rational Choice* (Chicago: Haymarket Books, 2009).

60. For another rejection of culturally relativist accounts of reason, see Kwasi Wiredu, *Cultural Universals and Particulars: An African Perspective* (Bloomington: Indiana University Press, 1996).

61. N.Y. Louis Lee and P.N. Johnson-Laird, "Are There Cross-Cultural Differ-

ences in Reasoning?" in *Proceedings of the 28th Annual Conference of the Cognitive Science Society*, ed. Ron Sun and Naomi Miyake (Hove, East Sussex: Psychology Press, 2006), 459–64; Philip Johnson-Laird, *How We Reason* (Oxford: Oxford University Press, 2011); and Jean-Baptiste Van der Henst, Yingrui Yang, and P.N. Johnson-Laird, "Strategies in Sentential Reasoning," *Cognitive Science* 26, no. 4 (2002): 425–68.

62. McCain and Poston, eds, *Best Explanations*, 1; and John R. Josephson and Susan G. Josephson, eds., *Abductive Inference: Computation, Philosophy, Technology* (Cambridge: Cambridge University Press, 1996), 7–12. See also Hugh Gauch, *Scientific Method in Brief* (Cambridge: Cambridge University Press, 2012); Jerry R. Hobbs, "Abduction in Natural Language Understanding," *Handbook of Pragmatics* (2004): 724–41; Peter Lipton, "The Epistemology of Testimony," *Studies in History and Philosophy of Science* 29, no. 1 (1998): 1–31.

63. See James Robinson, Paul Hoffmann, and John Kloppenborg, *The Critical Edition of Q* (New York: Fortress Publishers, 2000).

64. For example, I have argued elsewhere that part of the reason the myth of disenchantment has held on so long is because scholars have historically presumed that modernity meant a rupture and that cultures become more rational over time. Instead, we would likely have formulated better possible theories had we tried to rule out possibilities such as that disenchantment is the exception, not the rule. See Josephson-Storm, *The Myth of Disenchantment*.

65. Adapted from Josephson and Josephson, *Abductive Inference*, 14–15.

66. Josephson and Josephson, *Abductive Inference*. See also John R. Josephson, "On the Proof Dynamics of Inference to the Best Explanation," *Cardozo Law Review* 22 (2000): 1621–43.

67. Here I am agreeing with the critique of sterile debates about observability discussed in Jim Bogen, "'Saving the Phenomena' and Saving the Phenomena," *Synthèse* 182, no. 1 (2011): 7–22.

68. Josephson and Josephson, *Abductive Inference*, 13–14.

69. Josephson and Josephson, *Abductive Inference*, 15.

70. Douglas Adams, quoted in Victoria de Rijke, *Duck* (London: Reaktion Books, 2008), 12.

71. Van Fraassen has argued that the problem with IBE is that the real explanation may include a hypothesis that no one has considered. While I agree that many philosophers are too confident in conclusions determined by abduction, I don't think that this is a fatal problem. The best explanation might always be a theory we've never considered, but insofar as our current theory is doing some work to explain the data we are justified in consenting to it on Zetetic grounds, even if someday it may be overturned. Bas van Fraassen, *The Scientific Image* (Oxford: Clarendon Press, 1980).

72. Josephson, "Proof Dynamics," 1628.

73. Readers probably needn't worry about the implications of Duhem–Quine for excluding alternatives. Quine famously argued that "our statements about the external world face the tribunal of sense experience not individually but only as

a corporate body. . . . The unit of empirical significance is the whole of science" (Quine, "Two Dogmas of Empiricism," 41–42.) Part of Quine's justification for this view is that no single experiment can ever refute a scientific theory because one can always modify auxiliary hypotheses to justify the theory. For instance, if your experiment seemingly refutes the theory that all objects should fall at the same rate, then you can modify your theory by introducing a notion of wind resistance. One might worry that if this were the case no alternative hypothesis could ever be ruled out. But a Zetetic orientation to abduction would already take as given that *definitive* exclusion presumes certainty and is not an issue. All we need is the grounds to reasonably and preliminarily exclude an alternative. Moreover, Quine's extension of "significance" to require the whole of science runs into the same contradictions as the semantic holism discussed in chapter 5.

The smaller-scale version if this argument put forth by Pierre Duhem is more persuasive, but even then it tends to ignore the cost of adding theoretical baggage. While in principle it may be possible to produce alternative accounts to preserve the theory, this is not the case in practice (sure, geocentrists could have argued that all the heliocentrists were hallucinating, but to do so they would have had to come up with a very implausible counter-theory of hallucination). Furthermore, as Laudan has persuasively argued, any theory of science (except Popper's discredited falsification) suggests that you will typically have a reason to choose between rival theories or explanations (e.g., because one explains the evidence in more detail, is simpler, more portable across more domains, etcetera). (See Laudan, *Beyond Positivism*, 34–35.) This means that when falsifiability is understood as a component, rather than the whole of inference, then Duhem–Quine largely fails to be an issue.

74. Boaventura de Sousa Santos, *Epistemologies of the South: Justice against Epistemicide* (New York: Routledge, 2015), 190.

75. Peirce is well known for suggesting that even basic perceptual judgments are abductive inferences. Justus Buchler, *Charles Peirce's Empiricism* (New York: Harcourt, 1939).

76. John R. Josephson, "Smart Inductive Generalizations Are Abductions," in *Abduction and Induction: Essays on Their Relation and Integration*, ed. Peter Flach and Antonis Kakas (Dordrecht: Springer, 2000), 31–44. (

77. Hume called deduction "demonstrative reasoning."

78. See Harman, "Inference to the Best Explanation"; and Josephson, "Smart Inductive Generalizations." See also J. Adam Carter and Duncan Pritchard, "Inference to the Best Explanation and Epistemic Circularity," in *Best Explanations*, ed. McCain and Poston, 133–49; and Stathis Psillos, *Scientific Realism: How Science Tracks Truth* (London: Routledge, 1999). I'm not that worried about circularity, but we could adopt a modified "Reichenbach vindication" for abduction. If anything has a chance at knowledge, then inference to the best explanation would seem to be our best bet. As my father says: "what are you going to do, pick the worst explanation?"

79. Josephson and Josephson, *Abductive Inference*, 25.

80. Lorenzo Magnani, *Abductive Cognition* (Berlin: Springer Berlin, 2013); and Tommaso Bertolotti, *Patterns of Rationality* (Cham: Springer International Publishing, 2015).

81. Josephson, "Proof Dynamics," 1632.

82. See also Haraway, "Situated Knowledges."

83. Josephson and Josephson, *Abductive Inference*, 14.

84. See Larry Laudan, *Progress and Its Problems* (Berkeley: University of California Press, 1977), esp. 81.

85. Siebers, *Cold War Criticism*; and Christian Thorne, *The Dialectic of Counter-Enlightenment* (Cambridge: Harvard University Press, 2010).

86. For a recent discussion, see Brown, *Fallibilism*.

87. For examples, see Francisco Sánchez, *That Nothing is Known (Quod nihil scitur)* (Cambridge: Cambridge University Press, 2008); and for fallibilism in classical Indian philosophy, see Sundar Sarukkai, *Indian Philosophy and Philosophy of Science* (New Delhi: Centre for Studies in Civilizations, 2005).

88. For optimistic fallibilists, think Dewey, Karl Popper, and to a lesser extent Richard Bernstein.

CHAPTER SEVEN

1. Ethical relativism and nihilism are often sloppily conflated.

2. Gilles Lipovetsky, *Le Crépuscule du devoir: L'éthique indolore des nouveaux temps démocratiques* (Paris: Gallimard, 2007).

3. James Wilson, *The Moral Sense* (New York: The Free Press, 1993), 5, 9; see also John Cook, *Morality and Cultural Differences* (New York: Oxford University Press, 1999), 41.

4. Douglas Walton, *Ethical Argumentation* (Lanham, MD: Lexington Books, 2009), 36.

5. Emphasis added. This is not a very accurate summary of Nietzsche. Charles Upton, *The System of Antichrist: Truth and Falsehood in Postmodernism and the New Age* (Hillsdale, NY: Sophia Perennis, 2001), 52. Also, contra Upton, the phrase originated not in Nietzsche, but likely in Hassan-i Sabbāh. See also Raymond Williams, *The Writings of Carlos Fuentes* (Austin: University of Texas Press, 1996), 95–96.

6. See Honi Haber, "Richard Rorty's Failed Politics," *Social Epistemology* 7, no. 1 (1993): 61–74; and Andreas Huyssen, "Forward: The Return of Diogenes as Postmodern Intellectual," in Peter Sloterdijk, *Critique of Cynical Reason* (Minneapolis: University of Minnesota Press, 1988).

7. See Harvey, *Condition of Postmodernity*, and Jameson, *Postmodernism*.

8. See the title of Pluckrose and Lindsay below.

9. Michael Rectenwald, *Springtime for Snowflakes: "Social Justice" and Its Postmodern Parentage* (Nashville: New English Review Press, 2018), vii.

10. Helen Pluckrose and James Lindsay, *Cynical Theories: How Activist Scholarship Made Everything about Race, Gender, and Identity* (Durham, NC: Pitchstone, 2020), 13–14. Rectenwald, Pluckrose, and Lindsay are not wrong to identify a

changing tenor in the mid-2010s, but they generally seem to miss its continuities with previous movements.

11. Max Weber, "Science as Vocation" (*Wissenschaft als Beruf*), trans. in H.H. Gerth and C. Wright Mills, *From Max Weber: Essays in Sociology* (New York: Oxford University Press, 1946), 143.

12. William Arnal, Willi Braun, and Russell McCutcheon, eds., *Failure and Nerve in the Academic Study of Religion: Essays in Honor of Donald Wiebe* (New York: Routledge, 2014).

13. Luther Martin and Donald Wiebe, "Religious Studies as a Scientific Discipline: The Persistence of a Delusion," *Journal of the American Academy of Religion* 80, no. 3 (2012): 587–97.

14. For this debate, see Warren S. Goldstein, "What Makes Critical Religion Critical?" *Critical Research on Religion* 8, no. 1 (April 2020): 73–86.

15. See Milton Friedman, *Essays in Positive Economics* (Chicago: University of Chicago Press, 1953). For examples of subsequent critiques, see Sandra Harding, "Can Feminist Thought Make Economics More Objective?" *Feminist Economics* 1, no. 1 (1995): 7–32; Hilary Putnam and Vivian Walsh, eds., *The End of Value-Free Economics* (Abingdon: Routledge, 2014); and Daniel Hausman and Michael McPherson, *Economic Analysis, Moral Philosophy, and Public Policy* (Cambridge: Cambridge University Press, 2009).

16. The two quotations appeared in the reverse order in the interview. Michael Bess, "Power, Moral Values and the Intellectual: An Interview with Michel Foucault November 3, 1980," *History of the Present* 4 (1988): 1–2, 11–13.

17. Many of these terms were not initially understood as negative. Sexism originally meant belonging to a sex, homophobia originally meant fear of humans, patriarchy originally referred to the office of ecclesiastical patriarch, and racism was embraced (by people we would now call racists) but as a positive attribute.

18. For examples: Joe Dunn, "In Search of Lessons: The Development of a Vietnam Historiography," *Parameters* 9, no. 1 (1979): 28–40; and Otis Graham, ed., *The New Deal: The Critical Issues* (Boston: Little, 1971), 171–73. For value neutrality, see Francis Madigan, *Philippine Sociological Review* 7, no. 4 (1959): 38–40; and also Gunnar Myrdal, *Value in Social Theory* (London: Routledge, 1958) esp. 134–52; and Ernest Nagel, *The Structure of Science* (New York: Harcourt, 1961).

19. Barthes's sympathetic gloss on Brecht. Roland Barthes, *Critical Essays* (Evanston, IL: Northwestern University Press, 1972), 140.

20. To be fair, in many cases, this negative register is so pervasive and folded into how people have been taught to critique that this sort of value-laden work is not perceived as imbued with value.

21. This is a mild caricature of Sandra Harding, *The Science Question in Feminism* (Ithaca, NY: Cornell University Press, 1993). Her real argument is more subtle.

22. An Emory independent investigative committee seems to have agreed and forced Bellesiles's resignation. But a similar ethically motivated source critique from the Left could be seen in the Hypatia transracialism controversy.

23. The impetus toward "canceling" is not new. People may be calling for dif-

ferent things to be cancelled (norms have changed), but canceling itself does not represent a generational shift (e.g., think of the Nestle boycott of the late 1970s). Cancel culture is not a new culture. But what has changed is the algorithmic amplification of outrage to drive digital engagement (anger equals clicks equals advertising revenue, or at least increased attention). For instance, organizing an all-female screening of *Wonder Woman* (2017) with the intended goal of inspiring outrage from "men's right activists" in order to make watching a corporate superhero movie seem like a feminist statement; or when right-wing activists dug up James Gunn's old tweets to try and get him fired and get themselves more attention. These kinds of media strategies have been combined with the simplification of ethical argumentation promoted by superficial headline-driven news/blog media and the bandwidth constraints of Twitter. Put differently, people were always canceling/boycotting, but canceling has just gotten more efficient, with the unfortunate side effect of being more indiscriminate and hence easier to manipulate. For a thoughtful discussion of canceling, its limits, and the vital question of "can we release our binary ways of thinking of good and bad in order to collectively grow from mistakes?" see adrienne maree brown, *We Will Not Cancel Us: And Other Dreams of Transformative Justice* (Chico: AK Press, 2020), 17.

24. For example, Evelyn Barish, *The Double Life of Paul De Man* (New York: Liveright, 2014).

25. For a similar critique of critique see Felski, *Limits of Critique*.

26. Here I am arguing against Pluckrose and Lindsay. But note that I reject both race reductionism and class reductionism.

27. Indeed, much of contemporary theory promotes what amounts to a secularized Christian notion of universal sinfulness.

28. Michel Foucault, *Politics, Philosophy, Culture: Interviews and Other Writings* (London: Routledge, 2013), 49.

29. Foucault, cited in Neil Levy, "Foucault as Virtue Ethicist," *Foucault Studies* (2004): 20–31, 22.

30. See Josephson-Storm, *The Myth of Disenchantment*.

31. See Max Weber, *Gesammelte Aufsätze zur Wissenschaftslehre* (Tübingen: Mohr, 1922). Portions translated in Max Weber, *The Methodology of the Social Sciences* (New York: Free Press, 1969).

32. See Weber, *Methodology of the Social Sciences*, 7.

33. Emphasis added. Weber, *Methodology of the Social Sciences*, 51.

34. Weber, *Methodology of the Social Sciences*, 1.

35. Weber, *Methodology of the Social Sciences*, 52–53.

36. Robert Proctor, *Value-Free Science? Purity and Power in Modern Knowledge* (Cambridge: Harvard University Press, 1991), 97.

37. Wilhelm Dilthey, *Introduction to the Human Sciences* (Princeton, NJ: Princeton University Press, 1991).

38. Proctor, *Value-Free Science?*, 144–45.

39. Weber, *Gesammelte Aufsätze*, esp. 452–54.

40. See Jay Ciaffa, *Max Weber and the Problems of Value-Free Social Science* (London: Associated University Press, 1998).

41. See Weber, *Gesammelte Aufsätze*.

42. John Cook, *Morality and Cultural Differences* (New York: Oxford University Press, 2003).

43. See Marvin Harris, *The Rise of Anthropological Theory* (New York: Crowell, 1968), esp. 163; and Elvin Hatch, *Culture and Morality: The Relativity of Values in Anthropology* (New York: Columbia University Press, 1983), 38.

44. Franz Boas, *The Mind of Primitive Man* (New York: Free Press, 1963), 203. Boas himself refers to Edward Westermarck, who provides the example of elder abandonment I use above. Both cited in Cook, *Morality and Cultural Differences*, 69–70.

45. The origins of ethical relativism are themselves not necessarily an argument against it—although that argument has been made; see John Cook, "Cultural Relativism as an Ethnocentric Notion," in *The Philosophy of Society*, ed. Rodger Beehlar and Alan Drengson (London: Methuen, 1978), 289–315.

46. See Robert Proctor and Heather Douglas, *Science, Policy, and the Value-Free Ideal* (Pittsburgh: University of Pittsburgh Press, 2009).

47. Andrew Jewett, *Science, Democracy, and the American University* (New York: Cambridge University Press, 2012).

48. Emphasis in original. David Hume, *A Treatise of Human Nature*, vol. 1 (Oxford: Clarendon Press, 2010), 302.

49. The phrase "naturalist fallacy" having been appropriated from G.E. Moore, but now more often put to a different use than Moore intended.

50. See note 54 below.

51. See Alasdair MacIntyre, "Hume on 'Is' and 'Ought,'" *The Philosophical Review* 68, no. 4 (1959): 451–68; and Charles Pigden, "Hume on Is and Ought: Logic, Promises, and the Duke of Wellington," in *The Oxford Handbook of Hume*, ed. Paul Russell (Oxford: Oxford University Press, 2016), 401–15.

52. A is MacIntyre's conclusion above and B is Pigden's conclusion above.

53. To increase readability and because their arguments often overlap, full citation occurs in the notes, but the theorists cited are: Max Black, Patricia Hill Collins, Heather Douglas, Philippa Foot, Allan Gibbard, Sandra Harding, Donna Haraway, Larry Laudan, Helene Longino, Georg Lukács, Alasdair MacIntyre, Robert Merton, Iris Murdoch, Michael Polanyi, Hilary Putnam, John Searle, Amartya Sen, Daniel Steel, Christine Tappolet, Pekka Väyrynen, Cornel West, and Bernard Williams.

54. Allan Gibbard, "Truth and Correct Belief," *Philosophical Issues* 15 (2005): 338–50. Gibbard, however, makes a distinction between objective and subjective senses of ought that seems far-fetched.

55. John Searle, *Speech Acts: An Essay in the Philosophy of Language* (Cambridge: Cambridge University Press, 1969), 134–35.

56. Hilary Putnam, *The Collapse of the Fact/Value Dichotomy and Other Essays* (Cambridge: Harvard University Press, 2002), 31. For attempts to refine the notion of epistemic or cognitive values, see Daniel Steel, "Epistemic Values and the Argument from Inductive Risk," *Philosophy of Science* 77, no. 1 (2010): 14–34; and Heather Douglas, "The Value of Cognitive Values," *Philosophy of Science* 80, no. 5 (2013): 796–806.

57. One of the arguments that the Copernican model had over its rivals was that circles or ellipses were a simpler and more elegant description of planetary motion that multiplying epicycles.

58. Readers interested in historicizing the notion of a scientific spirit in US history should read Jewett, *Science, Democracy, and the American University*.

59. Robert K. Merton, "The Normative Structure of Science," in *The Sociology of Science* (Chicago: University of Chicago Press, 1973), 267–78; Larry Laudan, *Science and Values* (Berkeley: University of California Press, 1984); and Liam Kofi Bright, "Du Bois' Democratic Defence of the Value Free Ideal," *Synthese* 195, no. 5 (2018): 2227–45.

60. Michael Polanyi, "The Republic of Science: Its Political and Economic Theory," *Minerva* 1 (1962): 54–74.

61. Amartya K. Sen, "The Nature and Classes of Prescriptive Judgements," *The Philosophical Quarterly* (1950-) 17, no. 66 (1967): 46–62. See also Putnam, *Fact/Value Dichotomy*, esp. 76.

62. See Helen Goode, Hannah McGee, and Ciaran O'Boyle, *Time to Listen: Confronting Child Sexual Abuse by Catholic Clergy in Ireland* (Dublin, Ireland: Liffey Press, 2003).

63. Bernard Williams, *Ethics and the Limits of Philosophy* (Cambridge: Harvard University Press, 1985). Putnam, *Fact/Value Dichotomy*, esp. 34. See also Philippa Foot, "Moral Arguments," *Mind* 67, no. 268 (1958): 502–13; Iris Murdoch, *The Sovereignty of Good*, 2nd edition (London: Routledge, 2008), esp. 31–32.

64. To be fair, some philosophers have argued that it is possible to disentangle the evaluative and non-evaluative aspects of a given thick-ethical concept. See Christine Tappolet, "Through Thick and Thin: Good and Its Determinates," *Dialectica* 58, no. 2 (2004): 207–21; and Pekka Väyrynen, *The Lewd, the Rude and the Nasty: A Study of Thick Concepts in Ethics* (New York: Oxford University Press, 2015). I share some of their skepticism about the possibility of there being actual "thin" ethical concepts, and clearly "thick" is on a spectrum.

65. Max Black, "The Gap Between 'Is' and 'Should,'" *The Philosophical Review* 73, no. 2 (1964): 165–81, 173.

66. MacIntyre, "Hume on 'Is' and 'Ought,'" 463.

67. See Helene Longino, *Science as Social Knowledge: Values and Objectivity in Scientific Inquiry* (Princeton, NJ: Princeton University Press, 1990); Georg Lukács, *History and Class Consciousness: Studies in Marxist Dialectics* (Cambridge: MIT Press, 1972); Cornel West, *Ethical Dimensions of Marxist Thought* (New York: New York University Press, 1991), esp. 148–55.

68. I don't give much credence to the quasi-Nietzschean and self-refuting version of this argument that suggests that all facts are values, see chapter 6.

69. Donna Haraway, *Primate Visions: Gender, Race, and Nature in the World of Modern Science* (New York: Routledge, 1989).

70. Stephen Jay Gould, *The Mismeasure of Man* (New York: W.W. Norton & Company, 1996).

71. Sandra Harding, "Rethinking Standpoint Epistemology: What is 'Strong Objectivity'?" *The Centennial Review* 36, no. 3 (1992): 437–70; see also Patricia Hill

Collins, *Black Feminist Thought: Knowledge, Consciousness, and the Politics of Empowerment* (New York: Routledge, 2015), 290.

72. Collins, *Black Feminist Thought*, 274.

73. See Mary Hesse, *Revolutions and Reconstructions in the Philosophy of Science* (Bloomington: Indiana University Press, 1980), 33.

74. See Laudan, *Beyond Positivism*, 46–47.

75. Often it takes the form of a fallacy, such as: John Bull was a colonialist. John Bull taught Shakespeare. Therefore, teaching Shakespeare is colonialist. Alternatively, it can be produced by association as a kind of six degrees of Kevin Bacon, only with Hitler. Obviously, philosophy of ethics is much more sophisticated, but unfortunately this subfield is not widely read in the rest of the academy.

76. For instance, some scholars seem to have adopted what amounts to a one-drop rule for racism, which means calling out even inspirational leaders like W.E.B. Du Bois. See Ibram X Kendi, *Stamped from the Beginning: The Definitive History of Racist Ideas in America* (New York: Nation Books, 2017), and Carlos Lozada, "The Racism of Good Intentions," *Washington Post*, April 15, 2016. Similarly, as Rita Felski has observed, there has been increasing slippage between describing violence toward people and "symbolic violence" toward texts. See Felski, *Limits of Critique*, esp. 97–107. Thus condemnations of symbolic violence, while sometimes useful, can actually divert attention from actual systems of physical and psychological violence.

77. For Ludwig Klages as the actual originator of the term, see Josephson-Storm, *The Myth of Disenchantment*, 221.

78. Campbell Pryor, Amy Perfors, and Piers Howe, "Even Arbitrary Norms Influence Moral Decision-Making," *Nature Human Behaviour* 3, no. 1 (2019): 57–62.

79. One could ask this question of science/technology, but probably the unspoken goal of scientific progress is increasing power or domination over matter.

80. An exception is Volney Gay, *Progress and Values in the Humanities: Comparing Culture and Science* (New York: Columbia University Press, 2013).

81. J. Hillis Miller, *Tropes, Parables, and Performatives* (Durham, NC: Duke University, 1991), 79.

82. Pierre Hadot, *Philosophy as a Way of Life: Spiritual Exercises from Socrates to Foucault* (Oxford: Blackwell, 1995).

83. G.E.M. Anscombe, "Modern Moral Philosophy," *Philosophy* 33, no. 124 (1958): 1–19.

84. For some influential works which have shaped my account of what follows, see: Stephen Angle and Michael Slote, eds., *Virtue Ethics and Confucianism* (New York: Routledge, 2013); Michael Bishop, *The Good Life: Unifying the Philosophy and Psychology of Well-Being* (New York: Oxford University Press, 2015); Philippa Foot, *Virtues and Vices and Other Essays in Moral Philosophy* (Oxford: Clarendon Press, 2009); Rosalind Hursthouse, *On Virtue Ethics* (New York: Oxford University Press, 1999); Alasdair MacIntyre, *After Virtue: A Study in Moral Theory* (Notre Dame, IN: University of Notre Dame Press, 2012); Murdoch, *Sovereignty of Good*; Daniel Statman, ed., *Virtue Ethics* (Washington, DC: Georgetown University Press, 2007).

85. See, for example, Bryan Van Norden, *Virtue Ethics and Consequentialism in Early Chinese Philosophy* (New York: Cambridge University Press, 2007).

86. Aristotle, *Nicomachean Ethics*, trans. with commentary by Christopher Rowe and Sarah Broadie (New York: Oxford University Press, 2002). For an argument for translating of Eaudaimonia as flourishing see Hursthouse, *On Virtue Ethics*.

87. I say "most" because some people might reject one or the other of these terms—for example, those who believe they need to suffer to be happy. There may even be people who are sufficiently hurt that they think they want to reject all of these, but if so, I suspect that their rejection is really a sign that they need help.

88. I don't mean suggest that there are only two kinds of happiness. Nor do I mean to suggest that happiness$_1$ is reducible to a clearly delineated biological kind. But I think it likely has some common neurological basis. See Kent Berridge and Morten L. Kringelbach; "Affective Neuroscience of Pleasure: Reward in Humans and Animals," *Psychopharmacology* 199, no. 3 (2008): 457–80.

89. Here I'm thinking of both Daoist and Marxist arguments against stasis and alienation.

90. See also Vivasvan Soni, *Mourning Happiness: Narrative and the Politics of Modernity* (Ithaca, NY: Cornell University Press, 2010).

91. This is also perhaps what Nietzsche had in mind in his notion of eternal return.

92. See Jennifer Whiting, "Aristotle's Function Argument: A Defense," *Ancient Philosophy* 8, no. 1 (1988): 33–48.

93. Molefi Asante, *The Afrocentric Idea, Revised* (Philadelphia: Temple University Press, 1998), 200. See also Collins, *Black Feminist Thought*, 279.

94. Tu Weiming, *Humanity and Self-Cultivation: Essays in Confucian Thought* (Berkeley, CA: Asian Humanities Press, 1979), 35.

95. For Renaissance thought, see Giovanni Pico della Mirandola, *On the Dignity of Man* (Indianapolis: Hackett, 1998). For the Ojibwe community, Michael McNally, *Honoring Elders: Ojibwe Aging, Religion, and Authority* (New York: Columbia University Press, 2009), esp. 46–48. For Kant, see Robert B. Louden, *Kant's Human Being: Essays on his Theory of Human Nature* (Oxford: Oxford University Press, 2014), esp. 136–49. See also James Behuniak, *Mencius on Becoming Human* (Albany: State University of New York Press, 2005); Katherine McKittrick, ed., *Sylvia Wynter: On Being Human as Praxis* (Durham, NC: Duke University Press, 2015); and Paulo Freire, *Pedagogy of the Oppressed* (New York: Continuum, 2017).

96. Tibor Scitovsky, *The Joyless Economy* (Oxford: Oxford University Press, 1976) and Erlangga Landiyanto et al., "Wealth and Happiness: Empirical Evidence from Indonesia," *Southeast Asian Journal of Economics* 23, no. 1 (2011): 1–17.

97. David Graeber, *Bullshit Jobs: A Theory* (London: Penguin, 2019).

98. Marx and Engels, *The German Ideology*.

99. For a defense of virtue as human dispositions, see Joel J. Kupperman, "Virtue in Virtue Ethics." *The Journal of Ethics* 13, nos. 2–3 (2009): 243–55.

100. For an influential attempt at classification (although I think it is overly universalizing), see Christopher Peterson and Martin Seligman, *Character Strengths and Virtues* (New York: Oxford University Press, 2004). For contrast between Aris-

totelian and Confucian conceptions of virtue see Yu Jiyuan, "Virtue: Confucius and Aristotle," *Philosophy East and West* 48, no. 2 (1998): 323–47.

101. See Pierre Hadot, *The Inner Citadel: The Meditations of Marcus Aurelius* (Cambridge: Harvard University Press, 1998).

102. See Georges Dreyfus, "Meditation as Ethical Activity," *Journal of Buddhist Ethics* 2 (1995): 28–54.

103. Analects 7.22. Confucius, *Analects with Selections from Traditional Commentaries*, trans. Edward Slingerland (Indianapolis: Hackett, 2003), 71.

104. This is the main debate around Confucian notions of ritual 礼. For example, Xun Kuang, *Xunzi, A Translation and Study of the Complete Works* (Stanford, CA: Stanford University Press, 1988).

105. Śāntideva, *Bodhicaryāvatāra*. See Jay Garfield, "What Is it Like to be a Bodhisattva? Moral Phenomenology in Śāntideva's Bodhicaryāvatāra," *International Association of Buddhist Studies* (2010): 333–57; Georges Dreyfus, "Is Compassion an Emotion?" in *Visions of Compassion: Western Scientists and Tibetan Buddhists Examine Human Nature*, ed. Richard Davidson and Anne Harrington (New York: Oxford University Press, 2001), 31–45; Charles Goodman, *Consequences of Compassion: An Interpretation and Defense of Buddhist Ethics* (New York: Oxford University Press, 2014).

106. See Francesca Borgonovi, "Doing Well by Doing Good: The Relationship between Formal Volunteering and Self-Reported Health and Happiness," *Social Science & Medicine* 66, no. 11 (2008): 2321–34.

107. Steven Bein, *Compassion and Moral Guidance* (Honolulu: University of Hawai'i Press, 2013).

108. Collins, *Black Feminist Thought*, 282–283; and Annette Baier, *Postures of the Mind* (Minneapolis: University of Minnesota Press, 1985), 93–108. We can also see similar claims in Asante, *The Afrocentric Idea*,and elsewhere. That said, Virginia Held rejects the connection between compassion and care, but to my mind she is mistaking compassion for self-destructive forms of altruism. See Virginia Held, *The Ethics of Care* (Oxford: Oxford University Press, 2006).

109. Thích Nhất Hạnh, *Being Peace* (Berkeley, CA: Parallax Press, 1988).

110. Sara Ahmed, *The Promise of Happiness* (Durham, NC: Duke University Press, 2010).

111. By "Revolutionary" I mean to signal politically and ethically transformative. As has been pointed out by a colleague, my formulation also has positive resonances with Raoul Vaneigem's maxim that "the only real joy is revolutionary." Raoul Vaneigem, *The Revolution of Everyday Life* (Oakland, CA: PM Press, 2012), 32.

112. Hannah Arendt, *On Revolution* (New York: Penguin, 1990), 255. The work is best read alongside Hannah Arendt, *The Human Condition* (Chicago: University of Chicago Press, 1998).

113. Max Horkheimer, *Critical Theory: Selected Essays* (New York: Continuum, 2002), 248. We can see a parallel claim from a different political spectrum in John Milbank and Adrian Pabst, *The Politics of Virtue: Post-Liberalism and the Human Future* (London: Rowman & Littlefield, 2016).

114. For a critique, see David Harvey, *Spaces of Neoliberalization* (Stuttgart: Steiner, 2005).

115. Steven Pinker, *Enlightenment Now: The Case for Reason, Science, Humanism, and Progress* (New York: Penguin, 2018). Perhaps neoliberals on the center-left would also add that a certain percentage of the wealthiest CEOs should be women or from minoritized backgrounds.

116. Bruno Frey, *Not Just for the Money: An Economic Theory of Personal Motivation* (Cheltenham: Elgar, 2007).

117. Name in quotes because "Hanzi Freinacht" is a pseudonym used by a pair of Danish political activists. Hanzi Freinacht, *The Listening Society* (Copenhagen: Metamoderna, 2017), 72. Space prohibits a fuller engagement with Freinacht and his definition of metamodernism, but I hope to post something on my professional website.

118. There are reasons we might want to be skeptical of some of this whole stratum of discourse. For many European thinkers, "the Other" is other European thinkers. Referring to the unintelligibility of "the Other" without distinguishing between different kinds of othering thus can be a reification of difference and a reduction of it to a paradoxical self-similarity.

119. See Saidiya Hartman, *Scenes of Subjection: Terror, Slavery, and Self-making in Nineteenth-century America* (New York: Oxford University Press, 1997); Fred Moten, *Black and Blur* (Durham, NC: Duke University Press, 2017); and George Yancy, *Black Bodies, White Gazes* (New York: Rowman & Littlefield, 2016). Also remember, of course, the account of blackness in Ellison's famous novel: Ralph Ellison, *Invisible Man* (New York: Random House, 1952).

120. See Gayatri Chakravorty Spivak, "Can the Subaltern Speak?" in *Can the Subaltern Speak? Reflections on the History of an Idea*, ed. Rosalind Morris (New York: Columbia University Press, 2010).

121. Howard Adelman, *Knowledge, Aesthetics and Preventing Genocide* (Toronto: Centre for Refugee Studies, York University, 1997), 15.

122. Emphasis in original. Sönke Neitzel and Harald Welzer, *Soldiers: German POWs on Fighting, Killing, and Dying* (New York: Alfred A. Knopf, 2012), 149.

123. Victoria Esses and Richard Vernon, eds., *Explaining the Breakdown of Ethnic Relations: Why Neighbors Kill* (London: Blackwell, 2009).

124. Esses and Vernon, eds., *Ethnic Relations*.

125. Nelson Mandela, *Notes to the Future* (New York: Atria Books, 2014), 84. I also have in mind Huey P. Newton's revolutionary love and Che Guevera's famous statement that "the true revolutionary is guided by strong feelings of love." Quoted in Judson Jeffries, *Huey P. Newton: The Radical Theorist* (Jackson: University Press of Mississippi, 2002), 33.

126. Tanabe, *Zangedō*.

127. This presumes the possibility of mutual listening, of compassion, if not its actualization. See Cornel West, Jonathan Judaken, and Jennifer Geddes, "Black Intellectuals in America: A Conversation with Cornel West," in *Naming Race, Naming Racisms*, ed. Jonathan Judaken (London: Routledge, 2013), 227. West is para-

phrasing Adorno's statement *"Das Bedürfnis, Leiden beredt werden zu lassen, ist Bedingung aller Wahrheit."* Adorno, *Negative Dialektik*, 27.

128. See Sharon Cransow, "Feminist Contributions to Anthropology and Sociology," in *Philosophy of Anthropology and Sociology*, ed. Stephen Turner and Mark Risjord (Amsterdam: Elsevier, 2006), 755–89; and Marianne Janack, "Dilemmas of Objectivity," *Social Epistemology* 16, no. 3 (2002): 267–81. "Subjectivity" also means too many different things to be useful as a contrasting category.

129. Freire, *Pedagogy of the Oppressed*.

130. Max Horkheimer, "Traditionelle und kritische Theorie," *Zeitschrift für Sozialforschung* 6, no. 2 (1937): 245–94. For Tzotzil (also written Tsotsil) activists, *lekil kuxlejal*, and the Zapatistas more broadly, see: Juan López Intzín, "Ich'el-Ta-Muk': la trama en la construcción del Lekil-Kuxlejal," in *Prácticas otras de conocimiento(s)*, ed. Xochitl Leyva (Buenos Aires: CLACSO, 2018), 181–98; Mariana Mora, *Kuxlejal Politics: Indigenous Autonomy, Race, and Decolonizing Research in Zapatista Communities* (Austin: University of Texas Press, 2017), esp. 19; and Dylan Fitzwater, *Autonomy Is in Our Hearts: Zapatista Autonomous Government through the Lens of the Tsotsil Language* (Oakland: PM Press, 2019).

CONCLUSION

1. See for example, Hans Rosenhaupt, "Modern Foreign Language Study and the Needs of Our Times," *Monatshefte für Deutschen Unterricht* 32, no. 5 (1940): 205–16.

2. See Michael Bérubé, "Days of Future Past," *ADE Bulletin* (2002): 20–26; and Linda Pratt, "In a Dark Wood: Finding a New Path to the Future of English," *ADE Bulletin* (2002): 27–33.

3. Han Byung-Chul, *Was ist Macht?* (Stuttgart: P. Reclam, 2005).

Index